Time of Troubles

D0872862

Time of Troubles

A New Economic Framework for Early Christianity

Roland Boer and Christina Petterson

Fortress Press
Minneapolis

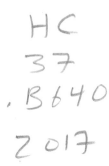

HC
37
.B640
2017

TIME OF TROUBLES
A New Economic Framework for Early Christianity

Copyright © 2017 Fortress Press. All rights reserved. Except for brief quotations
in critical articles or reviews, no part of this book may be reproduced in any manner
without prior written permission from the publisher. Email copyright@1517.media
or write to Permissions, Fortress Press, PO Box 1209, Minneapolis, MN
55440-1209.

Cover image: Parable of the Tenants (Parable of the Vineyard and Husbandmen).
16th CE engraving. Biblioteca Nacional Album / Art Resource, NY
Cover design: Tory Herman

Print ISBN: 978-1-5064-0631-2
eBook ISBN: 978-1-5064-0632-9

The paper used in this publication meets the minimum requirements of American
National Standard for Information Sciences — Permanence of Paper for Printed
Library Materials, ANSI Z329.48-1984.

Manufactured in the U.S.A.

This book was produced using Pressbooks.com, and PDF rendering was done by
PrinceXML.

JKM Library
1100 East 55th Street
Chicago, IL 60615

For Zachary Ian and Felix Hendrik

Contents

Preface

This book has been hard work, for a number of reasons. By the time we began researching and writing it, our minds were elsewhere —Christina's with the Moravians in Eastern Germany and throughout the world, and Roland's with the complexities of socialism in power in China. So it took a considerable effort of will and discipline to focus on this study. Further, we often found it necessary to wade through an enormous amount of material that was not particularly helpful in its overt content. So this required reading between the lines where the actual evidence ran against one or another author's theoretical framework. And we gradually found that we have somewhat different ways of working and thinking. We touch on one aspect at the other end of the book in the conclusion (on the nature of resistance), but we will not go into detail here. Suffice to say that we have had many, many conversations over the book, often via international vid-phone (as they used to call them), connecting from different parts of the world. Towards the closing stages, we kept our lines open day and almost all night, ready to discuss yet another aspect of the book. But we like the result. We hope and anticipate that it will stir debate since we often seek to think through matters differently and thereby provoke.

Over the years our interlocutors have been many and varied around the topic of the book, including Douglas Oakman, Richard Horsley, Alan Cadwallader, Zhang Shuangli, Zang Fengyu, Zhang Jing, Liang Gong, Hou Linmei, Li Panpan, Davis Hankins, Giovanni Bazzana, and James Harding. Niall McKay assisted us with some early research, related closely to his own work on the Gospel of Mark. Above all, Neil Elliott at Fortress press has urged us along, time and again. Neil is a unique person, a scholar and a publisher, and one who shares a passion for the work of this book.

Introduction

This work proposes nothing less than a new model for understanding the economy of the Greco-Roman era, in which Christianity arose. We do so on two foundations: empirical information, for what it is; and a theoretical model drawn from both *Régulation* economic theory and the work of G. E. M. de Ste. Croix.

In this light, we propose that the Greco-Roman economy had four key building blocks, or what we call institutional forms: subsistence survival agriculture; the reproduction of space entailed in the relations of *polis* and *chōra*; the permutations of tenure; and the slave relation. These building blocks came together in different constellations in which one institutional form dominated the others. These constellations we call regimes, which signal economic patterns with some staying power over time and place. Three such regimes can be identified: the slave regime; the colonial regime, dominated by *polis-chōra*; and the land regime, in which tenure comes to the fore, so much so that it leads eventually to the colonate. Only when we consider the regimes as a whole can we speak of the overarching category of mode of production. In other words, the economy had three articulated layers beginning with the most specific and moving to a more general framework: institutional forms, regimes, and mode of production. Our attention is primarily focused on the first two layers, for these provide detail on the nuts and bolts of the whole system.

Throughout this analysis, we deploy a couple of further distinctions. The first concerns the differences between allocation and extraction, which is more of a continuum than a stark opposition. Allocation designates the allocation and reallocation of labor, tasks, equipment, and produce. How they were reallocated was socially determined. By contrast, extraction is the process whereby those who do not labor rely upon the labor and produce provided by those who do labor. Extraction may appear as exploitation in which surplus is extracted from what one possesses and controls, while expropriation means the extraction of this surplus from what is possessed by another (plunder is the most obvious form, although it often falls under the euphemism of tribute). Of the institutional forms, only subsistence survival is dominantly allocative, while the remaining three—*polis-chōra*, tenure, and the slave relation—are extractive. The rest of the book seeks to unpack and explain in some detail this initial and somewhat dense statement for the sake of understanding the economic context in which Christianity arose, to which it responded, and of which it was to become the dominant and increasingly complex ideology.

Many have been the names given to this economic system, such as slave economy, pre-capitalist market economy, tributary economy, or indeed the ancient mode of production. We prefer not to give it a name immediately, since it is better to analyze what was actually taking place, insofar as that is possible in light of the nature of the evidence available. However, already at this point some may be wondering about our emphases, and indeed what appears to be left out. So let us make a few preliminary points as clearly as we can here (they will become clearer as the book proceeds).

First, agriculture is an economic activity; indeed, it was the primary economic activity in the ancient world. Too often do we find that agriculture is treated separately from the "economy," which is deemed to concern matters of commerce, of barter and trade. This approach misses the prime economic activity in the ancient world. *Second*, we do not treat "markets" driven by profit as a distinct phenomenon. Instead, they appear as part of the slave relation, for we make a strong argument for the determining role of slavery on the nature of exchange in the Greco-Roman era. In other words, markets were a logistical mechanism geared for the procurement of slaves. Since they were thoroughly shaped by the drive for slaves in the economic system, the markets themselves can be seen as byproducts or secondary phenomena. *Third*, we have not made patronage an institutional form in its own right despite the number of those urging what would count as such a position. This is not to say patronage was absent, but rather that it forms part of the reproduction of space in the relations between *polis* and *chōra*. More specifically, patronage belongs primarily to ruling class households where the patterns of honor and shame were the preserve of the obscenely rich, politicians, and criminals (usually rolled into one).

A word of warning is needed: as has been pointed out often, the ancient Greeks and Romans or indeed any other ancient people, did not operate within a horizon of thought, practices, and institutions that involved the categories many of us associate with economic analysis. Statistical analysis, quantitative data, economic models, arguments over economic policy—these and more simply do not appear in the literature. As Meikle puts it, "Scholars have shown empirically, over and over again, that antiquity did not have the institutions, ideas, and practices" of our modern capitalist world.[1]

As for the evidence available, despite its apparent richness, it remains lumpy, regionally uneven, and relatively sparse. In terms of literary resources, where figures actually appear, they are few and unreliable, functioning for different purposes and suffering the vagaries of millennia of transmission and contradictory manuscripts.[2] When they do discuss what we would now call economic matters, they do so in moral, social, and political terms. For example, in the drive of recent decades to shed light on the economic nature of the small corner of the Roman Empire known as Galilee, the literary material includes biblical texts, Josephus, later rabbinic material[3], Greco-Roman material from other regions such as Egypt, and texts that come overwhelmingly from the hands of the ruling class. The problems here are many: the interests of a new religious movement (Christianity), apologetics and propaganda (Josephus), the dangers of reading back later material concerning the idealized "genteel farmer" or, as we prefer,

1. Scott Meikle, *Aristotle's Economic Thought* (Oxford: Clarendon, 1995), 148. Or, as Cartledge observes in relation to slavery, "Thus we have no regular price series for the cost of purchase, cost of maintenance, or amortization of slaves (though we do have some individual figures, and isolated series, their specific interpretation and wider significance are disputed); and we have no figures for calculating the efficiency of slave-use (relevant variables would include labor-inputs, e.g., work in gangs; technological improvements; costs of supervision; size of estates; type of crops; manumission incentives; and slave-mortality)." Paul Cartledge, "The Political Economy of Greek Slavery," in *Money, Labour and Land: Approaches to the Economies of Ancient Greece*, eds. Paul Cartledge, Edward Cohen, and Lin Foxhall, 156–66 (London: Routledge, 2002), 161.
2. Geoffrey Lloyd, "Preface," in *Money, Labour and Land: Approaches to the Economies of Ancient Greece*, ed. Paul Cartledge, Edward Cohen, and Lin Foxhall, xv–xviii (London: Routledge, 2002), xvi; Edward Cohen, "Introduction," in *Money, Labour and Land: Approaches to the Economies of Ancient Greece*, ed. Paul Cartledge, Edward Cohen, and Lin Foxhall, 1–7 (London: Routledge, 2002), 4; Roland Deines, "Galilee and the Historical Jesus in Recent Research," in *Galilee in the Late Second Temple and Mishnaic Period, Volume 1: Life, Culture, and Society*, eds. David Fiensy and James Strange, 11–48 (Minneapolis: Fortress, 2014).
3. Ze'ev Safrai, "Urbanization and Industry in Mishnaic Galilee," in *Galilee in the Late Second Temple and Mishnaic Period, Volume 1: Life, Culture, and Society*, eds. David Fiensy and James Strange, 272–96 (Minneapolis: Fortress, 2014).

the exploitative big peasant (rabbinic material),[4] the risks of drawing from regions that had their distinct histories and emphases (Egyptian papyri),[5] and the many traps of working with material produced by a tiny slice of ancient life (ruling-class texts). By contrast, if we rely on archaeological material, significant extrapolation is required. Such evidence favors the ceramic rather than the aceramic, the durable over the makeshift. Yet, the primary economic activity—in agriculture—was undertaken by those whose lives were makeshift and aceramic. They did not leave behind stone and brick dwellings, expensive decorations, or indeed written texts.[6] The outcome is that for what passes as conventional economic analysis, the evidence is full of lacunae and bias.

So what is to be done? Not a few have sought other means to provide the type of quantitative analysis that passes for economic reconstruction. This task may involve population estimates based on a "density coefficient" or "carrying capacity," the one based on a rather arbitrary estimate of how many persons could live in a "house" and the other making assumptions concerning minimum required calorie intake (usually about 2,000 per day) in relation to soil productivity. Or the task may draw together scattered references concerning food requisitions and transport costs to come up with estimates in relation to the requirements of major centers such as Rome. These efforts remain hypothetical and subject to significant margins of error. With nothing else available, we too have occasionally made use of these estimates to make a point, but we warn that they are no more than educated guesses. Obviously, in this situation, the model one uses to understand the data makes a significant difference. More importantly, the model must not merely seek to squeeze results from resistant evidence, or seek alternative ways to produce the data economic analysis desperately desires. It must also be sensitive to what can be done with what is

---

4. For examples, over-reliance on later rabbinic material vitiates the analyses of Ze'ev Safrai, *The Economy of Roman Palestine* (London: Routledge, 1994); Ze'ev Safrai, "Agriculture and Farming," in *The Oxford Handbook of Jewish Daily Life in Roman Palestine*, ed. Catherine Hezser, 246–63 (Oxford: Oxford University Press, 2010); Ben-Zion Rosenfeld and Joseph Menirav, *Markets and Marketing in Roman Palestine*, trans. Chava Cassel (Leiden: Brill, 2005). For useful warnings in using idealistic rabbinic material, see Philip Harland, "The Economy of First-Century Palestine: State of the Scholarly Discussion," in *Handbook of Early Christianity: Social Science Approaches*, ed. Anthony Blasi, Jean Duhaime, and Paul-André Turcotte, 511–27 (Walnut Creek: Altamira, 2002), 522–25.

5. For good introductions and methodological surveys of the Egyptian papyri, see Roger Bagnall, *Reading Papyri, Writing Ancient History* (London: Routledge, 1995); Roger Bagnall, ed., *The Oxford Handbook of Papyrology* (Oxford: Oxford University Press, 2009).

6. On the question of literacy per se, see the fine survey by Carol Bakhos, "Orality and Writing," in *The Oxford Handbook of Jewish Daily Life in Roman Palestine*, ed. Catherine Hezser, 482–501 (Oxford: Oxford University Press, 2010), 483–87.

available. Our sense is that the approach we use is most appropriate to this situation.

So let us lay out our assumptions before turning to a synopsis of the book as a whole. To begin with, we do not buy into the ever-shifting distinction between "ideological" and "empirical" studies. This distinction may be framed in terms of sociological versus archaeological, theological versus scientific, and so on. It is a simple point but often needs repeating: we all work with models and frameworks through which we process information. Ideally, the information assists in reshaping the model in question. We constantly seek to be aware of the theoretical model we are using, but we feel that this is far better than eschewing interest in theoretical frameworks, for then they are all the more powerful.

As a related point, we find curiously naïve the suggestion that one should use approaches that have been applied by the ancients themselves. This proposal is supposed to avoid methodological anachronism without being aware that all of the approaches we use are anachronistic. Far better, then, to develop an approach that is constantly aware of such anachronisms, so much so that it is built into the approach itself. The best way this can be achieved is via a narrative of difference in which the very difference between ancient and modern worlds (or, rather, modes of production) is written into and is always present in any analysis. In other words, the critic's work involves a necessary anachronism that cannot be avoided, while at the same time being aware of the function of this anachronism in light of the historical and qualitative difference between distinct modes of production. At the same time, we would like to give this approach a dialectical twist, opting not for a sharp distinction between identity and difference, but rather, in Lévi-Strauss's terms, to observe that it is "not the resemblances, but the differences, which resemble each other."[7]

Finally, our approach is deeply Marxist. We see no need to give apologies for this approach, for its explanatory power far exceeds whatever else is available. Above all, Marxist methods enable us to identify the more substantial and deeper economic structures instead of imposing theoretical constructs on the material and—like the proverbial bed of Procrustes— forcing it to fit. However, the dialectical secret is that an approach like this can deal with the evidence because of the heuristic framework provided by the theory. At the same time,

7. Claude Lévi-Strauss, *Totemism*, trans. Rodney Needham (Harmondsworth: Penguin, 1962), 149.

the apparent confidence of our reconstruction should always be taken with a sense of "maybe" or "possibly." Our direct statements function as a mechanism to convince readers of our proposal, which should be taken as a rhetorical strategy in its own way. Yet this strategy should always be qualified by the "maybe" that underlies it.

In terms of practical matters, we have made some terminological choices to which we remain consistent. We prefer Greco-Roman to Hellenistic, since the latter term assumes a primarily cultural referent; our interest is in economics. We do not distinguish between the Roman Republic and the Empire, of which the principate forms a part, roughly 27 BCE to 235 CE, to be followed by the outright emperors. These are political distinctions that have little bearing on economic realities. And when we do refer to the region of the southern Levant, we have opted for the widely-used term Syria-Palestine. This is a descriptive term for a particular region, which underwent many name changes over time and colonial overlord: these include, but are not limited to, Persian-era Yehud, the Roman-era Judea and then Syria-Palaestina. Indeed, the locations in which Christianity first gained traction cannot be isolated from the wider context of the Mediterranean and ancient Southwest Asia. So we do not give preference to the "search for the historical Galilee," for this makes little sense without understanding how this backwater related to the eastern Mediterranean and indeed the Roman Empire as a whole. Indeed, there is a logic within the Christian movement that behooves a wider perspective, in terms of the *longue durée*—since our time-frame runs into the fourth century CE, Christianity itself was by that time an empire-wide creed.

Many times did we quail before the task we set ourselves. Surely, we thought, the time scale is too vast and the regional variations too bewildering for a study such as this. Surely, there are scholars better equipped than us to deal with the matters at hand. And why did we find that we were pushing against what seemed at times like an overwhelming tide of approaches that we designate "economics imperialism," deploying neoclassical economic approaches without being aware of the limits and, indeed, the history of such an approach. But each time we wavered, we once again took courage from Wallerstein's observation that one's ability to participate intelligently in the development of one's own system depends upon the ability to understand the whole: "The more difficult we acknowledge this task to be, the more urgent it is that we start sooner rather than later."[8]

It remains to offer a synopsis of the chapters that follow. The first chapter is theoretical, always a necessity in ventures such as this. Here we explain in some detail why a neoclassical economic approach falls well short, not merely for understanding the economies of the ancient world but also capitalism. This has much to do with its imperializing tendencies—known as "economics imperialism"—in which the specific conditions of its emergence were systematically forgotten in the process of desocializing, individualizing, and dehistorizing. We also give careful attention to the primitivist-modernist debate, running from the nineteenth century only to morph in the twentieth century into the substantivist-formalist distinction with a Weberian turn. This long-running debate turns on the distinction between difference and identity with most preferring to see the terms as qualitatively distinct rather than dialectically related. The upshot is that while our work does not fall into the perimeters of the primitivist-modernist—or substantivist-formalist—debate, we do draw some insights from it. The final section of this chapter introduces a careful overview of both the unjustly neglected work of G. E. M. de Ste. Croix and the Marxist-inspired economic model provided by *Régulation* theory. Ste. Croix's great insights are into the inescapable class structure of the ancient Greek world, in terms of unfree labor (seen in terms of slavery) and the small ruling class. *Régulation* theory provides us with the subtle framework of institutional forms, regimes, modes of production, and mode of *régulation*.

With this theoretical material in mind, the following few chapters deal with the institutional forms. Thus, in the second chapter we present subsistence survival, which was resolutely agricultural, primarily an allocative institutional form and the reality for the majority of people. To be clear, subsistence survival relies not on a vague idea of subsistence, but designates a specific economic reality. This reality involves what was already a millennia-old practice of animal husbandry and the cultivation of crops. As for animals, the preferred combination was sheep and goats, with ratios of two-thirds sheep and one-third goats. Crops involved what one would expect in ancient Southwest Asia and the Mediterranean: wheats, barley, legumes, and olive and grape orchards. Crucially, the process of allocating labor and produce turned on field-shares that were reallocated every one or two years depending on requirements and available labor. At the same time, we also identify a tension in which the equalization of realloca-

---

8. Immanuel Wallerstein, *The Modern World-System I: Capitalist Agriculture and the Origins of the European World-Economy in the Sixteenth Century* (Berkeley: University of California Press, 2011), 10.

tion ran against the distinctions between exploitative big peasants and the middle-to-small peasants.

The next chapter deals with the two institutional forms that arise from the reproduction of space. The first of these concerns *polis* and *chōra*, which we initially draw from Ste. Croix and then develop in light of Henri Lefebvre's argument that space is produced and reproduced by each economic formation. We are particularly interested in the colonial shape of the *polis-chōra* relation, for the *poleis* in question were Greek impositions from the time of Alexander of Macedon. Here we find that the cultural aspect of the *polis* (language, architecture, institutions) was part and parcel of the far more significant economic function, which was to demand produce to support the *polis* from the colonized hinterland, the *chōra*. The Romans subsequently modified the functions of the *poleis* so that they became more closely enmeshed with Rome so as to enable imperial administration. However, we do not take sides in the ongoing argument over whether the relations between *polis* and *chōra* were conflictual or symbiotic, exploitative or beneficial. Instead, both apply, for the most effective form of exploitation is the smoothest: symbiotic relations without disruptions are by far the most effective way to ensure exploitation continues.

The other type of reproduction of space was tenure, which we define as an extractive situation in which land is worked (requiring labor) for the benefit of the one controlling the land. We begin by identifying three main types of tenure that applied towards the beginning of our period: those not under tenure (really anti-tenure); those under lifetime tenure in return for certain obligations, such as military service; those under short-term tenure, the conditions of which could be changed at any time. It was clearly in the interest of the ruling class to reduce the first category and force as many as possible into the third. In this chapter we examine two such mechanisms—estates and debt—with debt functioning to secure labor, ensure the flow of wealth to none other than the wealthy ruling class, and the reinforcing of class hierarchies. In the chapter on regimes, we pick up the most sustained effort to reduce as many as possible to the third category: the development of the colonate.

The fourth chapter concerns what we call the slave relation on which much has been written. After dealing with some theoretical matters (indeed, objections to the importance of slavery from some Marxist critics), and after stressing the sheer ubiquity of slaves in terms of the tasks they undertook and the commonality of slave exchange, we develop our argument for the shaping of Greco-Roman markets by slavery. Ancient markets did not exist as entities unto themselves, for which slaves happened to be "commodities" in "demand." Instead, the very nature of markets was determined by the overwhelming need to procure slaves. The Greeks and Romans could not imagine a world without slaves. But how did such a determination function? We identify the inescapable role of slavery in the Roman invention (late second century) of absolute private property. Tellingly, this property was defined as a relation between a human being and an object, with the crucial caveat that the thing (*res*) in question was a slave. This invention had profound ramifications for everything else exchanged in Roman times. Even more, this move entailed a new level of abstraction. While a significant leap in perceptions of abstraction took place with the invention of coinage (at the same time in China, India, and Lydia), with the concomitant discovery of monotheisms and universal religions in the "axial age," another shift took place with regard to private property: now abstract value could be attached to a human being, on the condition that the human being in question was none other than a thing (*res*). The effect on exchange was as profound as it was unexpected: the slave became the hand of the master, the embodiment of Aristotle's sentient tool or automaton that enacted without direction the will of the master. The reason is that the slave did not have *potestas*, but was part of the master's *potestas*. Thus a slave did not count as an agent in his or her own capacity, but acted only in the capacity of the master. The apparent paradox is that this situation enabled slaves to act in exchange, because they did so as the hand of the master. The markets that were shaped by slavery were also the locations where slaves acted as the extension of their masters.

In the fifth chapter we move to more obviously synchronic concerns, identifying the regimes that were constituted by different constellations of the four institutional forms. A regime marks a period of relative economic stability, with its attendant compromises and reasonably effective efforts to deal with crisis. These are the slave, colonial, and land regimes with the respective dominant institutional forms being the slave relation, *polis-chōra*, and tenure. Missing here is a subsistence survival regime, yet it remains the ghost that forever haunted the three others. Each of the three was mostly extractive, seeking different approaches to negating and subsuming the constitutive resistance of subsistence survival. The slave and colonial regimes arose and existed side by side in different parts of the Greco-Roman world.

Thus, the slave regime emerged in the wake of the long "dark age" of Greek history, which went longer than the "collapse" and "crisis" of ancient Southwest Asia. Of course, the centuries-long period (end of second millennium BCE to the early centuries CE) was a boon for the majority of people engaged in agriculture along subsistence survival lines. But with the emergence of the "classical" age in Greece, the slave regime had appeared as a new way to deal with subsistence survival. The regime underwent many modifications into Roman times, transforming Italy by the second century BCE and many other areas under Rome's increasing sway. By contrast, the colonial regime became the norm in many of the colonized areas, first in the eastern Mediterranean and ancient Southwest Asia with Greek conquests, and then in regions conquered by the Romans beyond these areas. Here the colonial form of *polis-chōra* relations dominated, drawing the slave relation, tenure, and subsistence survival under its sway. However, another tendency was already underway, seeking to draw those not enslaved into the orbit of tenure. By the late third century CE, this process was officially enacted by Diocletian's reform, according to which all rural laborers were to be tied to specific land (estate or, more commonly, in Egypt and Syria-Palestine to villages) and entered in the census accordingly, with such a status becoming hereditary. Ostensibly a fiscal reform it was also aimed at restricting the movement of peasants, which was one of their most effective weapons when exploitation became too onerous. In light of the fundamental shift from being subject to a master or landlord to being tied to land, we call this the land regime. It did not negate slavery for this institutional form continued, even at an ideological level, for the peasants so tied were designated as "slaves of their land." Finally, only when we have all of the regimes are we able to speak of a mode of production, which we prefer to call the ancient mode of production.

Although the matter of early Christianity and its texts lies behind our analysis in the previous chapters, in chapter six we address this matter directly. Here the mode of *régulation* comes into play, which we understand as the various cultural assumptions, social norms and networks, institutions, patterns of conduct, and, especially, belief systems that enable the stability of specific regimes. We also see mode of *régulation* as a potential facilitator of change in the way it anticipates at ideological and organizational levels the shape of a new order. Usually unwitting, this anticipation embodies the tensions of the change in question. In this light do we understand early Christianity, which became a major aspect of the mode of *régulation* of the later Roman Empire. Thus, Christianity may initially have bolstered the slave regime, and it may have been a *polis*-based movement (so much that the Gospel representations of the *chōra* are provided from the perspective of the *polis*), but it was most effective in facilitating the later change to the land regime, which in turn opened up some of the myriad lines that would lead to that unique European mode of production, feudalism.

The conclusion takes a slightly different tack, drawing out a debate that has been with us throughout the writing of the book: is there any form of resistance embodied in the texts of early Christianity, and, if so, what might they be. Christina prefers to see resistance as generated out of the dominant framework, so much so that resistance serves that framework. Roland agrees with the pervasiveness of the ruling ideology and economic system, but prefers to seek out the inconsistencies and breaks—particularly in the way they reveal efforts to contain and subdue potential resistance. The conclusion by no means seeks to resolve this debate, but we raise it because not a few scholars of the Bible and early Christianity have an interest in this question.

1

Economic Theory

The theoretical basis for this study is provided by the work of G. E. M. de Ste. Croix and *Régulation* theory, both of which come out of the rich tradition of Marxist economic analysis. Our reason is simply that Marxist approaches are the most flexible, provide the most adequate analysis of the data, and are able to produce insights outside the purview of other approaches. But is Marxism not too "ideological"? Would it not be better to pursue a more "scientific" approach, if not simple empiricism? We prefer to identify our framework clearly, examining its potential and refining it for the task at hand. This is far preferable to leaving our approach assumed and unexamined, under the cover of focusing on unadorned "facts." Indeed, we find that the tendency to leave a framework untouched makes it so much stronger.[1] Some may feel a knee-jerk resistance to a Marxist-inspired approach, due perhaps to political predilections, to a witting or unwitting allegiance to a liberal or conservative project or indeed prejudice. In response, we take in the present work a minimal position: the analytic power

---

1. The best elaborations on this situation remain Hayden White, *Metahistory: The Historical Imagination in Nineteenth-Century Europe* (Baltimore: The Johns Hopkins University Press, 1973); Hayden White, *Tropics of Discourse: Essays in Cultural Criticism* (Baltimore: The Johns Hopkins University Press, 1978); Hayden White, *The Content of the Form: Narrative Discourse and Historical Representation* (Baltimore: The Johns Hopkins University Press, 1987). For an insightful deliberation relating to ancient historical study and especially early Christianity, see Elizabeth A. Clark, *History, Theory, Text: Historians and the Linguistic Turn* (Cambridge: Harvard University Press, 2004).

of our approach should be assessed in light of its ability to generate new insights. Indeed, we would argue that the sophistication of Marxist approaches grows with each generation, not least in the context of the revival of such approaches in the last decade or more.[2] Since we do not claim to have produced the definitive study beyond which no further discussion is possible, our hope is that we will at least produce some new questions which require further debate and analysis.

Our theoretical analysis has three main parts. We begin by analyzing the shortcomings of neoclassical economic approaches to the period of early Christianity. Why not begin with Marxist approaches? The reason is that neoclassical economics remains the dominant and mostly unexamined model for efforts to reconstruct this part of the ancient economy. The burden of the first section is to establish why and how this dominance has been achieved; suffice to note here that it is part of a wider ideological and political triumphalism that arose in the last years of the twentieth century. We seek to denaturalize what seems natural to many, to destabilize the comfort of working within an apparently un-transcendable horizon of "given" assumptions concerning economic analysis. In short, a neoclassical economic approach is woefully inadequate for reconstructing the economic situation of early Christianity, let alone for the world in which we live. The second section tackles the perennial debate over primitivism and modernism in relation to studies of the ancient world. Many are those who have announced the supersession of this debate, only to take a position within it once again or to champion a revised neoclassical economic approach. We prefer to interpret the primitivist-modernist debate as a dialectic that reveals an inescapable dimension of any work on the distant past. This approach to the debate is enabled by the Marxist framework within which we operate—the topic of the third section. Here we engage critically with the magisterial but unjustly neglected work—at least in biblical studies—of G. E. M. de Ste. Croix. Many are his insights into the complex dimensions of the class struggle in the ancient world, but we also seek to situate his work within the methodological insights of *Régulation* theory, our final topic in this chapter. With our critical

---

2. For example, see Chris Wickham, ed., *Marxist History Writing for the Twenty-First Century* (Oxford: Oxford University Press, 2007). For insightful analyses of the long and rich legacy of Marxist approaches to archaeology, see Randall McGuire, *A Marxist Archaeology* (New York: Percheron, 2002); Thomas Patterson, *Marx's Ghost: Conversations with Archaeologists* (Oxford: Berg, 2003). See also the symposium on Marxism and Archaeology in *Rethinking Marxism* 17, no. 3 (2005). And for a general survey of economic studies that relate in some way to early Christianity and the Bible, see Harland, "Economy of First-Century Palestine."

development of Ste. Croix and *Régulation* theory, we are then able to begin the reconstruction of the ancient Greco-Roman economy, within which Christianity arose, in the remaining chapters of the book.

Neoclassical Economics

[There] is . . . a certain propensity in human nature, . . . the propensity to truck, barter, and exchange one thing for another.[3]

Although many biblical scholars and historians of ancient economies draw upon neoclassical economics, we do not.[4] The reasons for its inadequacy are many but we emphasize its claims to a form of disciplinary and ideological imperialism, which has become known as economics imperialism. A dual process is involved with such imperialism in which radical reductionism produces a set of basic premises which are then applied to all human activity at all times. In other words, economics imperialism involves a false universal, which simultaneously draws upon the specific, limited conditions of a particular approach and negates those specifics to claim universality.

In a little more detail, economics imperialism is premised on the three reductions of individualizing, desocializing, and dehistoricizing.[5] Thus, the individual—as rational, self-interested, and determined by utility—becomes the focus of analysis; the "market" becomes an entity unto itself with its own dynamics and without any social basis; and this "market" is regarded as without history since it exists whenever any individual exchanges something with another individual. Now the dialectical twist appears: on the basis of this triple reductionism, the universalizing and imperializing mission of neoclassical economics can take place. With the removal of history, society, class, politics, institutions, and even religion, this retooled version of neoclassical economics engages in colonizing precisely the areas it has so systematically cut

3. Adam Smith, *An Inquiry into the Nature and Causes of the Wealth of Nations* (Oxford: Oxford University Press, 1979), 1.2.1.
4. The following criticism of neoclassical economics is summarized from Roland Boer, *The Sacred Economy of Ancient Israel*, Library of Ancient Israel (Lousville: Westminster John Knox, 2015), 11–18; Roland Boer and Christina Petterson, *Idols of Nations: Biblical Myth at the Origins of Capitalism* (Philadelphia: Fortress, 2014).
5. Dimitris Milonakis and Ben Fine, *From Political Economy to Economics: Method, the Social and the Historical in the Evolution of Economic Theory* (London: Routledge, 2009); Ben Fine and Dimitris Milonakis, *From Economics Imperialism to Freakonomics: The Shifting Boundaries between Economics and Other Social Sciences* (London: Routledge, 2009). For the connection to archaeology, where individual "agency" is the code for neoliberal individualizing, see Thomas Patterson, "The Turn to Agency: Neoliberalism, Individuality, and Subjectivity in Late-Twentieth-Century Anglophone Archaeology," *Rethinking Marxism: A Journal of Economics, Culture & Society* 17, no. 3 (2005): 373–82.

away. Even more, in an extraordinary example of disciplinary chauvinism, it launches itself into every conceivable corner of human existence. Its basic and narrow principles of individual rationality and equilibrium—that human motivation is primarily economic[6]—are applied to history, geography, institutions, human psychology, functions of the brain (neuroeconomics), and now to religion itself.[7] While these developments first appeared in the earlier twentieth century, they became rampant from the late 1980s, especially in the wake of the triumphalism that followed the "fall" of communism. The signal of this economics imperialism is the self-description as "mainstream" economics or even to universalize this particular approach without acknowledging any others and simply call it "economics."

In order to understand the universalizing assumptions of neoclassical economics, we need to go back to some of the key points in classical economic theory.[8] The surprising feature of this work is its concern with human nature—surprising because neoclassical economics asserts a "scientific" basis for its assumptions rather than indeterminable philosophical questions. The key here is the work of the moral philosopher Adam Smith (1723–1790), especially what may be called his "fable of the dogs." This fable follows the well-known saying concerning human nature: there exists, Smith writes, a "certain propensity in human nature," which is "the propensity to truck, barter, and exchange one thing for another."[9] However, Smith does not back up this dubious assertion with careful argumentation, but rather with a fetching fable concerning dogs. These dogs represent all animals, whose nature is supposed to be distinct from that of human beings. Do animals too exchange with one another? "Nobody ever saw a dog make a fair and deliberate exchange of one bone for another with another dog." Indeed, "Nobody ever saw one animal by its gestures and natural cries signify to another, this is mine, that yours; I am willing to give

---

6. To which Polanyi's succinct response is that "No human motive is per se economic." Karl Polanyi, *Primitive, Archaic and Modern Economies* (Boston: Beacon, 1971), 63.
7. For example, see Lionel Charles Robbins, *An Essay on the Nature and Significance of Economic Science* (London: Macmillan, 1935); Gary S. Becker, *The Economic Approach to Human Behavior* (Chicago: University of Chicago Press, 1976); Rachel McCleary, ed., *The Oxford Handbook of the Economics of Religion* (Oxford: Oxford University Press, 2010); Larry Witham, *Marketplace of the Gods: How Economics Explains Religion* (Oxford: Oxford University Press, 2010).
8. Classical economic theory developed slowly from the early seventeenth century (arguably with Hugo Grotius, 1583–1645) to come to full flower in the nineteenth century. Neoclassical economic theory arose in the early twentieth century, seeking to affirm the basic postulates of classical economics, albeit shorn of the latter's moral, social, and political agenda.
9. Smith, *Wealth of Nations*, I.ii.1. Later he writes of the "natural inclinations of man," by which he means this initial assertion (III.i.3; see also II.i.2).

this for that."[10] A dog can only obtain what it wants by fawning over its master—exchange or barter is simply not the way dogs, or indeed any other animals, operate.

Our point is not merely the problematic nature of Smith's argument, but also the way his economic arguments are based on assumptions concerning human nature. Indeed, this assertion concerning the "natural" propensity for human beings to truck, barter, and exchange, is actually part of what may be called the "founding myth of Adam Smith," which structures the magnificently flawed storybook called *Wealth of Nations*.[11] The myth concerns a "tribe of hunters of shepherds" which undergoes a benign process of specialization and then exchange.[12] Eventually, "every man thus lives by exchanging, or becomes in some measure a merchant, and the society itself grows to be what is properly a commercial society."[13] Add to this stockpiling and the invention of money and credit and our entrepreneurial tribesmen have revealed their inherently capitalist nature. There is a small problem with this "most important story ever told,"[14] for it is no more than a myth. True, it has entered into the realm of common sense through thousands of repetitions, but this tribe or village simply never existed and will never exist. It is pure fantasy, but this is precisely the power of myth, for myth is remarkably resilient to factual evidence.[15] At the same time, myth operates—in light of its curious history—in a dialectic between fiction and deeper truth.[16] We do not mean that Smith provides an insight into human nature, as many would assert, but that the deeper truth of this myth is the creation of an entity called "the economy"—an entity distinct from the state, politics, social dynamics,

10. Smith, *Wealth of Nations*, I.ii.2.
11. It is not a work of science in any conventional sense, for it overflows with fables, sayings, moral tales, vignettes, parables, and especially myths. See especially Murray Rothbard, *An Austrian Perspective on the History of Economic Thought I: Economic Thought Before Adam Smith* (Auburn: Ludwig von Mises Institute, 2010), 435–74; Jacob Viner, *Essays on the Intellectual History of Economics* (Princeton: Princeton University Press, 1991), 101.
12. Smith inherited the myth from a longer tradition that may be traced back to Grotius and Locke, although they were explicit in their efforts to retell the story of Genesis 2-3 so that private property, freedom, labor, law, human society, and commerce were the result of God's will and not of the Fall. Hugo Grotius, *Commentary on the Law of Prize and Booty*, ed. Martine Julia Van Ittersum, trans. John Clarke (Indianapolis: Liberty Fund, 2006), 315–21; John Locke, *Two Treatises of Government and A Letter Concerning Toleration*, ed. Ian Shapiro (New Haven: Yale University Press, 2003 [1691]). See further, Boer and Petterson, *Idols of Nations*.
13. Smith, *Wealth of Nations*, I.iv.1.
14. David Graeber, *Debt: The First 5,000 Years* (New York: Melville House, 2011), 24.
15. Georges Sorel, *Reflections on Violence*, trans. T. Hulme and J. Roth (New York: Collier, 1961).
16. Bruce Lincoln, *Theorizing Myth: Narrative, Ideology, and Scholarship* (Chicago: University of Chicago Press, 2000); Roland Boer, *Political Myth: On the Use and Abuse of Biblical Themes* (Durham: Duke University Press, 2007).

and ideology. But why? A new discipline needed an object to study with distinct features such as exchange, trade, and profit. And this realm could come into its own only if it was free from "interference," whether by the state, social dynamics, or institutions. The seeds of economics imperialism had already been laid, but we note here that many who work on ancient economics, particularly in relation to early Christianity, continue to be beguiled by this understanding of "the economy." They assume that what counts as "the economy" is autonomous and self-regulating, where individual "entrepreneurs" engage in trade and commerce, following their natural inclinations in terms of rational self-interest and comparative advantage without any consideration for socially determining forces.[17]

Smith's *Wealth of Nations* has become in many respects the "Bible" of capitalism, although it usually functions as a source of slogans for neoliberals keen to bolster their approach to economics, all of which is guided by the infamous "invisible hand." But how did this "Bible" of capitalism lead to the economics imperialism we have today? The development was substantial,[18] although a notable feature is the way "Adam Smith" has become a master-slogan in his own right. A few subsidiary slogans are drawn from his work without careful study of their context: invisible hand of the market; the power of self-interest; and the core of human nature to truck, barter, and exchange. The process of such sloganeering acts as a result and symptom of a process that initially sought to excise the moral, social, and political dimensions of "political economy." The reductionism soon gained pace at the hands of the Marginalists: William Stanley Jevons, Carl Menger, and Léon Walras. They proposed that a newly dubbed "neoclassical economics" should focus on problem-solving, drawing upon statistical analysis, quasi-scientific calculations, and mathematical formulae, focusing attention on price mechanisms, money, credit, and exchange. These were seen as the "true" concerns of economic research.[19] No longer would such a discipline be at home among the moral philosophers

17. Eduard Meyer, *Geschichte des Altertums* (Stuttgart: J.G. Gotta'sche Buchhandlung Nachfolger, 1907), IV: 516–17; Kajsa Ekholm and Jonathan Friedman, "'Capital' Imperialism and Exploitation in Ancient World Systems," in *Power and Propaganda: A Symposium on Ancient Empires*, ed. Mogens Trolle Larsen, 41–58 (Copenhagen: Akedemisk Forlag, 1979), 41; George Gotsis and Sarah Drakoupolou Dodd, "Economic Ideas in the Pauline Epistles of the New Testament," *History of Economics Review* 35 (2002): 13-34; George Gotsis and Gerasimos Merianos, "Early Christian Representations of the Economy: Evidence from New Testament Texts," *History and Anthropology* 24, no. 3 (2012): 467–505; Guillermo Algaze, *Ancient Mesopotamia at the Dawn of Civilization: The Evolution of an Urban Landscape* (Chicago: University of Chicago Press, 2008), 42.
18. For the details, see Milonakis and Fine, *From Political Economy to Economics*; Fine and Milonakis, *From Economics Imperialism to Freakonomics*.

or even the arts and humanities. Instead, it sought to migrate to the applied sciences. Now an "economist" simply deployed specific techniques, so that "economics" would become a "scientific" discipline.[20] Of course, banishing politics and advocacy never succeeds, for it finds another way of being present. In this case, the concern with providing theoretical guidelines for policy, if not policy and direct advice itself, served to bolster the assumed coordinates of liberal democracies and capitalist economies. Wallerstein puts it best: economics took the form of a university discipline in which "the Western world studied itself, explained its own functioning, the better to control what was happening."[21] The groundwork was laid for the economics imperialism that came into its own at the end of the decade of the 1980s.

The Greco-Roman era has not been immune from economics imperialism, especially since 1989. In recent decades, more and more scholars have used the cover of an apparent methodological liberalism to apply the terminology of a "market economy", assuming one or more slogans from the meager arsenal of neoclassical economics. These include "scarcity," "maximization of profit," "commodification," "monetization," "economic capital," "fixed capital," "human capital," "supply and demand," "comparative advantage," "labor market," "market exchange," "specialization of labor," "net profit," "economic rationality," "international competition," "economic growth," "GDP," and, of course, "market economy."[22] The terminological array gives the air of

---

19. Or as Braudel observed, "nothing is intelligible until it has been put into statistics." Fernand Braudel, *The Structures of Everyday Life*, trans. M. Kochan, revised ed. (New York: Collins, 1981), 23.
20. Mark Blaug, "The Formalist Revolution of the 1950s," *Journal of the History of Economic Thought* 25, no. 2 (2003): 145–56; E. Roy Weintraub, *How Economics Became a Mathematical Science* (Durham, North Carolina: Duke University Press, 2002).
21. Immanuel Wallerstein, *The Modern World-System IV: Centrist Liberalism Triumphant, 1789–1914* (Berkeley: University of California Press, 2011), 264. See also Ben Fine and Dimitris Milonakis, "From Freakonomics to Political Economy," *Historical Materialism* 20, no. 3 (2012): 81–96.
22. Séan Freyne, "Herodian Economics in Galilee: Searching for a Suitable Model," in *Modelling Early Christianity: Social-Scientific Studies of the New Testament in Its Context*, ed. Philip Esler, 22–44 (London: Routledge, 1995), 31, 41; Edward Harris, "Workshop, Marketplace and Household: The Nature of Technical Specialization in Classical Athens and Its Influence on Economy and Society," in *Money, Labour and Land: Approaches to the Economies of Ancient Greece*, eds. Paul Cartledge, Edward Cohen, and Lin Foxhall, 67–99 (London: Routledge, 2002), 323–48; William Harris, "The Late Republic," in *The Cambridge Economic History of the Greco-Roman World*, eds. Walter Scheidel, Ian Morris, and Richard Saller, 511–39 (Cambridge: Cambridge University Press, 2007); William Harris, *Rome's Imperial Economy: Twelve Essays* (Oxford: Oxford University Press, 2011), 257–87; Walter Scheidel, "Slavery in the Roman Economy," *Princeton/Stanford Working Papers in Classics* (2010), https://www.princeton.edu/~pswpc/pdfs/scheidel/091003.pdf: 10–12; Chris De Wet, "Slavery in John Chrysostom's Homilies on the Pauline Epistles and Hebrews: A Cultural-Historical Analysis" (PhD, University of Pretoria, 2012); Peter Temin, *The Roman Market Economy* (Princeton: Princeton University Press, 2013). Perhaps the most sustained example of economics imperialism is the large collection by Walter Scheidel, Ian Morris, and Richard Saller, eds., *The Cambridge Economic History of the Greco-Roman World* (Cambridge: Cambridge University Press, 2007). While Morris initially finds such

being rather hazy, all of it based on the assumed entrepreneurial and rational spirit at the heart of "human nature." This is embodied in the mythical incompetent, *Homo oeconomicus*, who would not last a day in the real world. It is worth noting that the majority of these works appeared during the most significant phase of economics imperialism after 1989.[23] Communism had "failed," it was assumed, and even China, Vietnam, and North Korea seemed to be embarking on the "capitalist road." The truth of "human nature" had at last become clear: human beings are capitalists at heart. Given the opportunity, we will engage in commerce for the sake of self-betterment (never mind that human beings usually make the worst choice rather than the best). So also for our forebears in the Greco-Roman world, including those living in the southern Levant. They too were capitalists of a sort, although they did not quite realize how much.

It should be clear by now that we find neoclassical economics rather bereft of real insights into the ancient world (we would add that it is quite inadequate for analyzing our own context). Our criticism is not merely that this approach is anachronistic, for this is a persistent

---

an approach inadequate, he ultimately uses a neoclassical framework, spiced with Finleyesque, Malthusian, and institutional economic touches, to explain the rise of slavery in classical Greece. Ian Morris, "Hard Surfaces," in *Money, Labour and Land: Approaches to the Economies of Ancient Greece*, eds. Paul Cartledge, Edward Cohen, and Lin Foxhall, 8–43 (London: Routledge, 2002), 20–22, 30–40. For a curious effort to suggest "exchange value" existed even with palaeolithic hunters, see Andrew Sherratt, "Cash-Crops Before Cash: Organic Consumables and Trade," in *The Prehistory of Food: Appetites for Change*, eds. Chris Gosden and Jon Hather, 12–32 (London: Routledge, 1999).

23. As with studies of ancient Southwest Asia, a number of projects were attempted, all with the aim of reconsidering Greco-Roman economics from "new" perspectives and attempting to overcome the terms and binaries of "old" debates. The context in a supposedly post-Cold War Europe is unavoidable. For example, in France a series of conferences on the "ancient economy" was held from 1994, focusing on quantitative analysis. J. Andreau, Pierre Briant, and R. Descat, eds., *Économie antique. Les échanges dans l'Antiquité: le rôle de l'État* (Saint-Bertrand-de-Comminges: Musée Archéologique Départemental, 1994); J. Andreau, Pierre Briant, and R. Descat, eds., *Économie antique. Prix et formation des prix dans les économies antiques* (Saint-Bertrand-de-Comminges: Musée Archéologique Départemental, 1997); J. Andreau, Pierre Briant, and R. Descat, eds., *Économie antique. La guerre dans les économies antiques* (Saint-Bertrand-de-Comminges: Musée Archéologique Départemental, 2000). Further, there is the ongoing Oxford Roman Economy Project, also focusing on quantitative analysis. Alan Bowman and Andrew Wilson, eds., *Quantifying the Roman Economy: Methods and Problems* (Oxford: Oxford University Press, 2009); Alan Bowman and Andrew Wilson, eds., *Settlement, Urbanization, and Population* (Oxford: Oxford University Press, 2011); Alan Bowman and Andrew Wilson, eds., *The Roman Agricultural Economy: Organization, Investment, and Production* (Oxford: Oxford University Press, 2013); Paul Erdkamp, Koenraad Verboven, and Arjan Zuiderhoek, eds., *Ownership and Exploitation of Land and Natural Resources in the Roman World* (Oxford: Oxford University Press, 2015). And the Italian project, Incontri Capresi di Storia dell'Economia Antica. Elio Lo Cascio, ed., *Innovazione tecnica e progresso economico nel mondo romano: Atti degli Incontri capresi di storia dell'economia antica (Capri 13-16 aprile 2003)* (Bari: Edipuglia, 2006); Elio Lo Cascio, ed., *Credito e moneta nel mondo romano: Atti degli Incontri capresi di storia dell'economia antica (Capri 12-14 ottobre 2000)* (Bari: Edipuglia, 2003). See also the celebration of a new-found liberal diversity of approaches in Paul Cartledge, Edward Cohen, and Lin Foxhall, eds., *Money, Labour and Land: Approaches to the Economies of Ancient Greece* (London: Routledge, 2002).

problem for all approaches,[24] but that the reductionist-cum-imperialist nature of neoclassical theory renders it highly suspect. Its individualizing, desocializing, dehistoricizing, and even detheologizing mean that it has conveniently erased the historical conditions of its own emergence, if not the account of its own particular development.[25] The result is a false universal, which entails applying historically conditioned ideas to the broad economic experience of human history. Crucially, it attempts to do so without any sense of historical and spatial difference, or without an adequate account of how human beings moved from such situations to what we have now.

Primitivism or Modernism?

A second major feature of economic research into the Greco-Roman world turns on the perpetual opposition between primitivism and modernism. So persistent is this opposition—despite numerous proclamations in the era of economics imperialism that it has been overcome—that our work may erroneously be regarded by some as yet another manifestation of primitivism: to wit, the assumption that the ancients were so different from us that it becomes nearly impossible to understand their economic lives. Conversely, the modernists suggest that the ancients were largely the same as us ("human nature" again) and so it becomes possible to use a large array of economic terminology from the context of capitalism to understand their economies. As will become clear, we do not take sides in this debate for it traps one within a particular framework that is not very helpful. In order to see why, we offer a critical survey of the primitivist-modernist debate.

Oikos Debate

Stemming from the nineteenth century, the debate was initially called the *oikos* debate.[26] Classicists, historians, and political economists were

---

24. This also means that we cannot in some way escape such anachronism. Instead, approaches need to be constantly aware of this reality and include a "narrative of difference" that accounts for such anachronism. See further Boer, *Sacred Economy*, 41–44.
25. Here Marx's observation in *The Eighteenth Brumaire of Louis Bonaparte* is pertinent: they "performed the task of their time in Roman costume and with Roman phrases, the task of unchaining and setting up modern *bourgeois* society. . . . And in the classically austere traditions of the Roman Republic its gladiators found the ideals and the art forms, the self-deceptions that they needed." Karl Marx, "The Eighteenth Brumaire of Louis Bonaparte," in *Marx and Engels Collected Works*, vol. 11, 99–197 (Moscow: Progress Publishers, 1979), 104.
26. A number of useful accounts of this debate are available, but we have preferred to study the original texts for the sake of highlighting features important to our argument. The best survey is by

divided: was the ancient Greek economy (and then later ancient economies more generally) based on *oikoi*, or households and estates, or was it essentially a market economy that can be analyzed using neoclassical theory? In more detail, was the household economy primary with its focus local and agricultural, and exchange restricted to specific goods produced by craft workers out of local raw materials and for local use? Or was the economy international with large-scale and rationalized industry overtaking agriculture and aiming primarily at export for profit in competition with other ventures?

The initial framework for the debate was set a century and a half ago with an article by the conservative socialist, Johann Karl Rodbertus.[27] His immediate concern was taxation or tribute in the time of the Roman Emperor Augustus in comparison with capitalism. But tax structures were the window through which he sought to espy social and economic structures. As may be expected for a new idea, Rodbertus produced some distinct insights but also mistakes that bedeviled the debate that would ensue. The insights were two: the social determination of economic life, and the sheer differences between economic systems. The mistake was also twofold: the assumption that "economy" refers to exchange, trade, and commercial practice, and the use of a narrative of differentiation. We deal initially with his insights. If one begins with social determination, argued Rodbertus, then one is led to argue for significant economic differences between the modern (capitalist) and ancient worlds. In other words, economics itself does not provide the answer, for economic activity cannot be separated from the social, legal, and political context in which it functions. As we will see, Rodbertus in his own way anticipates a key feature of the *Régulation* theorists upon whom we draw. The economy in any time and place does not exist as an entity unto itself, for it is always socially determined.

In order to make his point, Rodbertus begins with modern taxation. It has multiple quantitative and qualitative distinctions, which rely on the diversity of the multiple layers of social life under capitalism.[28] This

Neville Morley, *Theories, Models and Concepts in Ancient History* (London: Routledge, 2004), 31–47. See also Harry Pearson, "The Secular Debate on Economic Primitivism," in *Trade and Market in the Early Empires: Economies in History and Theory*, eds. Karl Polanyi, Conrad Arensberg, and Harry Pearson, 3–11 (New York: Free Press, 1957); Mohammad Nafissi, "On the Foundations of Athenian Democracy: Marx's Paradox and Weber's Solution," *Max Weber Studies* 1, no. 56–83 (2000): 56–83, 63–65; Gareth Dale, *Karl Polanyi: The Limits of the Market* (Cambridge: Polity, 2010), 137–40.

27. Johann Karl Rodbertus, "Untersuchungen auf dem Gebiete der Nationalökonomie des klassischen Alterthums. II. Zur Geschichte der römischen Tributsteuern seit Augustus," *Jahrbücher für Nationalökonomie und Statistik* 4 (1865): 341–427.

"money economy" cannot function without distinct social, legal, and political arrangements. Items in this variegated economy pass from one part to the other through buying and selling in which each part or layer makes a claim to a share of the income. Legal structures had to come into place over centuries to delineate and consolidate the many parts and their relations to one another. Political structures had to gain definition and strength to ensure the interchange of products within and across borders. Customs, logistics, policing were the roles of the new type of state. And, socially, human beings had to become accustomed to very different ways and patterns of working, socializing, living, and seeing themselves as units in an economy and citizens of a state.

By contrast, ancient economic and social life did not have such differentiation. The social basis was slavery, specifically in the vast slave-worked and slave-run estates of the Roman era. Slaves were responsible for the whole process from raw materials through manufacture to distribution. This meant that the products did not pass through many hands in different layers of the economy, indeed that workers, landowners, and owners of capital were one and same person. As a result, the Romans did not distinguish between different types of taxes for there was only one: the *tributum*. This was paid by the head of such an economic unit, which Rodbertus designated as *oikos*, following Aristotle. This term, by which Rodbertus meant the slave estates of the Roman era, caught the imagination of subsequent scholars. It came to designate a self-sufficient system, predicated on the original Greek meaning of *oeconomia*: the concerns of the household or the estate (the latter was seen as an extended household). Contrary to some earlier dismissals of the household as both a construct and a red herring,[29] we suggest that it was an important theoretical move, especially in light of the burgeoning of household studies over the last three decades.[30] Of course, the meaning of household has undergone significant development in comparison with Rodbertus but his genius was to indicate the importance of the term.

28. In more detail, he distinguished between personal and property taxes; property taxes as either on land or capital; capital as either industrial or commercial; and commercial as either goods (industry) or money (finance). So also with incomes: personal income versus that from impersonal property; the latter in turn produces rent from land or capital gains (profit); and profit in its turn may be divided according to interest or company profits. Rodbertus, "Untersuchungen auf dem Gebiete der Nationalökonomie des klassischen Alterthums," 342–43, 345.

29. Pearson, "Secular Debate on Economic Primitivism," 5.

30. The founding work of modern household studies is that of Richard Wilk and William Rathje, "Household Archaeology," *American Behavioral Scientist* 25 (1982): 617–39.

At the moment of his discovery, Rodbertus stumbled. He assumed that economic activity concerns exchange, trade, and commercial activity more generally. Given the lack of differentiation in an "*oikos* economy," he made this controversial proposal:

> The national product in the course of all its stages of production never changed owners. . . . The inevitable consequence of such a situation had to be an economy-in-kind [*Naturalwirthschaft*]. Now no money was needed to enable the national product to proceed from one production stage to another, since there was no change of ownership.[31]

The problem here is not so much that Rodbertus assumed one needed modern capitalism to enable the exchange of commodities, production and consumption, and financial transactions, but that such activity is the very definition of "economy." Rarely in subsequent debates do we find analyses of agriculture (both crop-growing and animal husbandry) as the main feature of ancient economies. The second problem with Rodbertus's approach is systemic: he deploys a narrative of differentiation. Ancient economies and societies were largely undifferentiated, failing to make the distinctions with which capitalism is familiar. Thus, the process to our "complex" world is one of increasing differentiation of yet more and more distinct features. Unfortunately, such narratives are still common in scholarship today. The catch with Rodbertus is that the narrative of differentiation provides him with the reason for distinguishing the ancient Roman world from his own. There is no cause to do so, for one may be fully aware at every analytic step of the disparity between capitalism and ancient economies.

Rodbertus's pioneering ideas may well have disappeared into the hidden alleys of scholarship were it not for the furious debate that erupted towards the end of the nineteenth century and spilled well into the twentieth. This debate too was characterized both by new insights and by the traps that bedeviled Rodbertus's argument: economics as commercial activity and narratives of differentiation. These traps afflicted proponents of both primitivist and modernist approaches. The most erudite and influential of the former was Karl Bücher's *Die Entstehung der Volkswirtschaft*, which went through seventeen editions between 1893 and 1926.[32] Bücher proposed, in true nine-

---

31. Rodbertus, "Untersuchungen auf dem Gebiete der Nationalökonomie des klassischen Alterthums," 343, 345.
32. The third German edition was translated into English as Karl Bücher, *Industrial Evolution*, trans. Samuel Morley Wickett (New York: H. Holt and Company, 1901).

teenth century style, a grand narrative from "primitive" (or "natural") to modern economics, a process that was characterized by increasing differentiation and complexity. He identified significant economic activity within the framework of this "natural economy," which moves from reciprocal gift exchange in the framework of hospitality to exchange, markets, shares, fees for the use of roads and bridges, the transportation of goods, and even the communication of news. Yet none of this constitutes a *Volkswirtschaft*, a "national" or "public economy," characterized by the complexity of modern economic life on a large territorial scale.[33] Within this schema he located Greek and Roman economies. Given that they were closer to primitive rather than modern forms of the *Volkswirtschaft*, which required the power and influence of the modern state (from 1000 CE onwards),[34] it followed that the ancient economy could not in any sense be regarded as similar to a national or "market" economy. Although exchange existed, especially with slaves, and although wages were paid for professional services, the Greeks and Romans remained bound to a closed domestic economy (*geschlossene Hauswirtschaft*). This was the stage of an independent domestic economy, based on the autonomous household community, the *oikos* (with acknowledgement of Rodbertus). It entailed production solely for the household's own needs in which the goods are consumed where they are produced.[35]

At the same time, Bücher also had a distinct insight: he challenged the myth of *Homo oeconomicus*—the assumption that human beings are by nature economic animals acting rationally for their self-interest.[36] This challenge, articulated clearly in the book's opening pages,[37] structures the whole study. In other words, the debate turned on the question of human nature, which for Bücher changes due to historical conditions. We can only agree, although we add that such changes are marked by intensified disputes over human nature, which is usually

33. Bücher, *Industrial Evolution*, 60–79.
34. "National economy [*Volkswirtschaft*] is the product of a development extending over thousands of years, and is not older than the modern State; for long epochs before it emerged man lived and laboured without any system of trade or under forms of exchange of products and services that cannot be designated national economy." Bücher, *Industrial Evolution*, 88.
35. Bücher, *Industrial Evolution*, 96–102. In the following pages (102–14), Bücher also locates European medieval economics.
36. He even offers a prescient warning of the dangers of what would much later become economics imperialism: "They have almost unwittingly applied to past times the current classifications of modern national economy; . . . they have kneaded away so long at conceptions of commercial life that these perforce appear applicable to all economic periods." Bücher, *Industrial Evolution*, 84–85.
37. See also the specific criticisms of Adam Smith and David Ricardo. Bücher, *Industrial Evolution*, 87–88.

understood to be eternal in such disputes. Bücher's challenge is cast in terms of his narrative of primitive-to-modern, but the point can be made without such a narrative.

Despite the potential to develop economic analysis outside the framework of commercial exchange, Bücher fails to do so. Even with his natural economy, he is concerned to show that what looks like modern commerce is actually couched in terms of gift exchange. This assumption concerning the nature of economics enabled his critics to argue for a "modernist" position, the most telling of whom was Eduard Meyer.[38] In 1895, Meyer launched a lengthy refutation of Rodbertus and Bücher, arguing that the "market", not the *oikos*, was the central economic institution of ancient economies.[39] He marshalled the evidence available at the time (extended now to the whole of ancient Southwest Asia and the Mediterranean) for exchanges of possessions such as slaves, land and buildings, for dealing in weights of gold and silver and then coinage, manufacturing, transportation, and long distance exchange. For Meyer, these indicated "sophisticated industry," "comprehensive commodity exchange," and an "articulated economic life." In short, later antiquity was "thoroughly modern," so much so that ancient Athens of the fifth and fourth centuries lived "under the sign (*unter dem Zeichen*) of capitalism."[40]

Some forty years later, Mikhail Rostovtzeff agreed wholeheartedly. This staunch anti-communist (an exile from the Soviet Union) constructed monumental studies of the Greek and Roman empires that ranged over social, political, and economic matters.[41] Rostovtzeff identified class as a core issue, which will be a feature of our analysis, but how he dealt with class is another matter entirely. His main argument was that the ancient "bourgeoisie" was responsible for the proto-capitalist features of Greco-Roman expansion. It enabled the great success of Greek economics and then the Roman Empire, but it was also responsible for their respective collapses. The reason is that the "bour-

38. For a detailed study of the Bücher-Meyer debate, see André Reibig, "The Bücher-Meyer Controversy: The Nature of the Ancient Economy in Modern Ideology" (PhD, University of Glasgow, 2001).
39. Eduard Meyer, "Die wirtschaftliche Entwicklung des Altertums," in *Kleine Schriften zur Geschichtstheorie und zur wirtschaftlichen und politischen Geschichte des Altertums*, 79–168 (Halle: Niemeyer, 1910). Hard on Bücher's heels came an equally modernist attack by Julius Beloch, "Zur griechischen Wirtschaftsgeschichte," *Zeitschrift für Sozialwissenschaft* 5 (1902): 1–97.
40. Meyer, *Geschichte des Altertums*, IV: 516–17.
41. Mikhail Rostovtzeff, *The Social and Economic History of the Hellenistic World*, 3 vols. (Oxford: Clarendon, 1941); Mikhail Rostovtzeff, *The Social and Economic History of the Roman Empire*, 2 vols. (Oxford: Clarendon, 1957). For a similar approach, see John D'Arms, *Commerce and Social Standing in Ancient Rome* (Cambridge: Harvard University Press, 1981).

geoisie" failed to enable the rural "proletariat" to rise above their lowly status and thereby overcome class conflict, with the result that ancient Greece and the Alexandrian Empire was conquered by the Romans and that subsequently Rome was seized by the rural "proletariat" in allegiance with the army. But who was this ancient "bourgeoisie"? For Rostovtzeff, a "bourgeois" man was an average citizen, "a middle class landowner, a business man, or a rentier, well-to-do but not extremely rich."[42] Although members of this "bourgeoisie" fostered liberty, learning and high culture, and were devoted to the traditional Greek pantheon of gods, building new temples, and maintaining the traditional festivals and games in honor of their gods, Rostovtzeff's argument concerning their identity is primarily economic. The members of this class had become successful due to their own efforts or by means of an inheritance that they had effectively invested. The bourgeoisie was distinguished from other classes by the fact that they were not craftsmen or employees, but the owners of capital, investors, and employers of labor.[43] They enabled industry of all types, foreign and local trade, and even banking—although Rostovtzeff constantly admits that the evidence is scant indeed. In other words, this ancient "bourgeoisie" implemented nothing less than a profit-motivated capitalism.[44]

The time of Rostovtzeff's studies marked almost a century of the "*oikos* debate" with proponents or either side keen to show how the other was grossly mistaken. Despite occasional insights (such as the social determination of the economy, the role of the household, or the importance of class), they all shared some basic assumptions that hobbled the debate. We have noted the persistence of the assumption that the "economy" means industry, trade, and commerce. None of them paid any serious attention to the dominant form of economic life: agriculture.[45] As a consequence of this sense of what the "economy" should

---

42. Rostovtzeff, *Social and Economic History of the Hellenistic World*, I:163. Or in more detail: "This typical citizen for whom Menander wrote his comedies and whom he and Theophrastus chiefly portrayed in their works is not an aristocrat by birth and wealth, nor is he a pauper or a proletarian. . . . He draws his income from his farm, which he manages personally in a rational way with the help of slaves or hired labour, from his commercial operations, mostly marine ventures, or from money-lending. . . . The Athenian *bourgeois* is well-to-do. He lives in a small comfortable residential house and owns one or two domestic slaves. He is not stingy, and on great occasions spends money freely; but he is careful about his affairs. His family is not very large; he generally has one or two children" (I:163). For a more recent effort to resuscitate a comparable "middling farmer," with his ideology of independence and individualism as the roots of "Western civilization," see Victor Davis Hanson, *The Other Greeks: The Family Farm and the Agrarian Roots of Western Civilization*, revised ed. (Berkley: University of California Press, 1999).
43. Rostovtzeff, *Social and Economic History of the Hellenistic World*, II:1115–16.
44. Ibid., II:453.
45. For example, out of the thousands of pages of Rostovtzeff's studies, only twenty pages are devoted

be, they assumed that if one can identify certain features that seem familiar to us, such as exchange, surplus and markets, then this must mean that the system as a whole was in essence the same as capitalism, in which these items also appear. Those who tried to argue that it was not capitalist were forced to deny or at least minimize the presence of such items. But they failed to examine the significant conceptual step between the individual features and the system as a whole. A basic question remained unanswered: is it possible that the function, arrangement, and relations between these and other features operated in a rather different system?

Weberian Insights and Traps

The attempt to answer this question was the genius of Max Weber's engagement with the debate, whose work picked up Rodbertus's emphasis on the social determination of economics. He was quite prepared to accept all of the evidence available for commercial activity, such as trading, markets, and tax farming, even to the point of suggesting that "capitalism shaped whole periods of Antiquity, and indeed precisely those periods we call 'golden ages'."[46] At the same time he warned that seeing similarities with modern economies is quite misleading, for the system as a whole had characteristics that "sharply differentiate" it from medieval and modern forms.[47] Thus, in ancient economies trade was limited in volume and rarely involved bulk goods,[48] long-distance trade was mostly in high-quality and high-labor goods, major acquisitions such as grain were administered by the state, the dominance or pervasiveness of slavery (precisely during high points of "free" political systems), the absence of industrial factories in the technical and operational sense of the term, limited banking in

to agriculture. Even here he is not interested in the "rural proletariat" but in the activities of the "bourgeois" free citizen. Ibid., II:1180–1200.

46. Max Weber, *The Agrarian Sociology of Ancient Civilizations* (London: Verso, 1976), 51.

47. The use of "capitalism" is thus unfortunate and vague, despite his effort at a minimal and non-systemic definition: it involved property as an object of trade for the sake of profit in a market situation. He adduces nine features that may be regarded as capitalist in this sense: 1) government contracts for taxes and public works; 2) mines; 3) sea trade; 4) plantations; 5) banking; 6) mortgages; 7) overland trade; 8) leasing out slaves or establishing them as artisans in return for a percentage of the income; 9) exploitation of slaves in crafts. Yet each item had its own distinct limits that prevented them from becoming full capitalism. Weber, *Agrarian Sociology*, 51–58. For a careful study of Weber's equivocations over "ancient capitalism," see John Love, "Max Weber and the Theory of Ancient Capitalism," in *Max Weber: Critical Assessments*, ed. Peter Hamilton, 270–290 (London: Routledge, 1991), 279–83.

48. See further Max Weber, *General Economic History*, trans. Frank Knight (New York: Collier, 1961), 149–69.

the hands of a few tax farmers,[49] the absence of large scale enterprises based on "free" labor, the cities as sites of consumption rather than production, and the role of *oikoi*, which he redefined in terms of the economic institutions of the political ruling class.[50] In short, "nothing could be more misleading . . . than to describe the economic institutions of Antiquity in modern terms."[51] It would seem that it was actually far from capitalism in any real sense.

Thus far, we have stressed Weber's insight in terms of arguing for the importance of the economic system as a whole and the functions and relations within such a system of the different parts.[52] When he attempted to describe the system his shortcomings come into view. In terms of the Greco-Roman world, he preferred to speak of a form of feudalism based on fortified centers settled by professional warriors who made widespread use of slaves.[53] Military, political, and agrarian concerns were primary in such a feudalism—all of them turning on one of Weber's favored categories, patronage as the concrete manifestation of "status."[54] The purpose of the economic system was to collect goods, whether through trade, tribute or conquest, which were then distributed among the citizens of the "feudal" city-state. The problems are many. First, feudalism becomes a catch-all term, applicable to nearly all precapitalist economic forms and thereby requiring continual distinctions.[55] Second, his treatment of slavery is vitiated by a curious tension: while he acknowledges the central role of slavery, he sets it in contrast with "free" labor. Indeed, Weber conjures up "free" laborers as a distinct force that often challenged the dominance of slaves, although he does so primarily from the perspective of slave owners.[56] This leads to the third problem, which is the overwhelming

---

49. See further Weber, *General Economic History*, 191–200.

50. For Weber, the *oikos* was an authoritarian household of a local or central ruler based around "want satisfaction" rather than profit making.

51. Weber, *Agrarian Sociology*, 45. The reason often adduced is the statist bureaucracy, which he constantly contrasts with individual initiative.

52. Nafissi goes too far in suggesting that eventually Weber's synthesis resolved the *oikos* debate. Nafissi, "On the Foundations of Athenian Democracy," 65.

53. It should be noted that Weber traces the development of three stages in the *polis*: aristocratic, hoplite, and democratic.

54. Weber, *Agrarian Sociology*, 39, 154–55, 161–68. He argues that patronage was strongest with the Romans (275–92).

55. For example, he also describes the Persian era as "feudal," with specific features. Ibid., 220–21, 228.

56. Ibid., 202–6. For a later effort to revive the importance of "free" laborers, see Peter Garnsey, ed., *Non-Slave Labour in the Greco-Roman World* (Cambridge: Cambridge Philological Society, 1980); Peter Garnsey, *Cities, Peasants and Food in Classical Antiquity* (Cambridge: Cambridge University Press, 1998), 135–50. Love describes Weber's thoughts on slavery as "rather weak." Love, "Max Weber and the Theory of Ancient Capitalism," 277.

focus on the ruling class, from the *polis* or imperial city. When the majority involved in agriculture come into view, they challenge a ruling class that must constantly adapt. Fourth, the category of patronage is somewhat overdone, especially in raising it to the overarching economic framework. Instead, it may have functioned as part of one institutional form (as we will argue). Fifth, the much-debated *Stand*, which is almost untranslatable but may be rendered as "status group," speaks of lifestyles determined by esteem or honor.[57] This category should be read as a good description of class consciousness rather than an adequate explanation and analysis of the economic dynamics of class itself. In other words, *Stand* deals with the ideological dimensions of class identity, largely from a ruling class perspective in which status determines the characterization of one's class enemies. Thus, it may give the impression of stratification, if not a spectrum of honor, but this ideological dimension serves to consolidate distinct class identity of the group that imposes patterns of stratification.[58]

Weber had clearly recalibrated the primitivist-modernist debate, so much so that subsequent scholarship was deeply in his debt. Yet, in doing so, he also bequeathed the problems of his proposal to two scholars who were among the most influential in dealing with the ancient economies: Moses Finley and Karl Polanyi.[59] Finley was extremely careful to avoid the tendency to parallelism: when one encounters features of ancient economies that resemble that of capitalism, one should be wary indeed of analyzing them in the same way.[60] Terms such as banking system, investment, credit, labor market, money market, joint stock companies, and capital conjure up a whole range of associations that simply did not exist in the ancient world. For Finley, the ancient Greeks had no idea of what "economic policy" might be, or indeed of an "economy" as it is understood now. He goes on to argue that there is scant evidence for the creation of capital for they sought to amass

57. Richard Swedborg, *The Max Weber Dictionary: Key Words and Central Concepts* (Stanford: Stanford University Press), 269. The key text for Weber's thoughts on *Stand* is Max Weber, *Economy and Society: An Outline of Interpretive Sociology* (New York: Bedminster, 1968), 302–7, 926–40.

58. Ste. Croix argues that *Stand* is a static rather than a dynamic and relational category; it functions as a descriptive rather than explanatory category; and it has distinct shortcomings in relation to class. Our point is that it speaks primarily of the dimension of class consciousness and thereby does not provide an adequate economic analysis of class. G.E.M. de Ste. Croix, *The Class Struggle in the Ancient Greek World: From the Archaic Age to the Arab Conquests* (London: Duckworth, 1981), 85–96.

59. A more immediate predecessor to Finley was Hasebroek, who argued that conquest and colonization constituted the prime motive for Greek expansion. In this "thalassocratic" world, "plain robbery and exploitation" was the driving force rather than "the peaceful activities of commerce." Johannes Hasebroek, *Trade and Politics in Ancient Greece*, trans. L.M. Fraser and D.C. MacGregor (London: G. Bell, 1933), 140.

60. Moses Finley, *The Ancient Economy* (Berkeley: University of California Press, 1999).

wealth and promptly used it to acquire land. Absent, too, is evidence for long-distance transport of bulk goods; business loans (for the sake of producing "capital"); statistical analysis; reflections on price variation from a business perspective; the justification of land holding in terms of maximizing income; or even cost analysis for state ventures such as conquest.

Like Weber, Finley fell on the side of arguing for systemic differences between modern capitalism and the ancient economy of the Greeks and Romans (although they both sought reasons why the ancient economies did not develop into capitalism).[61] But what was the system in question? He was not interested in the "slave mode of production," since, he argued, slaves were not statistically dominant in many periods and regions, slavery has existed in other economic formations, and the need to account for transitions into and out of such a mode of production.[62] Part of this resistance was due to a Weberian inspired rejection of Marxist categories, including that of (a misinterpreted category of) class,[63] but since we will use such categories in our analysis, a brief reply is in order. To begin with, while Finley admits that slavery was in many ways the dominant social and economic form of ancient Greece and Rome, he offers no sustained analysis of the economic function of slaves in the production of surplus, let alone the overwhelming ideological framework in which even agrarian workers in villages were seen in terms of slaves. To be sure, when pressed he emphasizes that "slaves provided the bulk of the immediate income from property . . . of the elites, economic, social and political."[64] But all this depended on location, in terms of owners and role. Beyond this he does not dare to go, settling on the vague "slave society" as the most one can say concerning a system. Further, the presence of slavery in feudalism or capitalism is no real argument, for each mode of production incorporates the contradictions of former modes of production within itself, let alone constellations of what we will call institutional forms into regimes within a mode of production. Still, we have not found an answer to the systemic question. In many respects, we will not find an overt system in Finley's works, since he is peculiarly resistant to systematizing in light of a concern for variation and particularity, all of which is enhanced by a studied "pointillist" approach.

61. Morley, *Theories, Models and Concepts in Ancient History*, 44.
62. Finley, *Ancient Economy*, 62–94, 179–80.
63. Ibid., 183–89. As Ste. Croix points out, Finley's suggestion that slaves and wage laborers were of the same class is a curious misreading of Marx. Ste. Croix, *Class Struggle*, 58.
64. Moses Finley, *Ancient Slavery and Modern Ideology* (Princeton: Markus Weiner, 1998), 150.

Yet a system there is, partially concealed. It appears via a curious move, which is to defer to the self-consciousness of the ancients. The solution: "the social institutions and values make up a coherent system."[65] And how are the "values" manifested? In the very Weberian notion of *Stand* or status group, which was primarily a moral rather than an economic category. Thus the highest moral status was one of a "free man," not dependent on any other, who owned agricultural land as the basis of wealth, which he had acquired rather than produced, and engaged in politics. The lowest was of course the slave.[66] The problem is that status is unable to account for the dynamic of exploitation, let alone the patterns of social and economic change in dealing with the rise and decline of slavery (the undefined notion of "demand" is hardly an answer).[67] Further, as Finley admits, status focuses on the perspective of the elites, for it is difficult indeed to know what the majority actually thought. The ruling class was of course responsible for leaving us their opinions, texts, and ideological framework, but Finley's case would have been strengthened had he made the move to point out that this material reflects the contradictory nature of ruling class consciousness (as Ste. Croix does so well). In our analysis, we are interested in precisely the other side—the ones constantly denigrated and despised by this ideological framework. And Finley's focus on class consciousness says little about economic factors, which is a whole other dimension alongside such consciousness.

Karl Polanyi finally offered what Weber promised and Finley avoided: a systemic answer to what ancient economies might have been. Polanyi's work on ancient economies ranged over ancient Southwest Asia, ancient Greece and eighteenth century West Africa, always seeking to provide a framework for debate.[68] Under the influence of

65. Moses Finley, *The World of Odysseus* (New York: New York Review Books, 2002), xix.
66. Finley, *Ancient Economy*, 47–61, 144.
67. Ste. Croix, *Class Struggle*, 81–98. The best that Finley can do is suggest that status underwent transformations from the time of the Greeks and early Romans, with the two clear statuses of free and slave, to the continuum of status under the later Roman Empire. See Moses Finley, *Economy and Society in Ancient Greece*, eds. Brent Shaw and Richard Saller (London: Chatto & Windus, 1981), 132.
68. Karl Polanyi, Conrad Arensberg, and Harry Pearson, eds., *Trade and Market in the Early Empires: Economies in History and Theory* (New York: Free Press, 1957); Polanyi, *Primitive, Archaic and Modern Economies*; Karl Polanyi, *The Great Transformation: The Political and Economic Origins of Our Time* (Boston: Beacon, 2001). This section is a summary of the discussion of Polanyi in Boer, *Sacred Economy*. Such is the influence of Polanyi that Liverani observes: "Polanyi's influence on economic and political anthropology has now become so pervasive as to make use of many indirect channels—so that an essay could easily be written about 'The impact of Polanyi's theory upon scholars who did never read it.'" Mario Liverani, *Prestige and Interest: International Relations in the Near East ca. 1600–1100 B.C.* (Padua: Sargon, 1990), 20. The best critical assessments of Polanyi remain Maurice Godelier, *The Mental and the Material: Thought, Economy and Society*, trans. Martin Thom (London: Verso, 1986), 179–207; Dale, *Karl Polanyi*.

Malinowski's anthropological studies,[69] Polanyi distinguished three economic patterns that interacted with one another in ever-changing ways: reciprocity (gift-exchange), redistribution (central appropriation and subsequent distribution), and the market.[70] Into this triad he introduced another, differentiating between trade, money, and markets. In contrast to the assumption thus far that these three are always integrated in a market mechanism, with trade seen as a movement of goods through markets and facilitated by money, Polanyi argued that they are not necessarily so connected except under capitalism. Instead, trade operated in very different ways, in terms of reciprocal gift giving or state-controlled acquisition and redistribution (thus as "embedded" trade); markets functioned largely as marginal or peripheral features of ancient life, with customary price; money was a special-purpose or heterogeneous object with specific functions rather than a generalized medium of exchange.[71]

By now it should be clear that Polanyi was deeply concerned with a systemic answer—unlike Finley—to the problems that had come through to him from almost a century of debate. Indeed, he astutely sought to shift the very terms of that debate: instead of the modernism and primitivism divide of the *oikos* debate, he proposed the distinction between formalism and substantivism. Thus, the ancients in those parts of the world either made use of the same economic forms as capitalism (due to the eternity of human nature), or they were substantively different from us, so much so that it becomes difficult indeed to understand how they really functioned. One may also cast the opposition in terms of quantity and quality: both sides did indeed see differences, but was it a matter of quantitative or qualitative difference, of merely having less of the same or not being the same at all? And

69. Bronislaw Malinowski, *Argonauts of the Western Pacific; an Account of Native Enterprise and Adventure in the Archipelagoes of Melanesian New Guinea* (London: Routledge, 1932).
70. Karl Polanyi, "The Economy as Instituted Process," in *Trade and Market in the Early Empires: Economies in History and Theory*, eds. Karl Polanyi, Conrad Arensberg, and Harry Pearson, 242–70 (New York: Free Press, 1957), 245–56; Polanyi, *Primitive, Archaic and Modern Economies*, 207–37; Polanyi, *The Great Transformation: The Political and Economic Origins of Our Time*, 49–58; George Dalton, "Introduction," in Karl Polanyi, *Primitive, Archaic and Modern Economies*, ix–liv (Boston: Beacon, 1971), xxxi–xxxvi. In *The Great Transformation* (55–57). Polanyi also mentions a fourth category, householding, which not only draws on Aristotle's reflections on *oeconomia* but also evokes the *oikos*. The category remains undeveloped. For an effort to develop a Polanyian approach to the economy of Roman Syria-Palestine, see Ekkehard Stegemann and Wolfgang Stegemann, *The Jesus Movement: A Social History of Its First Century*, trans. O.C. Dean, Jr (Minneapolis: Fortress, 1999), 15–52.
71. He does so in three works: Karl Polanyi and Abraham Rotstein, *Dahomey and the Slave Trade: An Analysis of an Archaic Economy* (Seattle: University of Washington Press, 1966); Karl Polanyi, *The Livelihood of Man*, ed. Harry Pearson (New York: Academic Press, 1977); Polanyi, Arensberg, and Pearson, *Trade and Market in the Early Empires*. For a useful discussion, see Dale, *Karl Polanyi*, 141–87.

this is the key, for in his effort to recast the debate Polanyi continued the opposition and clearly opted for the position of substantivist difference.

Let us use the example of ancient Greece, since this is germane to our interests.[72] For Polanyi, Athens first discovered "market methods" as a way for Greek democracy to manage redistribution. Note that he does not speak of an integrated market system. The issue was how to ensure the acquisition of slaves, grain, and metals so to make them available for the citizens of Athens. Even with commoditization, monetization, freight insurance, and shipping (or bottomry) loans, the *polis* itself was the prime mover, rather than any mechanisms of supply and demand in the market itself. Here price is a crucial indicator. With the assumption of customary price, fluctuations were permitted within a limited range, and when they did move precipitously (due to political events) the *polis* intervened to ensure the customary price. In other words, the Athenian *agora* was primarily a device for redistribution, subject to political drivers. Why? The *polis* was the main economic actor, which needed to ensure that its citizens were provisioned, since most of them relied on their own *polis* for their livelihoods.[73]

Polanyi may have filled the systemless void of Finley's work, if not of Weber's, but he produced a new set of problems.[74] *First*, the category of redistribution assumes a centralized authority that appropriates surplus from a population in order to "redistribute" it in various ways, from state building projects through to grain supplements and even in Greece and Rome to theater tickets. This model does not quite work: in the context of the ever-changing and vague boundaries of ancient states, the practice of aspiring despots was acquisition, not redistribution. The overwhelming tendency was centripetal, not centrifugal. And the purposes were the vast building projects, provisioning of armies (which themselves functioned to acquire more wealth), feeding the urban poor (in Rome), and the ostentatious displays of the relatively wealthy lives to which the ruling class and their hangers-on had

---

72. Here we follow Dale, who draws upon Polanyi's manuscripts. Dale, *Karl Polanyi*, 162–72. Dale finds that Polanyi's depiction, even in light of the expected criticism that seeks to find greater evidence of a "market system," largely holds up.

73. Dale notes a caveat in the late fourth century, leading into the subsequent centuries, of a market determined by supply and demand. But this was due not to a "natural" outgrowth of Athenian markets, but the use of the market by Ptolemaic "super-planners," who extended the use of Athenian markets for their own redistributive needs. Dale, *Karl Polanyi*, 166–67.

74. We leave aside Polanyi's erroneous assumption that market-based capitalism arose in the nineteenth century (with the so-called "industrial revolution") and that all precapitalist forms until then entailed various combinations of reciprocity, redistribution, and householding.

become, rather quickly accustomed. *Second*, Polanyi assumed not merely that the market is by nature a profit-generating exercise (through most of history markets have not primarily been profit-making ventures), but he is ambivalent on the crucial issue of embeddedness of the market. His basic position is that no market is a self-regulating entity unto itself. Such an idea is a "stark utopia" since this "institution could not exist for any length without annihilating the human and natural substance of society; it would have physically destroyed man and transformed his surroundings into a wilderness."[75] But he also hints that an autonomous market may well be possible, insofar as it subsumes social relations within itself.[76] Many have turned this ambivalence into a clear opposition: reciprocity and redistribution constitute economic practices determined by social relations, but "market" economies are not so embedded. Trade—assumed to be a key indicator of economic activity—is usually the focus, so that the former triple distinction now appears as an opposition between embedded and disembedded trade. The misreading should be obvious. Polanyi castigates the classical and neoclassical economists for their efforts to disembed the economy, to the point of encouraging governments and decision makers that such an act is possible. For Polanyi, this is a futile quest, for an autonomous market economy would destroy what holds it together, namely, its social and natural environment.

Third, Polanyi excludes any sustained discussion of class or of the economics of agriculture. The avoidance of class is (like Finlay) due to his Weberian framework, but it leaves Polanyi unable to deal with the dynamics of economic exploitation, with unequal and hierarchical patterns of economic activity. The absence of agriculture as an economic activity is a feature endemic to the whole history of the debate we have been tracing. This is largely due to the assumption that economics involves the various dimensions of commerce—such as trade, markets, and money—even if they are differentiated and seen to function in very different ways within the proposed categories of reciprocity and redistribution. We do not mean the activities of landlords, estates, and slave-owners, for this is still to focus on the commercial aspects.

75. Polanyi, *Great Transformation*, 3; see also Polanyi, *Primitive, Archaic and Modern Economies*, 72–74; Fred Block, "Introduction," in *The Great Transformation: The Political and Economic Origins of Our Time*, xviii–xxxviii (Boston: Beacon, 2001).
76. "Instead of economy being embedded in social relations, social relations are embedded in the economic system." Polanyi, *Great Transformation*, 60; Polanyi, "The Economy as Instituted Process," 266–70. It may be possible to reinterpret Polanyi as saying that capitalism does indeed attempt to subsume social relations, with the dire consequence of environmental destruction, but this is a step beyond Polanyi.

Instead, we mean actual organization and agricultural activity to which we devote much of our attention.

We have devoted considerable space to the permutations of the primitivist-modernist debate for they are still with us in so many ways, albeit now divided in terms of neoclassical economists and anthropologists, or archaeologists and sociologists—although such distinctions are misleading. In our analysis, we have sought to highlight shortcomings and insights. The problems were many: narratives of differentiation (Rodbertus and Bücher); the retrofitting of capitalism into the ancient world on the assumption that human nature is always the same (Meyer and Rostovtzeff); the mistaking of ruling class ideology in terms of an overarching framework of patronage or values (Weber and Finley); the assumption, with all its twists, of the primitivist-modernist distinction; and the universal assumption that "economy" refers to commerce, with a resultant inability to deal with agriculture adequately. At the same time, we found useful some items that need further development: the inescapable social dimension, if not determination, of economic life (Rodbertus and Weber); the challenge to *Homo oeconomicus* as a feature of human nature (Bücher); the importance of class (Rostovtzeff) and indeed of slavery (Weber and Finley); the need for an alternative model or system within which the various items functioned (Weber and Polanyi). Indeed, Polanyi's great contribution was to dare a systemic answer to the question of ancient economies, an answer that did not simply seek to retrofit neoclassical categories into contexts where they clearly do not fit. While we find significant problems with this answer, we acknowledge the need for it. We hope that our answer is at least a little more adequate.

Marxist Economic Theory and Early Christianity

> It is not the resemblances, but the differences, which resemble each other.[77]

Given the inadequacies of neoclassical economics and the whole framework of the primitivist-modernist debate (with its later Weberian turn), we find that more adequate theoretical resources may be found within Marxist approaches.[78] Rather than positing a simple opposition

---

77. Lévi-Strauss, *Totemism*, 149.
78. While we appreciate Morris's occasional mentions of Marxism, we find his observations not as helpful as they might be. Morris, "Hard Surfaces."

of resemblance and difference or perhaps a golden mean between them, these approaches offer a dialectical engagement in which, as Lévi-Strauss puts, the differences resemble each other—by which we mean the historical and economic differences of the ancient world, which strangely come to resemble our own. We draw on two main sources: the work of G. E. M. de Ste. Croix and the *Régulation* school of economic theory.

Ste. Croix

> These are the voiceless toilers, the great majority—let us not forget it—of the population of the Greek and Roman world, upon whom was built a great civilization which despised them and did all it could to forget them.[79]

Among the many contributions of Geoffrey Ernest Maurice de Ste. Croix (the name is of Huguenot background), his importance for us lies in the sustained and largely persuasive argument for the importance of class in the economies of ancient Greece and Rome.[80] This is not to say that Ste. Croix leaves a few questions hanging, which we address after identifying his main argument.

For Ste. Croix, the central feature of analysis is class. He defines it as "the collective social expression of the fact of exploitation" in which exploitation designates the appropriation of part of the product

---

79. Ste. Croix, *Class Struggle*, 210.
80. The core text we use is Ste. Croix, *Class Struggle*. His other works are equally insightful: G. E. M. de Ste. Croix, *The Origins of the Peloponnesian War* (London: Duckworth, 1972); G. E. M. de Ste. Croix, *Athenian Democratic Origins and Other Essays*, eds. David Harvey, Robert Parker, and Peter Thonemann (Oxford: Oxford University Press, 2004); G. E. M. de Ste. Croix, *Christian Persecution, Martyrdom, and Orthodoxy*, eds. Michael Whitby and Joseph Streeter (Oxford: Oxford University Press, 2006). Ste. Croix attempts to strike a delicate balance between the detail of empirical historical analysis and the necessary search for overarching theoretical frameworks for understanding such material. For an insightful defense of the use of class for analyzing the ancient world, see Harris, *Rome's Imperial Economy*, 15–26. Despite our use of a number of his points, Bradley's liberal framework according to which slavery is the most extreme of domination, vitiates his analysis. Keith Bradley, *Slaves and Masters in the Roman Empire: A Study in Social Control* (New York: Oxford University Press, 1987); Keith Bradley, "Roman Slavery: Retrospect and Prospect," *Canadian Journal of History/Annales canadiennes d'histoire* 43, no. 3 (2008): 477–500; Keith Bradley, "Slavery in the Roman Republic," in *The Cambridge World History of Slavery. Volume 1: The Ancient Mediterranean World*, eds. Keith Bradley and Paul Cartledge, 241–64 (Cambridge: Cambridge University Press, 2011). Less useful is Dimitris Kyrtatas, "Modes and Relations of Production," in *Handbook of Early Christianity: Social Science Approaches*, eds. Anthony Blasi, Jean Duhaime, and Paul-André Turcotte, 529–54 (Walnut Creek: Altamira, 2002); Dimitris Kyrtatas, "Domination and Exploitation," in *Money, Labour and Land: Approaches to the Economies of Ancient Greece*, eds. Paul Cartledge, Edward Cohen, and Lin Foxhall, 140–55 (London: Routledge, 2002). Freyne's valiant effort at class analysis misses the insights provided by Ste. Croix. Séan Freyne, *Galilee from Alexander the Great to Hadrian, 323 BCE to 135 CE: A Study of Second Temple Judaism* (Wilmington and Notre Dame: Michael Glazier and University of Notre Dame Press, 1980), 194–200.

of others' labor.[81] In other words, a particular class is determined by a twofold relationship: to the conditions or means of production, and to other classes. A class society exists when a particular (usually small) class controls the conditions or means of production and is thereby able to appropriate a surplus at the expense of other classes which do not control or own the means of production. The forms of exploitation may be direct in which slaves, debtors, serfs, or peasants are exploited by individual masters, moneylenders, or landlords, or it may be indirect, through taxation, military service, or forced labor. This definition of class is conventionally Marxist, albeit with a twist: in terms of the control over the means of production, it seeks to identify how surplus is produced and to determine who benefits from that surplus and who is exploited in order to produce it. Now for the twist: Ste. Croix insists that a sufficient condition for class is the economic fact of exploitation. Political and subjective factors (ideology and class consciousness) may complete the picture, but they are not necessary for the existence of class.[82] Thus, class struggle may be defined in economic terms, designating a situation when the system of exploitation is perpetuated and, most importantly, when it meets resistance. Class struggle is endemic to classes, involving constant tensions, struggles, and violence in the everyday experience of life. In terms of ancient Greece and Rome,[83] Ste. Croix argues that the principal means of production was land (controlled by the "propertied" classes) as well as "unfree" labor through which a relatively limited surplus was extracted *by force*. Indeed, force is crucial, for only by compulsion was the level of surplus enabled and sustained. He distinguishes four often overlapping forms of unfree labor: slaves, debt-bondage, indentured laborers (serfs), and "small independent producers."[84]

Slaves, their labor, and other activities were completely under the

---

81. Ste. Croix, *Class Struggle*, 43. See the full explication on pp. 43–69.
82. He goes to some length to refute the idea that class and especially class struggle is primarily political. Ste. Croix, *Class Struggle*, 55–69.
83. Ste. Croix (*Class Struggle*, 19–30) also manages a welcome reclaiming of Marx as a classicist (with a PhD on Democritus and Epicurus). Quotations and expositions of Marx saturate the text. Reading and rereading Ste. Croix is an intimate pleasure, with rigorous scholarship seasoned with the personality of the author. The section on Marx provides a window into the 1970s, when Marxist approaches were once again making their way in European studies after a long period of contemptuous silence and occasional mocking footnotes. For some background on Marx and antiquity, see Padelis Lekas, *Marx on Classical Antiquity: Problems of Historical Methodology* (Brighton: Wheatsheaf, 1988); Neville Morley, "Marx and the Failure of Classical Antiquity," *Helios* 26, no. 3 (1999): 151–64.
84. As a useful footnote to Ste. Croix, see Peter Garnsey, Richard Saller, and Martin Goodman, *The Roman Empire: Economy, Society and Culture* (Oakland: University of California Press, 2015), 132–36. The economic category of class should not be confused with legal and political definitions, or the Roman "orders," such as senators, equestrians, decurions, citizens, non-citizens, and slaves.

control of their masters.[85] Unlimited control rather than ownership was the key, for this enabled the master to direct the slave as he or she wished. Slaves were put to work without any recompense and would thereby generate surplus well beyond their purchase price and cost of upkeep.[86] Although Ste. Croix argues that slavery was more systemic and widespread than is often understood (due to significant under-representation in the records), he is fully aware that slaves at times numbered less than other forms of labor, such as peasants and artisans,[87] so he proposes that the ruling classes above all lived on the surplus produced by "unfree" labor, of which slaves formed a highly significant and often dominant part—from Homer's texts onwards. This position relies on the crucial theoretical point that it "is not so much *how the bulk of the labour of production is done, as how the dominant propertied classes,* controlling the conditions of production, *ensure the extraction of the surplus* which makes their own leisured existence possible."[88] Domestic slaves were one dimension, but far more important for overwhelmingly agricultural societies was agricultural production in which slaves were ubiquitous.[89] While the relatively poor farmer of fifth century Athens usually had at least one slave,[90] the possessors of the largest tracts of land in later centuries were the ruling class and the preferred way of working land was through slave labor, because it was the most efficient way to extract maximum surplus in a context with limited technology.[91] Often they did not supervise the slaves them-

---

85. As we will show later, slavery was central to the first legal definition of private property by the Romans in the late second century BCE. Ste. Croix does not notice this point.
86. The following paragraph is based on Ste. Croix, *Class Struggle*, 133–62.
87. He finds (*Class Struggle*, 179-204) that hired labor played a minor role, and that it was scarce, unskilled, lacking mobility, and thoroughly despised. As Cohen points out, the key was not the type of labor, but whether one was supervised or not. Edward Cohen, "Free and Unfree Sexual Work: An Economic Analysis of Athenian Prostitution," in *Prostitutes and Courtesans in the Ancient World*, eds. Christopher Faraone and Laura McClure, 95–124 (Madison: University of Wisconsin Press, 2006), 100–101.
88. Ste. Croix, *Class Struggle*, 52. The terminology of "surplus" may give the impression that what is produced is extra to a person's daily requirements for basic survival. Ste. Croix is careful to define surplus: first, in a strictly relative sense, designating the product of an individual person's labor, which such a person does not enjoy and of which the benefits are enjoyed by another; second, the condition under which a primary producer is compelled under compulsion to give up a portion of the produce; third, the smallness of the surplus produced, due to the limits of technology available, a condition in which force was crucial. Ibid., 37–40.
89. Jameson points out that in fifth-fourth century Athens, the distinction between domestic and agricultural slaves is somewhat artificial, since slaves undertook a range of tasks. Michael Jameson, "Agriculture and Slavery in Classical Athens," *The Classical Journal* 73, no. 2 (1976–1977): 122–45, 137.
90. Cartledge estimates that of the 25–30,000 adult males in fifth-century Athens, more than half had at least one slave. Cartledge, "The Political Economy of Greek Slavery."
91. For instance, ancient Greece and Rome did not know the wheelbarrow (known in China in the fourth century CE), or indeed the windmill, which appeared in Europe only in the twelfth cen-

selves, preferring to appoint overseers who were themselves slaves (a form of "slave aristocracy" which effectively divided slaves[92]). In this way was the ruling class able to live free of despised daily labor—for labor itself was regarded as servile[93]—and undertake the assumed roles of a leisured and "civilized" life, such as politics, military leadership, literature, the arts, hunting, and athletics—all tasks that were possible only on the backs of the slaves who worked the estates.[94] The slaves directly supported the existence of a uniformly brutal ruling class who produced all the art, literature, science, and philosophy of the classical world.

Debt bondage was far more widespread than is often realized.[95] Ste. Croix distinguishes two main forms among the variety in the ancient world. The first was indefinite bondage in light of debt forfeiture and limited bondage in which the person may hope for release from the debt at some time. Given that the former is a type of slavery, he limits the usage of "debt bondage" to the second type. This category is primarily a juridical one, which Ste. Croix introduces into the material to clarify the different forms of exploitation. For the Greeks and Romans, it made no difference whether one's servitude was temporary or permanent: they were all seen as *douloi* and *servi*. This point is crucial for understanding a mode of production, which concerns not merely the economic and social factors, but also ideological, legal, political, and religious dimensions. In particular, the way in which the Greeks and Romans understood their system is an indicator not of the true nature of the system, but of the way its dominant economic forms shaped and were given shape by ideological factors. To add more strictly economic

tury. The Greeks and Romans could not imagine any other form of production as efficient, except (in Aristotle) tools that worked of their own accord, or automatons like those produced by the legendary sculptor, Daedalus. Aristotle, *Politics*, trans. Harris Rackham, Loeb Classical Library (Cambridge: Harvard University Press, 2005), 1253b34–1254a1. Despite all his twists and turns on the matter of "natural slavery," Aristotle cannot imagine a system without it. Aristotle, *Politics*, 1254a14–1255a2; Wayne Ambler, "Aristotle on Nature and Politics: The Case of Slavery," *Political Theory* 15, no. 3 (1987): 390–410; Malcolm Heath, "Aristotle on Natural Slavery," *Phronesis* 53, no. 3 (2008): 243–70.

92. This slave aristocracy was also manifested in the way slaves would prefer to be owned by wealthy masters with many slaves rather than a "poor" man who had perhaps two or three. Ste. Croix, *Class Struggle*, 143–44.

93. Perry Anderson, *Passages from Antiquity to Feudalism* (London: Verso, 1974), 26–27; John Bodel, "Slave Labour and Roman Society," in *The Cambridge World History of Slavery*, eds. Keith Bradley and Paul Cartledge, vol. 1, 311–36 (Cambridge: Cambridge University Press, 2011), 312.

94. Ste. Croix (*Class Struggle*, 117–20) tracks how such levels of wealth based on land increased from the relatively low levels of the Greek era to the vast fortunes of the Roman era.

95. It is easy, suggests Ste. Croix (*Class Struggle*, 137, 162), to be misled by Solon's reform in Athens, in which he forbade pledging the body as security. This reform was uncharacteristic of the ancient world. See the extensive examples of debt-bondage (ibid., 162–70).

dimensions to Ste. Croix's analysis, we would argue that debt-slavery, as it is commonly known, had the primary economic function of compulsion for labor. In a situation where labor was usually in short supply, the onerous loans for which surety was one's own body or the body of someone in the household ensured that the debtor had to "repay" the loan through labor. This dimension of debt—known as "personal execution" in which one became an *addictus* to the lender—carried through in various ways into later Roman times.[96] This means that debt as a mechanism for ensuring the flow of wealth from debtor to lender, as well as providing another dimension of economic and social hierarchy, were secondary developments of debt.[97]

The third category of "unfree" labor concerns indentured laborers (or serfs), who are distinct from slaves in the sense that they were not owned by masters, but rather legally bound to serve on specific land and not free to change their status. This category is actually a modification in Ste. Croix's schema required in light of the stretch of time covered by his "Greek world," from the seventh century BCE to the mid-seventh century CE. In the later phase, during the early centuries of the Christian era, the development of *coloni* (indentured rural laborers) increased. However, since we deal with this topic later, we note the following points here.[98] Crucial to the colonate was the tying of peasants to land rather than to a master (as with slavery). Ste. Croix makes his own proposals for the development of the colonate—drying up slave sources, slave tenants, dispersed estates, increase in "barbarian" settlements—to which many more have been added before and after his work. All of this culminated in the great reform of Diocletian (284–305) in which the whole of the agricultural population of the Roman Empire was legally tied to the land on a hereditary basis.[99] "Freehold" peasants were tied to their villages (at least in theory) and "leasehold" peasants were tied to the plot or farm so rented or to the village in which they resided. The purpose was economic, to ensure the

96. Ibid., 165–69.
97. See our more detailed discussion of debt in chapter 3.
98. Ibid., 226–59.
99. With this development, Ste. Croix attempts to read serfs back into the earlier period, especially groups such as the Spartan and Messenian helots, the Thessalian *penestai*, the *klarotai* of Crete, and the *mariandynoi* of Heraclea Pontica. See further Susan Alcock, "A Simple Case of Exploitation? The Helots of Messenia," in *Money, Labour and Land: Approaches to the Economies of Ancient Greece*, eds. Paul Cartledge, Edward Cohen, and Lin Foxhall, 185–99 (London: Routledge, 2002). Ste. Croix also makes the rather dubious argument that the economic form of ancient Southwest Asia before the Greeks was based on serfdom, but that it initially fell away due to Greek influence. At the same time, he avoids the terminology of "feudalism." See Ste. Croix, *Class Struggle*, 147–62, 267–69. For a different position that forms the backdrop to this study, see Boer, *Sacred Economy*.

systemic collection of new taxes, although it did not mean that slavery disappeared, for it continued to comprise a significant part of the economy. While the distinction was initially juridical, it was enmeshed with economic factors of class.[100] Further, the Greeks and Romans did not identify any difference. For them, as we will see, everyone was either free or slave.

The question of the *coloni* brings us to what is actually a fourth dimension of class exploitation, which Ste. Croix initially describes as "small independent producers," such as peasants, artisans and traders.[101] Above all, he is interested in the peasants, which he is careful to define in the following terms: they possess their means of production; are not enslaved but may be serfs or bondsmen; occupy land in various ways, from freehold to lease to tenancy; work in family units; are collectively defined by village communities (*kōmae*); remain peasants even if they take up ancillary labor; tend to support the superimposed classes who exploit them.[102] Clearly, the peasantry as a class overlaps with, if not forming the substratum of, debt bondage and serfdom. At one level, this overlap is to be expected with classes (similar to the way debt bondsmen can easily slip into slavery). But at another level, the reason is to be found in the way Ste. Croix defines the different classes. Earlier, we emphasized that the definitions of debt-bondage and serfdom were initially legal, albeit with real economic dimensions. By contrast, the definition of peasantry is primarily economic, dealing with the means and relations of production.[103] The outcome (not developed explicitly by Ste. Croix) is that peasants form an economic and social class with subsequent legal variations that indicate debt-bondage and serfdom. This means that the two basic exploited classes—economically and socially—were slaves and peasants, with significant internal variations that Ste. Croix is keen to emphasize.[104]

---

100. Thus, for Ste. Croix, indentured laborers exercised more "rights" than slaves or those under debt-bondage.
101. He also discusses traders, courtesans, craftsmen (including artists, doctors, architects, builders, and so on) and pliers of other trades (from ferrymen to bakers), who, although mostly living close to poverty, did not comprise a distinct class.
102. Since we discuss peasants in detail in chapter 2, we deal with the pertinent items of definition here.
103. Ste. Croix, *Class Struggle*, 212.
104. For example, he begins with Engels's influential distinction between small, middle, and big peasants, with the latter really forming a distinct type of exploitation within the peasantry. Ste. Croix's focus is on the small and middle peasants. From there he proceeds to make further distinctions: "freeholders," holders of land on condition of performing military service, tenants (who then break down into paying fixed rent in money or kind, part of the crop, or labor service), and *emphyteusis* (uncultivated or derelict land on long term lease). Friedrich Engels, "The Peas-

Except for conditions of debt bondage and the later colonate, he argues that the peasants were often in the majority (except during times of masses of cheap slaves, such as fifth-fourth centuries BCE in some Greek cities and in Italy in the first century BCE) and that they were at times not exploited and did not exploit others, for they lived at a subsistence level somewhat outside the exploitation of unfree labor.[105] But just when he has opened a zone relatively free of exploitation, he closes it down again, albeit with an ambivalence that we are keen to emphasize. Peasants were often exploited, primarily indirectly—by which he means exploitation by the state for the collective benefit of the ruling classes. Specific types of indirect exploitation were taxation, military conscription, and compulsory labor services extracted by the city administrations (regular and occasional labor rents, as well as specifically requisitioned *angareia*). This was particularly the case in the Greco-Roman era, in the context of colonial and imperial expansion (after Alexander) when the residents of the largely non-Greek speaking hinterland (*chōra*) were systemically exploited in order to maintain the sparkling life of the colonial and Greek-speaking cities (*poleis*).[106] So also during the Roman Empire, for Ste. Croix argues that it developed very efficient techniques of exploitation for precisely such people, thereby enabling the move to *coloni* in the Christian era. While peasants living under a tried and tested subsistence-survival method (our terms) can normally put away surpluses for the bad year that is always only a season away, Ste. Croix suggests that the Romans managed to exploit them in a way hitherto not seen.[107]

At this point, a note of ambivalence appears in his analysis. The evidence given for such exploitation is literary (Ste. Croix's main source of information). He refers to a number of sources indicating that during famines, the peasants would move to the *poleis* in order to find food. The implication is that no food was to be found in the countryside because the rich and powerful hoarded grain in order to sell at high prices during times of shortage. What this limited evidence does not

---

ant Question in France and Germany," in *Marx Engels Collected Works*, vol. 27, 481–502 (Moscow: Progress Publishers, 1852 [1894]); Ste. Croix, *Class Struggle*, 211–26.

105. We deliberately do not use the terminology of "free labor," since this is a fictional category in all epochs. See Jairus Banaji, *Theory as History: Essays on Modes of Production and Exploitation*, Historical Materialism Book Series (Leiden: Brill, 2010), 131–54.

106. Add to these linguistic and cultural differences, which is particularly germane to Syria-Palestine, and the "clear-cut difference between 'Hellene' and '*barbaros*' (Greek and native) that was gradually transformed into a more purely class distinction, between the propertied and non-propertied." Ste. Croix, *Class Struggle*, 17.

107. Ibid., 208–26.

tell us is how many peasants did so and how close they were to the centers of power. We tend to assume too readily the mechanisms of modern nation-states with patterns of administration, logistics, and policing of relatively firm borders that enable systemic taxation and tribute. Power in the ancient world—even under the Romans—was far more uncertain, shifting, and vague, with outer borders never clear (despite grandiose claims). To be sure, those closer to centers of power would be under onerous pressure, but those further away less so. Crucially, Ste. Croix notes the common practice of *anachōrēsis* or *secessio*, an "exodus" by tenant farmers who would collectively refuse to work and even depart until a grievance had been remedied. This would entail an appeal to a landlord against officials and soldiers, a provincial governor or even the emperor himself. Obviously, such appeals were not necessarily or always successful, so other strategies came into play, in which village communities (tenant or "freehold") would remove themselves from exploitation by relocating out of harm's way. Other age-old practices included not harvesting crops that were to be requisitioned, melting away when labor service was required, hiding small surpluses put aside for a bad season, or absconding entirely and resettling in a more remote area. They knew full well that the glittering *poleis* of Greek colonization and of imperial Roman rule could not exist without their produce and labor. Such acts of collective resistance rose to critical levels during the collapse of the Roman Empire. Above all, this feature of the village communities distinguishes peasants sharply from slaves, who, according to Ste. Croix, did not regularly and systematically engage in revolts. Of course, there are frequent examples of micro-resistance and escape, but revolts as such were relatively rare. Ste. Croix adduces a number of factors to account for this difference between peasants and slaves, such as the ethnic mix of slaves, the effective collective management and "citizen policing" of the slave population by all masters, and the absorption of slaves into the dominant ideological framework in which they competed with one another for influence and even wealth.[108] But we suggest another factor not considered by Ste. Croix:

108. Since Ste. Croix's work, some studies have focused on micro-acts of resistance and slave agency, indicating that it was widespread. Missing is the awareness that these activities are constituent features of day-to-day class conflict. Keith Bradley, *Slavery and Rebellion in the Roman World, 140 BC–70 BC* (Bloomington: Indiana University Press, 1998); Keith Bradley, "Resisting Slavery at Rome," in *The Cambridge World History of Slavery*, eds. Keith Bradley and Paul Cartledge, vol. 1, 362–84 (Cambridge: Cambridge University Press, 2011); Keith Bradley, "Engaging with Slavery," *Biblical Interpretation* 21, no. 4–5 (2013): 533–46, 534–38; Niall McKeown, "Resistance Among Chattel Slaves in the Classical Greek World," in *The Cambridge World History of Slavery*, eds. Keith Bradley and Paul Cartledge, vol. 1, 153–75 (Cambridge: Cambridge University Press, 2011).

the tried and tested method of subsistence survival included thousands of years of collective history and memory of how one should respond to excessive exploitation.

In outlining the key features of Ste. Croix's effort to identify classes in the ancient Greek (and indeed Roman) world, we have already engaged in some critical assessment, especially in terms of his methods in distinguishing classes (economic and juridical). In what follows, we engage in more direct assessment with an eye on what we will use in the rest of this study. To begin with, it is to Ste. Croix's immense credit—in contrast to nearly all of the material we have discussed thus far—that he acknowledges the centrality of agriculture in the *chōra*, *kōmae*, and *agroi*. He would have agreed with Lynn White's observation that antiquity was "agricultural to a degree which we can scarcely grasp."[109] Even in the most prosperous regions more than ten people were required to enable a single person not to live on the land, and of the total population no more than three percent formed the ruling class.[110] Two dimensions of the centrality of agriculture appear in Ste. Croix's work: the perspective of the ruling classes and that of unfree labor. For the former, the possession of land was the *sine qua non* of wealth, leisure, and the "civilized" life of the *kalos kagathos*. Wealth acquired by other means was immediately turned to the acquisition of land, for agriculture was the basis of virtue, nobility, valor, prudence, and intellect. Of course, this assumed that one did not actually work the land from dawn to dusk, although one might occasionally assist with a task as a virtuous act of leisure or amusement (so as not to lose touch with one's "roots"). Cicero sums it up best: "of all means of acquiring wealth there is nothing better, nothing more profitable, nothing sweeter, nothing more worthy of a free man, than *agricultura*"—by which he means possessing and managing land.[111] For the ruling class, it was crucial that they possessed land but did not *need* to work on it.

An angle on the sheer importance of land for agriculture—from a ruling class perspective—is provided by his observations on trade (the persistent focus of others who deal with ancient economics). Here

109. Lynn White, "The Expansion of Technology 500–1500," in *The Fontana History of Europe, I: The Middle Ages*, ed. Carlo Cipolla, 143–74 (London: Fontana, 1972), 144–45; quoted in Ste. Croix, *Class Struggle*, 10–11.
110. Carolyn Osiek and David Balch, *Families in the New Testament World: Households and House Churches* (Louisville: Westminster John Knox, 1997), 37.
111. M. Tullius Cicero, *De Officiis*, trans. Walter Miller, Loeb Classical Library (London: William Heinemann, 1928), I.151. The translation here is that of Ste. Croix (*Class Struggle*, 122).

33

Ste. Croix tacks closer to the work of Finley and Polanyi, although he otherwise cannot be counted as a primitivist or substantivist. Against repeated assertions that trade was the driving force of ancient Greek economies, Ste. Croix draws on what was already a substantial body of work concerning the physical limitations imposed on trade. Simply put, the transport of goods overland was prohibitively expensive. The evidence is impressive: the cost of a cargo of wheat would double every 340 kilometers, if one could keep the oxen and then donkeys from eating the whole load before the end of the journey; according to the price edict of Diocletian of 301 CE, it was cheaper to ship the same quantity of wheat by ship from one end of the Mediterranean to another—from Syria to Spain—than it was to transport it 120 kilometers (or 75 miles) overland; travelling by raft downstream took half the time the same journey could be covered by land; even so, it was cheaper to haul goods upstream than overland.[112] Milevski calls this the "friction of distance," which designates an exponential relationship between distance and the amount of labor involved, to which may be added the social factors entailed in passing through region after region with inevitable negotiation, protection money, obstruction, and violence.[113] Was water-borne trade then the preferred method? It was and especially under the Romans became relatively extensive.[114] Yet, the prime purpose remained the supply of a *polis*, of which Rome was the supreme example. Those engaged in such exchange were systematically despised, especially if they grew wealthy from the process. The

112. Ste. Croix, *Class Struggle*, 11–12; Ste. Croix, *Athenian Democratic Origins*, 349–70; Michael Roaf, *Cultural Atlas of Mesopotamia and the Ancient Near East* (London: Equinox, 1990), 18; Marc van de Mieroop, *The Ancient Mesopotamian City* (Oxford: Clarendon, 1997), 169. Ste. Croix draws his initial observation on the price edict of Diocletian of 301 CE from Arnold Hugh Martin Jones, *The Roman Economy: Studies in Ancient Economic and Administrative History* (Oxford: Blackwell, 1974), 37; Arnold Hugh Martin Jones, *The Greek City* (Oxford: Clarendon, 1966), 260. For a useful study of the edict, which suggests it concerns sailing time rather than distance, see Walter Scheidel, "Explaining the Maritime Freight Charges in Diocletian's Prices Edict," *Journal of Roman Archaeology* 26 (2013): 464–68. For criticism from a neoclassical economic perspective (if profits were sufficient, land transport would be used), see Harris, *Rome's Imperial Economy*, 161; Harris, "The Late Republic," 535–36.
113. Ianir Milevski, *Early Bronze Age Goods Exchange in the Southern Levant: A Marxist Perspective* (London: Equinox, 2011), 32; Peregrine Hordern and Nicholas Purcell, *The Corrupting Sea: A Study of Mediterranean History* (Oxford: Palgrave, 2000), 377; Stegemann and Stegemann, *The Jesus Movement*, 22–24. The papyri from "customs houses" in Egypt (18–214 CE) indicate that goods were moved by donkey and camel for local use. Agnes Choi, "Never the Two Shall Meet? Urban-Rural Interaction in Lower Galilee," in *Galilee in the Late Second Temple and Mishnaic Period, Volume 1: Life, Culture, and Society*, eds. David Fiensy and James Strange, 297–311 (Minneapolis: Fortress, 2014). A useful tool to estimate distance and costs of transport, with overland transport notably the highest cost, can now be found at http://orbis.stanford.edu.
114. See the detailed archaeological evidence in Kevin Greene, *The Archaeology of the Roman Economy* (Berkeley: University of California Press, 1990), 17–44. Greene estimates that the cost ratio of sea:river:overland was 1:4.9:28 (39–40).

overwhelming Greek preference was for a *polis* to be supplied with foodstuffs by its surrounding *chōra*. As Alexander the Great pointed out when considering the location of what became Alexandria (Mt Athos had been proposed): just as a child needs milk, so a *polis* without fields and abundant produce cannot grow or sustain a population.[115] Further, significant resources were required for even a half-decent riverboat, let alone a sea-going vessel. Only a *polis* or state could manage any level of serious ship-building, as also the control of ports. Once built, methods of navigation (capping or kenning—moving from seen headland to headland) were basic, especially without compasses, charts, and weather forecast, and the risks high indeed, as the many shipwrecks even in a pond such as the Mediterranean suggest. Even the Romans who made much greater use of sea transport had their profound misgivings. After a particularly harrowing voyage in July, Cicero observed, "A sea journey is a serious matter [*negotium magnum est navigare*]."[116]

More significantly, Ste. Croix makes use of an important distinction between imports, exports, and commercial exchange.[117] The primary concern of Greek *poleis* was clearly imports, rather than commercial exchange for profit in view of the balance of trade. The Greeks were interested in what they could acquire, not what they could send out. But how was one to pay for aforesaid imports? The means of payment was fortuitous. Athens at least had silver mines and tribute from colonies, but if all else failed, the necessary evil of exports became a last resort. Absent was the primary desire to profit (it was secondary), as is shown by the fact that Athens of the fourth century BCE imposed the same duty of two percent on exports and imports.[118] Perhaps merchants were the ones who were focused on profit. The catch is that merchants were despised, peripheral figures in the eyes of the ruling classes.[119] Indeed, the assumption was that the pursuit of profit pure and simple was a threat to the social order. No merchant was ever

---

115. Ste. Croix, *Class Struggle*, 12–13.

116. Ibid., 12. For a rather benign recent overview of the benefits and hazards of land and sea travel, see Catherine Hezser, "Travel and Mobility," in *The Oxford Handbook of Jewish Daily Life in Roman Palestine*, ed. Catherine Hezser, 210–28 (Oxford: Oxford University Press, 2010), 211–14.

117. The following is based on Ste. Croix, *Athenian Democratic Origins*, 352–58.

118. Ste. Croix also notes the absence of adequate accounting, with no distinction between what would now be called "capital" and "income," or even a sense of "net profit." Double or even single accounting was not known. Ste. Croix, *Class Struggle*, 114. Note also Kyrtatas, "Modes and Relations of Production," 541.

119. A trace of the opprobrium embodied in the very terminology of "merchant" from ancient Southwest Asia (where *shr* and *rkl* in Hebrew means "groveling busybody," while in Akkadian *tamkāru* also means one who betrays) may be found in the Latin *negotior* (*negotiator*, *negotium*). Its semantic field includes the senses of difficulty and pains, as well as feathering one's own nest.

a politician, nor was a statesman a merchant. Merchants were useful for ensuring imports, but *poleis* did not think of them as "their own" and they did not form a "mercantile class."[120] The fact that most who actually engaged in merchant activity were slaves or ex-slaves adds another layer to the disdain shown, well into Roman times. But Ste. Croix goes further: even imports were regarded as a necessary evil, for the *poleis* were ideally self-sufficient. The reason for such an ideal lay with land. To make his point, Ste. Croix develops a conventional assumption in studies of the ancient world.[121] It is a commonplace that Greek colonization was primarily due to population pressures rather than trade. He gives the example of the first settlement on the Propontis or Black Sea coast. If one were to select a trade-oriented location, one would opt for the point whither the currents naturally lead, the north-western coast where Istanbul now stands. But the first settlement in 651 BCE was at Chalcedon on the other side where it is difficult indeed to land a boat. The reason: Chalcedon has far more arable land. Only seventeen years later did they settle Byzantium. If a town did develop trade, it was secondary, arising from the needs of provisioning and imports (as Polanyi argued) rather than any primary intention to engage in trade. In Roman times, very similar assumptions applied. The reality was that food was primarily produced locally for local consumption, with exceptions being the larger *poleis*, and Rome the greatest exception. It was a parasite that drew immense resources from the rest of its empire— symbolized by grain imports and the grain dole. It could do so because its empire was overwhelmingly a water-based one, on the inland lake known as the Mediterranean and the major rivers.

But what of agriculture from the perspective of the exploited classes? Ste. Croix's main interest is in how exploitation was effected, which always includes the relations between exploiters and exploited. However, he rarely speaks directly of the economic factors involved in agriculture itself. He admits that vast literary and archaeological materials are available even in his time (he was writing in the 1970s), but that the work of integration had not yet been done.[122] Indeed, his study is notable for its focus on literary sources, regarded as the proper domain for a historian, and the relative absence of treatments of archaeology. Some insights may be gained from time to time in his

---

120. See the evidence in Ste. Croix, *Class Struggle*, 124–32.
121. For a relatively recent study of population growth and colonization, see Walter Scheidel, "The Greek Demographic Expansion: Models and Comparisons," *Journal of Hellenic Studies* 123 (2003): 120–40.
122. Ste. Croix, *Class Struggle*, 218–19.

work, especially in terms of the importance of the *chōra* and *kōmē*. In colonized areas, the *chōra* was the relatively vast area of land outside the Greek-speaking *poleis*. Here local populations lived, worked the land, spoke their own languages, and shared cultural assumptions from well before the Greeks or Romans arrived (it is also the area in which Jesus focuses, at least as represented in the Gospels). Central to the *chōra* was the *kōmē*, which we prefer to translate as village community or commune. Ste. Croix mentions briefly their modes of self-governance in terms of assemblies, an elected or hereditary *kōmarchos*, and the persistence of such practices, but he says little about economic or social organization. When we examine this context in later chapters, we will need to go well beyond Ste. Croix.

We close our discussion with the issue of ideology, for it is crucial in understanding the functions of a mode of production.[123] As we indicated earlier, a mode of production concerns not merely economic and social elements (the means and relations of production), but also ideological, legal, political, and religious factors. We would like to recalibrate Ste. Croix's work in light of such a framework, even though he studiously avoids the term. He is in two minds concerning what may be called the objective and subjective dimensions. On the one hand, he insists that class and class struggle are primarily due to the objective economic reality of exploitation and that the subjective factors of ideology and politics are not sufficient or primary.[124] On the other hand, he is fully aware that his reading risks a form of economism, neglecting the power of ideas, which would be a misreading of Marx.[125] In this light, he introduces legal distinctions for the categories of debt-bondage and serfdom, as well as devoting considerable space to examining precisely the subjective factors of ideology and class consciousness.[126] We seek to knit both sides into a larger picture, a mode of production.

Beginning with the perspective of the ruling classes, the crucial point is that they viewed the whole system through the lens of slavery. They operated with the fundamental distinction between free and slave. Thus, all of the exploited classes distinguished by Ste.

123. Ste. Croix studiously avoids the terminology of mode of production, yet his analysis works well within such an established term and would even have been enhanced if he had deployed it.
124. Ste. Croix, *Class Struggle*, 3, 44, 55–69. This insistence was aimed at those who understand political factors and ideology as primary.
125. This has led some, such as Perry Anderson, to suggest that Ste. Croix misses subjective factors entirely. Perry Anderson, *A Zone of Engagement* (London: Verso, 1992), 17–18.
126. Our focus here is chapter 7, "The Class Struggle on the Ideological Plane" (*Class Struggle*, 409–52).

Croix—slavery, debt-bondage, serfdom, and exploitation of peasants—were seen in terms of slavery.[127] This class consciousness
appeared in different forms, such as the advocacy of systemic violence;
efforts to ensure "unfree" labor assumed the perspective of the ruling
class (*philosdespotos*); the denigration of the "bald-headed little tinker"
(so Plato); the argument that inequality is real equality; the fear of any
manifestation of even the very limited democracy of ancient Greece;
but above all the assumption that slavery was an accident of Fortune.
The last item in particular provided the overarching ideological position that a good and wise person was never "really" a slave, while the
bad person, even if "free," was a slave to passions. This perspective
carries through from Greek writers, through the Romans, to Christian
approaches, which "helped to rivet the shackles rather more firmly"
on the slave's feet.[128] The importance of this ideological framework
is revealed by the way moral, political, and economic terminology
meshed with one another. Thus, *agathos* and *kakos* are not merely moral
terms for they are connected in a host of ways that indicate the differences between free and slave—down to physical appearance. Thus,
the "good" are also wealthy, noble, brave, well-born, blessed, lucky,
upright, elite, beautiful, and the pillars of society, while the "bad" are
poor, ignoble, cowardly, ill-born, cursed, unlucky, lowly, the masses,
ugly, and the dregs of society.[129] In short, the former are the "free," the
latter slaves—even at a metaphorical level. Thus, in terms of ideology
and class consciousness, slavery is the archetypal form of unfree labor,
which was "omnipresent in the psychology of all classes."[130]

As for the exploited classes, Ste. Croix has surprisingly little to say.
Few and far between are actual expressions of their consciousness.
He mentions a few inscriptions and epigraphs that indicate pride by
craftsmen in their skills, even if they were despised by the ruling class
for "earning" a living.[131] Above all, he emphasizes the fable—albeit far

---

127. Thus, the range of terms for slaves signals the importance of slavery on the ideological plane.
These include but are not limited to *doulos, andropodon, oiketēs, pais, sōma, servus* and *mancipium.*
128. Ibid., 420.
129. Elsewhere, Ste. Croix provides a host of related terms: *hoi tas ousias echontes, plousioi, pacheis, eudai-
mones, gnōrimoi, eugeneis, dunatoi, dunatōtatoi, kaloi kagathoi, chrēstoi, esthloi, aristoi, beltistoi, dexiōtatoi,
charientes, epieikeis*—all for the "good" ruling classes; for the "bad" exploited classes seen through
the lens of slavery, they used *hoi penētes, aporoi, ptōchoi, hoi polloi, to plēthos, ho ochlos, ho dēmos,
hoi dēmotikoi, mochthēroi, ponēroi, deiloi, to kakiston.* Ste. Croix, *Christian Persecution, Martyrdom, and
Orthodoxy,* 338–39; Ste. Croix, *Origins of the Peloponnesian War,* 371–76.
130. Ste. Croix, *Class Struggle,* 173, 259; Paul Blackledge, *Reflections on the Marxist Theory of History* (Manchester: Manchester University Press, 2006), 105.
131. For Aristotle, such pursuits make one vulgar and degrade the mind, for one acts in a "menial and
servile manner." Aristotle, *Politics,* 1337b4–22; see also 1254b28–31; Stegemann and Stegemann,
The Jesus Movement, 24–26.

too briefly[132]—as a form of popular protest literature, especially those collected by Phaedrus, an ex-slave in the early first century CE who drew in part on the work another ex-slave, Aesop (from the early sixth century BCE). Although fables were readily appropriated by the ruling classes, many of them have managed to survive in which animals represent human situations of oppression and resistance. Apart from fables (and biblical parables, he suggests), the problem is that by far the bulk of the material was produced and preserved by the ruling class. This situation requires a dialectical reading against the dominant position (first championed by Ernst Bloch[133]), recognizing that texts dealing with resistance and revolt only to close it down again enable the preservation of precisely such stories. Mostly, Ste. Croix does not take this approach with one major exception.[134] In his persuasive treatment of the decline of the Roman Empire, he picks up his earlier comment on forms of peasant resistance (see above). A major factor in that decline was the sheer absence of affection for the state and a consequent welcoming of the invaders.[135] Ste. Croix presents an impressive range of evidence of continual "defections" to "barbarian" invaders, revolts, assistance, and profound indifference to the disintegration of the empire—reflected in the increasingly harsh penalties for doing so. Let us pick up a fable to give a clear expression of this sentiment. A timid old man is pasturing a donkey when an invading army appears. The old man urges the donkey to flee with him so as not to be captured. The donkey refuses, and asks in a leisurely manner: "Do you suppose that the conqueror will place double panniers upon me?" The old man replies in the negative, to which the donkey says: "Then what matters it to me, so long as I have to carry my panniers, whom I serve?"[136]

Summing up, we have focused on Ste. Croix's theoretical contribu-

---

132. Ste. Croix, *Class Struggle*, 444–45.

133. Ernst Bloch, *Atheism in Christianity: The Religion of the Exodus and the Kingdom*, trans. J. T. Swann (London: Verso, 2009).

134. Minor exceptions include some rare comments in Sallust and Tacitus, in which the anti-Roman perspective of a conquered people appears (only to be dismissed); protests against foreign imperialism, such as the "Acts of the Pagan Martyrs of Alexandria"; and apocalyptic literature, which usually came from the ruling classes but may on occasion manifest a form of class struggle if the voices of victims of exploitation appear. However, he feels that theological differences, especially in the early struggles over doctrine, were a distraction from, rather than an expression of, class struggle.

135. Ste. Croix, *Class Struggle*, 453–503. He adduces a range of other factors that exacerbated the situation: the inability and lack of desire by the ruling class to improve the standards of peasant life in order to ensure a sufficiently strong army; the increasingly brutal exploitation of unfree labor in order to support an expensive and burdensome state apparatus (the final straw being the creation of a whole new bureaucracy in the form of the Christian church after Constantine's conversion); the increasing pressure on the richer members of local communities ("curial class") who were not senators and equestrians.

tion, pinpointing insights that even now go beyond other Marxist studies of ancient economies.[137] But we have also identified some problems and gaps, especially in terms of the interconnectedness of economics, social forces, and ideology (in terms of mode of production), the actual economic workings of rural agriculture, and the absence of sustained use of archaeological material. In the following chapters, we return to these issues in order to fill out the reconstruction, as well as drawing upon features of Ste. Croix's analysis that could be mentioned only at a theoretical level here. These include spatial production in terms of *polis* and *chōra*, synchronic factors in relation to slavery, the question of property, and the development of the colonate.

Régulation Theory

The second major theoretical feature of our reconstruction draws upon *Régulation* theory.[138] This approach operates with four critically articulated bases: economic activity is inescapably social; contradiction and therefore crisis is the norm; temporary stability is the exception and needs to be analyzed; stability is enabled by institutional, behavioral, and ideological practices. Before examining these positions, let us indicate the reason for using "*régulation*" and not "regulation."[139] The English risks misrepresenting the French, for the former designates juridicopolitical regulation at a microeconomic level.[140] By contrast, *régulation* means the social, institutional, and ideological factors that determine the stabilities and transformations of a system.[141]

136. Phaedrus, *The Fables of Phaedrus*, trans. Henry Thomas Riley and Christopher Smart (Urbana-Champaign: Gutenberg, 2002), I:15. Ste. Croix, *Class Struggle*, 444.
137. For example, Kautsky argued that slavery developed out of debt bondage in both ancient Greece and ancient Israel, while Hindess and Hirst argue on theoretical grounds that slavery as an economic system is untenable. Meiksins Wood goes so far as to suggest that slavery was not a dominant feature of her favored ancient Athens. Karl Kautsky, *Foundations of Christianity*, trans. H. F. Mins (London: Socialist Resistance, 2007); Barry Hindess and Paul Q. Hirst, *Precapitalist Modes of Production* (London: Routledge and Kegan Paul, 1975), 109–77; Wood, *Peasant-Citizen and Slave*.
138. The following draws on and revises Boer, *Sacred Economy*, 31–41. The reader interested in insightful surveys of *Régulation* theory should also consult Robert Boyer and Yves Saillard, eds., *Régulation Theory: The State of the Art* (London: Routledge, 2002); Bob Jessop and Ngai-Ling Sum, *Beyond the Regulation Approach: Putting Capitalist Economies in their Place* (Cheltenham: Edward Elgar, 2006), 13–57.
139. Here we follow the practice established in Robert Boyer, "Introduction," in *Régulation Theory: The State of the Art*, eds. Robert Boyer and Yves Saillard, 1–10 (London: Routledge, 2002), 1.
140. The better French word for such realities would be *réglementation*.
141. Or as Jessop and Sum put it, *régulation* theorists "typically refer to a wide range of economic and extraeconomic mechanisms in seeking to explain the 'regularities' of economic behaviour. They aim to show how these mechanisms interact to normalize the capital relation and guide (govern) the conflictual and crisis-mediated course of accumulation." Jessop and Sum, *Beyond the Regulation Approach*, 15; see further Robert Boyer, *The Regulation School: A Critical Introduction*, trans. Craig Charney (New York: Columbia University Press, 1990), 20–21, 47–48, 117–23.

40

We will not outline the background of *Régulation* theory here, with its emergence from Marxist economics and philosophy (with debts to Louis Althusser, Kaleckian economics, and the Annales school), its response to the intellectual and practical *bankruptcy* of neoclassical economics in the context of the economic crisis of the early 1970s after the collapse of Fordism, and the many debates, works, and schools.[142] But it is worth noting that *Régulation* theory challenges the three impractical assumptions of economics imperialism that we outlined earlier: (1) the rational nature of the fictional *Homo oeconomicus*; (2) equilibrium as the norm, based on interactions between rational individuals, and crisis as an anomaly caused by external irrational factors and "interference"; (3) the independence of a network of markets in which such actions take place. Indeed, a fictional *Homo oeconomicus* released into the messy reality of life would not survive for a single day.

To return to the principles of *Régulation* theory, we quote from Alain Lipietz's succinct formulation:

> First, we consider society and, within society, economic activities, to be a network of social relations. That is, we do not say that there are individuals who from time to time connect with each other and engage in exchanges, but we consider that exchange is itself a social relation, of a very particular sort.

> A second major thesis is that each of these social relations is *contradictory*, and therefore it is not easy to live within this network of social relations. . . . If social relations are contradictory in this way, the usual situation should be a crisis. In other words, crisis is the normal, natural state and non-crisis is a rather chance event.

> This proposition leads to a third idea that there are long periods of time when things work. I mean, there are times when the configuration of social relations that defines capitalism, for instance, reproduces itself in a stabilized way. We call such a continuing system a *regime of accumulation*. This refers of course to economics but I think this methodology can be extended to politics, diplomacy, and so on.

> Fourth, we have to think about the ways this regime of accumulation is achieved. The problem is that individual expectations and behavior must take shape so that they are in line with the needs of each particular regime of accumulation. There are two aspects of the process. The first operates

---

142. For some more detail with references, see Boer, *Sacred Economy*, 33–34. Fordism is the name given for the approach to manufacturing and industrial production that breaks down the work of assembly-line construction into small unskilled tasks that are interlocked within a whole.

as *habitus*, as Bourdieu would say, in the minds of individuals with a particular culture and willingness to play by the rules of the game. The other operates through a set of institutions and may vary widely, even within the same basic pattern of social relations. Wage relations, market relations, and gender relations have, for example, changed a lot since they first developed. We call a set of such behavioral patterns and institutions a *mode of régulation*.

With these four notions or theses we can speak of different models of development through history.[143]

The final observation frames (for us) the four main points since it indicates that a *Régulation* approach may be developed for different historical epochs and their economic systems. With this in mind, let us see how each of the theoretical bases might be deployed for the economic realities of early Christianity. First, social relations are determinative of economic relations (a point first made by Rodbertus). Or in more conventional Marxist terms, the means of production cannot be thought without the relations of production or class—a point implicit in Ste. Croix's foregrounding of class. This social determination pertains as much to exchange and trade as it does to agriculture, spatial reproduction, and slavery. If this is true of capitalist economics, it is even truer of precapitalist systems. Here we see the core criticism of *Homo oeconomicus*, for an individual reduced to economic rationality is pure myth (as Bücher had already argued). Instead, our economic arrangements "arise from the construction and maintenance of a social bond."[144] In this light, the Polanyi-derived terminology of "embedded"

---

143. Alain Lipietz, "Rebel Sons: The Regulation School," *French Politics and Society* 4 (1987): 17–26, 18–19. http://lipietz.net/spip.php?article750. Or, as Jessop and Sum put: "Overall, starting from real social relations rather than abstract economic men, they aimed to achieve four goals: (1) describe the institutions and practices of capitalism; (2) explain the various crisis tendencies of modern capitalism and/or likely sources of crisis resolution; (3) analyse different stages (periods, phases and so on) of capitalism and compare accumulation regimes and modes of regulation in a given period of capitalist development; and (4) examine the social embedding and social regularization of economic institutions and conduct." Jessop and Sum, *Beyond the Regulation Approach*, 14–15.

144. Robert Boyer and Yves Saillard, "A Summary of *Régulation* Theory," in *Régulation Theory: The State of the Art*, eds. Robert Boyer and Yves Saillard, 36–44 (London: Routledge, 2002), 37; see also Boyer, *Regulation School*, 44. The connections with (new) institutional economics are worth noting here, although such an approach assumes a neoclassical framework (in terms of institutions and law functioning to assist or hinder the "market"). Maurice Baslé, "Acknowledged and Unacknowledged Institutionalist Antecedents of Régulation Theory," in *Régulation Theory: The State of the Art*, eds. Robert Boyer and Yves Saillard, 21–27 (London: Routledge, 2002); Marie-Claire Villeval, "*Régulation* Theory Among Theories of Institutions," in *Régulation Theory: The State of the Art*, eds. Robert Boyer and Yves Saillard, 291–98 (London: Routledge, 2002); Robert Boyer, "The Regulation Approach as a Theory of Capitalism: A New Derivation," in *Institutional Economics in France and Germany: German Ordoliberalism Versus the French Regulation School*, eds. A. Labrousse and J.-D. Weisz, 49–92 (Berlin: Springer, 2001). Advocates of institutional economics in Greek and Roman

economic practices is misleading since it may give the false impression that such practices can be undertaken and understood outside the "bed" independently before being "put to bed."

Second, crisis is the norm. Glaringly obvious with regard to capitalism, but is this so with other modes of production? In ancient Southwest Asia, before the era of the Greeks and Romans, crisis was often the only reality one could expect. Empires collapsed with alarming abruptness and centuries-long periods of "crisis" were often the case. By contrast, the infamous *pax Romana*, let alone the cultural hegemony of Hellenism seem to indicate relative stability. However, our argument is twofold: the very stability of the *pax Romana* both enabled more systemic patterns of exploitation and it was based on significant covert violence, repression, and terror. The fact that such repression was necessary indicates the constant reality of crisis and disruption. In other words, the veneer of the *pax Romana* was enabled by the need to keep crisis in check. Following *Régulation* theory, we propose four types of crisis: (1) exogenous (ranging from conquest to environmental shifts), which do not of themselves endanger a system; (2) endogenous, which enable a system to manage its extremes and are not intrinsically dangerous; (3) structural, in which the creative internal tensions of a system become exacerbated and threaten its viability, so that another system or regime must be found; (4) ultimate, which lead to the collapse of a whole mode of production and its absorption into another.[145] While we occasionally touch on the first two types of crisis, our interest is mainly in the third.[146] In particular, we are interested in the way institutional forms were constantly in tension, especially those of allocative and extractive natures. And we are concerned with tensions and ruptures between regimes, especially what we will call the slave and colonial regimes, but also the shift from both of these to a land regime in the late Roman Empire.

Given that instability, tension, and crisis are the norm during the timeframe of our study, the question arises as to how even a relative

economic analysis include Morris, "Hard Surfaces"; Dennis Kehoe, *Law and the Rural Economy in the Roman Empire* (Ann Arbor: University of Michigan Press, 2007); Bruce Frier and Dennis Kehoe, "Law and Economic Institutions," in *The Cambridge Economic History of the Greco-Roman World*, eds. Walter Scheidel, Ian Morris, and Richard Saller, 113–43 (Cambridge: Cambridge University Press, 2007).

145. Boyer and Saillard, "A Summary of *Régulation* Theory," 41–42.

146. *Régulation* theorists tend to focus on the third, seeking the dynamics of the self-undermining nature of specific regimes and the efforts to find new regimes in their place. The reason is that they attempt to understand the workings of the capitalist mode of production, which still seems to have some life in it. Jessop and Sum, *Beyond the Regulation Approach*, 209.

stability can be achieved and maintained for a while. In order to analyze such stability, *Régulation* theory uses two categories: regime and
mode. A regime designates the mechanisms by which a specific economic constellation is able for a time to manage exogenous and
endogenous crises so that the regime may reproduce itself. Crucially,
each regime is constructed by units or building blocks called "institutional forms." These forms are codifications of the fundamental social
relations that underpin economics. They may be quite discrete, with
little in common with one another, or they may overlap in significant
ways. The key is to find a combination in which they are able to work
together, at least for a time. Usually, one institutional form dominates
a regime with the other forms finding a place within that structure. It
should be obvious that the relations between the institutional forms
produce much of the tensions and potential crises of a regime. Most of
the time, these tensions are endogenous and manageable, but at times
the contradictions become too much and the regime enters structural
crisis, collapse, and replacement with another regime. Following the
lead of the *Régulation* theory, we give a good deal of attention to these
building blocks since they enable significant specificity and attention
to particular variations.[147] We distinguish the following institutional
forms: subsistence survival, which was profoundly disrupted by the
slave economy and new mechanisms for exploiting peasants; *polis-
chōra*; tenure; and the slave-relation.[148]

Institutional forms may come together in different constellations
called regimes, but the question left begging is how they achieve such
combinations and actually stay together. This brings us to the fourth
feature of *Régulation* approach, which is called a mode of *régulation*.
It may be defined as "an emergent ensemble of norms, institutions,
organizational forms, social networks and patterns of conduct that can
temporarily stabilize an accumulation regime despite the conflictual

147. By contrast, the main institutional forms of capitalism are the wage-labor nexus, money, forms
of competition, the state, and international relations with other regimes. Boyer, *Regulation School*,
38–42; Boyer and Saillard, "A Summary of *Régulation* Theory," 38–40.
148. Studies of the Greco-Roman world from time to time tend to elevate one of these institutional
forms into an overarching economic and cultural system. These include patron-client (based on
honor-shame), peasant mode of production, and even the household. Bruce Malina and Jerome
Neyrey, "Honor and Shame in Luke-Acts: Pivotal Values of the Mediterranean World," in *The Social
World of Luke-Acts: Models for Interpretation*, ed. Jerome Neyrey, 25–66 (Peabody: Hendrickson, 1991);
Richard Saller, *Patriarchy, Property, and Death in the Roman Family* (Cambridge: Cambridge University Press, 1994); Richard Saller, "Household and Gender," in *The Cambridge Economic History of the
Greco-Roman World*, eds. Walter Scheidel, Ian Morris, and Richard Saller, 87–112 (Cambridge: Cam-
bridge University Press, 2007); Chris Wickham, *Framing the Early Middle Ages: Europe and the Mediterranean, 400-800* (Oxford: Oxford University Press, 2005), 535–47.

and antagonistic character."[149] More succinctly, a mode of *régulation* is a dynamic and "active process of adjusting disequilibriums on a day-to-day basis."[150] This constant adjustment and effort at temporary stabilization takes place through the institutional forms, which mediate between the socioeconomic dimensions of a regime and the institutional and cultural factors of a mode of *régulation*. Such a mode operates in three ways: 1) compromises and constraints, such as laws and rules;[151] 2) learned and established assumptions about the world and acceptable patterns of behavior; 3) the mechanisms of socially reinforcing and indeed challenging such assumptions, behavior patterns, and compromises.[152] Here religion plays a crucial role, especially in the ancient world. This reality enables us to argue that Christianity functioned as a highly effective and supple mode of *régulation*.

To sum up, *Régulation* theory is notable not for being a Procrustes bed onto which one attempts to force the various pieces, but rather for its flexibility, in terms of developing its categories from the data available and ensuring that such categories remain supple. In particular, *Régulation* theory argues that the normal state of affairs is not stability disrupted by crisis, but rather assumes the normal state as one of economic instability and crisis, interspersed with periods of controlled stability. The key question is, therefore, how specific economic systems stabilize crises in order to establish continuity for certain periods. Thus, an economic system (mode of production) is made up of key building blocks (institutional forms) that come together in unique formations (regimes) to provide very limited continuity for a time within the larger scale of a mode of production. Due to internal contradictions, these regimes face constant tensions and crises. In those efforts at continuity, a whole series of compromises have to be made, which

149. Jessop and Sum, *Beyond the Regulation Approach*, 42. Or in Lipietz's words, it is "the totality of institutional forms, networks, and norms (explicit or implicit), which together secure the compatibility of typical modes of conduct in the context of an accumulation regime, corresponding as much to the changing balance of social relations as to their more general conflictual properties." Alain Lipietz, "Accumulation, Crises, and Ways Out: Some Methodological Reflections on the Concept of 'Regulation'," *International Journal of Political Economy* 18, no. 2 (1988): 10–43, 30.
150. Boyer and Saillard, "A Summary of *Régulation* Theory," 41.
151. These institutionalized compromises result from "situations of tension and conflict between socioeconomic groups over a long period, at the conclusion of which a form of organisation is established, creating rules, rights and obligations for those involved. Institutionalised compromises act as frameworks in relation to which the population and groups involved adapt their behaviour and strategies; their founding principles remain unchanged over the long term." Christine André, "The Welfare State and Institutional Compromises: From Origins to Contemporary Crisis," in *Régulation Theory: The State of the Art*, eds. Robert Boyer and Yves Saillard, 94-100 (London: Routledge, 2002), 95.
152. Boyer, *Regulation School*, 44–45.

are enabled and sustained by cultural assumptions, social forces, and above all, religious beliefs (mode of *régulation*). But there is a catch: the regimes and modes of *régulation* in question do not merely offer stability against constant disequilibria, which threaten to tear the system apart. Instead, the situation is much more dialectical, for the modes and regimes generate their own instability. Economic fluctuations "depend upon the reigning mode of regulation in each historical era."[153] The solution is at one and the same time a cause of further problems.

Conclusion

While our theoretical approach is inspired primarily by Ste. Croix and *Régulation* theory, earlier insights play a role, such as the social determination of economic life (Rodbertus and Weber) and the need for perceiving and elaborating on a distinct economic system (Weber, Finley, and Polanyi). However, we find that the proposals by Ste. Croix and *Régulation* theory to be the most useful with their emphases on exploitation, class, and slavery as the archetypal form of unfree labor (Ste. Croix), as well as a supple framework of social determination, crisis as the norm, institutional forms, regimes, and modes of *régulation*. In this light, we identify four institutional forms, framing Ste. Croix's insights in terms of *Régulation* theory. These are subsistence survival (peasants), *polis* and *chōra*, tenure (leading to the colonate), and the slave-relation. Each of these we have discussed to some extent above, especially in our engagement with Ste. Croix. However, we have left the bulk of analyzing these institutional forms to the chapters that follow. We draw our initial insights from Ste. Croix, but seek to elaborate much further and, where necessary, correct his work in light of subsequent research.

We close this outline of economic theory in relation to the Greco-Roman world with a couple of theoretical points. To begin with, we have thus far not elaborated directly upon the question of mode of production. Nonetheless, it has been implicit throughout our deliberations, for the work of Ste. Croix and *Régulation* theory (together with the questions posed by the Weberians) work best with mode of production as a distinct category. Such a category is of course the most basic, abstract, and overarching category. It is also the most inclusive, since a mode of production deals with economics, social relations,

153. Boyer, *Regulation School*, 69.

ideology, politics, culture, and belief.[154] Further, we do not seek to approximate our written words to whatever reality was in the ancient world. Common enough in historical, economic, and even scientific analysis, this crude assumption—that theoretical model and empirical facts should align with one another—will ensure that the researcher will always fail.[155] Instead, we prefer a Hegelian-Marxist approach in which historical reconstruction must first undergo a process of complete abstraction, pulling away from a supposed world "out there." For this reason, the terms we use such as exploitation, class, religion, economy, mode of production, household, slavery, regime, and so on, are abstract terms. A dialectical turn remains: the most abstract (*pace* Georg Lukács) is at the same time the most concrete at a new and deeper level. Now the task of real reconstruction can take place, to which we turn.

154. In other words, we have little time for the common distinction between idealist and materialist approaches.
155. Thus, we do not assume that the less data one has, the less is one able to approach a supposed reality; or, conversely, the greater the amount of data, the closer one may edge to a reality out there.

2

Out in the Wilds

And the Spirit immediately drove him out into the wilderness. (Mark 1:12)

Agriculture was the *sine qua non* of ancient economic life. An obvious statement perhaps, but too often is it ignored in treatments of economics, in which the latter is for some strange reason restricted to or focused upon commercial activity and thereby blown out of proportion.[1] By contrast, agriculture—as both crop growing and animal husbandry—is an economic activity.[2] In order to understand how it was

---

1. As a sample of recent studies, see Cartledge et al., *Money, Labour and Land*; Freyne, "Herodian Economics in Galilee"; David Mattingly, "The Imperial Economy," in *A Companion to the Roman Empire*, ed. David Potter, 283–97 (London: Blackwell, 2006); Hezser, "Graeco-Roman Context," 40–41; Mordechai Aviam, "People, Land, Economy, and Belief in First-Century Galilee and Its Origins: A Comprehensive Archaeological Synthesis," in *The Galilean Economy in the Time of Jesus*, eds. David Fiensy and Ralph Hawkins, 5–48 (Atlanta: Society of Biblical Literature, 2013), 28; Garnsey, Saller, and Goodman, *Roman Empire*, 71–90.

2. As Marx and Engels observed, human labor is an intimate interaction with nature: "One can look at history from two sides and divide it into the history of nature and the history of men. The two sides are, however, inseparable; the history of nature and the history of men are dependent on each other so long as men exist." Karl Marx and Friedrich Engels, *The German Ideology: Critique of Modern German Philosophy According to Its Representatives Feuerbach, B. Bauer and Stirner, and of German Socialism According to Its Various Prophets*, in *Marx and Engels Collected Works*, vol. 5, 19–539 (Moscow: Progress Publishers, 1974 [1845–46]), 28; see aso Karl Marx, "Economic and Philosophic Manuscripts of 1844," in *Marx and Engels Collected Works*, vol. 3, 229–346 (Moscow: Progress Publishers, 1975 [1844]), 303–4; Yicheng Qin, "Archaeological Research and Guidance of Marxism," *Marxist Studies in China* 2014 (2014): 287–307, 303–4. For an emphasis on agriculture, see further Marie-Claire Amouretti, "L'agriculture de la Grèce antique: bilan des recherches de la dernière décennie," *Topoi* 4, no. 1 (1994): 69–93; Harland, "Economy of First-Century Palestine"; John Davies, "Classical Greece: Production," in *The Cambridge Economic History of the Greco-Roman World*, eds.

so, we focus on the basic building blocks, or institutional forms, of economic life. This chapter concerns the institutional form of subsistence survival—the first of four such forms and the only one that was predominately allocative in its economic practice.

By subsistence survival, we mean a specific economic practice or structure, and not vague notions of "subsistence" evoked in the mind of the beholder.[3] It was an ancient institutional form with techniques honed over millennia to ensure that human beings could survive and be collectively self-sufficient in the face of significant uncertainty. Before we examine subsistence survival in detail, we need to deal with a potential challenge from an economics imperialist direction, which simultaneously trails the dust of the old modernist position and espouses a curious empiricism.[4] In proclaiming a "post-Finlay" approach,[5] some suggest that the Romans and their puppets provided "investment" in regions of the empire, and that the rural areas (chōra) in a Keynesian moment benefitted from the economic incentives or "intervention" by petty despots. In response, the entrepreneurial and "profit-minded" villagers and townspeople engaged in "vigorous home industry" and "trade" in goods such as olive oil, bread, dried fish, woolen garments, pottery, and glass. So dense was the population, suggest some, and so great was the surplus, that a diverse and complex economy buzzed along in a way was not again seen until the twentieth century. This "coherent economic and cultural integration" with its vibrant "capital flows" produced "thriving" proto-capitalist economies and villagers living in symbiosis with the towns and happy with their lives and their relative prosperity.[6] As Fergus Millar puts it, albeit in

Walter Scheidel, Ian Morris, and Richard Saller, 333–61 (Cambridge: Cambridge University Press, 2007), 342.

3. Thus, the criticism of "subsistence" as a generic category misses the mark. Sherratt, "Cash-Crops Before Cash," 12–13; Hordern and Purcell, Corrupting Sea, 271–74.

4. This empiricism appears via a curious effort to distinguish between "sociological" and "archaeological" approaches. "Sociological" becomes a code for "ideological" and thereby misdirected, while "archaeological" becomes "scientific," "empirical," and miraculously free from any assumed framework, nationalist or otherwise. For instance, see Morten Hørning Jensen, Herod Antipas in Galilee: The Literary and Archaeological Sources on the Reign of Herod Antipas and Its Socio-Economic Impact on Galilee, WUNT 2.215 (Tübingen: Mohr Siebeck, 2006). Jensen's own conservative theological agenda is nowhere made explicit.

5. Occasionally, one still encounters the more honest awareness that this is a revamped modernism. See Jack Pastor, "Trade, Commerce, and Consumption," in The Oxford Handbook of Jewish Daily Life in Roman Palestine, ed. Catherine Hezser, 297–307 (Oxford: Oxford University Press, 2010), 297–98.

6. Magen Broshi, "The Role of the Temple in the Herodian Economy," Journal of Jewish Studies 38, no. 1 (1987): 31–37; Douglas Edwards, "The Socio-Economic and Cultural Ethos of the Lower Galilee in the First Century: Implications for the Nascent Jesus Movement," in The Galilee in Late Antiquity, ed. Lee Levine, 53–73 (New York: Jewish Theological Seminary of America, 1992); Douglas Edwards, "Identity and Social Location in Roman Galilean Villages," in Religion, Ethnicity, and Identity in Ancient Galilee: A Region in Transition, eds. Jürgen Zangenberg, Harold Attridge, and Dale Mar-

quotation marks, it was a "capitalist-market economy without factories," or indeed, as John Love suggests, "political capitalism."[7] These suggestions beg at least two crucial questions: *cui bono?* For whose benefit was this apparent "prosperity"? Indeed, what is missing from such analyses is the awareness that the most effective forms of exploitation take place in situations of integration and symbiosis. Further, if everyone was so content, why were there intermittent rebellions and flourishing apocalypses, culminating in the revolts against Rome, with the typical Roman response of occupation and terror, and continuing with subsequent criticisms of Rome?[8] In contrast to this proto-capitalist utopia, the basic reality of the 90 percent or more of the work-

tin, 357–74 (Tübingen: Mohr Siebeck, 2007); Safrai, *Economy of Roman Palestine*; Eric Meyers, "Jesus and His Galilean Context," in *Archaeology and the Galilee: Texts and Contexts in the Graeco-Roman and Byzantine Periods*, eds. Douglas Edwards and C. Thomas McCollough, 57–66 (Atlanta: Scholars Press, 1997); James Strange, "First Century Galilee From Archaeology and From the Texts," in *Archaeology and the Galilee: Texts and Contexts in the Graeco-Roman and Byzantine Periods*, eds. Douglas Edwards and C. Thomas McCollough, 39–48 (Atlanta: Scholars Press, 1997); Mordechai Aviam, "First Century Jewish Galilee: An Archaeological Perspective," in *Religion and Society in Roman Palestine: Old Questions, New Approaches*, ed. Douglas Edwards, 7–27 (New York: Routledge, 2004), 293–300; Aviam, "People, Land, Economy, and Belief"; Mordechai Aviam, "The Transformation from *Galil Ha-Goyim* to Jewish Galilee: The Archaeological Testimony of an Ethnic Change," in *Galilee in the Late Second Temple and Mishnaic Periods. Volume 2: The Archaeological Record from Cities, Towns, and Villages*, eds. David Fiensy and James Strange, 9–21 (Minneapolis: Fortess, 2015); Peter Richardson, "Khirbet Qana (and Other Villages) as a Context for Jesus," in *Jesus and Archaeology*, ed. James Charlesworth, 120–44 (Grand Rapids: Eerdmans, 2006); Ann Killebrew, "Village and Countryside," in *The Oxford Handbook of Jewish Daily Life in Roman Palestine*, ed. Catherine Hezser, 189–209 (Oxford: Oxford University Press, 2010), 202–3; Sharon Lee Mattila, "Jesus and the 'Middle Peasants': Problematizing a Social-Scientific Concept," *Catholic Biblical Quarterly* 72 (2010): 291–313; Sharon Lee Mattila, "Capernaum, Village of Naḥum, from Hellenistic to Byzantine Times," in *Galilee in the Late Second Temple and Mishnaic Periods. Volume 2: The Archaeological Record from Cities, Towns, and Villages*, eds. David Fiensy and James Strange, 217–57 (Minneapolis: Fortess, 2015); Harris, *Rome's Imperial Economy*; Morten Hørning Jensen, "Rural Galilee and Rapid Changes: An Investigation of the Socio-Economic Dynamics and Developments in Roman Galilee," *Biblica* 93, no. 1 (2012): 43–67, 58–61; C. Thomas McCollough, "City and Village in Lower Galilee: The Import of the Archeological Excavations at Sepphoris and Khirbet Qana (Cana) for Framing the Economic Context of Jesus," in *The Galilean Economy in the Time of Jesus*, eds. David Fiensy and Ralph Hawkins, 49–74 (Atlanta: Society of Biblical Literature, 2013); David Fiensy, *Christian Origins and the Ancient Economy* (Eugene: Cascade, 2014), 91–95; Bradley Root, *First Century Galilee* (Tübingen: Mohr Siebeck, 2014), 166–67; J. Andrew Overman, "Late Second Temple Galilee: A Picture of Relative Economic Health," in *Galilee in the Late Second Temple and Mishnaic Period, Volume 1: Life, Culture, and Society*, eds. David Fiensy and James Strange, 357–65 (Minneapolis: Fortress, 2014). Freyne offers an intriguing twist: recognizing the central role of agriculture, he speaks of "agribusiness," first fostered by "state monopolies" under the Ptolemies. Freyne, *Galilee from Alexander the Great to Hadrian*. And for a welcome dissenting view, see Emilio Gabba, "The Social, Economic and Political History of Palestine, 63 BCE–CE 70," in *The Cambridge History of Judaism*, eds. William Horbury, W.D. Davies, and John Sturdy, vol. 3, 94–167 (Cambridge: Cambridge University Press, 1999), 107–11.

7. Fergus Millar, "The World of The Golden Ass," *The Journal of Roman Studies* 71 (1981): 63–75, 73; John Love, *Antiquity and Capitalism: Max Weber and Sociological Foundations of Roman Civilization* (London: Routledge, 1991), 165–72.

8. For a salutary situating of such revolts within the endemic patterns of unrest across the Roman Empire, see Garnsey, Saller, and Goodman, *Roman Empire*, 56–63.

ing rural population was quite different. The first component concerns subsistence survival.[9]

Sociable Quadrupeds and Amenable Grains

There are after all two roads to satisfaction, to reducing the gap between means and ends: producing much or desiring little.[10]

In order to understand how subsistence survival functioned in the era of our concern, we need to backtrack a few thousand years to what V. Gordon Childe called the "Neolithic Revolution."[11] By this he meant a profound shift in mode of production in which agriculture arose as the prime concern of human production.[12] This required the mutual and symbiotic domestication of human animals, other sociable animals, and amenable grains—a process that dates from the beginning of the Holocene era (c. 9,500 BCE) and took place simultaneously in different parts of the world but at different speeds.[13] Through mutual agency, the techniques of production became more intensive, and human beings and animals began to live collectively in villages, with consequent creativity in technology and social forms, but also a whole new range of diseases that use human and other animal bodies for their life cycles. In ancient Southwest Asia, the animals in question—sheep and goats—gradually mutated, genetically and culturally, from wild versions.[14] This was due to restricted movement, controlled breeding, and

9. Although we may differ on specific points, the underlying drive and reason for beginning with subsistence survival shares the methodological focus of Horsley and Hanson on the majority, that is, the exploited, whether slaves, peasants, or any other form of unfree labor. Richard Horsley and John Hanson, *Bandits, Prophets, and Messiahs: Popular Movements in the Time of Jesus* (Philadelphia: Trinity Press International, 1985).

10. Marshall Sahlins, "Tribal Economics," in *Economic Development and Social Change: The Modernization of Village Communities*, ed. George Dalton, 43–61 (New York: Natural History Press, 1971), 49.

11. V. Gordon Childe, *Man Makes Himself* (New York: Mentor, 1936), 59–86. A revolution may take millennia, as was the case here. On the gradual nature of the process, see George Willcox, "Agrarian Change and the Beginnings of Cultivation in the Near East: Evidence from Wild Progenitors, Experimental Cultivation and Archaeobotanical Data," in *The Prehistory of Food: Appetites for Change*, eds. Chris Gosden and Jon Hather, 468–89 (London: Routledge, 1999). The most considered recent work on Childe is Patterson, *Marx's Ghost*, 33–62.

12. Walter Scheidel, "Demography," in *The Cambridge Economic History of the Greco-Roman World*, eds. Walter Scheidel, Ian Morris, and Richard Saller, 38–86 (Cambridge: Cambridge University Press, 2007), 27. Too often lip service is given to this point, without serious engagement with agriculture.

13. See especially Melinda A. Zeder, "The Origins of Agriculture in the Ancient Near East," *Current Anthropology* 52 (2011): 221–35. This process appears separately and with different animals and crops in Afro-Eurasia, the Americas, Australia and Papua New Guinea, and the Pacific (from 2,000 BCE). The distinction indicates the possibility of contact within each zone. A useful overview, with some qualifications, may be found in David Christian, *Maps of Time: An Introduction to Big History* (Berkeley: University of California Press, 2011), 207–44; Bruce Smith, *The Emergence of Agriculture* (New York: W.H. Freeman, 1994).

selective feeding, so that they became smaller, lactated nearly all year, and their usable fibers grew longer and no longer molted.[15] The later heavier bovines, descendants of the auroch, were used for traction, and the pig also became a source of meat, although sheep and goats were the most versatile in terms of milk, fiber, and meat. As a result, such animals could no longer survive without human involvement.

Domestication of plants took place at the same time, with the processes of planting, weeding and harvesting, giving such plants favored treatment but also cutting off genetic contact with others.[16] With the resultant shifts in genetic structure and morphology, these plants became dependent on human beings for their existence, as did human beings on the plants. Thus, archaeobotanists look for larger seeds with thinner husks ("naked" seeds), clustered together and held to the stem by thicker and stronger stalks. Such seeds germinate better, do not scatter to the ground easily, ripen longer, and typically produce larger yields. Plants became fatter, fruitier, and fast-sprouting. In the part of the world that interests us, the main crops so developed were barley, emmer and einkorn wheats, lentils, peas, chickpeas, bitter vetch, and flax. The wider environment too was significantly altered, with limitations in biodiversity through weeding, grafting of olive trees and vines, hunting of predators, and the need for fertilization of the soil, but also resultant degradations such as erosion.

The outcome of this long process was subsistence survival agriculture, with sedentary and nomadic features woven together in a continuum.[17] It should be seen as a creative and tested response to both old and new problems rather than a narrative of progress. The problems that subsistence survival had to face were many: more labor for

14. Not to be forgotten here is the dog, derived from wolves, which preceded sheep and goats. But dogs serve a rather different function for human beings.
15. With sheep, descendants of the mouflon (*Ovis gmelini*), plucking the fine wool beneath an outer layer of long stiff hair during molting gave way to sheering that was required for regrowth. Genetic changes ensured that the fine wool dominated and the outer layer diminished. Andrew Sherratt, "Plough and Pastoralism: Aspects of the Secondary Products Revolution," in *Pattern of the Past*, eds. I. Hodder, G. Isaac, and N. Hammond, 261–306 (Oxford: Oxford University Press, 1981), 282.
16. This process was dependent also on soil types, or pedology, the knowledge of which grew over millennia of trial and error. Soils can, of course, be modified through fertilization. For useful introductions, see Edwin Michael Bridges, *World Soils*, 3 ed. (Cambridge: Cambridge University Press, 1997); Jean-Paul Legros, *Major Soil Groups of the World: Ecology, Genesis, Properties and Classification*, trans. V. A. K. Sarma (Boca Raton: CRC, 2012), 180-205, 265-90; Choi, "Never the Two Shall Meet?"
17. David Hopkins, "Agriculture," in *The Oxford Encyclopaedia of Archaeology in the Near East*, ed. Eric Meyers, vol. 1, 22–30 (Oxford: Oxford University Press, 1997), 28. The variations in this continuum over time and place were many, ranging between the ideal poles of full sedentarism and full nomadism.

new technologies such as the plow;[18] new diseases and plagues as the result of collective living in well-watered and fertile areas—such as Galilee[19]—and the attendant refuse (and absence of toilets),[20] along with the increasingly temperate climate; droughts and famines, which had a greater effect than on a more mobile population; a more limited diet and physical problems from repetitive tasks of agriculture and carrying heavy loads;[21] limited life expectancy of 25–30, with almost half of the children dying before maturity.[22] Life was not easy.[23] Subsistence survival then was as much a way of organizing the profound shift in economic life as it was a response to these problems. Its adaptability and creativity to changing conditions are part of its very structure.[24]

When we turn to the period of this study, we are faced with a conun-

18. David Hopkins, *The Highlands of Canaan: Agricultural Life in the Early Highlands* (Sheffield: Almond, 1985), 38–41.

19. Flavius Josephus, *Bellum Judaicum*, trans. H. St. J. Thackeray, 2 vols., Loeb Classical Library (London: William Heinemann, 1978), 3.42–43; Overman, "Late Second Temple Galilee," 358.

20. For sobering evidence, from osteoarchaeology from the first centuries of the common era, which reveals the widespread effects of malaria as well as gastrointestinal diseases, brucellosis (from infected animal products such as goat's milk), typhus, typhoid, dysentery, tuberculosis, and plague, see Alex Scobie, "Slums, Sanitation and Mortality in the Roman World," *Klio* 68, no. 2 (1986): 399–433; Mirko Grmek, *Diseases in the Ancient Greek World* (Baltimore: Johns Hopkins University Press, 1989), 86–89; Robert Sallares, *Malaria and Rome: A History of Malaria in Ancient Italy* (Oxford: Oxford University Press, 2002); Scheidel, "Demography," 33–37; François Retief and Louise Cilliers, "Malaria in Graeco-Roman Times," *Acta Classica* 47 (2004): 127–37; Walter Scheidel, "Population and Demography," *Princeton/Stanford Working Papers in Classics* (2006), http://www.princeton.edu/~pswpc/pdfs/scheidel/040604.pdf., 2; Walter Scheidel, "Epigraphy and Demography: Birth, Marriage, Family, and Death," *Princeton/Stanford Working Papers in Classics*(2007), http://www.princeton.edu/~pswpc/pdfs/scheidel/060701.pdf; Walter Scheidel, "Disease and Death in the Ancient Roman City," *Princeton/Stanford Working Papers in Classics*(2009), http://www.princeton.edu/~pswpc/pdfs/scheidel/040901.pdf; Jonathan Reed, "Mortality, Morbidity, and Economics in Jesus's Galilee," in *Galilee in the Late Second Temple and Mishnaic Period, Volume 1: Life, Culture, and Society*, eds. David Fiensy and James Strange, 242–52 (Minneapolis: Fortress, 2014); Eric Meyers and Carol Meyers, "Meiron in Upper Galilee," in *Galilee in the Late Second Temple and Mishnaic Periods. Volume 2: The Archaeological Record from Cities, Towns, and Villages*, eds. David Fiensy and James Strange, 379–88 (Minneapolis: Fortess, 2015), 381. Nonetheless, we do not wish to fall into the trap of attributing too much to disease cycles (the same applies to climate). As with other risks, subsistence survival had developed strategies for dealing with disease, such as avoiding the more pestilential areas.

21. For example, even in Roman times the production of usable fiber from flax was labor intensive and time consuming, as described in Pliny, *Naturalis Historia*, trans. Harris Rackham, W. Jones, and D. Eichholz, 10 vols., Loeb Classical Library (London: William Heinemann, 1949–54), 19.16–19.

22. Even in the *poleis*, infant mortality remained high in the Greco-Roman era. Beryl Rawson, "Death, Burial, and Commemoration of Children in Roman Italy," in *Early Christian Families in Context: An Interdisciplinary Dialogue*, eds. David Balch and Carolyn Osiek, 277–297 (2003), 279.

23. It is not for nothing the some "affluent" foragers appropriated only a few intensive features of agriculture but preferred not to adopt it wholesale. Christian, *Maps of Time*, 223–29. Many are the proposals as to why such a shift was made when the advantages are by no means clear. Although treatment of these proposals is beyond our remit, the collective needs for producing alcohol should not be discounted. About forty percent of early crops were devoted to alcohol production. See the fuller discussion and references in Boer, *Sacred Economy*, 67–70.

24. We stress that this institutional form is a far cry from the ideal patriarchal farmer of later rabbinic texts. Jacob Neusner, *Judaism: The Evidence of the Mishnah* (Chicago: University of Chicago Press, 1981), 252–55.

drum: the core institutional form of subsistence survival has left relatively little by way of conventional archaeological evidence. This way of life by its very nature was "aceramic," leaving minimal archaeological and recorded data.[25] So where is the evidence? The first is historical, for the practice is found in the earliest human settlements, through to medieval Europe, seventeenth-century North America, pre-1873 Japan, twentieth century Russia, Greece, the Maghreb, and Iraq. Notably for our purposes, it was a feature of agriculture in pre-Ottoman and Ottoman periods, and twentieth-century Greater Syria, including the Levant.[26] In light of the "extraordinary continuity" of village life,[27] it would seem strange that such practices suddenly disappeared in our area of interest for a few centuries, only to reappear afterwards. Further, we draw upon the relatively new fields of zooarchaeology (or archaeozoology) and archaeobotany (or palaeobotany) to glean information.[28]

As for zooarchaeology, the more sustained work has been done on earlier stages in the eastern Mediterranean, so we rely upon this material in order to gain a sense of the situation in the Greco-Roman era.[29] Sheep and goats were the key, with a 2:1 ratio of sheep and goats.[30] Both

25. This applies as much to peasants as to laborers, itinerants, and slaves. See Alan Cadwallader, "Peasant Plucking in Mark: Conceptual and Material Issues," in *Scriptural Radicalism*, eds. Sean Durbin and Robert Myles (New York: Palgrave Macmillan, In Press).

26. Abraham Granott, *The Land System of Palestine in History and Structure* (London: Eyre and Spottiswood, 1952); Jerome Blum, *The End of the Old Order in Rural Europe* (Princeton: Princeton University Press, 1978); Hopkins, *The Highlands of Canaan*, 257–58; Brian Roberts, *Landscapes of Settlement: Prehistory to the Present* (London: Routledge, 1996), 15–37; Tony Wilkinson, *Archaeological Landscapes of the Near East* (Tucson: University of Arizona Press, 2003); Michael R. Fischbach, *State, Society and Land in Jordan* (Leiden: Brill, 2000), 38–41; Philippe Guillaume, *Land, Credit and Crisis: Agrarian Finance in the Hebrew Bible* (Sheffield: Equinox, 2012), 28–42.

27. A. M. T. Moore, "Villages," in *The Oxford Encyclopaedia of Archaeology in the Near East*, ed. Eric Meyers, vol. 5, 301–3 (Oxford: Oxford University Press, 1997), 303.

28. Where necessary, we also draw on more conventional archaeological work in the Greco-Roman era, although much of it tends to focus on the artificial construct of "Galilee," which was not regarded as a distinct region in the ancient world. Obviously, the intense focus on Galilee is driven by the fact that Jesus came from this area, but the danger is that it isolates Galilee, if not Syria-Palestine, from the context of Greco-Roman economics and colonization. See Harland, "Economy of First-Century Palestine," 514–15; Jürgen Zangenberg, "Review of David A. Fiensy and James Strange, eds. Galilee in the Late Second Temple and Mishnaic Periods, Volume 1: Life, Culture, and Society," *Review of Biblical Literature* 2016, no. 2 (2016): 1–7. See also Weber, *Agrarian Sociology*, 66–135; McCollough, "City and Village in Lower Galilee," 56–57, 71.

29. Zooarchaeology focuses on bones of animals consumed by human beings, since the remains were tossed aside close to the place of consumption—albeit keeping in mind effects of the passage of time from the initial toss to arrival in the laboratory. Aharon Sasson, *Animal Husbandry in Ancient Israel: A Zooarchaeological Perspective on Livestock Exploitation, Herd Management and Economic Strategies* (London: Equinox, 2010); Brian Hesse and Paula Wapnish, *Animal Bone Archaeology from Objectives to Analysis* (Washington, DC: Taraxacum, 1985); Paula Wapnish and Brian Hesse, "Archaeozoology," in *Near Eastern Archaeology: A Reader*, ed. S. Richard, 17–26 (Winona Lake, IN: Eisenbrauns, 2003); Terry O'Connor, *The Archaeology of Animal Bones* (Stroud: Sutton, 2000). For the Greco-Roman era, see Killebrew, "Village and Countryside," 201.

species are versatile, providing milk, fibers, meat, hide, and bones. Goats especially are able to eat almost anything, and manage survival in a unique fashion during shortages of food and water and during extreme heat and cold.[31] Sheep may not be as flexible as goats, but they have higher levels of proteins and fats, eat pastures that goats may skip (regenerating grass), and can travel far from water resources. Why such a ratio, which is uniform wherever these two species are found? If disease afflicted one of the species, the other part of the herd would survive. Due to the high breeding rate of both animals, herd size could be restored in a few seasons. Analysis of bone remains indicates that sheep and goats were culled regularly to maintain a healthy herd, with most females favored with longer lives due to breeding and the provision of milk and fiber.[32] All parts of the animals were used, rather than select portions characteristic of luxury consumption and breeding for commercial reasons.

We have not mentioned our porcine and bovine friends. As for the much-debated pig, its popularity was patchy and periodic. Only in the Greco-Roman era did it come into its own, to the extent that in Syria-Palestine pig remains are also found.[33] The reason for its varied popularity is that pigs have significant limitations: they may provide good quality meat, but do not provide milk or fiber for human consumption. More importantly, they do not cope well with temperature extremes and require high levels of water. Thus, they tend to be found in well-watered areas (Egypt is a good example),[34] above the 250mm isohyet, well beyond what is required by sheep and goats. The heavy and lum-

30. Richard Redding, "Theoretical Determinations of a Herder's Decisions: Modeling Variation in the Sheep/Goat Ratio," in *Animals in Archaeology 3: Early Herders and Their Flocks*, eds. J. Clutton-Brock and C. Grigson, 223–41 (Oxford: British Archaeology Reports, 1984).

31. Goats can modify metabolism to deal with food shortage and can survive with the loss of 30 percent in body weight (for other animals the limit is 15 percent). They also ensure low moisture loss through sweating, urine, and feces, and recover swiftly after water shortage–drinking up to 40 percent of body weight at one go.

32. Being a male was clearly not an advantage, unless one had been selected for the pleasure of a long career of insemination. This situation was altered in some situations, especially in the first centuries of the common era, leading to the colonate: the production of wool for *poleis* led to a higher proportion of sheep achieving senility. Aviam, "People, Land, Economy, and Belief," 29.

33. For example, in the lower Levant, pigs were abundant during the Chalcolithic period, declined to a low in the Late Bronze Age, rebounded for a while in the early Iron Age in a few places, until they resurged fully in the Greco-Roman era. Brian Hesse, "Pig Lovers and Pig Haters: Patterns of Palestinian Pork Production," *Journal of Ethnobiology* 10 (1990): 195–225; Brian Hesse and Paula Wapnish, "An Archaeozoological Perspective on the Cultural Use of Mammals in the Levant," in *A History of the Animal World in the Ancient Near East*, ed. Billie Jean Collins, 457–91 (Leiden: Brill, 2002), 468–70. Safrai struggles to deal with the archaeological and literary evidence of pigs in the province of Judea. Safrai, "Agriculture and Farming," 258.

34. Douglas Brewer, "Hunting, Animal Husbandry and Diet in Ancient Egypt," in *A History of the Animal World in the Ancient Near East*, ed. Billie Jean Collins, 427–56 (Leiden: Brill, 2002), 441–43.

bering cow was even more of a drain on fodder and water than the pig.[35] Remains of bovines indicate that they were usually few in each village and that they lived to a relatively ripe old age, when they were finally slaughtered for a repast of tough old meat at a festival or two.[36] In other words, the relatively few oxen were used primarily for traction, being shared around in the village for plowing and hauling heavy loads.[37]

For the archaeobotanical evidence,[38] we focus on three matters: actual land use for cropping, olive growing, and viticulture; the village dynamics of field shares; and the class dynamics of changes in crops. Many of the patterns of crop and land use in ancient Southwest Asia and the Mediterranean continued from earlier millennia. The range of crops mentioned above were still grown, namely, cereals such as barley and wheat (which thrive in what are variously called Calcisols or Pale Renzina soils),[39] legumes like broad beans, chickpeas, and lentils, along with the ubiquitous vines and olives. Of these, high quality wine and olive oil could be exchanged over longer distances, and grain was sequestered by the larger *poleis* (especially Rome). However, the predominant consumption of food was local—in this respect human beings were "locovores." It was, in short, a tried and risk-averse practice of polyculture with significant enough staying power that it spread—beginning in the first millennium BCE—from the eastern Mediterranean to the west. Alongside this development, two other changes may also be identified: one in regard to fruit trees and the other with grains (which we address in a moment). The practice of grafting, probably borrowed from eastern Asia, appeared in the Levant and Mediter-

---

35. Paul Halstead, "Traditional and Ancient Rural Economy in Mediterranean Europe: Plus ça Change?," *Journal of Hellenic Studies* 107 (1987): 77–87, 84; Paul Halstead and Glynis Jones, "Agrarian Ecology in the Greek Islands: Time Stress, Scale and Risk," *Journal of Hellenic Studies* 109 (1989): 41–55, 49. The species of cow in the ancient Mediterranean and Southwest Asia had five times the body mass of a sheep or a goat, yet it sucked up to 25 times the amount of water. A cow needs approximately 50 liters of water per day, more in hot weather, while a sheep or a goat needs two to three liters. For this reason, a cow can range no more than 16 kilometers from a water source, while sheep and goats can be up to 30 kilometers away. Conspicuous consumption of fatted calves and cows was a mark of ruling-class identity (Luke 15:23, 27, 30).

36. By contrast, more consistent use of traction animals is associated with estates. In other words, they were used for producing food for those who did not work. Paul Halstead, *Two Oxen Ahead: Pre-Mechanized Farming in the Mediterranean* (Oxford: Wiley Blackwell, 2014), 60.

37. Sasson (*Animal Husbandry*, 56) estimates that a village of 100 people would need 300 sheep and goats, and only 12 bovines. Thus, they were highly prized, with specific laws concerning bovines (Exod 21:28–36).

38. For a useful survey of archaeobotany in light of comparative models, see Ann Butler, "Traditional Seed Cropping Systems in the Temperate Old World: Models for Antiquity," in *The Prehistory of Food: Appetites for Change*, eds. Chris Gosden and Jon Hather, 452–67 (London: Routledge, 1999).

39. Hopkins, "Cereals."

ranean in the first millennium. Grafting was the most effective way to spread olive cultivation, but it was also done with a range of trees, such as apple, plum, pistachio, pear, and the sweet and sour varieties of cherry.[40]

Given that the economic life of agriculture was inescapably social, how was crop growing organized? Many simply assume, somewhat uncritically, that peasants had "private lots," "holdings" or "small farms" for "nuclear families," estimating what the size of such a "holding" might be, with the expected result that it would be too small to support a "family."[41] The reality was somewhat different: in many areas it turned on an ancient practice of field shares, based on what Soviet-era Russian scholars call the village commune (*mir* or *obshchina*) and others describe as *musha'* farming.[42] In short, the field shares—understood as social units rather than land as such—were periodically reallocated within the context of a village community or even a collection of villages. Every one to five years and in light of the needs and capabilities of households, as well as the need to spread risk (natural and human) and to optimize labor, soil conservation and consistent crops, the allocation of field shares would be debated—often at length—and then apportioned to able-bodied members of the commu-

40. Wild varieties had been gathered for much longer, but they all began to be grafted at the same time. At another level, as the Roman Empire spread, the Romans brought back with them more exotic fruit trees, at times parading them in triumphs. See Pliny, *Naturalis Historia*, 12.54.111; Daniel Zohary, Maria Hopf, and Ehud Weiss, *Domestication of Plants in the Old World*, 4 ed. (Oxford: Oxford University Press, 2012); Scheidel, "Demography," 27–34.

41. Freyne, *Galilee from Alexander the Great to Hadrian*, 155–80; Shimon Dar, *Landscape and Pattern: An Archaeological Survey of Samaria, 800 BCE–636 CE*, BAR International Series (Oxford: BAR, 1986), 230–45; Peter Garnsey, *Famine and Food Supply in the Graeco-Roman World: Responses to Risk and Crisis* (Cambridge: Cambridge University Press, 1988), 46; David Fiensy, *The Social History of Palestine in the Herodian Period: The Land is Mine* (Lewiston: Edwin Mellen, 1991), 93–95; Lin Foxhall, "The Dependent Tenant: Land Leasing and Labour in Italy and Greece," *Journal of Roman Studies* 80(1991); Safrai, *Economy of Roman Palestine*, 357, 360–63.

42. The literature on such farming is immense, but see the following material that is relevant for the period under consideration, including Greece and Italy: Samuel Bergheim, "Land Tenure in Palestine," *Palestine Exploration Fund Quarterly* 26, no. 3 (1894): 191–99; Tarif Khalidi, ed. *Land Tenure and Social Transformation in the Middle East* (Beirut: American University of Beirut Press, 1984); Ya'akov Firestone, "The Land-equalizing Mushâ' Village," in *Ottoman Palestine*, ed. Gad Gilbar, 91–130 (Leiden: Brill, 1990); Foxhall, "Dependent Tenant," 108; Carol Palmer, "Whose Land Is it Anyway? An Historical Examination of Land Tenure and Agriculture in Northern Jordan," in *The Prehistory of Food: Appetites for Change*, eds. Chris Gosden and Jon Hather, 282–99 (London: Routledge, 1999); Birgit Schäbler, "Practicing Musha': Common Lands and the Common Good in Southern Syria under the Ottomans and the French (1812–1942)," in *Rights to Access, Rights to Surplus: New Approaches to Land in the Middle East*, ed. Roger Owen, 241–309 (Cambridge: Harvard University Press, 2000); Amos Nadan, "Colonial Misunderstanding of an Efficient Peasant Institution," *Journal of the Economic and Social History of the Orient* 46 (2003): 320–54; Amos Nadan, *The Palestinian Peasant Economy under the Mandate: A Story of Colonial Bungling* (Cambridge: Harvard University Press, 2006); Halstead, *Two Oxen Ahead*, 304–8. For painstaking detail in regard to practices in Arab villages in the early twentieth century, see Gustaf Dalman, *Arbeit und Sitte in Palästina*, 8 vols. (Gütersloh and Berlin: Bertelsmann and De Gruyter, 1928–2012). For a full bibliography, see Excursus 7 in Boer, *Sacred Economy*.

nity. The shares tended to be non-contiguous and relatively long, so as to ensure a relatively even spread of different types of land.[43] Methods of allocation varied, from gathering of the whole village, through elders, to the casting of lots. The produce of such shares would also be reallocated among households at harvest times. Common projects, such as grape, olive, and fruit orchards, required shared labor, as did the production of alcoholic beverages and bread. And grazing grounds for the herds of sheep and goats were held in common, often variable and shared with other villages.[44]

Here we would like to introduce a feature of crop growing that anticipates the analysis of exploitation below (and marks the second change of this era). It concerns the increasing class dimensions of such crops—the granarian class struggle—when subsistence survival is considered in light of its relations with other institutional forms. When we enter our era, barley and two basic types of hulled wheat—emmer (*Triticum dicoccum*) in wetter areas and einkorn (*Triticum monococcum*) in the Levant and Greece—were dominant. Apart from areas under irrigation (such as Egypt or lower Mesopotamia) or well-watered by other means,[45] the average yield was between 4:1 and 5:1 or a net product of 400-500 kilograms per hectare.[46] Both barley and wheat can be used for the staples of beer and bread, although barley was much preferred for beer. Indeed, it may be argued that a major motive for human beings opting to live in such villages with all their problems was precisely the desire to produce alcoholic beverages from cultivated grains. At the same time, class factors began to determine the preferences for barley or wheat. Barley (*Hordeum vulgare*) was already regarded by the Greeks as a food fit for slaves, peasants, the poor, and animals.[47] Bar-

---

43. This practice makes sense of what is sometimes called "splitting" or "fragmentation" of peasant "holdings" into small, non-contiguous strips. Rather than the result of inheritance breakdown, it marks the effects of the farming practices outlined here. Safrai, "Agriculture and Farming," 250.

44. All of this helps in understanding the fine radial tracery of village paths, trails, and tracks, which were the primary means of getting to fields and other villages some 2–4 kilometers apart—on foot. Nucleated villages were surrounded by an apparently fragmented landscape of land shares and pastures, with an absence of clear boundaries and no conventional remains of temporary structures for shelter and other purposes. To our eyes, such landscape may seem fragmented and haphazard, but they constituted complex units. See Tony Wilkinson, "The Tell: Social Archaeology and Territorial Space," in *Development of Pre-State Communities in the Ancient Near East*, eds. Dianne Bolger and Louise C. Maguire, 55–62 (Oxford: Oxbow, 2010), 56–57; Wilkinson, *Archaeological Landscapes of the Near East*; Jesse Casana, "Structural Transformations in Settlement Systems of the Northern Levant," *American Journal of Archaeology* 112 (2007): 195–222; James Strange, "The Galilean Road System," in *Galilee in the Late Second Temple and Mishnaic Period, Volume 1: Life, Culture, and Society*, eds. David Fiensy and James Strange, 263–71 (Minneapolis: Fortress, 2014).

45. These areas were also the ones most prone to disease.

46. At the same time, we should be wary of such rough generalizations, for regional variations were significant and could run up to 8:1. Garnsey, Saller, and Goodman, *Roman Empire*, 104–5.

ley is tougher than wheat and requires less water and labor, and ripens earlier—precisely why it was preferred by those who knew its value. Both alcohol and bread played crucial roles in the class struggle over the granary. As for alcohol, the Romans and indeed Greeks preferred wine to beer, and with the spread—at least in the *poleis*—of Hellenistic cultural assumptions, wine displaced beer as the preferred beverage for the citified—on occasion threatening grain supplies since so much land was given over to viticulture.[48] As a consequence, barley was not needed for such refined folk, although it remained a staple in the countryside and among peasants. Further, the same classes and their aspirants preferred fine-floured bread rather than the coarse and tough loaves of the village dwellers. On estates and in villages required to provide produce for the local *polis*, the pressure was on to grow so-called naked grains rather than hulled grains, especially high-yield bread wheat (*Triticum aestivum*), poulard wheat (*Triticum turgidum*), and durum wheat (*Triticum durum*).[49] Not only do they require less labor to provide finer flour than hulled grains, but depending on the type they produce relatively fine-floured breads and semolina. In particular, the most desired bread was the Roman *panis siligneus* (*siligo* designated wheat flour), which was produced best in colder zones such as the Crimea, northern Italy, and Gaul. If this type of wheat flour was not available, a local variant would have to do.[50] By contrast, the peasants continued to grow the tougher hulled wheats[51] along with barley and oats, which were coarser, more durable, and resistant to disease. Their breads the Romans called with some disdain—*panis plebeius*. Slaves and city poor would also eat such bread, along with types of porridge. It

---

47. Halstead, *Two Oxen Ahead*, 181; Sitta Von Reden, "Classical Greece: Consumption," in *The Cambridge Economic History of the Greco-Roman World*, eds. Walter Scheidel, Ian Morris, and Richard Saller, 385–406 (Cambridge: Cambridge University Press, 2007), 390–91. Nonetheless, the Greeks continued to grow much barley. For example, in the fourth century CE, Attica produced ten times more barley than wheat, given the favorable conditions. Jameson, "Agriculture and Slavery in Classical Athens," 130.

48. The Romans fostered the spread of viticulture into much of Europe, while the Greeks had already seen it spread to the Black Sea. For the spread of viticulture in Palestine, see John Kloppenborg, "The Growth and Impact of Agricultural Tenancy in Jewish Palestine (III BCE–I CE)," *Journal of the Economic and Social History of the Orient* 51, no. 1 (2012): 31–66, 46–47.

49. For the marked shift to wheat and wine under the Ptolemies in Egypt, which had been a beer-swilling and barley-munching locale for millennia, see Joseph Gilbert Manning, "Hellenistic Egypt," in *The Cambridge Economic History of the Greco-Roman World*, eds. Walter Scheidel, Ian Morris, and Richard Saller, 434–59 (Cambridge: Cambridge University Press, 2007), 440.

50. For an insightful study into the metaphorical function of wheat for the Romans, see Brent Shaw, *Bringing in the Sheaves: Economy and Metaphor in the Roman World* (Toronto: University of Toronto Press, 2013).

51. Safrai mentions that wheat was the primary grain grown in the province of Judea, although he does not specify what type. Safrai, "Agriculture and Farming," 251–52.

is not for nothing that Josephus noted in the first century CE that in Galilee the rich ate wheat while the poor ate barley.[52]

To return to the internal dynamics of subsistence survival: all of these activities concerning amenable plants and sociable quadrupeds revolved around the extended-family household commune, or village communes, as Soviet-era Russian scholars called them.[53] In the midst of myriad variations, we discern two features: flexibility and the need to share. And in order to show how, we turn to consider the dynamic of households in the countryside—in the *chōra*. We do so for the specific reason that the dynamics of households are primarily cultural, social, and economic—from the choice of building materials to the spatial production they entail. Indeed, household architecture is a material form of ideology and social practice.[54]

Households of Rural Laborers

The classical world was massively, unalterably rural in its basic quantitative proportions.[55]

Let us begin with the question of flexibility. Our definition: a household comprises the rhythms of life and flexible constructions of space in and around distinct structures or collections of structures that are less or more permanent, which is made possible by the social and economic context in which it is found. To elaborate: a household comprises human beings, animals, and the items of everyday life from cooking pots to animal droppings (and the associated rich, earthy smells and tastes). None are static,[56] as even the archaeological evidence reveals with the sporadic spread of items found. They were constantly in movement, flowing into and out of places, constantly reproducing space in the process of such rhythms.[57] We emphasize this

---

52. Josephus, *Bellum Judaicum*, 5.427. The inversion of values in our day means that course whole grains and baked products are regarded as desirable by the elites who used to desire refined flours. Halstead, *Two Oxen Ahead*, 164-65; Jack Pastor, *Land and Economy in Ancient Palestine* (London: Routledge, 1997), 5.

53. However, the various *poleis* also had significant agricultural activity, with many residents working the fields nearby. Safrai, "Urbanization and Industry in Mishnaic Galilee." Patterns from the *chōra*, from where many of those who dwelt in the *poleis* came, usually applied to such agriculture.

54. Serena Love, "Architecture as Material Culture: Building Form and Materiality in the Pre-Pottery Neolithic of Anatolia and Levant," *Journal of Anthropological Archaeology* 32 (2013): 746–58.

55. Anderson, *Passages from Antiquity to Feudalism*, 19.

56. This static tendency is a legacy of the influential definition of Wilk and Rathje, who focus on: 1) the social unit constituting the household; 2) the material reality of the dwelling and its contents; 3) human behavior. Wilk and Rathje, "Household Archaeology," 618.

57. Henri Lefebvre, *Rhythmanalysis: Space, Time and Everyday Life*, trans. Stuart Elden and Gerald Moore

flexibility as a contrast to tendencies see them as static, for items were constantly reused for many purposes, and so reshaping internal and external space in light of current needs. The constructed features of a household may be more or less permanent, ranging from tents and shelters for a period, or structures of wood, mud, plaster, and stone. At the same time, a household is not constrained by these spaces for the external is as important as the internal. And households are not private or discrete units for they were determined by their socio-economic context.

Let us say a little more concerning villages and households. Archaeological surveys indicate that villages of less than 4 hectares (10 acres)—including orchards, fields, and grazing lands—comprised more than 90 percent of all settlements.[58] Ancient population patterns indicate 75–150, although by the Greco-Roman era and with pressure to supply the increasing number of *poleis*, some villages expanded over time to become near towns with estimated populations of up to 2,000.[59] A typical village featured dwelling clusters around courtyards, with the pathways between no more than two-three meters wide. They were unpaved and had no channels (for the heady brew of human and animal excrement, tossed-away body parts from repasts, water from rain, and whatever else one cared to drop). Common structures tended to be

---

(London: Continuum, 2004); Henri Lefebvre, *Éléments de rythmanalyse* (Paris: Éditions Syllepse, 1992); Scott Branting, "Agents in Motion," in *Agency and Identity in the Ancient Near East: New Paths Forward*, eds. Sharon R. Steadman and Jennifer C. Ross, 47–59 (London: Equinox, 2010).

58. By contrast, Sepphoris was no more than 60 hectares. For a useful surveys of village sizes, see Killebrew, "Village and Countryside," 196–98; David Fiensy, "The Galilean Village in the Late Second Temple and Mishnaic Periods," in *Galilee in the Late Second Temple and Mishnaic Period, Volume 1: Life, Culture, and Society*, eds. David Fiensy and James Strange, 177–207 (Minneapolis: Fortress, 2014).

59. Douglas Knight, *Law, Power, and Justice in Ancient Israel*, Library of Ancient Israel (Louisville: Westminster John Knox, 2011), 122–23. Population estimates are notoriously difficult and speculative. The two methods used are speculative: a "density coefficient" working with the static average of five persons for a "house," or "carrying capacity" estimates based on required calorie intake (roughly 2000 per day) in relation to product area and density (neglecting in the process optimal rather than maximal use). For a recent studies concerning the complexities of issues surrounding ancient demography, see Walter Scheidel, ed. *Debating Roman Demography* (Leiden: Brill, 2001); Scheidel, "Demography." It is worthwhile to recall Amartya Sen's observation: "The mesmerizing simplicity of focusing on the ratio of food to population has persistently played an obscuring role over centuries." Amartya Sen, *Poverty and Famines: An Essay on Entitlement and Deprivation* (Oxford: Clarendon, 1981), 8. See further, see David Goodblatt, "Population Structure and Jewish Identity," in *The Oxford Handbook of Jewish Daily Life in Roman Palestine*, ed. Catherine Hezser, 102–21 (Oxford: Oxford University Press, 2010), 105–6; Elio Lo Cascio, "The Size of the Roman Population: Beloch and the Meaning of the Augustan Census Figures," *The Journal of Roman Studies* 84 (1994): 23–40. The assumed daily calorie requirement of 2000 is based on a rough estimate made some decades ago. Harris, *Rome's Imperial Economy*, 41. See also Von Reden, "Classical Greece: Consumption," 388–90, 403.

rare, although villages that grew in size in the later Roman and Byzantine periods could boast one or two such structures.[60]

As for households within such villages, people usually lived in simple and unadorned dwellings with common courtyards that were less static structures for nuclear families[61] than flexible clusters or compounds with common space for human and other animals. So we find in Syria-Palestine[62] that such a structure had a main room in which many overlapping tasks were performed—gathering with others and eating when the weather did not permit doing so outside, processing of food, making and repairing the items needed for daily life, sleeping, and so on. Often, this was the only room, but at times there may have been an additional small room for sleeping, perhaps in a loft. A key feature was the need for storage, for the foodstuffs produced locally and kept for the time in between harvests and for a potential bad season or unexpected event (human or otherwise). Anywhere would do, whether in the courtyard, corners, in underground holes (also used for hiding), or in space to the side of the common room. Over time, simple rooms could be added to the cluster—or *insulae*—around the courtyard, perhaps for another mating couple and their offspring or for some other relatives (or even non-relatives) who had suffered decimation from disease, disaster, war or state-sponsored terror, and in need for a workshop (baking, pottery, oil production, and so on). The most crucial feature of all was the courtyard, usually shared with other simple structures to make a common area.[63] With such a focus, external fenestration in the structures themselves was not necessary. In the courtyard the vast majority of the constantly changing activities took place: cooking, storage (water as well), washing, growing vines, keeping animals, talking, drinking, arguing, and farting (at times they had basic toilets too). Needless to say, it would have been a feast of noises, smells, tastes, and sights.

As mentioned above, the available evidence for such dwellings

60. Jonathan Reed, *Archaeology and the Galilean Jesus: A Re-Examination of the Evidence* (Harrisburg: Trinity Press International, 2000), 139–69; Killebrew, "Village and Countryside," 197–98.
61. Killebrew, "Village and Countryside," 197; David Fiensy, "The Galilean House in the Late Second Temple and Mishnaic Periods," in *Galilee in the Late Second Temple and Mishnaic Period, Volume 1: Life, Culture, and Society*, eds. David Fiensy and James Strange, 216–41 (Minneapolis: Fortress, 2014). Fiensy does note occasionally the common nature of clustered dwellings and shared courtyards.
62. Eric Meyers, "The Problems of Gendered Space in Syro-Palestinian Domestic Architecture: The Case of Roman-Period Galilee," in *Early Christian Families in Context: An Interdisciplinary Dialogue*, eds. David Balch and Carolyn Osiek, 44–70 (Grand Rapids: Eerdmans, 2003), 44–49; Katharina Galor, "Domestic Architecture," in *The Oxford Handbook of Jewish Daily Life in Roman Palestine*, ed. Catherine Hezser, 393–402 (Oxford: Oxford University Press, 2010), 431–35.
63. Meyers, "Problems of Gendered Space," 51–54; Galor, "Domestic Architecture," 430.

favors the durable rather than the flimsy, so the basic constructions of branches, straw, and mud do not survive, let alone the tents and periodic dwellings of people on the move.[64] Occasionally traces appear, such as the reclaimed places of the rich and even "public" buildings in towns and cities after they had been abandoned. Behind the facades of larger buildings, people created smaller and more familiar inter-connected dwellings by simple partition walls, in what may be called "subdivision."[65] These dwellings produced space through multiple rhythms—movements and flows of animate and inanimate items with constant reuse and reproduction of the same space.[66] Here the dynamic and transient nature of such existence points to the ease with which the poorest farmers would readily move away from the burdens of req-uisitions, *angareia*[67] and disease, and to the possibility of better food and conditions, if not to join bandit groups which had been a consistent feature of subsistence survival for millennia.[68]

In making this definition, we seek to answer some of the problems with household research in the Greco-Roman period. Time and again we find the assumption not only that the household was the smallest economic unit and thereby "foundation" of ancient societies,[69] but also

---

64. A.C. Bouquet, *Everyday Life in New Testament Times* (London: Batsford, 1953), 27; Garnsey, Saller, and Goodman, *Roman Empire*, 101. Richardson offers the most detailed typology of rural housing: cave, tent, beehive house, workshop house, farmhouse, villa, fortress-palace, apartment, and monastery. Peter Richardson, "Towards a Typology of Levantine/Palestinian Houses," *Journal for the Study of the New Testament* 27 (2004): 47–68.

65. This process appears again and again, but especially in the dramatic changes throughout the Roman Empire in the fifth and sixth centuries CE. See Simon Ellis, "The End of the Roman House," *American Journal of Archaeology* 92, no. 4 (1988): 465–76, 567–69; Simon Ellis, "Late Antique Hous-ing and the Uses of Residential Buildings: an Overview," in *Housing in Late Antiquity: From Palaces to Shops*, eds. Luke Lavan, Lale Özgenel, and Alexander Sarantis, 1–23 (Leiden: Brill, 2007), 12–13; Andrea Berlin and Sharon Herbert, "Kadesh of the Upper Galilee," in *Galilee in the Late Second Tem-ple and Mishnaic Periods. Volume 2: The Archaeological Record from Cities, Towns, and Villages*, eds. David Fiensy and James Strange, 424–42 (Minneapolis: Fortess, 2015), 233.

66. In the surviving archaeological record, this is revealed notably in the *insulae* or dwellings with common courtyards. This flexible production of space may give the impression of the absence "town planning," but this imposes modern, angular assumptions and misses the need for "rhyth-manalysis." See Lefebvre, *Rhythmanalysis.*

67. On *angareia*, see Matt 15.21; Matt 27.32, and note especially Matt 5:41. The requisitioning of a don-key and its colt also fits within this framework (Matt 21:2–7). Indeed, a villager who went to a *polis* for whatever reason was always at risk of being drafted into compulsory labor service, not least because it was assumed that he or she was there for that reason. Safrai, "Urbanization and Indus-try in Mishnaic Galilee."

68. Moxnes's comment—"But Jesus left his own household and dislocated his would-be followers from their households"—was not as uncommon as he seems to feel. Halvor Moxnes, *Putting Jesus in His Place: A Radical Vision of Household and Kingdom* (Louisville: Westminster John Knox, 2003), 2.

69. With unmistakable echoes of religious "family values" that suggest the same for the modern fam-ily. Many are content simply to reiterate the claim that the household is the "most common social component of subsistence, the smallest and most abundant activity group." Wilk and Rathje, "Household Archaeology," 618; Santiago Guijarro, "The Family in First-Century Galilee," in *Con-structing Early Christian Families: Family as Social Reality and Metaphor*, ed. Halvor Moxnes, 42–65 (Lon-

that a household constitutes a building for a family. Depending on the size, the fixed dwelling becomes one for a "nuclear" or (the catchall) "extended" family without considering the dynamics of interaction and flexibility. These assumptions are exacerbated by the simple connection made between dwelling and family size. So a smaller structure (preserved in stone) becomes one for a "nuclear" family, while larger structures such as the *insulae* house "extended" families.[70] Indeed, this inbuilt assumption infamously led Ian Morris to argue that since the external dimensions of fixed swellings appear to have increased during the first centuries CE, there must have been an increase in the standard of living.[71] These are by no means the only problems. The very use of the opposition of "extended" and "nuclear" obfuscates the range of possible arrangements of relations. For example, the possibilities include mating couples, blood relations, those beyond such relations, the dead, animals, recent additions to genealogies, if not—as wider anthropological studies reveal—situations where fathers and mothers do not cohabit, the absence of any sense of the biological paternity of children or the central role of slaves in mediating social relations (as we will see with the *poleis* in the next chapter).[72] A household was very much a "houseful" in ways that we find it difficult to imagine.[73]

A further problem with household researchers is the great static temptation—almost irresistible—due to the inertia of ancient archaeological remains. Given modern assumptions concerning the "privacy" that walls provide, many assume that the household was hemmed in

don: Routledge, 1997), 43; Saller, "Household and Gender," 87; James W. Hardin, "Understanding Houses, Households, and the Levantine Archaeological Record," in *Household Archaeology in Ancient Israel and Beyond*, eds. Assaf Yasur-Landau, Jennie R. Ebeling, and Laura B. Mazow, 9–25 (Leiden: Brill, 2011), 10.

70. Some have weighed heavily on the side of nuclear families, which means that the *insulae* were occupied by unrelated families. Shemuel Safrai, "Home and Family," in *The Jewish People in the First Century: Historical Geography, Political History, Social, Cultural and Religious Life and Institutions*, eds. Shemuel Safrai and Menaḥem Stern, vol. 2, 728–92 (Leiden: Brill, 1988), 748–64; Hezser, "Graeco-Roman Context," 38; Alexei Sivertsev, "The Household Economy," in *The Oxford Handbook of Jewish Daily Life in Roman Palestine*, ed. Catherine Hezser, 229–45 (Oxford: Oxford University Press, 2010), 234–35. For a valiant effort to account for the variety of kinship structures, distinguishing between large, multiple, nucleated, and scattered, see Guijarro, "Family in First-Century Galilee," 57–61.

71. Ian Morris, "Archaeology, Standards of Living, and Greek Economic History," in *The Ancient Economy: Evidence and Models*, eds. Joseph Gilbert Manning and Ian Morris, 91–126 (Stanford: Stanford University Press, 2005).

72. See further Bonnie J. Fox, ed. *Family Patterns, Gender Relations* (New York: Oxford University Press, 2008); Susan McKinnon, *Neo-Liberal Genetics: The Limits and Moral Tales of Evolutionary Psychology* (Chicago: Prickly Paradigm, 2005); Halvor Moxnes, "What Is Family? Problems in Constructing Early Christian Families," in *Constructing Early Christian Families: Family as Social Reality and Metaphor*, ed. Halvor Moxnes, 13–41 (London: Routledge, 1997).

73. Peter Laslett, "Introduction: The History of the Family," in *Household and Family in Past Time*, eds. Peter Laslett and Richard Wall, 1–89 (Cambridge: Cambridge University Press, 1972), 36.

by walls, floor, and roof. Our definition of household, with its stress on flexible rhythms of continuously reproduced space, seeks to counter these temptations.[74] Such spaces included not merely human and animal bodies amongst the structures, but also the rich, earthy smells and tastes and feels of rural life where bacteria flourished. In the end, our ability to imagine what really went on fails us on so many occasions. For instance, when faced with villages containing curving walls, meandering lanes, bent structures, and traceries of myriad pathways, researchers fall back on categories such as "haphazard" and "unplanned" to describe the situation.[75] While landforms may have played a role, we propose that the nature and connections between these structures suggests quite a distinct approach to spatial production: oblique angles, jutting corners, irregular patterns, walls with minds of their own, structures that seem integrated in a way that is almost impossible to conceptualize. They could certainly construct places with right angles and straight lines, as some of the *poleis* indicate, but these were lines of control and calculated domination. Perhaps the villages in question offered a more layered and overlapping perception of life and production of space.

Flexibility leads to the need to share. We mean not some vague altruistic motive, but rather one of collective necessity: the individual would simply not survive on his or her own.[76] We prefer to call this the allocative need of subsistence survival economics. In terms of kinship, we find a malleable continuity, predicated on the assumption that "we have always done so" assumed a rather limited sense of "always." Thus, genealogies themselves were constantly adapted for the sake of stability, especially in the context of ethnic fluidity, if not the effects of disease and internecine warfare. Further, seen from the perspective of the household, a clan would undergo contraction and expansion, depending on life cycles. Capabilities for labor and reproduction, dependent on numbers of children, adults, and (very occasionally) genuinely old people, affected the needs and sizes of households.

As for gender, the situation was somewhat different than in the *poleis*

74. In their own way, by stressing the blurring of "public" and "private," Strange and Meyers unwittingly reinforce this point. James Strange and Eric Meyers, *Excavations at Ancient Meiron, Upper Galilee, Israel 1971–72, 1974–75, 1977* (Cambridge: American Schools of Oriental Research, 1981), 37–38.

75. Safrai, *Economy of Roman Palestine*, 46; John Dominic Crossan and Jonathan Reed, *Excavating Jesus: Beneath the Stones, Behind the Texts* (San Francisco: HarperSanFrancisco, 2001), 81; Killebrew, "Village and Countryside," 198; Fiensy, "Galilean Village."

76. Implicit in Freyne's comment concerning the dominance of "a peasant style of life with people living together in close ties of kinship in relatively small and isolated settlements." Freyne, *Galilee from Alexander the Great to Hadrian*, 16.

and among ruling class households. Women were both part of hierarchical households and part of the distinct fluidity in labor. Thus, they were subject, socially and economically, to a paterfamilias, in either patrilocal or virilocal forms.[77] At the same time, the sheer range of tasks required in agriculture, along with short life expectancy, meant that female hands were required wherever possible.[78] Both sexes were by definition multi-skilled, partaking in the sharing of labor, equipment, and produce—not without the obligatory bickering and differences.[79] If a neighbor needed to repair a roof or dig a pit, most able hands would assist. If one required the traction animal to plow one's allocated furrows, then this would fit in with the needs of others. If women with young children needed to keep working the fields, then one or more of the village wet-nurses would breastfeed their newborn children. Both sexes baked bread, harvested olives, brewed beer, trod grapes, wove cloth, made pottery, cut wood, hunted, fished, and even engaged in regime-sponsored building projects in the *poleis*.[80] In short, men and women overlapped in many areas of the actual work needed for subsistence survival in the framework of the household. The dictates of survival ensured that the produce of soil and animals, if not from the many other tasks undertaken, were reallocated within the village. Those who seemed to be slightly better off were tolerated insofar as their "wealth" was seen to benefit the village as a whole.[81]

---

77. In one, women were subject to their fathers and males came to live in such a household; in the other, women went to live in the households of their mating partners. By the Greco-Roman period, the latter was predominant. See the initial outline of this terminology, in contrast to the misleading "matrilocal" and "patrilocal," in Mieke Bal, *Death and Dissymetry: The Politics of Coherence in the Book of Judges* (Chicago: University of Chicago Press, 1988).

78. "The lower down the social scale we look, the less women were differentiated from their menfolk." Kyrtatas, "Domination and Exploitation," 153.

79. Milton Moreland, "The Galilean Response to Earliest Christianity: A Cross-cultural Study of the Subsistence Ethic," in *Religion and Society in Roman Palestine: Old Questions, New Approaches*, ed. Douglas Edwards, 37–48 (New York: Routledge, 2004), 39–40; Halstead, *Two Oxen Ahead*, 308–11.

80. On the many and flexible tasks of women, see Miriam Peskowitz, *Spinning Fantasies: Rabbis, Gender and History* (Berkeley: University of California Press, 1997), 193n19. Elsewhere, Peskowitz traces how the rabbis and Romans tried to distinguish such rural flexibility in terms of formal gender distinctions. Miriam Peskowitz, "Gender, Difference, and Everyday Life: The Case of Weaving and Its Tools," in *Religion and Society in Roman Palestine: Old Questions, New Approaches*, ed. Douglas Edwards, 129–45 (New York: Routledge, 2004). Less helpful is Harris, "Workshop, Marketplace and Household."

81. Governance of village communities seems—although the evidence is tantalizingly vague—to have operated in terms of various forms of village assemblies (especially in Asia Minor and the Levant), councils of elders (*gerousia*), and headmen (*kōmarchos*). All of these persisted despite changing situations in the *poleis*, and could also be found in the local districts of larger towns and cities. On ancient evidence, see Ninel Jankowska, "Communal Self-Government and the King of the State of Arrapha," *Journal of the Economic and Social History of the Orient* 12(1969): 233–82, 274–76; Igor M. Diakonoff, "The Structure of Near Eastern Society before the Middle of the Second Millennium BC," *Oikumene* 3 (1982): 7–100; Michael Heltzer, *The Rural Community in Ancient Ugarit* (Wiesbaden:

To sum up, the household provided the social determination of agricultural activities. Social determination may be seen in terms of three factors: communality of assent, economizing, and enforcement.[82] Assent appears in terms of collective needs for survival and the role of kinship; economizing in light of the needs of combined labor for myriad tasks from plowing to harvesting; and protection from raiders, landlords, tax agents, and military requisitions.

Exploitation Within

Whereat he said firmly: "When your excellency writes a book, you will not say: 'Here there is a beautiful church and a great castle." The gentry can see that for themselves. But you shall say: "In this village there are no hens." Then they will know from the beginning what sort of country it is.[83]

Thus far we have emphasized the durability, diversity, and flexibility of subsistence survival, but this is only half of the story. The other side concerns exploitation—both within subsistence survival itself and in relation to other institutional forms.[84] Obviously we have a tension between the equalizing tendency of collective concerns, and the differentiation of exploitation. By internal exploitation we mean the processes within the institutional form itself, especially with the big peasants who exploited the middle and small peasants. External exploitation was the result of other institutional forms within the larger regimes and within a mode of production itself.[85] We also stress that exploitation is systemic in, if not constitutive of, periods of apparent calm, stability, and even peace ("*pax Romana*"), for such periods

Dr Ludwig Reichert, 1976), 75–83. On later evidence concerning the Hellenistic and Roman eras, see Ste. Croix, *Class Struggle*, 221–22.

82. Roberts, *Landscapes of Settlement*, 35–37.

83. Gertrude Bell, *The Desert and the Sown* (London: William Heinemann, 1907), 93.

84. While our previous analysis touches on similar points made by Horsley, we differ in that this institutional form was not mostly separated from others. Indeed, through the regimes it was inescapably cheek-by-jowl with them. Richard Horsley, *Galilee: History, Politics, People* (Philadelphia, Pennsylvania: Trinity Press International, 1995), 203–7.

85. Most analyses of exploitation in the Greco-Roman world concern external exploitation. Douglas Oakman, "Late Second Temple Galilee: Socioarchaeology and Dimensions of Exploitation in First-Century Palestine," in *Galilee in the Late Second Temple and Mishnaic Period, Volume 1: Life, Culture, and Society*, eds. David Fiensy and James Strange, 346–56 (Minneapolis: Fortress, 2014), 346. See further, Moreland, "The Galilean Response to Earliest Christianity." Contra Jensen, "Rural Galilee and Rapid Changes" and "Climate, Drought, Wars, and Famines in Galilee as a Background for Understanding the Historical Jesus," *Journal of Biblical Literature* 131, no. 2 (2012): 307–24. Unfortunately, Freyne's somewhat useful account is vitiated by a caricature of peasant life. Freyne, *Galilee from Alexander the Great to Hadrian*, 176–83, 194–98.

(which we call regimes) serve to ensure that the ruling and propertied classes increase their wealth and power. During distinctly disruptive times, exploitation comes starkly into the light of day, being both challenged by those exploited and reconstituted by those who benefit from exploitation.[86] In other words, the fault lines of systemic exploitation would from time to time bring about the seismic shifts seen with the change of regimes.

Since we deal with external exploitation in subsequent chapters—in terms of *polis-chōra*, tenure (and the colonate), and the slave-relation —we focus here on internal exploitation. This form of exploitation was often a feature of subsistence survival, particularly in village communities where certain individuals accrued some influence and power through hereditary claims, clan structures, or election as village headman. These factors were not necessarily exclusive, since election would also recognize the claims of clan heads and inheritance. Indeed, the clan structures themselves were usually quite hierarchical with what the Romans called the paterfamilias functioning as clan leader. Such a position overlapped with patterns of patronage, which could work with existing structures or cut across them when they limited the desire of a patron to gain more power. We also find a pattern in which the big peasants made greater use of external sources for the sake of relative wealth. At the same time, the claims of the big peasants were usually mitigated by the equalizing tendencies of subsistence survival, such as the regular process of reallocating field shares. Try as they might to control the process—preferably by allocating field shares themselves—they were also subject to the collective will of the village community, which would in normal circumstances debate fiercely the relative merits and demerits of a new arrangement. Village communities would tolerate a big man as long as he was seen to contribute to the good of the village rather than focus on his own aggrandizement.

Archaeological evidence indicates that among the surviving and ubiquitous one-room dwellings in villages and towns a few buildings were constructed by those somewhat wealthier.[87] In order to under-

---

86. Oakman calls this distinction "inarticulate felt-oppression" and "articulate perception." Oakman, "Late Second Temple Galilee," 348.

87. This is the case, for example, in the Galilean villages of Yodefat (Jotapata), Gamla, Khirbet Qana (Cana), or Capernaum. See Aviam, "People, Land, Economy, and Belief," 21–29; Aviam, "The Transformation from *Galil Ha-Goyim* to Jewish Galilee," 17; McCollough, "City and Village in Lower Galilee"; Sharon Lee Mattila, "Revisiting Jesus' Capernaum: A Village of Only Subsistence-Level Fishers and Farmers?," in *The Galilean Economy in the Time of Jesus*, eds. David Fiensy and Ralph Hawkins, 75–134 (Atlanta: Society of Biblical Literature, 2013). This evidence has led to a curious argument: wealth and power differentiation means that the (caricatured) "half-starved peasant"

stand this internal differentiation within subsistence survival, we turn to the influential article by Friedrich Engels, "The Peasant Question in France and Germany."[88] He distinguishes between three main types: (1) the most important category of the small-holding peasants, who till land no smaller than self-sufficiency requires but who are under immense pressure in regard to land and labor; (2) middle peasants, who teeter on the edge of being small peasants but aspire to more; and (3) big peasants, who exploit small and faltering middle peasants as farm servants and day laborers. Crucially, these categories are not hard and fast distinctions, for "all these forms of production and ownership are found mixed in various proportions"[89] with some areas having large estates that go beyond the threefold distinction and exploit all and sundry, while in other areas the land is so insufficient for self-sufficiency that the peasants here must creatively find all manner of ways to survive. The important points that arise from Engels's analysis are that the small peasant is the key, rather than middle and big peasants; that the purpose of the categories is to indicate significant differentiation in terms of productive capacity and wealth; and that peasants are flexible in creating strategies of survival in different and difficult circumstances.

To apply Engels's insights to the ancient world, we draw upon Ste. Croix careful definition of peasant differentiation:

1. Peasants (mainly cultivators) possess, whether or not they own, the means of agricultural production by which they subsist; they provide their own maintenance from their own productive efforts, and collectively they produce more than is necessary for their own subsistence and reproduction.

living at an undefined "subsistence" level is theoretically and historically untenable. Mattila, "Jesus and the 'Middle Peasants': Problematizing a Social-Scientific Concept"; Sharon Lee Mattila, "Inner Village Life in Galilee: A Diverse and Complex Phenomenon" in *Galilee in the Late Second Temple and Mishnaic Periods: Life, Culture, and Society*, eds. David Fiensy and James Strange, vol. 1, 312–45 (Minneapolis: Fortress, 2014); Aviam, "People, Land, Economy, and Belief" 29. For astute rebuttals, see Cadwallader, "Peasant Plucking in Mark"; Douglas Oakman, "Execrating? or Execrable Peasants!," in *The Galilean Economy in the Time of Jesus*, eds. David Fiensy and Ralph Hawkins, 135–64 (Atlanta: Society of Biblical Literature, 2013).

88. Engels, "Peasant Question in France and Germany." Apart from first-hand research, Engels also draws upon material from Ireland and Russia. His insights were immensely influential in the Soviet Union, where the Bolsheviks worked hard to win over the small and even middle peasants. As a result, the dissenting position of Chayanov, which idealised peasant cooperation against collectivization, influenced foreign and usually anti-communist anthropologists. Aleksandr Vasilievich Chayanov, *The Theory of Peasant Economy*, eds. Daniel Thorner, Basile Kerblay, and R. E. F. Smith (Homewood: Richard D. Irwin, 1966); Aleksandr Vasilievich Chayanov, *The Theory of Peasant Co-operatives*, trans. David Wedgwood Benn (Columbus: Ohio State University Press, 1991).

89. Engels, "Peasant Question in France and Germany," 485.

2. They are not slaves . . . and are therefore not legally the property of others; they may or may not be serfs or bondsmen.
3. Their occupation of land may be under widely differing conditions: they may be freeholders, lessees (at a rent in money, kind or shares, and combined or not with labor services), or tenants at will.
4. They work their holdings essentially as family units, primarily with family labor, but occasionally with restricted use of slaves or wage-labor.
5. They are normally associated in larger units than the family, usually in villages.
6. Those ancillary workers (such as artisans, building and transport workers, and even fishermen) who originate from and remain among the peasants may be considered as peasants themselves.
7. They support superimposed classed by which they are exploited to a greater or less degree, especially landlords, moneylenders, town-dwellers and the organs of the State to which they may belong, and in which they may or may not have political rights.[90]

As Cadwallader observes with this supple definition, the blunt rigor of binaries evaporates as Ste. Croix "allows for significant degrees of variability in how peasants operate and who may be included within the definition and how."[91] Let us exegete Ste. Croix's definition with an eye on the tension between internal equalization and exploitation. On the one hand, peasants control the means of production (land, flocks, and crops), work the land collectively, associate in clans and villages, and produce sufficient surplus for bad years. On the other hand, differentiation appears in the way they hold land: occupation without subjection to another (later called "freehold"), rent (in produce, money, or labor), or tenancy. Further, peasants may work as agricultural or urban laborers, artisans, builders, transport workers, textile producers, and fishermen, so much so that the distinctions we like to make

---

90. Ste. Croix, *Class Struggle*, 210–11. These distinctions are more useful than the somewhat simplistic account of Kyrtatas, "Modes and Relations of Production," 537.
91. Cadwallader, "Peasant Plucking in Mark." Or, as Oakman puts it, "Although the term peasant is a shorthand conceptual model for a great variety of rural cultivator situations, it points to a complex of many typical features." Oakman, "Execrating? or Execrable Peasants!," 154. For key works and useful surveys of the immense literature on peasants, see Eric Wolf, *Peasants* (Englwood Cliffs: Prentice-Hall, 1965); James Scott, *The Moral Economy of the Peasant: Rebellion and Subsistence in Southeast Asia* (New Haven: Yale University Press, 1976); Teodor Shanin, ed. *Peasants and Peasant Societies: Selected Readings* (Harmondsworth: Penguin, 1971); Oakman, "Execrating? or Execrable Peasants!," 139–45; Oakman, "Late Second Temple Galilee."

(in the Taylorization of capitalism) between different professions make little sense in the ancient world.[92] These various tasks were both the result of economic necessity (in a village community or outside it) and simply part of what being a peasant entailed. Often, big peasants would be the ones making use of day laborers and indeed slaves. This point has significant ramifications for the Gospels, where we find fishers (Mark 1:16–20), artisans (τέκτων Mk 6:3), and day laborers (Matt 20:1–16), among others.[93] Finally, the working agricultural population formed the second of the two exploited classes in the ancient world, the other being slaves. Peasants may also become tenured laborers. By now we have moved to the category of external exploitation, which appears with Ste. Croix's last point that peasants tended to support the ruling classes—whether landlords, moneylenders, town-dwellers, and state organs—although we will come to disagree with Ste. Croix on this matter.

Conclusion

To sum up, the economics of subsistence survival can be seen in terms of three crucial features: diversity, security, and optimal use.[94] Diversity appears in the range of crops and in terms of animal species from which all parts can be used across all ages (rather than selecting specific parts more characteristic of luxury consumption). Diversity also leads to security, for failure in one part of the herd or crop is not a disaster for the whole. Optimal usage—rather than maximal usage for the sake of landlords, *poleis*, or even profit—ensures longer-term survival: pasture, water, and soil were not used until exhaustion, but always under-utilized for future use.[95] Such an optimal approach also affected

92. This is the important point made by Paul Erdkamp, "Agriculture, Underemployment, and the Cost of Rural Labour in the Roman World," *Classical Quarterly* 49, no. 2 (1999): 556–72; Moreland, "The Galilean Response to Earliest Christianity," 40. Oakman misses the point when he suggests that Jesus is forced to leave his peasant context in order to become an artisan: Douglas Oakman, *Jesus and the Peasants* (Eugene: Cascade, 2008), 171.

93. See further, Jonathan Draper, "Recovering Oral Performance from Written Text in Q," in *Whoever Hears You, Hears Me: Prophets, Performance and Tradition in Q*, eds. Richard Horsley and Jonathan Draper, 175–94 (Harrisburg: Trinity Press International, 1999), 179.

94. For variations on these three themes, albeit with the same point, see Clifton Wharton, "Risk, Uncertainty, and the Subsistence Farmer: Technological Innovation and the Resistance to Change in the Context of Survival," in *Studies in Economic Anthropology*, ed. George Dalton, vol. 7, 152–80 (Washington: American Anthropological Association, 1971); Halstead and Jones, "Agrarian Ecology in the Greek Islands," 50–52; Thomas Gallant, *Risk and Survival in Ancient Greece. Reconstructing the Rural Domestic Economy* (Cambridge: Polity, 1991); Hordern and Purcell, *Corrupting Sea*, 175–230; Lewis Binford, *Constructing Frames of Reference: An Analytical Method for Archaeological Theory Building Using Hunter-Gatherer and Environmental Data Sets* (Berkeley: University of California Press, 2001), 193.

human and animal populations when there were not external pressures, for such populations were usually kept below carrying capacity. Each of these practices also ensured small surpluses for the bad year that may be a season away.[96] These tried techniques have proved remarkably resilient and widespread, with human beings reverting to them even today in "times of trouble." We have stressed that this institutional form was adaptable and constantly reconfigured in light of prevailing and often difficult circumstances.[97] In terms of such difficulties we focused on internally extractive patterns of exploitation, which were in tension with the flexibility and allocative patterns of subsistence survival economics. In the following chapters we analyze three further institutional forms, each of them extractive and each of which sought to exploit subsistence survival externally.

95. Lack of awareness of this feature of subsistence survival has led some into the curious byway of suggesting that peasant agriculture was seasonally and structurally inefficient. Erdkamp, "Agriculture, Underemployment, and the Cost of Rural Labour in the Roman World"; Kloppenborg, "Growth and Impact of Agricultural Tenancy," 51–52. Note the warning against such assumptions in Garnsey, Saller, and Goodman, *Roman Empire*, 103.
96. Richard Redding, "A General Explanation of Subsistence Change: From Hunting and Gathering to Food Production," *Journal of Anthropological Archaeology* 7 (1988): 56–97; Richard Redding, "Subsistence Security as a Selective Pressure Favoring Increasing Cultural Complexity," *Bulletin on Sumerian Agriculture* 7 (1993): 77–98; Paul Halstead, "The Economy has a Normal Surplus: Economic Stability and Social Change Among Early Farming Communities of Thessaly, Greece," in *Bad Year Economics: Cultural Responses to Risk and Uncertainty*, eds. Paul Halstead and Paul O'Shea, 68–80 (Cambridge: Cambridge University Press, 1989); Brian Hayden, "On Territoriality and Sedentism," *Current Anthropology* 41, no. 1 (2000): 109–12. Even if one includes the small urban population, only five percent of food stocks typically lasted into the following year. Peter Foldvari, Bas Van Leeuwen, and Reinhard Pirngruber, "Markets in Pre-Industrial Societies: Storage in Hellenistic Babylonia in the English Mirror," *CGEH Working Paper Series* (2011), http://www.cgeh.nl/working-paper-series/.
97. Deaths, births, bad seasons, shortages of stored food, soil yield—these and many other factors meant changing strategies to ensure sufficient crops and animal products in any one year. Halstead, "Traditional and Ancient Rural Economy in Mediterranean Europe," 86; Halstead and Jones, "Agrarian Ecology in the Greek Islands," 50–52; Halstead, *Two Oxen Ahead*, 31–33, 238–51.

3

Re-Producing Space:
Polis-Chōra and Tenure

The second and third institutional forms are *polis-chōra* and tenure. Both concern the production and reproduction of space, for space is not so much a given that is then rearranged, but is constructed and produced by the social and economic relations of the mode of production in question.[1] The specific shaping of the urban-rural relation in the Greco-Roman period took place in terms of the complex interactions between *polis* and *chōra*, the latter of which provided the material foundations of the former. Tenure, which designates the conditions under which land is used and the obligations of labor related to such usage, is also a reproduction of space, so much so that it developed into what

---

1. In many respects, Ste. Croix anticipated a later Marxist-inspired approach to spatial analysis, inspired by Henri Lefebvre, *The Production of Space*, trans. David Nicholson-Smith (Oxford: Oxford University Press, 1991) first published in French in 1974. For developments of Lefebvre's work for English-speaking audiences, see David Harvey, *The Limits to Capital*, 2nd ed. (London: Verso, 1999), 373–445; Edward Soja, *Thirdspace: Journeys to Los Angeles and Other Real-and-Imagined Places* (Oxford: Basil Blackwell, 1996); Kim Knott, *The Location of Religion: A Spatial Analysis* (London: Equinox, 2005); Jon Berquist and Claudia Camp, eds. *Constructions of Space I: Theory, Geography, and Narrative* (London: T&T Clark, 2008); Jon Berquist and Claudia Camp, eds. *Constructions of Space II: The Biblical City and Other Imagined Spaces* (London: T&T Clark, 2009). This approach to the production of space is more dynamic than, but may also be seen as a way of sharpening, approaches such as gravity-based interaction, central-place theory, and rank-size distribution analysis. See Wade Kotter, "Settlement Patterns," in *The Oxford Encyclopaedia of Archaeology in the Near East*, ed. Eric Meyers, vol. 5, 6–10 (Oxford: Oxford University Press, 1997).

has been called the colonate. In this case, all of the rural working population was by the third century CE tied to a specific piece of land (*origo*) with significant restriction of movement. Both institutional forms constitute types of external exploitation of the working rural population (in contrast to the internal exploitation we analyzed at the close of the previous chapter). Before proceeding, we need to reiterate that our resolute focus is on the wider economic patterns of the Greco-Roman era with awareness of regional variations that include Syria-Palestine.

Chōra Versus *Polis*

If you seriously desire me to come to you, there are two hundred and four cities and villages (*poleis kai kōmai*) in Galilee.[2]

Too often are the material relations of production constituted by the *chōra* overlooked, not only in most surviving classical literature,[3] but also in many reconstructions of ancient economics. One notable exception is Ste. Croix's work, which relentlessly emphasizes the central role of the *chōra* in ancient economics.[4] Indeed, the reason we began the analysis of institutional forms with a treatment of subsistence survival is due to Ste. Croix's influence on our study, for that chapter is really a careful explication of the reality of economic life in the *chōra*. So we now examine the production of space involved in the complex relations of *polis* and *chōra*, before turning to the question of tenure.

Towards the Colonial *Polis*

The splendour and confidence of the early Hellenistic *polis* and the later Roman Republic, which dazzled so many in subsequent epochs, represented a meridian of urban polity and culture that was never to be equalled for another millennium.[5]

Here we develop the distinction between *chōra* and *polis* (*civitas*), draw-

2. Flavius Josephus, *Vita. Contra Apion*, trans. H. St. J. Thackeray, Loeb Classical Library (London: William Heinemann, 1999), 235.
3. As Ellen Meiksins Wood points out, albeit with a different agenda, "discussions of agriculture in general are surprisingly sparse in Greek literature." Ellen Meiksins Wood, *Peasant-Citizen and Slave: The Foundations of Athenian Democracy* (London: Verso, 1997), 47.
4. Both of us have previously engaged with Ste. Croix's work on *chōra* and *polis*, so we draw on that work here. Christina Petterson, *Acts of Empire: The Acts of the Apostles and Imperial Ideology* (Taipei: Chung Yuan Christian University Press, 2012); Roland Boer, *Criticism of Theology: On Marxism and Theology III* (Leiden: Brill, 2010).
5. Anderson, *Passages from Antiquity to Feudalism*, 19.

ing initially on Ste. Croix's insights.[6] While *chōra* clearly refers to the countryside with its *kōmai*, and *polis* designates a "city" (albeit much smaller than we would assume to be a city, for many had less than 10,000 inhabitants[7]), we would like to identify a crucial shift in the production of such a spatial opposition. In its initial Greek formation, the *chōra* involved the fields surrounding a *polis*, crucial to supplying the *polis* with its food, fibers, and usable tools. The relation was to provide the *polis* with its needs through a symbiotic connection—a combination of demand and symbiosis would remain in various ways throughout the history of *polia* and *chōra*. The terminology often used is one of "city-states" such as Athens and Corinth, in which the *chōra-polis* was a distinct unit. Citizens of the *polis* included those in the *chōra*, and many of the residents in the *polis* would make their way daily into the fields to farm. So important was the *chōra* for the viability of a *polis* that Greek colonies (most notably those of the Athenians) would only establish a new *polis* if it was surrounded by adequate arable land—*chōra*.

However, this earlier form of colonialism set in train a series of developments that eventually led to a somewhat different production of space, which was crucial for the structure of what we will call the colonial regime.[8] The conquests of Alexander the "Great" and feverish planting of *poleis* saw the most significant shift in the form of the *polis*, for now it became an instrument of empire and colonization throughout the conquered areas.[9] The potentates who squabbled over his legacy carried on his policy and established even more *poleis* or converted former cities into ones that resembled Greek forms. They began to administer the *chōra* through the royal bureaucracy (*chōra basilikē*), with substantial military presence to ensure such control.[10] By the time of the Romans, who both inherited much from the Greeks and introduced their own innovations in which the *polis* was even more subject

6. In doing so, we follow the Marxist insight that in the midst of apparent cultural, political, and social variation one may discern a basic opposition of exploitation in economic terms.
7. Even a *polis* like Pompey had only 8–10,000 inhabitants, while Tiberias and Sepphoris had at most 7,500–8,000 in the first century CE. Hans Eschebach, "Erlauterungen zum Plan von Pompeji," in *Neue Forschungen in Pompeji und den anderen vom Vesuvausbruch 79 n. Chr. vershutteten Stadten*, eds. Bernard Andreae and Helmit Kyrieleis, 331–38 (Recklinghausen: Verlag Aurel Bongers Recklinghausen, 1975); Jensen, *Herod Antipas in Galilee*, 26; Richard Horsley, *Covenant Economics: A Vision of Biblical Justice for All* (Louisville: Westminster John Knox, 2009), 87; Mattila, "Revisiting Jesus' Capernaum" 85. Rome was, of course, the glaring exception.
8. Indeed, the *poleis* in question underwent constant changes, with the founding of new ones, the dissolution of old ones, destruction, rebuilding, and—our focus—socio-economic shifts in the relationship between *polis* and *chōra*. See Hordern and Purcell, *Corrupting Sea*, 94.
9. Séan Freyne, "Cities of the Hellenistic and Roman Periods," in *The Oxford Encyclopaedia of Archaeology in the Near East*, ed. Eric Meyers, vol. 2, 29–35 (Oxford: Oxford University Press, 1997), 30.
10. Freyne, *Galilee from Alexander the Great to Hadrian*, 106–7.

to the dictates of Rome, the *chōra* came to designate all of the colonized territories under control of the *polis*.

Let us pause for a moment to consider the theoretical issues connected with this shift. The first concerns the continuing debate over symbiosis and antagonism: were *polis* and *chōra* integrated and symbiotic realities, or were they perpetually in socio-economic conflict?[11] One may describe these two approaches as functionalist and conflictual, although as Oakman points out that a functionalist approach is usually preferred by those interested in maintaining the status quo (usually those who benefit from the system), while a conflictual approach has more traction with those who have little to gain from the current system.[12] We do not take sides in this opposition, preferring a more dialectical reading: it was precisely through the symbiosis and integration of *polis* and *chōra* that economic exploitation was enabled and made even more efficient. Regimes of exploitation prefer relative stability and smooth operation, for this ensures that economic exploitation continues without disruption. The trick of such a system is to ensure that those exploited may even gain in some small way from the system ("trickle-down" economics), or at least believe that they gain from it, while their losses are in reality even greater. This pattern remained even with the changes in the *polis-chōra* relation we noted above. It is also revealed in the perceptions among the Greeks and Romans themselves: while they tended to see the world in binaries,[13] they also realized the interdependence of the two. For this reason we find that the distinction is not hard and fast, and that the terminology of what might count as a *polis* varied.[14] In one respect, however,

11. On the symbiotic and harmonious side, see Edwards, "Socio-Economic and Cultural Ethos"; Strange, "First Century Galilee"; Edwards, "Identity and Social Location in Roman Galilean Villages"; Jensen, "Rural Galilee and Rapid Changes," 59–61. On the conflictual side, see Séan Freyne, "Urban-Rural Relations in First-Century Galilee: Some Suggestions from the Literary Sources," in *The Galilee in Late Antiquity*, ed. Lee Levine, 75–91 (New York: Jewish Theological Seminary of America, 1992); Séan Freyne, "Jesus and the Urban Culture of Galilee," in *Texts and Contexts: Biblical Texts in Their Textual and Situational Contexts. Essays in Honor of Lars Hartman*, eds. Tord Fornberg and David Hellholm, 597–622 (Oslo: Scandinavian University Press, 1995); Séan Freyne, *Galilee and Gospel: Collected Essays* (Leiden: Brill, 2002), 59–72; Reed, *Archaeology and the Galilean Jesus*, 98; Richard Horsley, "Social Movements in Galilee," in *Galilee in the Late Second Temple and Mishnaic Period, Volume 1: Life, Culture, and Society*, eds. David Fiensy and James Strange, 167–74 (Minneapolis: Fortress, 2014).

12. Douglas Oakman, "The Countryside in Luke-Acts," in *The Social World of Luke-Acts: Models for Interpretation*, ed. Jerome Neyrey, 151–80 (Peabody: Hendrickson, 1991), 153–54. Oakman opts for a conflictual approach, which is more characteristic of some Marxist approaches.

13. As Cohen observes in relation to a somewhat different context (the relation between *pernanai* and *hetairein*), classical Greek economic "institutions accordingly tend to derive their meaning from their binomial interrelationships with their putative opposites." Cohen, "Free and Unfree Sexual Work," 96.

14. Josephus and Luke-Acts are often used as examples here, for they call the same place—Yodefat in Jospehus is a good example—both *polis* and *kōmē*. Further, Bethlehem is a *polis* in Luke 2:4 but a

the perception of the *chōra* did change from the classical Greek situation to the colonial: in their home territories, the aristocratic Greeks and indeed Romans maintained a fondness for the authenticity of a rural life,[15] while at the same time deriding those who actually lived and worked in the *chōra*. The reality was that they viewed one's rural roots in terms of managing farms and estates, and perhaps spending an afternoon picking a few grapes.[16] This may have been fine in Greece and Italy, but this valorization of simple rural values did not transfer so well to the colonial areas.

In this colonial situation, the *chōra* meant not the fields and villages in the vicinity of the *polis*, but all the colonized territory outside the *polis*, with peasant farming, village communities, as well as wilder areas at the limits of human presence.[17] In the eastern parts of the Empire, the *polis* meant a Hellenistic city, which could be either an existing *polis* that had become "Hellenized" or one that had been newly established, as happened often under the conquering Greeks and then Romans.[18] The largely Greek-speaking members of the *polis* saw themselves as a civilizing—literally "citifying"—force bringing sophisticated culture to the barbarians.[19] "Hellenization" betokened types of art[20] and the architectural appurtenances deemed necessary for a cultured life, such

kōmē in John 7:24; so also with Bethsaida in Luke 9:10 and Mark 8:23. See further, Ste. Croix, *Class Struggle*, 9; Fergus Millar, *The Roman Near East: 31 BC–AD 337* (Cambridge: Harvard University Press 1993), 18; Rami Arav and Carl Savage, "Bethsaida," in *Galilee in the Late Second Temple and Mishnaic Periods. Volume 2: The Archaeological Record from Cities, Towns, and Villages*, eds. David Fiensy and James Strange, 258–79 (Minneapolis: Fortess, 2015).

15. Hesiod, "Works and Days," in *Theogony, Works and Days, Testimonia, Loeb Classical Library*, 86–153 (Cambridge: Harvard University Press, 2006), lines 225–47; Horace, "Epodes," in *Odes and Epodes, Loeb Classical Library*, 270–320 (Cambridge: Harvard University Press, 2004), 11.

16. Bodel, "Slave Labour and Roman Society," 315.

17. The later rabbinic material distinguishes—to take the more common terms—between *kerakh* (large and walled urban settlement), *'ir* (town), and *kfr* (village). This leads Safrai to suggest that, in Galilee, one may also identify "local cities" in distinction from "Roman cities," while Killebrew goes even further and distinguishes three types of rural settlements apart from cities: village-towns of more than 5 hectares; small villages of 2-2.5 hectares; and farmhouses. Safrai, "Urbanization and Industry in Mishnaic Galilee," 195; Killebrew, "Village and Countryside." The risk here is to retrofit terms from the Byzantine era. See Yizhar Hirschfeld, "Farms and Villages in Byzantine Palestine," *Dumbarton Oaks Papers* 51 (1997): 33–71.

18. For a detailed survey that covers the periods of the Ptolemies, Seleucids, Hasmoneans, and Romans in Syria-Palestine, see Freyne, *Galilee from Alexander the Great to Hadrian*, 101–38; Jürgen Zangenberg and Dianne Van der Zande, "Urbanization," in *The Oxford Handbook of Jewish Daily Life in Roman Palestine*, ed. Catherine Hezser, 165-88 (Oxford: Oxford University Press, 2010).

19. The Romans devoted considerable energy to pacifying the local ruling class by means of citifying them—in terms of education, language, dress, and the temptations of lounge, bath, and well-appointed dinner table. As Tacitus drily notes, "The simple natives gave the name of 'culture' to this factor of their slavery." P. Cornelius Tacitus, *Dialogus, Agricola, Germania*, trans. William Peterson and Maurice Hutton (London: William Heinemann, 1914), *Agr.* 21.

20. Such as the famous Dionysius Mosaic from Sepphoris. Eric Meyers, E. Netzer, and Carol Meyers, "Artistry in Stone: The Mosaics of Ancient Sepphoris," *Biblical Archaeologist* 50 (1987): 223-31.

as council assembly halls, temples, market places, *cardi*, amphitheaters, gymnasia, hippodromes, stadia, bathhouses,[21] aqueducts, fountains of (relatively) fresh water, and the ever-present liturgies.[22] Culturally and linguistically, it meant that the language of governance, law courts, and intellectual matters was Greek (in the eastern Mediterranean).[23] From the purview of the *polis*, its inhabitants saw themselves as islands of "culture" in a sea of barbarians.

By contrast, in the *chōra*, the language spoken was anything but Greek (in Palestine, Aramaic), the architecture evinced older practices of the complex layers and intersections of daily life rather than the clear lines of a *polis*.[24] However, the preceding characterization risks perpetuating a form of culturism: the terminology of "Hellenization" and the presentation of the differences between *polis* and *chōra* suggests that culture was primary, manifested in language, architecture, layout, and even religion.[25] We cannot stress enough that such "Hell-

21. For an insightful study of the dynamics and importance of bathhouses, see Yaron Eliav, "Bathhouses as Places of Social and Cultural Interaction," in *The Oxford Handbook of Jewish Daily Life in Roman Palestine*, ed. Catherine Hezser, 605–22 (Oxford: Oxford University Press, 2010).

22. Maud Gleason, "Greek Cities Under Roman Rule," in *A Companion to the Roman Empire*, ed. David Potter, 228–49 (London: Blackwell, 2006).

23. See especially Richard Horsley, "The Language(s) of the Kingdom: From Aramaic to Greek, Galilee to Syria, Oral to Oral-Written," in *A Wandering Galilean: Essays in Honour of Seán Freyne*, eds. Zuleika Rodgers, Margaret Daly-Denton, and Anne Fitzpatrick McKinley, 401–26 (Leiden: Brill, 2009).

24. Already in 1896, Weber noted (*Agrarian Sociology*, 228–29) that the *chōra*, or *ethne* as he called it, was largely not Hellenized. In this light do we read Chancey's sustained challenge to a slightly earlier "pan-Hellenistic" hypothesis, to the point where Jesus styled himself on Cynic philosophy. Chancey's concern is Galilee where he suggests that even with all the interaction the countryside especially remained Aramaic speaking and Jewish. The situation could be replicated across the Roman Empire. Mark Chancey, *Greco-Roman Culture and the Galilee of Jesus*, SNTS Monograph Series 134 (Cambridge: Cambridge University Press, 2005).

25. Freyne and Chancey explicitly define "Hellenism" in cultural terms, while Chancey sees "Hellenization" as the intersections between Greek and local cultures. Freyne, "Urban-Rural Relations in First-Century Galilee"; Chancey, *Greco-Roman Culture and the Galilee of Jesus*, 18. An upshot of this cultural focus is to dwell on religious and ethnic questions, which obscure the economic dimension. As a sample, see Eric Meyers and Mark Chancey, "How Jewish was Sepphoris in Jesus' Time?," *Biblical Archaeology Review* 26, no. 4 (2000): 18033; Mark Chancey, *The Myth of a Gentile Galilee: The Population of Galilee and New Testament Studies*, SNTS Monograph Series 118 (Cambridge: Cambridge University Press, 2002); Mark Chancey, "Archaeology, Ethnicity, and First-Century CE Galilee: The Limits of Evidence," in *A Wandering Galilean: Essays in Honour of Seán Freyne*, eds. Zuleika Rodgers, Margaret Daly-Denton, and Anne Fitzpatrick McKinley, 205–14 (Leiden: Brill, 2009); Mark Chancey, "The Ethnicities of Galileans," in *Galilee in the Late Second Temple and Mishnaic Period, Volume 1: Life, Culture, and Society*, eds. David Fiensy and James Strange, 112–28 (Minneapolis: Fortress, 2014); Andrea Berlin, "Household Judaism," in *Galilee in the Late Second Temple and Mishnaic Period, Volume 1: Life, Culture, and Society*, eds. David Fiensy and James Strange, 208–15 (Minneapolis: Fortress, 2014); Idan Shaked and Dina Avshalom-Gorni, "Jewish Settlement in the Southeastern Hula Valley in the First Century CE," in *Religion and Society in Roman Palestine: Old Questions, New Approaches*, ed. Douglas Edwards, 28–36 (New York: Routledge, 2004); Aviam, "The Transformation from *Galil Ha-Goyim* to Jewish Galilee." For a timely warning on the limitations in using ethnic categories, see Nicola Denzey, "The Limits of Ethnic Categories," in *Handbook of Early Christianity: Social Science Approaches*, eds. Anthony Blasi, Jean Duhaime, and Paul-André Turcotte, 489–507 (Walnut Creek: Altamira, 2002).

enization" was primarily an economic reality: it entailed colonization[26] of conquered lands from which the significant needs of the *polis* were expropriated through state-sponsored strong-arm tactics and terror.[27] As Ste. Croix points out, we "should not exaggerate the strictly ethnic and linguistic factors . . . at the expense of economic and social ones" in distinguishing between the ruling classes of the *polis* and the exploited rural working population of the *chōra*.[28] Or as Perry Anderson observes, the "frieze of city civilisation always had something of the effect of a *trompe l'oeil façade*," for "behind this urban culture and polity lay no urban economy in any way commensurate with it: on the contrary, the material wealth which sustained its intellectual and civic vitality was drawn overwhelmingly from the countryside," which furnished the wealth of the *polis*.[29] Above all, the *polis* sought to extract what it could from the *chōra*, usually well beyond the thin surplus that was stored in the latter for the sake a bad harvest or disease among the herds. The beloved *polis* could not exist without the economic realities of rural exploitation.

From *Chōra* to *Polis*

At this point, we must introduce a further distinction: for the Romans, the *polis-chōra* relation operated on at least two levels. At the local level, the *poleis* had varying levels of autonomy (*municipium* and, especially in the east, *colonia*), providing simultaneously the administrative and economic mechanisms of empire.[30] At another level, the Roman Empire itself may be seen in terms of *polis* and *chōra*, with Rome—the "parasite city"[31]—being the *polis* par excellence and the rest of the empire its colonized *chōra*. The underlying reality was the same: the *polis* was primarily an extractive economic and centripetal economic force. Unable to supply its own needs, it simply had to be supplied to

---

26. It is not for nothing that most Roman cities in the east were called *colonia*, with constitutions modelled on Rome.
27. For a salient reminder of the brutal and systematic terror employed by the Romans in conquest and domination, see Richard Horsley, *Jesus and the Politics of Roman Palestine* (Columbia: University of South Carolina Press, 2014), 56–63. We propose that even the Hasmonean flash of independence, as also the possibility for regional variation in this corner of the Roman Empire, could take place only in the context of continuing colonization and thereby Hellenization. The very mechanisms of revolt, control, governance, and economic management are conceivable only within a colonizing framework.
28. Ste. Croix, *Class Struggle*, 16.
29. Anderson, *Passages from Antiquity to Feudalism*, 19.
30. Garnsey, Saller, and Goodman, *Roman Empire*, 40–46.
31. Ibid., 22, see also 109–14; Freyne, "Cities of the Hellenistic and Roman Periods," 33.

exist by whatever means were available: slavery, indenture, estates, or simple plunder. Or rather, to draw on Sen's distinction, Rome and indeed the other *poleis* in its empire felt entitled to what they demanded.[32]

Let us give a specific example of each of these two levels—the local and the imperial. We assume for the sake of argument that the average per capita consumption per annum in a *polis* was as follows: 200 kilograms of grain, 250 liters of wine, and 20 liters of olive oil. The first example concerns Sepphoris in Galilee, the population of which may be estimated at about 8,000.[33] Even a small population like this would require annually no less than 1,600,000 kilograms of grain, 2,000,000 liters of wine, and 160,000 liters of oil. Clearly, these amounts went beyond a simple rural "surplus." How many animal loads would this entail? Evidence from Egyptian papyri indicates that a donkey could carry 90 kilograms (3 artabae). This means that Sepphoris required on a daily basis just under 115 donkey loads (48.7 of grain, 60.9 of wine, and 4.9 of oil), or 41,975 per year.[34] The division of tasks adds to the imbalance: while the securing of goods was directed by overseers in the *polis*, the provision of animals and actual time and effort for transporting materials fell to the rural working population. Given the friction of distance, let alone the simple pathways (rather than Roman roads, which were constructed only towards the end of the first century CE), the

---

32. Sen, *Poverty and Famines*.

33. Choi, "Never the Two Shall Meet?" 304. For further recent archaeological material on Sepphoris, see especially Eric Meyers, "Roman Sepphoris in Light of New Archaeological Evidence and Research," in *The Galilee in Late Antiquity*, ed. Lee Levine, 321-38 (New York: Jewish Theological Seminary of America, 1992); Eric Meyers and Mark Chancey, *Alexander to Constantine*, vol. 3, Archaeology of the Land of the Bible (New Haven: Yale University Press, 2012), 141-45, 260-84; Eric Meyers, Carol Meyers, and Benjamin Gordon, "Residential Area of the Western Summit," in *Galilee in the Late Second Temple and Mishnaic Periods. Volume 2: The Archaeological Record from Cities, Towns, and Villages*, eds. David Fiensy and James Strange, 39-52 (Minneapolis: Fortess, 2015); Carol Meyers and Eric Meyers, "Sepphoris," in *The Oxford Encyclopaedia of Archaeology in the Near East*, ed. Eric Meyers, vol. 4, 527-36 (Oxford: Oxford University Press, 1997); Jensen, *Herod Antipas in Galilee*, 151-62; James Strange, "The Jewel of the Galilee," in *Galilee in the Late Second Temple and Mishnaic Periods. Volume 2: The Archaeological Record from Cities, Towns, and Villages*. David Fiensy and James Strange, 22-38 (Minneapolis: Fortess, 2015); Strange, "The Sepphoris Aqueducts"; Zeev Weiss, "From Galilean Town to Roman City, 100 BCE–200 CE," in *Galilee in the Late Second Temple and Mishnaic Periods. Volume 2: The Archaeological Record from Cities, Towns, and Villages*, eds. David Fiensy and James Strange, 53-75 (Minneapolis: Fortess, 2015). For the most recent material on Tiberias, see Katia Cytryn-Silverman, "Tiberias, from Its Foundation to the End of the Early Islamic Period," in *Galilee in the Late Second Temple and Mishnaic Periods. Volume 2: The Archaeological Record from Cities, Towns, and Villages*, eds. David Fiensy and James Strange, 186-210 (Minneapolis: Fortess, 2015). See also the thorough survey in Jensen, *Herod Antipas in Galilee*, 138-47. Freyne speaks of Sepphoris and Tiberias as "parasitical," thereby replicating Rome at a local level. Séan Freyne, *Jesus, a Jewish Galilean: A New Reading of the Jesus Story* (London: T&T Clark, 2004), 134.

34. It is not for nothing that Oakman ("Late Second Temple Galilee") writes of the solid prosperity of Sepphoris and Tiberias.

time and effort expended in such tasks meant that these sequestered goods were transported over relatively short distances. Further, on any visit to the *polis*, whether leading a few donkeys or for another unwelcome reason, the peasants in question were always under threat of the *angareia* or forced labor. They could very well be mistaken for such laborers when in the *polis* or simply dragooned into the latest building project.[35] This is but one example of a relatively small *polis*, which must be multiplied many times across the colonized spaces of Roman control. In the small corner of the empire around Sepphoris (later renamed Diocaesarea) with its minimal distances, we also find the new or re-founded *poleis*: Tiberias, Caesarea Philippi, Caesarea Maritima, Julias, and Sebaste (obviously named after Roman emperors or family members), as well as Ptolemais (Acco), Philoteria (Beth Yerach), Phasaelis, Archelais, Magdala (Tarichae), and of course the Dekapolis—a situation that can be seen again and again across the empire.[36]

The second example concerns the supply of grain, especially the preferred wheat, to Rome.[37] If we assume that the population was up to one million, this would require (in line with the estimates above) 30 million *modii* (200,000 tonnes) of grain. Part of this amount was for the *frumentationes*, the "grain dole." Established by the law of C. Gracchus in 123 BCE, it was consistently expanded over the following centuries. By the time of Augustus (27 BCE to 14 CE), some 200,000 people in Rome were listed as recipients of five *modii* (3.3 kg) per person per month. This was enough to feed up to two people, which means that the grain handouts could feed up to 400,000 people. This gives us an amount of 12 million *modii* (80,000 kg) just for the *frumentationes*. The remaining population required an extra 18 million *modii* (120,000 kg). Obviously, these mountains of grain needed considerable processes of procure-

35. This was certainly a "dynamic" process, but not in the way usually imagined. Zangenberg and Van der Zande, "Urbanization," 178-80. At the same time, the *polis* offered the vague promise of "opportunity" for disrupted lives in the *chōra*, a promise that was rarely if ever realized. Displaced members of the *chōra* would occasionally drift to the *polis*, only to find that they would be relegated to the fringes, providing necessary services that had little benefit for themselves.

36. Apart from the eagerness to rename themselves after emperors or indeed local hitmen (governors) after 63 BCE, many *poleis* minted coinage with busts and inscriptions of aforesaid colonial masters, dating them from the time of Roman occupation. Notably, Tiberias changed its name to honor Claudius in the second century, and Sepphoris became a distinctly Greco-Roman *polis* (now called Dioceasaria) by the reign of Emperor Hadrian (117-38 CE). Mark Chancey, "City Coins and Roman Power in Palestine: From Pompey to the Great Revolt," in *Religion and Society in Roman Palestine: Old Questions, New Approaches*, ed. Douglas Edwards, 103-12 (New York: Routledge, 2004), 105-6; Weiss, "From Galilean Town to Roman City."

37. On details concerning Rome, see Peter Garnsey, "Grain for Rome," in *Trade in the Ancient Economy*, eds. Peter Garnsey, Keith Hopkins, and C.R. Whittaker, 118-30 (Berkeley: University of California Press, 1983); Paul Erdkamp, *The Grain Market in the Roman Empire: A Social, Political and Economic Study* (Cambridge: Cambridge University Press, 2005), 237-57.

ment. In the early stages of expansion, Etruria, Umbria, and Tuscany were requisitioned, but soon enough this was not sufficient, so Sicily, Sardinia, and North Africa became sources. With the conquest of the eastern Mediterranean by the late first century BCE, Egypt became a major bread basket. From Egypt alone, 20 million *modii* (133,000 kg) or more were sequestered per annum, which suggests that grain was piled up in Roman storage places in case of shortages. Everything within the power of Rome's governance was brought to bear on the issue of grain supply, although the approach was opportunistic rather than calculated on the basis of needs, available stocks, and storage facilities.[38] Grain officials played the key role, who in turn contracted merchants in the system of procurement and supply. This went so far as to provide special privileges (replacement of loss in storm, payment for cargo if lost, exemption from tax, and so on) for ships large enough to transport significant volumes of grain.[39] The distribution of grain and especially bread was also controlled by city functionaries, since those who were not recipients of the handouts had to pay for their bread. Prices, although subject to fluctuation due to shortages and attempted hoarding, were closely watched and controlled.

It would not be an exaggeration to say that the *polis* sucked its needs from the *chōra*. However, would it not be possible for the various agents, *negotiatores*, *navicularii*, and *publicani*, to cut a profit from the whole process, whether we are speaking of Rome or one of the far-flung and smaller *poleis*? Of course, and some did very well indeed. However, such gain was clearly a by-product of the needs of the *polis* (an issue we examine in the chapter on the slave-relation). To suggest that Rome or indeed a local *polis* instituted policies—at times misnamed "intervention in the market"—that would foster private merchants, with the result (as Adam Smith would have it) that their own greed or "self-interest" had an inherently social benefit, is to prioritize what was clearly secondary. Further, while the widely despised merchants and their hangers-on could on occasion make themselves very rich indeed, the effort to find entrepreneurial farmers in such a situation has as much chance of success finding that later invention, *homo oeco-*

---

38. Against assertions from the perspective of neoclassical economics that the grain supply was due to "private enterprise," albeit fostered by the city government. Harris, *Rome's Imperial Economy*, 182–63.

39. In the first century CE, special privileges were granted to ships of more than 10,000 *modii* (68 tonnes) if they shipped grain for six years. By the end of the second century CE, ships with 50,000 *modii* or more (340 tonnes of wheat) were granted privileges, as also an operator with five ships of 10,000 *modii* each. Gaius Suetonius, *De Vita Caesarum*, Loeb Classical Library (London: William Heinemann, 1914), Claud. 18.2. Scaevola *Digest* 50.5.3. Gaius, *Inst.* 1.32c.

nomicus. We have indicated in an earlier chapter why this suggestion is implausible, not least because of the nature of subsistence survival agriculture. The increase in the number of villages in precisely such areas in the first century CE thus becomes not so much a self-interested move on the part of peasants from areas that were less pestilential (and less productive), but was due to pressure from the *poleis* to produce the goods they required. The fact that peasants had not occupied such land earlier speaks volumes as to their awareness of the risks involved.[40] To these earlier observations we now add the reproduction of space entailed in the *polis-chōra* institutional form. This was inescapably a colonizing economic form in which the *poleis* marked the imposition of new and disruptive economic practices. For those in the *chōra*, the *poleis* were alien impositions by a foreign power and culture, sucking vital produce from the land. In short, the exploiting ruling classes in colonial spaces (including Judea and the backwater of Galilee) were largely of the *polis*, and they did their best to exploit and despise those upon whom their brittle "culture" depended.

By this point, it may seem as though we have embraced the idea of a "consumer city," first advocated by Karl Bücher, and then pursued by Werner Sombart, Max Weber, and Moses Finley.[41] Due to limited production capacities, *poleis* relied on the *chōra* for their very existence, if not the wealth of the congeries of land holders in such cities. So we stress once again that we do not opt for either side in the debate over symbiosis and exploitation, but prefer a dialectical analysis in which the relations between *poleis* and *chōra* was both symbiotic and exploitative, indeed that the depth of integration was a mechanism for ensuring the exploitation of the *chōra* for the needs of the *poleis*.

Polis Household

The primary and smallest parts of the household are master and slave, husband and wife, father and children.[42]

---

40. Josephus's observation that Galilee was fertile and intensively farmed should be seen in this light. Josephus, *Bellum Judaicum*, 3.41-44.

41. Finley, *Economy and Society in Ancient Greece*, 3-40. See the references to Bücher, Sombart, and Weber in Finley's study. See further C. R. Whittaker, "The Consumer City Revisited: The *Vicus* and the City," *Journal of Roman Archaeology* 3 (1990): 110-18; Paul Erdkamp, "Beyond the Limits of the 'Consumer City'. A Model of the Urban and Rural Economy in the Roman World," *Historia: Zeitschrift für Alte Geschichte* 50, no. 3 (2001): 332-56. Erdkamp suggests the idea goes back to Richard Cantillon in 1735.

42. Aristotle, *Politics*, 1253b2.6-8.

The *polis-chōra* was not necessarily determined by the boundary lines of the *polis* precinct, for we also find it, albeit recalibrated, within the limits of the *polis* itself. Let us examine this situation in terms of the household. In the peripheral parts of the *polis* lay the poorer households—of artisans, freedmen, smalltime merchants, day laborers, and those displaced from the *chōra* and seeking a few crumbs from the tables of rich. One-room structures may have been their abodes, with artisans both sleeping and working in the same room (at times called loosely a "shop"), or indeed the densely crowded apartment blocks with much common space (often called *insulae*), or simply "shanty" constructions that have not been preserved in the archaeological record.[43] Their purpose too was to provide goods for the unemployed ruling class, functioning in some ways as an element of the *chōra* internal to the *polis*. Often separated from the poorer zones by an internal wall were the larger structures of the rich and the ruling class.[44] Our interest in these households is due not merely to the wider social determination of economic life, but also because of the importance of the *polis* household for early Christianity and its spread. We focus on four features: architecture; the hierarchical nature of the *polis* household; the indispensable role of slaves; and sharp gender segregation.

The built structures of these *polis* households had multiple rooms and more ornate features. The most popular, from the second century BCE to the mid-sixth century CE,[45] was the Roman peristyle *domus*. An inner courtyard was festooned with columns (*peristylos*) and surrounded on four sides by wings of the dwelling and often with an upper storey. They were also introduced into Syria-Palestine, although at times the courtyards did not feature columns.[46] In a village context such an occasional dwelling was clearly the abode of what we have earlier called the "big peasant." In the *poleis* these dwellings were more common and preferred by the obscenely rich and powerful, and even

43. Simon Ellis, *Roman Housing* (London: Duckworth, 2000), 93, 97; Steve Roskams, "The Urban Poor: Finding the Marginalised " in *Social and Political Life in Late Antiquity*, eds. William Bowden, Adam Gutteridge, and Carlos Machado, 487–532 (Leiden: Brill, 2006).

44. In a study of Rome, Wallace-Hadrill pushes against such a position, suggesting that poor and rich mingled throughout the city in cellular neighborhoods. Andrew Wallace-Hadrill, "*Domus* and *Insulae* in Rome: Families and Housefuls," in *Early Christian Families in Context: An Interdisciplinary Dialogue*, eds. David Balch and Carolyn Osiek, 3–18 (Grand Rapids: Eerdmans, 2003).

45. Ellis, "The End of the Roman House."

46. Guijarro, "Family in First-Century Galilee," 52–53, 55; Meyers, "Problems of Gendered Space," 54–58.

those somewhat less so.[47] Indeed, a sign of one's socio-economic position was to be able to acquire or construct such a dwelling.

At the same time, like the village compounds, human beings milled in the ostentatious structures of the powerful within the *polis*. And like them, there was still no clear separation between the uses of different spaces in ways that we might assume. It is easy to list the various rooms of a peristyle house: entrance (*atrium*), courtyards, reception rooms (*tablina*) with one functioning as the location for feasts (*triclinium*), bedrooms (*cubicula*), shrine (*lararium*), kitchens, workshops, and perhaps latrines.[48] Yet their spatial function constantly shifted. For instance, the Romans sat and slept on couches so a *cubiculum* might function as a place in which to sit with family and guests, engage in discussion, drink, or indeed sleep. Toilets—if a place had them at all—hovered over a cesspit, while in public baths they were shared in common, and one sat side by side with fellow evacuators,[49] although any walk on the streets and alleys would reveal steaming piles of similar materials deposited in passing.[50] Slaves may have their own small and dark quarters at the back of a building, but more often they slept on the floor, whether in the kitchen, reception rooms, or indeed at the doors of the *cubicula*. Further, there was no separation between what we would call the domestic and work spaces.[51] Without an "office" in a separate place, landlords, merchants, bishops, and others had to carry on their activity within the household or meet in public spaces in the *polis* or, where necessary, in the *chōra*.[52] Thus, a ruling class household was simultaneously home and office where the exercise of that typical practice of the powerful and over-wealthy—patronage—could be practiced. The same structure may be a Governor's "palace" (*praetorium*), bishop's "residence" (*episkopeion*), or a landlord's abode, although the roles often overlapped.

Such a household was determined primarily by hierarchical rela-

---

47. Yizhar Hirschfeld, *The Palestinian Dwelling in the Roman-Byzantine Period* (Jerusalem: Franciscan Printing Press, 1995), 57–85. Galor's functionalist argument, in which size and placement of courtyards depended on space and topography, is unconvincing as a sole determinant. Galor, "Domestic Architecture," 429.
48. The houses of the local ruling class in Jerusalem differed little, especially in light of their fetish for Roman decoration. Jodi Magness, *Stone and Dung, Oil and Spit: Jewish Daily Life in the Time of Jesus* (Grand Rapids: Eerdmans, 2011), 10. Yet, we should not be fooled by the occasional toilet, since ancient cities were largely filthy, smelly, unhealthy, and given to endemic diseases.
49. As Martial put it: "You read to me as I stand, you read to me as I sit, You read to me as I run, you read to me as I shit" *Epigr.* 3.44.
50. Magness, *Stone and Dung, Oil and Spit*, 130–32.
51. Meyers, "Problems of Gendered Space," 59.
52. Ellis, "Late Antique Housing," 7–8.

tions of domination and subordination or patron-client relations. Kin had to find their place among the pervasive slaves, clients (sometimes former slaves), tenants, and occasional hired laborers—in what was clearly a "houseful."[53] Indeed, the very terminology of *oikos, oikia, domus,* and *familia* refer primarily to the large conglomerations of the ruling class.[54] These households centered on the *paterfamilias,* who exercised the *patria potestas,* an extraordinarily powerful role in legal theory[55] that extended to matters of life and death over an ever larger number of perpetual dinner guests and flunkies. All of them were *alieni juris,* "in another's right,"[56] although the reality of human engagements meant that the flows of power were mediated and redistributed in complex patterns. This structure appears again and again in New Testament texts, which assume a hierarchical household (Acts 10–11; 16:25–34; Eph 5:22–6:9; Col 3:18–4:1; 1 Pet 2:18–3:7), ruled almost always by a male (but see Acts 16:13–15), and with Paul acting as paterfamilias—the "broker of heavenly relations"—in his correspondence.[57] When conversions take place, the head "with all his household" feared God (Acts 10:2; 11:14; 16:33–34; 18:8).[58] It also becomes clear that the relations of patron and client, based on the ideology of honor and shame, was the preserve largely of the ruling class.[59] Much has been made of the honor-shame dynamic to the point of suggesting that

53. Wallace-Hadrill, "*Domus* and *Insulae* in Rome," 4. Cicero clearly indicates the place of kin among the larger *domus.* In specifying one's duty and loyalty, the order is country, parents, and then "children and the whole *domus,* who look to us for support and can have no other protection; finally, our kinsmen." Quoted in Wayne Meeks, *The First Urban Christians: The Social World of the Apostle Paul* (New Haven: Yale University Press, 2003), 30. On the wider sense of Latin *familia,* with a focus on the complex and pervasive roles of slaves, see Jonathan Edmondson, "Slavery and the Roman Family," in *The Cambridge World History of Slavery,* eds. Keith Bradley and Paul Cartledge, vol. 1, 337–61 (Cambridge: Cambridge University Press, 2011).

54. Jerome Neyrey, "Managing the Household: Paul as Paterfamilias of the Christian Household Group in Corinth," in *Modelling Early Christianity: Social-Scientific Studies of the New Testament in its Context,* ed. Philip Esler, 208–18 (London: Routledge, 1995), 209–11; Moxnes, "What Is Family?" 21.

55. For an implicitly Foucauldian analysis of the actual complexities and mitigations of the power of the *paterfamilias,* see Saller, *Patriarchy, Property, and Death;* Richard Saller, "Pater Familias, Mater Familias, and the Gendered Semantics of the Roman Household," *Classical Philology* 94, no. 2 (1999): 182–97.

56. Eva Marie Lassen, "The Roman Family: Ideal and Metaphor," in *Constructing Early Christian Families: Family as Social Reality and Metaphor,* ed. Halvor Moxnes, 103–20 (London: Routledge, 1997), 104–6. For a comparable situation with the Greek *kurios,* at least according to Aristotle, see Mark Golden, "Slavery and the Greek Family," in *The Cambridge World History of Slavery,* eds. Keith Bradley and Paul Cartledge, vol. 1, 134–52 (Cambridge: Cambridge University Press, 2011), 136–37.

57. Neyrey, "Managing the Household."

58. Indeed, Paul seems to construct the new "household" of the church on a comparable model. Lone Fatum, "Brotherhood in Christ: A Gender Hermeneutical Reading of 1 Thessalonians," in *Constructing Early Christian Families: Family as Social Reality and Metaphor,* ed. Halvor Moxnes, 183–97 (London: Routledge, 1997).

59. For a detailed study of Roman patronage, see Richard Saller, *Personal Patronage Under the Early Empire* (Cambridge: Cambridge University Press, 1982).

it was the determining socio-cultural feature of the ancient Mediterranean world.[60] This is to fall victim to seeing all social relations through the eyes of the powerful and wealthy. We need to remind ourselves that honor-shame is the preserve of the wealthy, politicians, and gangsters who were (and are) usually embodied in one and the same person.[61]

Further, without slaves such a polis-household is unimaginable. One or more head slaves ran the day-to-day workings of the household—including the acquisition and preparation of food, engagement with outsiders, building and repairs, cleaning, care of the children, and interaction with the estates. Many were the slaves who undertook the myriad tasks needed, but they were also available for the penetrating paterfamilias should he feel the need to remind a slave—female or male—of his priapic authority. Indeed, the relationship was very much an active-passive one. The dominant male was the active penetrator, while the anus, mouth, or vagina in question was the passive receptacle. Any sign of energetic response from the penetratee was deemed highly inappropriate, if not an expression of subordination.[62] Hierarchies also pertained to the internal relations among slaves themselves, in what may be called a "slave aristocracy."[63] They much preferred to be owned by a wealthy and powerful master with many slaves, especially if they could make it to the top of the servile pecking order. They were thankful indeed that they were not the slaves of a "poor man," who might be found in the outer parts of a polis and engaged in the more despised roles of artisan or small-time merchant, and who might have only two or three slaves. These slaves were at times depicted as insolent, given to drunkenness, and perhaps even reciprocating a penetrating master. Above all, slaves functioned as the embodiment of what we call social mediation. So much of the social interaction within and between such households was undertaken by slaves. A paterfamilias may wish to contact his wife, to arrange for a

---

60. Malina and Neyrey, "Honor and Shame in Luke-Acts"; Osiek and Balch, *Families in the New Testament World*, 38–40, 48–54; Zeba Crook, "Honor, Shame, and Social Status Revisited," *Journal of Biblical Literature* 128, no. 3 (2009): 591–611.

61. The parable of the "Unjust Steward" is the signal example. See John Kloppenborg, "The Dishonoured Master (Luke 16:1–8a)," *Biblica* 70 (1989): 474–95; David Landry and Ben May, "Honor Restored: New Light on the Parable of the Prudent Steward (Luke 16:1–8a)," *Journal of Biblical Literature* 119, no. 2 (2000): 287–309.

62. David Halperin, *One Hundred Years of Homosexuality: And Other Essays on Greek Love* (New York: Routledge, 1989). In relation to the New Testament, see Joseph Marchal, "The Usefulness of an Onesimus: The Sexual Use of Slaves in Paul's Letter to Philemon," *Journal of Biblical Literature* 130, no. 4 (2011): 749–70.

63. Ste. Croix, *Class Struggle*, 143–44.

meeting with a neighbor, invite guests to dinner, inspect an estate, go to the forum, bathhouse or temple, or communicate with one of his children. In these and many other situations, the slave was the medium of communication and social interaction. All relations were systemically mediated, so much so that they went well beyond the physical acts of a slave: the very ways of thinking, writing, and speaking also functioned in a mediated fashion. In other words, the realms of ideology, belief, language, social relations, along with the means of production (in shorthand, all parts of infrastructure and superstructure) were infused with slaves and the slave-relation. The *polis*-household was no exception.

The implications for non-slave women in the *polis*-household should by now be obvious. Given the strong hierarchical system which ensured a pervasive sense of solidarity among those of the same class, the mediated interaction with others via slaves, and the limited engagement with those outside one's own class, women had little room to move.[64] Marriage was very much an intra-class reality with serious loss of status if one should marry outside one's class. Women were both part of the wider household in its relations of domination and submission, and specific bearers of the paterfamilias's seed. Needless to say, such women needed to be curtailed and sequestered in all manner of ways. A woman always knows which child is hers, but a man is never completely certain. The implications for inheritance, especially where significant property was involved, were not negligible.

One of the best indications is the use of veils, which was first attested in a Middle Assyrian law code from between 1400 and 1100 BCE when the state itself saw fit to legislate for women in a household.[65] The code distinguishes between five types of women: respectable women (married or concubines), widows, daughters of free men, prostitutes (both temple and street), and slaves. The first three types were to wear a veil, the other two not. If the latter were caught wearing a veil, the prostitute would be beaten fifty times with a stave and have pitch poured over her, while the slave had her ears cut off. Notably, the code specifies no punishment for respectable women, widows, and wives of freemen if they did not wear a veil. But veiling came into its own in another society somewhat later but with similar approaches to women— ancient Greece, especially at its height in the fifth century BCE. Ruling class males and heads of households found it perfectly

64. Contra Meyers, "Problems of Gendered Space," 67–69.
65. Graeber, *Debt*, 184-85.

acceptable to penetrate a variety of orifices around them, while their women were sequestered at home, chaste and modest, away from the sordid life of the streets. And if she went outside, a woman in a democratic city like Athens would never be seen without a veil, for it signaled potently that she was still very much within the controlled sphere of the household.[66]

While the households of *chōra* and *polis* may in some respects have been similar, particularly in terms of the assumed hierarchical structure under a male head or paterfamilias, they also differed in many ways. We have suggested that a *chōra* household was *functionally* equalizing, in the sense that all able hands were needed for the many tasks of subsistence survival agriculture (albeit in tension with internal exploitation). By contrast, the *polis* household could afford (literally) a division of labor, between the many and complex layers of domination and subordination. This situation applied particularly to women, who undertook many of the same tasks as the men in a village community, while they were sequestered away and guarded in a *polis* household. And while slaves appear in the households of the big peasants in the *chōra*, they were hardly seen among the small peasants.

Tenure or, Controlling the *Chōra*

The *chōra* was organized in a number of ever-changing patterns, as the ruling classes and *poleis* sought new ways to respond to the constitutive resistance of the working rural population. The aim was extraction: taxation was one way, enforced by various means, slavery was another, but here we focus on tenure. By tenure we mean an extractive relation in which land is worked (entailing labor) for the sake of the one controlling the land. The trick of tenure is that it is presented as a reciprocal and contractual relationship of mutual benefit: the one who does not work (landlord or the state) benefits from the produce of the land, while the tenant benefits from apparent security through the use of the produce left over. However, tenure is a deeply unequal relationship of economic exploitation, let alone in terms of the hierarchies of power (we return to this inequality in the discussion of debt).[67] The apparent

---

66. Lloyd Llewellyn-Jones, *Aphrodite's Tortoise: The Veiled Woman of Ancient Greece* (Swansea: Classical Press of Wales, 2003).
67. Luigi Capogrossi Colognesi, "Grandi proprietari, contadini e coloni nell'Italia Romana (I–II d.C.)," in *Società romana e impero tardoantico. Vol. I, Istituzioni, ceti, economie,* ed. Andrea Giardina, 326–65, 702–23 (Bari: Editori Laterza, 1986); Willem Jongman, *The Economy and Society of Pompeii* (Amsterdam: J. C. Gieben, 1988); Elio Lo Cascio, "Considerazioni sulla struttura e sulla dinamica dell'affitto

security and stability of some forms of tenure were the most effective ways of ensuring long-term extraction. Before we proceed, a caveat is in order: the danger of some recent studies is that tenure takes precedence over slavery, especially if tenure is seen as somewhat benign.[68] We stress that slavery remained the primary form of expropriation and exploitation, and that tenure was another form of unfree labor.

Forms of Tenure

Tenure applied primarily to peasants, as individuals, village communities, or estates. Even so, what seems to be individual tenure turns out to be collective, since the individual in question usually involved a collective entity such as an "extended" family that was included in the agreement. Following Ste. Croix, we distill the following categories:

1. Village communities and their clans and individuals not under any form of tenure.
2. Permission to dwell and work on specific land for a lifetime, on condition of military service with the inheritance of such land dependent on the will of the local despot.
3. Tenants who a) worked land on lease for a lifetime, or more commonly for a set number of years with the option of renewal, and b) tenants who could be ejected from the land at any moment or have the terms changed, usually on more onerous conditions. The type of payment demanded for such tenure could be in coin, kind, percentage of the crop, labor service, or combinations of these.[69]

The first category indicates the institutional form of subsistence survival, which was not always subject to external exploitation. From the perspective of the ruling classes, non-tenured villages of the *chōra* were unacceptable, for they could be taxed only at the relatively low rate of ten percent. The measures introduced to overcome this situation

agraria in età imperiale," in *De Agricultura: In Memoriam Pieter Willem de Neeve*, eds. Heleen Sancisi-Weerdenburg, et al., 296–316 (Amsterdam: J.C. Gieben, 1993); C.R. Whittaker, *Land, City and Trade in the Roman Empire* (Aldershot: Variorum, 1993).

68. As found, for example, in Foxhall, "Dependent Tenant"; Kehoe, *Law and the Rural Economy in the Roman Empire*.

69. Ste. Croix, *Class Struggle*, 213–14. For a discussion of three types payment—fixed return, coin, or percentage of the actual harvest—in the Mishnah, see Kloppenborg, "Growth and Impact of Agricultural Tenancy," 34–36. The third type typically required one third to a half, which was a very old practice from ancient Southwest Asia.

would lead eventually to the colonate. In regard to the second and third categories, we add that tenure was usually layered (an old practice that went back thousands of years in ancient southwest Asia). A client despot would be under tenure to the Roman Emperor, while local lands and their *instrumentum* (including slaves) were tenured to landlords, who may in turn produce another layer by renting out people, equipment, and land to groups and individuals.

Estates

Estates, debt, and the colonate—these three features of tenure are the most significant for our analysis. While estates and debt relate to the second and, especially, third categories of tenure noted above, the colonate was concerned to overcome the situation of the first. The overall drive was to increase the number of rural laborers in the third category. Indeed, each of the strategies examined here constitute different angles on this same drive.

The primary purpose of an estate was to supply those who did not labor with what they regarded as the necessities of life. Estates had the advantage—from the perspective of the ruling class and the *poleis*—of providing higher yields. Yet, the forms taken by estates varied considerably: an estate may be controlled by the state or landlords (often overlapping); managers may be slaves, freedmen, or tenants; they may involve slave labor, some tenants, and even hired labor during agricultural peak seasons; they may be constituted by tracts of land (at times fragmented) with slave gangs, tenured families, or whole villages under tenure; they may have the *instrumentum* supplied by the landlord or state (where slaves were dominant) or by the tenants themselves, in which case slaves may be included along with agricultural tools and livestock; and they may have used large central facilities such as olive presses which the various occupants would use. Each of the many combinations of these variables had their obligatory legal prescriptions, especially from those lovers of legalese, the Romans.

Out of this variety, we discern three trajectories concerning estates, which will set up the treatment of the colonate (in chapter five). The first trajectory comes from the long history of ancient Southwest Asia,[70] which was inherited and modified by the Seleucids. Initially, temple and then palatine estates were the institutional forms of extraction preferred by the small ruling class from the time of Ur

---

70. The first part of this paragraph summarizes Boer, *Sacred Economy*, 202–14.

onwards (fourth millennium BCE). The reasons were obvious, since estates were expected to hand over one third to a half of the produce to temple and palace, in contrast to the intermittently enforced taxation on the village communes of ten percent. The system was, however, chronically unstable, since labor for such estates was drawn from village communities with the result that their preferred forms of subsistence survival were often undermined. Thus, estate systems would collapse periodically, only to be reinstated once again. By the end of the second millennium BCE, the dominant estate system was no longer viable with the result that a centuries-long absence of palatine estates led to the flourishing of subsistence survival. After this welcome break, a rather new economic structure appeared in the first millennium with its regime of plunder in which taxation refers to internal plunder and tribute to external plunder. Perfected by the Persians over a relatively vast and diverse territory, it involved a complex system of administration, taxation, and tribute (usually via markets using coinage) to ensure revenue. In this situation, palatine estates did not disappear but were recalibrated to a relatively minor role in the new regime. Under the Seleucids, this regime of plunder underwent its own modification, in light of the four levels of monarch, satrap, *polis*, and individual.[71] While the first level dealt with minting coins and "public" expenditure, and the individual covered immediate agricultural produce, the lion's share of economic administration fell to the satrap and—notably—the *polis*. Thus, the satrap had to deal with agricultural "tithes" (*ekphorion* or *dekatē*), tariffs from exchange, individual poll taxes (*epikephalaion*), and taxes on artisans and merchants (*cheirōnaksion*). As for the *polis*, it drew its entitlements from the territory under its control, including taxes on roads and markets.[72] In other words, the Seleucid domination entailed the consolidation of the colonial *polis* that we outlined earlier.

In Egypt, the Ptolemies worked with many assumptions and structures similar to the Seleucids, especially in terms of the importance of the *polis* (developing Alexandria and Ptolemais) and the introduction of Greek administration.[73] However, the situation of Egypt was also unique (as the Persians found before them) in light of the crucial role

71. Peter Schäfer, *The History of The Jews in the Greco-Roman World*, revised ed. (London: Routledge, 2003), 28.

72. For further detail on Seleucid colonization and imperialism, see Susan Sherwin-White and Amélie Kuhrt, *From Samarkhand to Sardis: A New Approach to the Seleucid Empire* (Berkeley: University of California Press, 1993); Paul Kosmin, *The Land of the Elephant Kings: Space, Territory, and Ideology in the Seleucid Empire* (Cambridge: Harvard University Press, 2014).

73. For a strong argument for the fusion of Egyptian and Greek practices, see Manning, "Hellenistic Egypt."

of the Nile's flood cycles in an arid and flat land. Thus, estates functioned in a somewhat different fashion. The whole land was in theory the despot's *oikos*, although he tenured out "royal land" to officials and farmers, which became "conceded land".[74] In practice, this entailed an elaborate system of administrative regions (hyparchies or *nomoi*) with simultaneous military and economic governance (although to separate them so is foreign to the situation). The coexistence of the *stratēgos* and the *oikonomos* indicates how closely economic matters were connected with, fostered by, and enforced through the military—although this did not prevent rural uprisings and removal of labor from the land by peasants. Above all, the whole country was seen as a collection of estates, with temple estates remaining important and not a few large estates tenured to self-important hangers-on. Crucially, for the later development of the colonate, this meant that villages (the smallest administrative unit) and "royal farmers" were seen as functioning within the estate system.[75] Thus, they farmed the land under ultimate tenure to the despot, a situation which was formally established through the *kōmomisthōtēs*, the tax farmer who ensured the required revenue was extracted. Due to the significant agricultural resources of Egypt and the efficiency of the system, the Romans perpetuated much of it.[76] Notably and in contrast to their practices elsewhere, the Romans dragged their feet in recognizing and establishing *poleis*. The *nomoi* of the administrative districts were granted municipal institutions, some self-government, and control over their hinterlands only late in the piece (by the beginning of the third century CE, by Septimius Severus).

By contrast, the Roman estate or "villa" system was somewhat distinct, which was established as a result of Roman expansion in the last two centuries BCE. With Rome's rapid imperial expansion, the

---

74. The complexity of the Egyptian situation, in light of its long history, Persian rule, the Ptolemies, and the Romans defies easy statements. For an effort to sort out some of the complexity, albeit with neoclassical assumptions, see Andrew Monson, *From the Ptolemies to the Romans: Political and Economic Change in Egypt* (Cambridge: Cambridge University Press, 2012).

75. Jones, *Roman Economy*, 294–95; Manning, "Hellenistic Egypt," 451–54. An excellent example of villages within estates in the Ptolemaic period is provided by the Zenon archive, with reference to the estate of Beth Anath. The entire Zenon archive comprises about 2000 documents, of which 40 relate to "Syria and Palestine." They mark Zenon's inspection tour (with a host of officials) in 259–58 BCE. The result of the tour included updates in technology (irrigation and sowing), reconfiguring the administration of royal estates, and a resultant improvement in revenue. See Viktor Tcherikover, *Palestine Under the Ptolemies: A Contribution to the Study of the Zenon Papyri*, Mizraim IV–V (New York: G.E. Stechert, 1937). Examples of specific estates visited by Zenon include those of Beth Anath and Kedasa in Lower Galilees. See John Kloppenborg, *The Tenants in the Vineyard: Ideology, Economics, and Agrarian Conflict in Jewish Palestine*, WUNT 195 (Tübingen: J. C. B. Mohr, 2006), 284–90, 359–64, 367–76.

76. This feature is another indicator of the uniqueness of Egypt, which should make one wary of extrapolating from its situation.

landscape of Italy changed irrevocably: the small village landholders found themselves marginalized by an increasing number of ever larger estates, worked most often by slave gangs (although also with tenants[77]), and managed by a slave, freedman, or tenured overseer, who took orders from absentee landlords or the state.[78] This transformation marked the arrival of Rome's "classical" era.[79] The estates that tended to cluster on the river valleys closest to water transport were concentrated in the hands of ever fewer members of the ruling class, became larger over time (*latifundium* was coined mid-first century CE, albeit as a morally reprobate term), and became fragmented, with the resultant need to ensure connections between them.[80] The function of these new economic engines was to supply the *poleis* (*civitates*) with the items that those who did work on the land "needed"—above all, Rome, although it soon needed far more than Italy could supply, so large estates emerged throughout the empire.[81] The economic reason for such estates was obvious, for they were expected to produce thirty to fifty percent "surplus" of a range of crops and animal products, in contrast to taxes on villages of ten percent (these figures were ancient indeed, running back millennia in ancient Southwest Asia).[82]

Thus far we have emphasized the diversity of estate practices and histories. Not unexpectedly, such diversity also shows up in scholarship. Let us take the situation of Syria-Palestine. Given the long history of conflict between Seleucids, Ptolemies, Hasmoneans, and Romans, it should come as no surprise that the practices in estates varied in this corner of the empire, showing traces of distinct influences. Thus, the three strands identified above appear in various forms: in one, inherited from ancient Southwest Asia (and the Seleucids), estates actu-

---

77. Bradley, "Slavery in the Roman Republic," 248–49. For a suggestion that the prime move was from "free peasants" to "new"—that is, tenured—peasants, see Garnsey, *Cities, Peasants and Food in Classical Antiquity*, 96–105. The effort to reduce the role of slavery is not new, dating back at least to Weber. Banaji wishes to see greater flexibility in labor on the estates, which reflects shortage of adequate labor. Banaji, *Theory as History*, 105–7.

78. Jean-Jacques Aubert, *Business Managers in Ancient Rome: A Social and Economic Study of Institores, 200 BC–AD 250* (Leiden: Brill, 1994), 117–200. Aubert distinguishes between "steward" (*procurator*), "bailiff" (*vilicus*), and "overseer" or "foreman" (*praefectus, monitor,* and *magister*). Their tasks were extensive, ranging over supervising produce, record-keeping, registering transactions, buying equipment, dealing with debt, finding extra labor, maintenance of work contracts, and, of course, ensuring the required supply of produce to the landowners. See also Dennis Kehoe, "Landlords and Tenants," in *A Companion to the Roman Empire*, ed. David Potter, 298–311 (London: Blackwell, 2006).

79. Anderson, *Passages from Antiquity to Feudalism*, 59–60.

80. Garnsey, Saller, and Goodman, *Roman Empire*, 93–95.

81. Mattingly, "The Imperial Economy," 289–90; Kehoe, "Landlords and Tenants," 298–99.

82. Erdkamp gives the example of Roman Egypt, where estates were expected to produce 30–40 percent and villages ten percent. Erdkamp, *Grain Market in the Roman Empire*, 237.

ally played a relatively minor role; in another, from Egypt (Ptolemies), estates included whole villages under tenure; and in another, from Rome, slaves predominated but also included tenure. As a result, opinions vary regarding the nature and extent of estates. Some frame the situation in terms of a contrast between "small private land owners" and large estates, the latter being exceptions due to historical influences.[83] Others argue that estates became widespread, especially on the plains of Palestine.[84] In support of the latter position, some suggest that the fragmentation of estates means that they were not always obvious.[85]

It is all too easy to focus on the nature and management of estates, since the available written material concerns such matters, let alone the increasing complexity of Roman law that attempted to regulate practices in regard to tenure in general.[86] But what was the reality for the actual laborers under tenure? Through all the variety, we find a consistent drive to push untenured peasants into situations of tenure, preferably (from the perspective of the ruling class) into the third category noted above. Indeed, where possible, the preference was for tenants who were not tenured for a lifetime, but for an indeterminate period so they could be ejected at any time or have the terms changed at the whim of a landlord or the state. The mechanisms for doing so included the participation of whole villages within estates, forcing families and clans into tenure, and the patterns of debt. Tenants and would-be tenants were often caught between a bad situation and one that was worse. With such a limited range of options, the bad situation—tenure—was often the only viable one. Further, the production of space in terms of *polis* and *chōra* emerges in the nature of tenure and estates, for the landlords in question were almost always residents in

83. Freyne, *Galilee from Alexander the Great to Hadrian*, 155–77; Séan Freyne, *Galilee, Jesus, and the Gospels: Literary Approaches and Historical Investigations* (Philadelphia: Fortress, 1988), 135–75; Séan Freyne, "Galilee, Jesus, and the Gospels: Literary Approaches and Historical Investigations," in *Studying the Historical Jesus: Evaluations of the State of Current Research*, eds. Bruce Chilton and Craig Evans, 75–121 (Leiden: Brill, 1988).

84. Shimon Applebaum, "Economic Life in Palestine," in *The Jewish People in the First Century: Historical Geography, Political History, Social, Cultural and Religious Life and Institutions*, eds. Shemuel Safrai and Menahem Stern, vol. 2, 631–700 (Assen: Van Gorcum, 1976), 633–38; Kloppenborg, *Tenants in the Vineyard*; Kloppenborg, "Growth and Impact of Agricultural Tenancy"; Jensen, "Rural Galilee and Rapid Changes," 56; Fiensy, *Social History of Palestine in the Herodian Period*, 21–73.

85. Douglas Oakman, *Jesus and the Economic Questions of His Day* (Lewiston: Edwin Mellen, 1986), 49–57; Oakman, "Late Second Temple Galilee." For an assessment of the various arguments, see David Fiensy, "Did Large Estates Exist in Lower Galilee in the First Half of the First Century CE?," *Journal for the Study of the Historical Jesus* 10 (2012): 133–53. For an earlier trace in biblical material, see the parable of the tenants (*geōrgoi*) in Mark 12:1–12 and *Gospel of Thomas* 65.

86. Aubert, *Business Managers in Ancient Rome*, 117–200; Kehoe, *Law and the Rural Economy in the Roman Empire*.

a *polis* and the land under tenure was in the *chōra*. The managers and workers in the estates ultimately worked for the sake of the demands of the landlords and their respective *poleis*.

Debt

A second feature integrally bound up with tenure concerns debt. We propose that debt in the ancient world had three functions, with the priority varying over time and place. In ancient Southwest Asia, the primary function of debt was compulsion for labor, especially in a situation where labor was in relatively short supply. With short life expectancy and the ever-present threat of disease, let alone the economic desire of peasants to stay out of harm's way in order to engage in subsistence-survival agriculture, the shortage of labor was a constant problem. Tying a person's muscle power and skill into debt ensured that the land would be worked (of course, there was always the possibility of the debtor simply absconding).[87] Labor may be secured in this fashion either by interest rates that could simply not be repaid, thereby ensuring that the debtor remained in a permanent state of laboring for another (state or landlord),[88] or by constant adjustments to ensure that the burden of debt was not intolerable.

Initially, these two strategies may seem contradictory, but let us consider for a moment the typical Roman loan contract.[89] It contained clauses concerning late or non-payment, with an increase in interest (up to 50 percent) and potential seizure of the property and person of the debtor.[90] Putting the debtor into debt slavery was an old practice indeed, so much so that in third millennium Babylon the person pledged was simply called a "hostage" or "captive."[91] But Roman con-

---

87. We could describe this approach as one focused on gaining control of the "security" or "collateral" of the loan, except that the terminology breaks down here, for the prime purpose of the loan was qualitatively different.

88. "Assuming that most loans were made with other objectives than the interest-generated profit in mind, it follows that, in such circumstances at least, interest was a tool and not an economic end in itself, being therefore devoid of real economic value. Its rate was largely irrelevant vis-à-vis the amount of the loan, except that it had to be sufficiently high to make it impossible for the borrower to repay the capital." Piotr Steinkeller, "The Ur III Period," in *Debt and Economic Renewal in the Ancient Near East*, eds. Michael Hudson and Marc van de Mieroop, 109–38 (Bethesda: CDL, 2002), 113. The loan was determined by the need to ensure an obligation, in this case for labor.

89. The very need for a contract evinces a basic mistrust between two parties. See Julie Vélissaropoulos-Karakostas, "Merchants, Prostitutes and the 'New Poor': Forms of Contract and Social Status," in *Money, Labour and Land: Approaches to the Economies of Ancient Greece*, eds. Paul Cartledge, Edward Cohen, and Lin Foxhall, 130–39 (London: Routledge, 2002).

90. These come from Roman Egyptian contracts. See John Goodrich, "Voluntary Debt Remission and the Parable of the Unjust Steward (Luke 16:1–13)," *Journal of Biblical Literature* 131, no. 3 (2012): 547–66, 554.

tracts could also be subject to various types of alleviation, whether statutory, obligatory, or voluntary. The first item—enacted by the state or aspiring despot—is also an ancient practice, appearing with the spasmodic *mīšarum* (or *andurārum*) or jubilee, which was not a complete abolition but a partial and selective amelioration.[92] However, for the Romans obligatory or voluntary amelioration depended on circumstances, particularly climactic forces beyond the debtor's control (*vis maior*), with either formal legal proceedings by the debtor or an act by the lender of his own will.[93] The prime purpose of such amelioration was to ensure the continued productivity of those under tenure and thereby the income of the lender—the second role of debt (see below). Thus, it functioned as a safety-valve to ensure the system continued in the face of constant instability and crisis.[94] At the same time, we suggest that debt amelioration also played a role in labor compulsion: the myth of eventual repayment had to be kept alive so that debtors would at least continue to work the fields in question. If they ceased believing in the myth, they would simply sell the equipment, keep the produce for themselves, or abscond.

The second function of debt was to secure the flow of produce, money, and thereby wealth to the lender—a feature of debt perfected and raised to primary importance by the Romans and their civil law. Here interest comes into its own, although it was originally a foreign and "unnatural" idea,[95] and subject not to "market forces" but to royal decree and customary practice.[96] In many respects, the Romans continued with such assumptions, but being legal and ritual obsessives

---

91. Piotr Steinkeller, "The Money-Lending Practices in Ur III Babylonia: The Issue of Economic Motivation," in *Security for Debt in Ancient Near Eastern Law*, eds. Raymond Westbrook and Richard Jasnow, 47–61 (Leiden: Brill, 2001), 49. See also laws 114–16 of Hammurabi's code. Martha Roth, *Law Collections from Mesopotamia and Asia Minor*, 2nd ed., SBL Writings from the Ancient World Series (Atlanta, Georgia: Scholars Press, 1997), 102–3.

92. Knight, *Law, Power, and Justice in Ancient Israel*, 218–22; Boer, *Sacred Economy*, 160–61.

93. Goodrich, "Voluntary Debt Remission," 554–63.

94. They also enabled extraordinary spin, in which the despot or ruling class in question—inveterate propagandists all—claimed to bring justice, joy, and even food for the common people. Norman Yoffee, *Myths of the Archaic State: Evolution of the Earliest Cities, States, and Civilizations* (Cambridge: Cambridge University Press, 2005), 160.

95. For instance, the Hebrew Bible bans charging interest: Exodus 22:24 [ET 25]; Leviticus 25:36–37; Deuteronomy 23:20–21 [ET 19–20]; Ezekiel 18:17; Psalm 15:5.

96. For millennia in ancient Southwest Asia, it had been one-third for produce and one-fifth for silver and then coin— the former due to agricultural produce expected from estates and the latter from the sexagesimal system. Roth, *Law Collections*, 97; Marc van de Mieroop, "A History of Near Eastern Debt?," in *Debt and Economic Renewal in the Ancient Near East*, eds. Michael Hudson and Marc van de Mieroop, 59–94 (Bethesda: CDL, 2002), 84; Robert Englund, "Proto-Cuneiform Account-Books and Journals," in *Creating Economic Order: Record-Keeping, Standardization, and the Development of Accounting in the Ancient Near East*, eds. Michael Hudson and Cornelia Wunsch, 23–46 (Bethesda: CDL Press, 2004), 32–37.

they turned debt and its attendant interest into an utterly complex myriad of rules and regulations—all with the purpose of ensuring that the ruling class continued to gain, from those under tenure and in debt, the resources it felt perfectly justified in acquiring. The prime form of economic extraction may have been slavery, but the mechanism of debt tenure also played a significant role. For example, Pliny the Elder found himself constantly distracted by the concerns of his estates, their slaves, and their tenants so that he was often frustrated in his effort to continue his immensely valuable role in life as a writer.[97] Clearly, wealth went in one direction—from debtor to lender—and the lender would do all in his power to ensure the flow was relatively uninterrupted.

By now the third function of debt should be clear: to reinforce economic hierarchy. To be sure, some lenders did come from the ruling class, but the vast bulk of debts were loaned out by well-placed lenders to those outside their own ruling class structures. The previous two features of debt—compulsion for labor and the flow of wealth—function in terms of and ensure the economic hierarchy between tenants and landlords, between agricultural laborers and those who did not labor. It should come as no surprise that debt too was a feature of class conflict—the initial acts of popular uprisings have been and remain to cancel debts, destroy records, and reallocate land.[98]

Thus far, we have examined the way estates and debt sought to push the many rural laborers who were not slaves into tenure. The direction was clearly into the third category of tenure with its variable time frames and conditions. The third strategy—the colonate—was both a culmination of estates and debt and arguably the most effective one. It involved tying *coloni* (farmers or tenants) to the land and restricting their movement. However, since the colonate was the basis of the land regime, we leave the full analysis of this development to the chapter on regimes.

Conclusion: Towards the Colonate

To sum up, we have argued that the re-production of space led to two institutional forms: *polis-chōra* and tenure. The first underwent a significant transformation in the phase of Greek and then Roman colonization, so that the *polis* became a means for and representation of

---

97. Goodrich, "Voluntary Debt Remission," 555–59; Garnsey, Saller, and Goodman, *Roman Empire*, 95.
98. Graeber, *Debt*, 8; Finley, *Ancient Economy*, 80.

such colonization—in which economic matters were part and parcel of the cultural process of Hellenization. Indeed, so important was the *polis-chōra* relation that it became the determining institutional form of what we will call the colonial regime. We will argue in chapter 6 not merely that Christianity was a *polis*-based movement, but that its depictions of the *chōra* (especially in the Gospels) operate through the eyes of the *polis*. The second institutional form is tenure, which was targeted at the village communities not under any explicit form of compulsion apart from taxes. Estates and debt bent towards the inexorable process towards the colonate, which became a reality by the third century CE. This would eventually provide not only the basis for the land regime but also for feudalism, which is nothing less than a transition in modes of production.

4

The Slave-Relation

An ox is a poor man's slave.[1]

Slavery—or what we prefer to call the "slave-relation"—is the final institutional form of the Greco-Roman period. Although slavery was one of several forms of unfree labor, we follow Ste. Croix (as we already indicated in the first chapter) in showing that slavery in the course of the Greco-Roman era became the prime mode of extracting surplus, to the extent that one may speak of a slave economy.[2] In other words, this institutional form became the determining feature of one of the core regimes we identify in the next chapter. It operated at a number of levels from the economic to social consciousness and social interaction. Due to its pervasiveness, we call it the "slave-relation" and contend that the increasing work on the subject of slavery in early Christianity tends, with few exceptions, to treat slavery in isolation from the wider economic framework and thus focuses only on slavery either as an economic feature or as an element of cultural production.[3] What is lacking

---

1. Aristotle, *Politics*, 1252b.13. Jowetts's translation.
2. Among others, the following agree with Ste. Croix: Chris Wickham, *Land and Power: Studies in Italian and European Social History, 400–1200* (London: British School at Rome, 1994), 85; Wickham, *Framing the Early Middle Ages*, 261–62; David Turley, *Slavery* (Oxford: Wiley-Blackwell, 2000), 4–5, 62–63, 76–100; Scheidel, "Slavery in the Roman Economy," 2, 16.
3. Jennifer Glancy, *Slavery in Early Christianity* (Philadelphia: Fortress, 2003); Jennifer Glancy, *Corporal Knowledge: Early Christian Bodies* (Oxford: Oxford University Press, 2010); J. Albert Harrill, *The Manu-*

is not only more engagements of the relationship between the two as well as the connections with social interactions,[4] but also of the deeper ways in which the ideology of slavery saturated patterns of thought and interaction—or what de Wet calls "doulology."[5]

Our reconstruction approaches slavery in three ways. First, at an economic level, we return to theory to investigate how slavery was the main method of extracting surplus for the ruling class—a situation revealed through its ubiquity and variety. However, our key argument is that slavery determined the nature of markets themselves. This determination can be seen in the function of slave markets and the key role of slavery in developing the legal definition of private property, which in itself indicates a new level of abstraction in which a human being (like coinage) may possess an abstract value. Finally, we argue that the supposed humanization of slaves was actually part of the process, for the slave had no *potestas* apart from the master. In their very activities, slaves were the hands of the master, or Aristotle's automaton. In our later chapter on mode of regulation, we develop further the social mediation of slavery, as well as the ideological, intellectual, and psychic dimensions in which the slave-relation became integral to ways of thinking and being.

Theory: Slavery and Surplus

For all the wealth that Rome took from tributary Asia, three times as much shall Asia take from Rome . . . and for all the men who were taken from Asia to go and dwell in Italy, twenty times so many men of Italy shall serve in Asia as penniless slaves.[6]

In the first chapter, which was devoted to theory, we examined the arguments of Ste. Croix for the role of slavery in the Greek world as the prime means for extracting surplus.[7] We also noted Finley's admis-

---

mission of Slaves in Early Christianity (Tübingen: J.C.B. Mohr, 1995); J. Albert Harrill, *Slaves in the New Testament: Literary, Social and Moral Dimensions* (Minneapolis, Minnesota: Fortress, 2006).

4. As in Dale Martin, *Slavery as Salvation: The Metaphor of Slavery in Pauline Christianity* (New Haven: Yale University Press, 1990).

5. Chris De Wet, *Preaching Bondage: John Chrysostom and the Discourse of Slavery in Early Christianity* (Oakland: University of California Press, 2015). It is a pity that De Wet's chapter on economic dimensions in his PhD thesis did not appear in the book. De Wet, "Slavery in John Chrysostom's Homilies," 323–48.

6. *Sibylline Oracles*, 3.350–55.

7. Although slavery can be found in different times and places, it did not become the prime means of extracting surplus as in the Greco-Roman era. For instance, slavery is found in ancient Southwest Asia before the Greco-Roman era, but it never formed a significant part of the economy. This has not prevented some scholars from suggesting otherwise. Muhammad Dandamaev, *Slavery in Baby-*

sion that slavery provided the bulk of the immediate "income" from property of the "elites," although he, like Polanyi and others in the Weberian tradition, do not offer any systemic analysis of class in relation to slavery. At this point, we return to theory for a while, since the dominance of slavery in this period has also been questioned, not least by Marxists. Apart from the strictly theoretical objections of Hindess and Hirst,[8] Ellen Meiksins Wood criticizes the proposal that slavery was the main method for extracting surplus, at least with regard to classical Athens. In the midst of her discussion of freedom and slavery, she offers an intriguing footnote in which she mentions—and then seeks to dismiss—the key Marxist proponents of slavery as the prime means for extracting surplus: Ste. Croix, Anderson and Yvon Garland.[9] At the same time, Wood is clearly not in favor of the proposition that "Athenian democracy rested on the material foundation of slavery."[10] Instead, implicitly drawing on a tradition that goes back at least to Weber (see the chapter on theory), she insists that the category of free labor played an unprecedented, and since unequalled, role in her model location, Athens.[11] Her position against slavery is set forth more strongly in the second chapter of her *Peasant-Citizen and Slave* where she takes particular issue with Michael Jameson's study into agriculture and slavery, and Ste. Croix's analysis of class struggle.[12] Jameson's argument, as distilled by Wood, is "the proposition that 'slaveholding enabled the

Ionia: From Nabopolassar to Alexander the Great (626–331 BC), trans. Victoria A. Powell (DeKalb: Northern Illinois University Press, 2009); Gregory C. Chirichigno, *Debt-Slavery in Israel and the Ancient Near East* (Sheffield: JSOT, 1993). Many are the works on Greco-Roman slavery, although we have not found the following particularly useful: Niall McKown, *The Invention of Ancient Slavery?* (London: Duckworth, 2007).

8. Hindess and Hirst, *Precapitalist Modes of Production*, 109–77.

9. "For example, Finley describes Greece and Rome as 'slave societies', not because slavery predominated over free labour but because these societies were characterized by 'an institutionalized system of large-scale employment of slave-labour in both the countryside and the cities.' . . . G. E. M. de Ste. Croix argues that, although 'it would not be technically correct to call the Greek (and Roman) world "a slave economy"', because 'the combined production of free peasants and artisans must have exceeded that of unfree agricultural and industrial producers in most places at all times', nevertheless this designation remains appropriate because slavery was, he maintains, the dominant mode of surplus extraction or exploitation. . . . Perry Anderson . . . chooses to retain the Marxist concept, 'slave mode of production', but, again, not on the grounds that slave labour predominated in Greek or Roman production but because it cast its ideological shadow over other forms of production. See also Yvon Garland, *Slavery in Ancient Greece* [. . .], especially the Conclusion, for a consideration of such concepts as 'slave mode of production' as applied to ancient Greece." Ellen Meiksins Wood, *Democracy Against Capitalism: Renewing Historical Materialism* (Cambridge: Cambridge University Press, 1995), 183n1.

10. Wood, *Democracy Against Capitalism*, 186.

11. Wood also argues that any slavery was restricted to the domestic sphere. But, as Anderson points out, this would have added an intolerable non-productive workforce to the Athenian economy without agricultural slave labor. Perry Anderson, *In the Tracks of Historical Materialism* (London: Verso, 2016), 37.

12. Jameson, "Agriculture and Slavery in Classical Athens"; Ste. Croix, *Class Struggle*.

Athenian to be a participant in a democracy.'"[13] However, while Jameson's article is carefully argued and deploys a range of classical sources, Wood's refutation relies on postulates, misleading references to secondary literature and no engagement with the source material, leaving her refutation rather unconvincing. Her battle with Ste. Croix turns on agricultural slavery, which unwittingly helps to make sense of her position. Apart from her insistent misreading of Ste. Croix's category of unfree labor as referring solely to slavery, Wood also does not take into account the fact that Ste. Croix's analysis is one of class struggle and the way the various forms of labor must always be seen in relation to surplus extraction.[14] This not only suggests that she does not appreciate and engage with Ste. Croix's resolutely economic argument, but also that her own argument is not an economic one, but rather is founded on apologetics and social-democratic morals—circumstances odd and troubling for a Marxist historian. Her main desire is to deploy Athenian democracy as a source for social democracy,[15] and in order to do so she edentates and defuses the works of Ste. Croix, Anderson, and Garlan, by placing them under the aegis of Moses Finley.

So let us return to Finlay: towards the end of his article on Greek civilization and slave labor, he rhetorically ponders distinguishing between slavery as *a* basic institution of Greek civilization or as *the* basic institution, suggesting that the debate has been pre-empted by Marxism.[16] His response: the question is a fruitless one, for we should consider how slavery *functioned*, a point that enables him to conclude:

> The Greeks, it is well known, discovered both the idea of individual freedom and the institutional framework in which it could be realized. The pre-Greek world—the world of the Sumerians, Babylonians, Egyptians, and Assyrians; and I cannot refrain from adding the Mycenaeans—was in a very profound sense, a world without free men, in the sense in which the west has come to understand that concept. It was equally a world in which chattel slavery played no role of any consequence. That too, was a Greek

13. Wood, *Peasant-Citizen and Slave*, 52.
14. See, for example, her representation of Ste. Croix's argument for the unimportance of hired labor. She understands his point in absolute terms, while Ste. Croix means the unimportance of hired labor in relation to surplus extraction. Wood, *Peasant-Citizen and Slave*, 72.
15. Compare Foxhall's proposal that ancient Athens did experience some forms of "radical democracy" decoupled from possession of land, but that these moves did not ultimately undermine the connection of land ownership and ruling class power. Lin Foxhall, "Access to Resources in Classical Greece: The Egalitarianism of the Polis in Practice," in *Money, Labour and Land: Approaches to the Economies of Ancient Greece*, eds. Paul Cartledge, Edward Cohen, and Lin Foxhall, 209–20 (London: Routledge, 2002).
16. Moses Finley, "Was Greek Civilization Based on Slave Labour?," *Historia: Zeitschrift für Alte Geschichte* 8, no. 2 (1959): 145–64, 161.

discovery. One aspect of Greek history, in short, is the advance, hand in hand, of freedom *and* slavery.[17]

This conclusion is unsatisfactory for both Yvon Garlan—who otherwise shows great admiration for Finley—and, less surprisingly so, for Ste. Croix. The former politely asks what might have "what sparked off this evolution,"[18] while the latter directly points out that Finley merely leaves the statement "as a kind of paradox, entirely without explanation" and attributes this to Finley's "refusal to think in terms of class consciousness," and his "curious disinclination to recognize exploitation as a definable characteristic of a class society."[19] As we indicated in the chapter on theory, for Ste. Croix the explanation to Finley's "paradox" is class: because the poorer citizens were protected by right in a democratic city such as Athens, the most had to be made of those who were outside the realm of citizenship, who did not enjoy the same rights as a citizen, namely slaves.[20] This explains the intensity of Athenian slavery.

Garlan's entire study on slavery in Ancient Greece is an attempt to address this "paradoxical" relation between freedom and slavery through the categories of exploitation and class.[21] Despite the admira-

---

17. Finley, "Was Greek Civilization Based on Slave Labour?," 164.
18. Yvon Garlan, *Slavery in Ancient Greece*, (Ithaca: Cornell University Press, 1988), 39.
19. Ste. Croix, *Class Struggle*, 141–42.
20. Free foreigners residing in the city, the so-called metics, were also privy to the rights of the citizen. They paid a small tax to the state, but were also desirable dwellers, and thus could not be excessively exploited (Ste. Croix, *Class Struggle*, 141).
21. Let us not be fooled by his facetious presentation of the problem on pages 39–40, where he approaches the "paradox" by posing two conceivable developments: either economic progress leads to the development of slavery, which leads to the progress of democracy; or, the progress of democracy leads to the development of slavery which leads to economic progress. In the first case, Garlan states that "it is easy to refer to an extension of commercial and artisan activities accompanied by a reduction in the available labor force in Greece, following the surge of colonization from the eighth to the sixth centuries" to which may be added a number of indications of technological progress in architecture, ceramics, and naval construction. In relation to the second process, he indicates that the reinforcement of the *demos* due to a variety of reasons (economic in terms of the increasing importance of artisans and commerce; the growing demand for soldiers due to the adoption of hoplite tactics; and "simply a renewal of community vitality and a taste for political liberty accompanied by all the material advantages that went with the status of a citizen") led to the deterioration of the aristocracy. He settles on the conclusion that we should take into account "a whole complex of possibilities (opened up by an increase in 'productivity' and hence also in surplus demand)" and that we should also take note of the fact that "these developments were favored by a powerful surge in both the military and the commercial sectors" that made Greek hegemony possible. The explanation to the first development falls short of explaining the transition from economic boom to slavery, and then from slavery to democracy. It seems that shortage of labor and technological progress are assumed to be the reasons for the development of slavery, but is that a necessary trajectory? Taking a look at the second process, we are again given the initial impetus (strengthening of the *demos*) and left to guess the rest. Further, the initial impetus is not what it seems, because the strengthening of the *demos* is seen to be the *result* of various preceding processes, such as economic, military, and civic. Garlan's problem is that while

tion for Finley,[22] it is nevertheless clear that Garlan's argument relies on Marxist categories, such as exploitation, surplus and mode of production, and is finely attuned to ideological interpretation and economics. The key is economic, in terms of the primary form of exploitation that provided the material conditions of existence for the ruling class.[23] Once this has been determined, it becomes possible to examine questions of ideology and culture. At this point we need to be exceedingly careful, for Garlan begins to use the terminology of mode of production for what we are calling institutional forms. Thus he is concerned that slavery did not necessarily predominate—numerically and in terms of the extraction of surplus—at all times and places in Greco-Roman antiquity. It was only one "mode of production" that, due to particular historical conditions and social forces, coexisted with "secondary modes of production."[24] The reason for being careful at this point is that it is a staple of Marxist analysis that subordinate modes of production do exist within a dominant mode in each time and place (as we will see with Anderson in a moment). However, Garlan makes the category mistake of confusing an institutional form—in this case the slave-relation—with the slave mode of production.[25] Our argument is that various institutional forms, which have been examined, come together in specific constellations to produce regimes. It is only the sum total of the regimes that constitutes a mode of production. Thus, we interpret Garlan's study in terms of the institutional form of the slave-relation, especially when he writes that it existed "within the framework of a particular social conditioning," that it bore "the mark of the historical conditions in which it developed," which were a "combination of more or less independent forces affecting various sectors of social life".[26]

Our final theoretical touchpoint is Perry Anderson, whom we read through the same lens with which we interpreted Garlan.[27] Thus, a reinterpreted Anderson argues that the Greek city-states transformed the institutional form of slavery from an ancillary facility (in ancient

he sees exploitation as a central category, he is reluctant to subscribe to what he sees as an economic determinist approach, which may be seen from his frequent invocation of "extra-economic constraints." Garlan, *Slavery in Ancient Greece*, 118, 202.

22. Ibid., 201–8.
23. Ibid., 202.
24. Ibid., 203, emphasis in original.
25. See the chapter on theory for other examples of such category mistakes, such as patron-client, household, or tribute.
26. Ibid., 203, emphasis in original.
27. Anderson, *Passages from Antiquity to Feudalism*, 22–23.

Southwest Asia and pre-Hellenistic monarchies) into a systematic mode of exploitation so much so that it came to determine a regime as such. This was particularly the case in Greece in the fifth and fourth centuries BCE and in Rome from the second century BCE to the second century CE. At the same time, it was not the only institutional form and not the only regime in operation at the time. We have indicated earlier that other institutional forms include subsistence survival, *polis-chōra*, and tenure, and we will outline distinct regimes in the next chapter. At the same time, we also recognize that slavery "gave its imprint to the whole civilization of the city-state."[28] On this point, we come back to Ste. Croix, who argues that slavery was the archetypal form of unfree labor, omnipresent in the psychology of all classes.[29]

Varieties of Slave Labor

To have slave help was considered the norm.[30]

When we turn to the specific function of slavery, we find that the tendency of so many studies of slavery in biblical studies is to focus on household slavery. At one level, this is understandable since the overwhelming majority of references in the New Testament deal with household slaves. Yet, we need to be wary of using such terminology, for the Greeks and Romans did not have a term for "domestic slave" or the euphemism "domestic servant"—as one who undertakes the tasks of cooking, cleaning, gardening, and personal assistance to the master. The usual word evoked in this context, *oiketēs,* is by no means limited to the space of the "domestic" or the "home." The term refers instead to the slave's place in the realm of the *oikos* with its rich connotations, and was not restricted to slaves. Only in the richest ruling households would it have been possible to have a slave able to dote on the master's every need. By contrast, the vast majority of slaves undertook many tasks and moved between different types of labor. They worked at agriculture (from individual managers to work gangs), hunting, mining where early death was guaranteed,[31] craftwork, pottery, brewing, teaching, medicine, wet-nursing, transportation, pri-

---

28. Ibid., 22.
29. Ste. Croix, *Class Struggle*, 173, 259.
30. Jameson, "Agriculture and Slavery in Classical Athens," 123.
31. For some detail, see T. E. Rihll, "Classical Athens," in *The Cambridge World History of Slavery*, eds. Keith Bradley and Paul Cartledge, vol. 1, 48–73 (Cambridge: Cambridge University Press, 2011), 68–69.

mary agents in market transactions, government roles,[32] the military as porters and assistants, food processing, construction and road-building, attendants in public baths, and religious rituals. They were owned by the state, communities, partnerships, and individuals. And they could be chained or given extensive responsibility, and anywhere in between.

Nonetheless, to put it this way suggests a level of specialization that was foreign to Greco-Roman economic reality. Let us take the example of agriculture, which we have argued was the inescapable economic foundation of ancient Greece and Rome. The ideal for a self-respecting Greek or Roman male was to engage in agricultural labor (although for the obscenely rich this was more of a genteel and occasional hobby). And every self-respecting male would have at least one or two slaves, although preferably many more. Yet we struggle to find a specific term for an agricultural slave. The generic *geōrgos* is often invoked, but the term refers in general to those who are engaged in tilling the soil and thereby agriculture. The reality is that the absence of a specific word indicates not that slaves were unimportant in agriculture, but that they were simply everywhere.[33] Agricultural work is what would now be called "unskilled," although we prefer multi-skilled.[34] The same slave may be required to sow and reap grain, deal with wine-making and olive oil presses, cut wood, work metal, make bricks, cut stone, gather salt, attend to bees, shepherd animals, mill flour, bake bread, shear sheep, make garments and shoes, repair equipment, provide lodgings and food for visitors, hunt and fish. And these tasks related merely to agricultural work in one place. They could also be required to work for another when not immediately needed—work on a construction site or road-building, purchase or sell items at the markets (often other slaves), or pull oars on a ship. In older periods when masters actually were present on estates (unlike the Roman Empire), if the master needed to undertake "civic" duty, such as jury work, assembly or liturgy, then the slaves in question would be left in charge of agricultural matters. Through all of this, we should not forget the brutality and pervasive violence—to the point of having professional slave

32. For a careful study of the Latin texts relating to roles of slaves in the Roman state, see Alexander Weiss, *Sklave der Stadt: Untersuchungen zur öffentlichen Sklaverei in den Städten des Römischen Reiches* (Stuttgart: Franz Weiner, 2004).

33. Indeed, the sheer range of terms for slaves also indicates the symbolic (in Lacan's sense) saturation of slavery in Greek and Roman society and culture. As we indicated in the first chapters, these include, but are not limited to, *andrapodon, doulos, therapōn, akolouthos, pais, sōma, servus, mancipium*.

34. A point made in his own way by Bodel, "Slave Labour and Roman Society," 329–30.

torturers (*tortores*)[35]—the assumed sexual use of slaves,[36] and the ever-present fate that awaited not merely a convicted criminal but a recalcitrant and errant slave: the mine gangs.[37]

Thus far, we have stressed the range of tasks demanded of slaves, so much so that distinguishing between household, agricultural, and perhaps "industrial" slaves as distinct categories becomes quite meaningless.[38] But we have done so for another reason that will become clearer in what follows: the sheer pervasiveness of slavery in the economic and social pores of Greece and Rome.[39] It should be no surprise that the Greeks and Romans thought slavery so utterly normal and unquestionable (Jews and Christians included[40]), and the Romans in particular could not imagine their own history without it.

Slave Markets

No one sails on the open sea just for the sake of crossing it.[41]

In the same way that slaves were expected to undertake myriad tasks of economic production, so also were they pervasive in the actual markets of the Greco-Roman world. At this point we begin to develop our argument that slavery determined and shaped the very nature of markets in this corner of the globe and at this time. In order to make what may seem like a counter-intuitive argument, we focus on the per-

35. Carolyn Osiek, "Female Slaves, *Porneia*, and the Limits of Obedience," in *Early Christian Families in Context: An Interdisciplinary Dialogue*, eds. David Balch and Carolyn Osiek, 255–75 (Grand Rapids: Eerdmans, 2003), 262.
36. Penetrating any slave within a man's purview has been a topic of some interest in biblical studies of late, especially in relation to Paul's assumptions and advice concerning slaves. Jennifer Glancy, "Obstacles to Slaves' Participation in the Corinthian Church," *Journal of Biblical Literature* 117, no. 3 (1998): 481–501; Jennifer Glancy, "The Sexual Use of Slaves: A Response to Kyle Harper on Jewish and Christian *Porneia*," *Journal of Biblical Literature* 134, no. 1 (2015): 215–29; Osiek, "Female Slaves, *Porneia*, and the Limits of Obedience," 262–64, 268–70; Marchal, "The Usefulness of an Onesimus."
37. The situation is quite similar in the late Roman Empire. See Cam Grey, "Slavery in the Late Roman World," in *The Cambridge World History of Slavery*, eds. Keith Bradley and Paul Cartledge, vol. 1, 482–509 (Cambridge: Cambridge University Press, 2011), 498–99.
38. Jameson, "Agriculture and Slavery in Classical Athens," 137; Michael Jameson, "On Paul Cartledge, 'The Political Economy of Greek Slavery'," in *Money, Labour and Land: Approaches to the Economies of Ancient Greece*, eds. Paul Cartledge, Edward Cohen, and Lin Foxhall, 167–74 (London: Routledge, 2002).
39. A point stressed by Neville Morley, "Slavery Under the Principate," in *The Cambridge World History of Slavery*, eds. Keith Bradley and Paul Cartledge, vol. 1, 265–86 (Cambridge: Cambridge University Press, 2011), 266–74.
40. Jennifer Glancy, "Slavery and the Rise of Christianity," in *The Cambridge World History of Slavery*, eds. Keith Bradley and Paul Cartledge, vol. 1, 456–81 (Cambridge: Cambridge University Press, 2011). For a full discussion of New Testament matters relating to slavery, see chapter 6.
41. Polybius, *The Histories*, trans. W. R. Paton, 6 vols., Loeb Classical Library (London: Heinemann, 1922–1929), 3.4.10.

vasiveness of slaves in the markets; the crucial role of the invention of private property the significant step in abstraction required to see human beings as exchangeable objects; and slaves as extensions of the master's *potestas*.

Before proceeding, let us address the assumption that we challenge in what follows. Where slavery and markets are connected (not as often as one would expect) one finds the argument that ancient markets were entities to themselves—a witness to the deep imprint of neoclassical economic theory. The fact that they often functioned primarily for the procurement and acquisition of slaves thereby becomes a historical accident in which slaves were merely one type of commodity among others. Thus, if there was a demand for slaves and they were profitable, then the market would find ways to supply them.[42] Seductive as this suggestion may be, imbued as it is with the myths of Adam Smith, we argue that it is profoundly misleading. Instead, the very nature of Greco-Roman markets was determined by slavery.

Our first point in developing this argument concerns the pervasiveness of slaves in markets, which was a given in Greece by the fifth and fourth centuries BCE. With the expansion of Greek colonies in the eastern Mediterranean, a whole new source of slaves arose from conquests. *Poleis* like Athens and Corinth needed ever more slaves in order to function at all, so the markets grew to enable such acquisition. Estimates for Athens range from 15 percent to 60 percent of the population,[43] but even at the minimal level slaves had already become the crucial mechanism for producing surplus for the ruling class. Given the realities of water-borne transport over relatively short distances, slaves could be captured, transported, displayed at markets, and sold—largely by sea. Significant transit points such as Chios and Delos (supplied by the Cilician pirates) functioned as massive slave markets, but many other places also had significant markets. This model was also applied to a port like Piraeus, which was used as a mechanism driven and controlled (even in terms of price) by the Athenian *polis* to ensure its own supplies.

As with the classical Greeks, debates continue concerning the num-

42. Hordern and Purcell, *Corrupting Sea*, 342–400; Astrid Möller, "Classical Greece: Distribution," in *The Cambridge Economic History of the Greco-Roman World*, eds. Walter Scheidel, Ian Morris, and Richard Saller, 362–84 (Cambridge: Cambridge University Press, 2007); Pastor, "Trade, Commerce, and Consumption," 297; Scheidel, "Slavery in the Roman Economy," 8; Harris, *Rome's Imperial Economy*, 162–75; Dimitris Kyrtatas, "Slavery and Economy in the Greek World," in *The Cambridge World History of Slavery*, eds. Keith Bradley and Paul Cartledge, vol. 1, 91–111 (Cambridge: Cambridge University Press, 2011), 94.
43. Rihll, "Classical Athens," 49–50; Anderson, *Passages from Antiquity to Feudalism*, 22–23.

ber of slaves in the Roman population and their relative percentage (due to the absence of what now counts as quantitative data). In the empire as a whole, estimates range from 5 million to 20 million, and the proportion from 10 percent to 30 percent of the total population. Debate also continues concerning the sources of slaves with proposals arguing for the prime sources in either prisoners of war, reproduction (*vernae*), exposed infants, or debt-slavery.[44] A realistic assessment would include a range of sources for slaves—including children sold by parents, adults giving themselves up to slavery, some criminals (theft, tax and military service evasion, even murder, depending on the court), kidnapping and slave-raiding, and acquisition across the frontiers[45]—all of which would push towards a higher number of slaves in the system. No matter what the source, slaves had to be exchanged and for this the markets of the Roman Empire were geared. They had to deal with both significant gluts[46] and periodic shortages for which the array of sources would be able to cope.

How were the slave markets structured? Here we follow Harris's fourfold schema: 1) local transactions in villages and towns in which a single slave was sold by one master to another; 2) opportunist markets such as the general and specialist slave traders who followed the Roman armies and snapped up human flesh for sale elsewhere; 3) periodic markets at fairs and in town squares in which slaves could be bought and sold and the traders would number slaves among their other wares; and 4) large-scale markets in major centers and at transit points.[47] This category included Rome and major Italian centers such

---

44. The arguments in either direction turn on the ratio of males to females, values given to female slaves, rates of manumission, and potential numbers from conquest. Keith Hopkins, *Conquerors and Slaves* (Cambridge: Cambridge University Press, 1978), 8–11; Walter Scheidel, "Quantifying the Sources of Slaves in the Early Roman Empire," *The Journal of Roman Studies* 87 (1997): 156–69; Scheidel, "Slavery in the Roman Economy," 5–7; Richard Saller, "Women, Slaves, and the Economy of the Roman Household," in *Early Christian Families in Context: An Interdisciplinary Dialogue*, eds. David Balch and Carolyn Osiek, 185–204 (Grand Rapids: Eerdmans, 2003); Harris, *Rome's Imperial Economy*, 62–65, 68–69, 88–109. The sources from warfare were many: newly conquered territories (especially during earlier years of expansion), suppression of endemic revolts, conflicts at the outer limits of the empire, captured brigands on land and sea, and so on. Military triumphs typically paraded the tens of thousands of captives to be enslaved, well into the common era. See Walter Scheidel, "The Roman Slave Supply," in *The Cambridge World History of Slavery*, eds. Keith Bradley and Paul Cartledge, vol. 1, 287–310 (Cambridge: Cambridge University Press, 2011), 294–97. For the late Roman Empire, see Grey, "Slavery in the Late Roman World," 495–97.
45. Harris, *Rome's Imperial Economy*, 70–81.
46. Such as Caesar's capture of 53,000 Aduatici in 57 CE, or the 97,000 captives as a result of suppressing the Jewish Revolt in 66–70 CE, and even more after the Bar-Kochba revolt of 135 CE—even when we allow for the usual unreliability of ancient estimates. Iulius Caesar, *De Bello Galico*, trans. H. J. Edwards, Loeb Classical Library (London: William Heinemann, 1958), 2.33; Josephus, *Bellum Judaicum*, 6.420. Indeed, it may be argued that in some cases the conquests had as one of their main purposes the search for new sources of slaves.

as Brundisium, Capua, Puteoli, and Pompeii as well as places in the eastern empire, especially the major slave market of Ephesus; but also Byzantium, Alexandria, Amphipolis, Mitylene (after the decline of Delos), Sardis, Thyatira, Samos, Rhodes, Xanthus, Myra, Side, Acmonia, Gaza, and many other places. These locations offer only a sample, but they illustrate how ubiquitous slave markets were. Slaves could be bought and sold in their hundreds if not thousands at the great centers, but they were also exchanged as an everyday affair in whatever corner of the empire one cared to look. In short, slave dealing took place everywhere and on every occasion, perhaps comparable to buying a cup of coffee or tea today.[48]

Origins of Private Property

The great, decisive accomplishment of the new Roman law was . . . its invention of the concept of "absolute property."[49]

Pervasiveness and ubiquity may indicate that slaves were simply everywhere in Greek and especially Roman markets, but quantitative presence does not necessarily produce—although it certainly assists in a Hegelian sense—the qualitative point that slavery determined the very nature of such markets. For this point we need to go further into the very invention of private property. It was the Romans who first invented and defined private property, a definition that arose late in the second century CE from the centrality of slavery in Roman markets and one that had its own profound effect on those markets. However, the Romans developed a unique definition: private property was first defined as a relationship between a human being and the object (*res*) owned—with the "object" in question being nothing less than another human being who had been reduced to such a status. In other words, private property began in the relationship between a master (human being) and slave (object). Thus, the Roman markets functioned to obtain through exchange objects also known as slaves. Let us explain in a little more detail.

---

47. Harris, *Rome's Imperial Economy*, 75–76; Scheidel, "Roman Slave Supply," 301–2. Slaves were displayed on platforms, with placards (*tituli*) stating their qualities, point of origin, health, and propensity to escape. New arrivals had their feet marked, while those who could not be guaranteed by the seller wore special caps (*pillei*). Slaves could be undressed for closer inspection.
48. David Braund, "The Slave Supply in Classical Greece," in *The Cambridge World History of Slavery*, eds. Keith Bradley and Paul Cartledge, vol. 1, 112–33 (Cambridge: Cambridge University Press, 2011), 124; Bradley, "Slavery in the Roman Republic," 242.
49. Anderson, *Passages from Antiquity to Feudalism*, 66.

The Latin term for private property is *dominium*—a later term with its own history. In Roman law, property—or *dominium*—is a relation between an individual person and a thing, characterized by absolute, inalienable power of that person over that thing. By private property, the Romans meant the legal and economic category of "absolute property," or *dominium ex jure Quiritium*—the right of absolute ownership for any individual Roman citizen.[50] The crucial distinction is between "possession" and "property": the former refers to the control of goods, while the latter entails full legal title to those goods.[51] Thus, possession is subject to all manner of qualifications and external constraints; property refers to the unqualified and absolute legal title to a thing. And if one has absolute rights to a piece of property, one is able to alienate it. The Roman jurists defined absolute ownership as the right to dispose perfectly of a material thing insofar as it not forbidden by law: *jus perfecte disponendi de re corporali nisi lege prohibeatur.*[52]

Now a problem emerges: how is it possible for a human being to have a relationship with a thing? Surely the issue is the way people relate to one another concerning things.[53] Does one not own a piece of property to the exclusion of others owning it? Yet these Roman jurists did not frame their law in such a fashion; they insisted that the relationship is between a human being and a thing—the reason why opens up the specificity of the history and nature of private property. The key is that

---

50. The term *Quiritium* has a long history, designating citizens after the combination of the Romans and Sabines (*Romani* referred to warriors and rulers). In the fragments that remain from the fifth-century BCE Twelve Tables of the Law, Quiritarian ownership referred to the specific ceremonial process that had to be followed for the transfer of a slave. This ceremony included oaths and striking scales with a piece of bronze. If it was not observed correctly, the slave remains the Quiritian property of the original owner. The formula, by which the property is transferred is found in Gaius's *Institutes* 1.119: "Mancipation, as before stated, is an imaginary sale, belonging to that part of the law which is peculiar to Roman citizens, and consists in the following process: in the presence of not fewer than five witnesses, citizens of Rome above the age of puberty, and another person of the same condition, who holds a bronze balance in his hands and is called the balance holder, the alienee holding a bronze ingot in his hand, pronounces the following words: This man I claim as belonging to me by right quiritary and be he (or, he is) purchased to me by this ingot and this scale of bronze (*hunc ego hominem ex iure quiritium meum esse aio isque mihi emptus esto hoc aere aeneaque libra*). He then strikes the scale with the ingot, which he delivers to the mancipator as by way of purchase money." For a good discussion see György Diósdi, *Ownership in Ancient and Preclassical Roman Law* (Budapest: Akadémiai Kiadó, 1970), 56–59.
51. David Johnston, *Roman Law in Context* (Cambridge: Cambridge University Press, 1999), 56–58.
52. One may well ask whether it is possible to have utterly inalienable property. The qualifier, *nisi lege prohibeatur*, suggests precisely such limitations. Yet, the qualifier also recognizes that the basic form of property is private property and that it is in the owner's absolute power to do anything he wants with it.
53. Gray and Gray simply dispense with this specific history and state mistakenly that "property" is an "abbreviated reference to a quantum of socially permissible power exercised in respect of a socially valued resource." Kevin Gray and Susan Francis Gray, "The Idea of Property in Land," in *Land Law*, eds. S. Bright and J. Dewar, 15–51 (Oxford: Oxford University Press, 1998), 15.

these Roman jurists were thinking about relationships between human beings, except that one of those human beings was a slave. Or rather, the slave may once have been a human being, but now he or she was a thing—a *res*.

Let us set the context. This unique legal and economic development was the product of specialized jurists, although the debate continues as to their actual function and relation to everyday Roman society. On one side are those who argue that the tradition of law should be understood within the juristic tradition, which set itself apart from society and dealt with matters within the tradition.[54] On this view, the jurists were legal theorists devoted to analytic and theoretical reflection on civil and economic law without concern for morality, justice, or economic welfare. In short, the law is an entity unto itself and not beholden to anyone. On the other side are those who argue that the law as elaborated by the jurists had everything to do with its context.[55] These theoretical reflections arose from the realities of everyday life, which in turn informed such life and its practice. These include, *inter alia*, duties of a proconsul, life expectancy, languages to be used, the taking of oaths, farm equipment, and the relations of masters and slaves. The great codes in question were gathered in a massive burst of energy during the early years of emperor Justinian (527–65 CE), resulting in the *Digest*, which sought the essence of more than three million lines of earlier texts in a mere 150,000 lines.[56] A second source is the *Institutes* by Gaius, written circa 161 CE.[57] These works deal with the full range of public and private law, but our concern pertains to disputes over property, over contracts, and exchange between Roman citizens.

For these theorists, the question of private property—as the relation between a human being and a thing—had arisen due to the increasing pervasiveness of slavery.[58] With the conquest of the Mediterranean

---

54. The most sustained proponent of this position in more recent work is Alan Watson, *The Spirit of Roman Law* (Athens: University of Georgia Press, 1995).
55. Johnston, *Roman Law in Context*, 9–11; John Matthews, "Roman Law and Roman History," in *A Companion to the Roman Empire*, ed. David Potter, 477–91 (London: Blackwell, 2006), 482–83.
56. A full and recent translation is now available in Alan Watson, *The Digest of Justinian*, 4 vols. (Philadelphia: University of Pennsylvania, 2009).
57. W. M. Gordon and O. F. Robinson, *The Institutes of Gaius* (London: Duckworth, 1988).
58. Indeed, the very origins of Roman law turns on the issue of slavery, as may be seen in the legendary tale related by Livy (*Ab Urbe Condita* 3:34–58). According to his tale, the trigger for the Twelve Tables was the capture and enslaving of a plebeian woman, Verginia, by the patrician, Marcus Claudius. This event led to the end of the decemvirate, the establishment of the republic, and the engraving of the Twelve Tables on bronze and their public display. See brief overviews in Hans Julius Wolff, *Roman Law: An Historical Introduction* (Norman: University of Oklahoma Press, 1951), 55–56; Alan Watson, *Rome of the XII Tables: Persons and Property* (Princeton: Princeton University Press, 1975), 96–97. We are not necessarily claiming historical reliability for the narrative, but

from 300 BCE onwards, the vast influx of conquered peoples who became slaves, the huge increase in economic transactions involving slaves, the central role of slaves in these transactions (as objects exchanged and as agents on behalf of masters), and the sheer volume of legal proceedings and decisions involving slaves in all manner of situations[59]—in this context the question of the relation between slaves and masters became pressing. Two specific developments enabled the discovery of private property by the Romans.

First, a new word for property was coined, *dominium*, which derives from *dominus*—master or slave-owner.[60] The *dominus* was, of course, the paterfamilias of the *domus* over which he had absolute power (see the discussion in the chapter on re-producing space). *Dominium* appeared late in the second century, soon after *dominus* (111 BCE).[61] The term embraced two older terms from the "archaic law" (fifth century BCE) of the legendary Twelve Tables of the Law.[62] Here a distinction was made between *res mancipi* and *res nec mancipi*.[63] To the category of *res mancipi*, which means ownership that has to be transferred through the ceremony of *mancipatio* (or *in iure cassio*), belong land, beasts of draft and burden, and slaves.[64] *Res nec mancipi* concerns all other items.[65] Crucially, slaves appear among the *res mancipi*, thereby enabling the conceptual and legal possibility for a human being to become an object possessed. Subsequently, both *res mancipi* and *res nec mancipi* became the property of the *dominus*, and by the time of Justinian (sixth century CE) the distinction was abolished.

---

emphasizing Livy's connection between the establishment of a code of law and the issue of slavery.

59. For a useful survey of some of these legal proceedings, see Jane Gardner, "Slavery and Roman Law," in *The Cambridge World History of Slavery*, eds. Keith Bradley and Paul Cartledge, vol. 1, 414–37 (Cambridge: Cambridge University Press, 2011), 415–19.

60. The very invention of the term *dominium* indicates exactly what was at stake, for the whole process served to secure the economic and political power of the ruling class. "Roman legislation served the purpose of adapting the structure of state and law to changed conditions, but never that of radically altering it." Wolff, *Roman Law: An Historical Introduction*, 67.

61. Orlando Patterson, *Slavery and Social Death: A Comparative Study* (Cambridge: Harvard University Press, 1982), 32.

62. The Twelve Tables are not extant, except in quotations and paraphrases in later authors, such as Cicero and Gaius. See H. F. Jolowicz and Barry Nicholas, *Historical Introduction to the Study of Roman Law*, 3 ed. (Cambridge: Cambridge University Press, 1972), 5, 108.

63. Diósdi, *Ownership in Ancient and Preclassical Roman Law*, 60.

64. Diósdi concludes (*Ownership in Ancient and Preclassical Roman Law*, 57), after surveying other options that the most convincing explanation for the particular items in the *res mancipi* is that "the most important means of production of a peasant economy belonged to the res mancipi." While we do not dispute this claim, it should be emphasized that the point of view is that of the master. Curiously, while De Wet notes the category of *res mancipi*, he fails to note the crucial role of slaves in the development of private property. This may be due to his preference for Bourdieu's terminology of economic and symbolic capital. De Wet, "Slavery in John Chrysostom's Homilies," 326–28.

65. Jolowicz and Nicholas, *Historical Introduction to the Study of Roman Law*, 137.

Second, the process towards the legal discovery of private property required the devaluing of slaves. In the period of the Twelve Tables, slaves were still regarded as both human beings and things, as the category of *res mancipi* indicates. However, their status as human beings was already diminished since injuries against slaves required only 50 percent of the recompense paid to a free person. By the time of the *lex Aquilia* (c. 287 BCE), slaves were equated with domestic animals with injuries against both having the same status.[66] The development was by now clear, so by the second century BCE, we find that a slave had been redefined as *res* at the same time that the new term *dominium* appeared. Now the Roman jurists regarded slaves as the "only human *res*."[67]

This huge theoretical and practical breakthrough was not restricted to the realm of legal theory, for it may be seen as both the theoretical culmination of what was already in practice and a further impetus to economic practice. Indeed, it had profound implications for the very nature of markets, if not for the class structure of Roman society. Graeber implicitly indicates the effect on markets:

> In creating a notion of *dominium*, then, and thus creating the modern principle of absolute private property, what Roman jurists were doing first of all was taking a principle of domestic authority, of absolute power over people, defining some of those people (slaves) as things, and then extending the logic that originally applied to slaves to geese, to chariots, barns, jewelry boxes, and so forth—that is, to every other sort of thing that the law had anything to do with.[68]

In other words, the Roman markets were now determined by *dominium* or private property, understood as the relation between *dominus* and *res*. The very possibility of doing so was created by the economic reality of slavery.[69]

66. Alan Watson, *Roman Slave Law* (Baltimore: Johns Hopkins University Press, 1987), 54–55.

67. William Warwick Buckland, *The Roman Law of Slavery: The Condition of the Slave in Private Law from Augustus to Justinian* (Cambridge: Cambridge University Press, 1908), 3. See also Raymond Monier, *Manuel élémentaire de droit romain* (Paris: Dalmat-Montchrestien, 1947), 211; Watson, *Roman Slave Law*, 46–66.

68. Graeber, *Debt*, 201. Or, as Orlando Patterson observes: "It can be no accident that the shift in the meaning of 'dominium' from slaveholding to the holding of all objects of property in an absolute sense perfectly correlates with the changeover of Roman economy from one in which slaves were simply one of many objects of property to a society in which slaves became one of the two most important sources of wealth and objects of property" Patterson, *Slavery and Social Death*, 32.

69. The history of private property after the Romans followed an even more devious path. With the fading of the Roman Empire, private property as so defined was lost for centuries, only to be rediscovered in the high Middle Ages under the "lawyer popes" of the "Papal Revolution" and in Italian universities. By adapting Roman law to feudalism, the murky area of property was clarified—in terms of land claims and due process for every minute aspect of daily life, all through the

Slavery and Abstraction

The solstice of classical urban culture always also witnessed the zenith of slavery.[70]

The redefinition of a human being and the reduction to the status of *res* requires a significant step in abstraction, let alone the abstraction concerned with the invention of private property, *dominium*, as the relation between *dominus* and *res*. We now wish to deepen the argument by connecting it with the invention of coinage, which signals in itself a major step in abstraction—usually connected with the "axial age"—a few centuries before the invention of private property. In this case, the attachment of a certain quality or value to a piece of metal shaped in a certain way is comparable to, and indeed connected with, the abstraction entailed in attaching a quality to another object, specifically a human being who functions as an object.

In order to get to this point, we need to take a necessary detour, tracing the way the invention of coinage determined in its own way the development of markets in the later part of the first millennium BCE. These markets arose as the byproduct of a significant logistical problem facing ancient states.[71] In order to provision an army on the move, as many people were needed as in the army itself. In a context of almost continual warfare—with the Neo-Assyrians, Neo-Babylonians, and especially the Persians—this reality required significant organization. The invention of coinage—almost simultaneously in about 600–500 BCE in three parts of the world from (China, India, and Lydia) without evident contact—provided the circuit-breaker.[72] Rulers—or their "advisors"—soon saw a distinct logistical benefit of this invention: instead of the immense resources devoted to provisioning armies, rulers began to demand taxes in coin from the people they controlled.[73]

---

pope's legal representatives (legates) who spread across Europe. This rediscovery fed into myriad strands, including the Enlightenment, the French civil code of Napoleon and the first stirrings of capitalism in the sixteenth century—a development first noted by none other than Proudhon. See further Pierre-Joseph Proudhon, *Qu'est-ce que le propriété? Recherche sur le principe du droit et du gouvernement. Premier mémoire* (Paris: J. F. Brocard, 1840); Nicholas Gianaris, *Modern Capitalism: Privatization, Employee Ownership, and Industrial Democracy* (Westport: Greenwood Publishing, 1996), 20; China Miéville, *Between Equal Rights: A Marxist Theory of International Law* (Leiden and London: Brill and Pluto, 2004), 95–97.

70. Anderson, *Passages from Antiquity to Feudalism*, 22.
71. Graeber, *Debt*, 49–50.
72. Coins were produced in different ways: casting in the Great Plain of China, punching in the Ganges River valley of northern India, and stamping in the terra firma surrounding the Aegean Sea, beginning in Lydia.
73. As Kraay pointed out more than 50 years ago, coinage first served political and indeed symbolic

At the same time, the soldiers were paid in coin, the first properly anonymous form of payment. So how could people get hold of such coins to pay taxes? Exchange agricultural produce with the soldiers for the aforesaid pieces of metal with a ruler's head imprinted upon them, usually for a customary price. Local, intermittent, and decentralized practices of exchange—usually with neighboring villages in view (2–4 kilometers apart)[74]—were now transformed into markets to supply passing armies, which could be quite large (the Roman armies numbered around 300,000 in total, with 24,000 in the province of Judea after 135 CE). The practice was soon extended by the Persians to many other areas of its administration of the relatively vast territory it claimed to control.[75] Indeed, it enabled the Persians to develop an extensive taxation system, which was far more stable than the loot-oneself-into-oblivion approach of the Neo-Assyrians (although the Persians could deploy terror with the worst of them).

The initial point is that markets arose as a byproduct of a logistical problem that faced states in an almost constant state of warfare. In a similar way, the markets of the Greeks and then Romans served to supply the economically necessary slaves. Of course, such markets were not invented as such, since they already existed for another logistical purpose, but they were bent, reshaped, and expanded to the new logistical exercise. Once again, they were the byproduct of a specific condition. At the same time, the Greeks and especially Romans continued to use and even expanded markets for the sake of supplying armies.[76] Time and again, we come across evidence that local people did not immediately adopt coinage with enthusiasm. Instead, they tended to

functions. Colin Kraay, "Hoards, Small Change and the Origin of Coinage," *The Journal of Hellenic Studies* 84 (1964): 76–91. See also Leslie Kurke, *Coins, Bodies, Games, and Gold: the Politics of Meaning in Archaic Greece* (Princeton: Princeton University Press, 1999).

74. For items not obtainable in specific phytogeographic regions, and transported via the local tracery of pathways, see Milevski, *Early Bronze Age Goods Exchange*, 132–45; McCollough, "City and Village in Lower Galilee," 65–67. In the western Mediterranean, periodic markets for mostly local agricultural produce were called *nundinae*. See Jean Andreau, "Markets, Fairs and Monetary Loans: Cultural History and Economic History in Roman Italy and Hellenistic Greece," in *Money, Labour and Land: Approaches to the Economies of Ancient Greece*, eds. Paul Cartledge, Edward Cohen, and Lin Foxhall, 113–29 (London: Routledge, 2002), 115–19.

75. Although the claims were usually grander than the reality, as was characteristic of ancient states, James Osborne, "Sovereignty and Territoriality in the City-State: A Case Study from the Amuq Valley, Turkey," *Journal of Anthropological Archaeology* 32 (2013): 774–90. The actual extent of the Roman Empire was also vague and wavering. David Cherry, "The Frontier Zones," in *The Cambridge Economic History of the Greco-Roman World*, eds. Walter Scheidel, Ian Morris, and Richard Saller, 720–40 (Cambridge: Cambridge University Press, 2007), 720–21.

76. Keith Hopkins, "Taxes and Trade in the Roman Empire (200 CE–400 AD)," *The Journal of Roman Studies* 70 (1980): 101–25. For a useful introduction to the Roman army, see Nigel Pollard, "The Roman Army," in *A Companion to the Roman Empire*, ed. David Potter, 206–27 (London: Blackwell, 2006).

resist coinage, which had to be forced upon them. For example, during the Roman Empire's expansion from the third century BCE onwards, the Romans demanded taxes in coin[77] and evidence shows that coinage followed in the path of Roman armies with hunters and local farmers taking up the use of coins only when they were forced to do so—hardly surprising, given the association between invasion, coins, and taxes.[78] In later centuries, when coinage was issued by *poleis* (with approval from imperial overlords), the mechanism of exploitation was also determined by the *polis-chōra* relationship.[79] Not only does the discovery of coinage indicate that armies and garrisons were present—with their needs for supply through markets and the inevitable taxes that had to be paid[80]—but also that the *poleis* reasserted their economic and political control over the *chōra*. Whether the coins were Hasmonean or (after 63 BCE) Roman, with the inevitable inscriptions and (in the case of Roman coinage) busts of emperors or local hardheads, the very fact that the *poleis* issued coins indicated that while the colonial master may have changed, the local master was still very much present.[81] That the nearby *polis* was usually keen to indicate its support of the new colonial master enabled it to claim a renewed source of power.[82]

Now we can address the issue of abstraction entailed with coinage.

77. Seth Schwartz, "Political, Social, and Economic Life in the Land of Israel, 66–c. 235," in *The Cambridge History of Judaism*, ed. Steven Katz, vol. 4, 23–52 (Cambridge: Cambridge University Press, 2006), 39. By the second century CE, the concentration of Roman forces in the province of Judea was one of the highest in the empire. Ze'ev Safrai, "The Roman Army in the Galilee," in *The Galilee in Late Antiquity*, ed. Lee Levine, 103–14 (New York: Jewish Theological Seminary of America, 1992), 104–5. Safrai's hypothesis that its presence was economically beneficial in all respects is somewhat fanciful.

78. Rui M. S. Centano, "De República ao Império: reflexões sobre a monetização no Ocidente da Hispânia," in *Barter, Money and Coinage in the Ancient Mediterranean (tenth–first Centuries BC)*, eds. María Paz García-Bellido, Laurent Callegarin, and Alicia Jiménez Díaz, 355–67 (Madrid: Instituto de Historia, 2011); M.a Isabel Vila Franco, "El proceso de monetización del noroeste de la Península Ibérica: las calzadas romanas," in *Barter, Money and Coinage in the Ancient Mediterranean (tenth–first Centuries BC)*, eds. María Paz García-Bellido, Laurent Callegarin, and Alicia Jiménez Díaz, 369–76 (Madrid: Instituto de Historia, 2011). This point is missed by Garnsey, Saller, and Goodman, *Roman Empire*, 114–19.

79. For the situation in Galilee, see Freyne, *Galilee from Alexander the Great to Hadrian*, 183–94; Fabian Udoh, "Taxation and Other Sources of Government Income in the Galilee of Herod and Antipas," in *Galilee in the Late Second Temple and Mishnaic Period, Volume 1: Life, Culture, and Society*, eds. David Fiensy and James Strange, 366–87 (Minneapolis: Fortress, 2014).

80. Richard Horsley, *Archaeology, History and Society in Galilee* (Philadelphia: Trinity Press International, 1996), 81–82. Of course, other archaeological evidence indicates the disruptive brutality of invasion and conquest. For instance, see Aviam, "The Transformation from *Galil Ha-Goyim* to Jewish Galilee."

81. This situation makes sense of Gresham's Law: high value coins (gold and silver) end up in political centers, while the countryside finds itself with low value copper coins. Oakman, "Late Second Temple Galilee," 354.

82. Thus, the supposed "integration" indicated by coinage was between *polis* and colonial overlord, whoever it might have been. For a useful study of the political and economic power associated with *polis*-minted coinage, see Chancey, "City Coins and Roman Power in Palestine."

This took place during the much-discussed and much-celebrated "axial age" in which abstraction is supposed to have been discovered with the consequent henotheisms, monotheisms and ethical codes of Confucius, Siddhartha Gautama (the Buddha), and Zoroaster. However, this was an extremely violent age with the breakdown and reforming of states and the reshaping of social and economic conditions. Armies, gangs, and bands cut swathes through the land and its peoples, while despots sought for new ways to extract plunder and tribute as ways of feeding larger state machines, and above all keeping the armies and bands fed and armed. In this situation, itinerant armed men were a distinct risk and the last thing one wanted to do was extend credit to such a person (credit was a much older practice that relies on people actually knowing one another). For any transaction, it was better to have something that was assumed to have an objective value, a value that was marked as such. Here coinage was ideal, much like the "drug dealer's suitcase full of unmarked bills: an object without a history, valuable because one knows it will be accepted in exchange for other goods just about everywhere, no questions asked."[83]

In this context, a new level of abstraction comes into its own. Coinage embodies an abstract value, a value instituted and guaranteed by a state (hence the ruler's head or at least an inscription) and thereby agreed upon by its users. Obviously, we are not persuaded by the suggestion that abstraction was first invented out of the air and ushered in during the "axial age." According to this suggestion, coinage could take place only after this wondrous step in the human ability of thinking in a sustained and abstract manner. But we also do not adhere to a mechanistic materialist argument, according to which the invention of coinage caused abstract speculation. Instead, the situation was a dialectical one in which material and idealist conditions interacted with one another in a complex fashion, the details of which are now lost to us. And we are not persuaded by the strange argument that human beings first learnt to think abstractly during this period, having previously operated only in concrete and immediate terms. Instead, it was a new level or new type of abstraction, moving into hitherto unexplored areas beyond the abstractions of language and the classification of the natural world. Thus, the coin with objective value signals in a concrete

83. Graeber, *Debt*, 213. Payments required "small change" as much as large denominations, as implied by H.S. Kim, "Small Change and the Moneyed Economy," in *Money, Labour and Land: Approaches to the Economies of Ancient Greece*, eds. Paul Cartledge, Edward Cohen, and Lin Foxhall, 44–51 (London: Routledge, 2002).

way the new type of abstraction. While a coin is objectively universal, with the same objective value for the peasant who produces food and the hungry mercenary seeking a feed (neither of whom will see each other again), so also were the new types of religious and ethical expression universal, with theological systems and their single gods who laid claim not to a tribe or region or palace-temple, but to the whole known cosmos.

An analogous process appears with slavery, especially with the slave as "human *res*" and the eventual definition of private property in response to slavery. This definition—in terms of the slave as *res* owned by a *dominus*—both took place within a wider context and pinpoints the specific moment when the abstraction underway was explicitly recognized. As for the context, this was not only the result of a long development relating specifically to slaves: the influx of slaves from Roman expansion, their saturation and consequent determining of markets, and the process of reducing a human being to the full status *res*. It was also made possible by the invention of coinage and the attendant new form of abstraction outlined above. Let us explain: it is no coincidence that the flourishing of Greek economy, society, and thought in the fifth century BCE took place not long after the invention of coinage in this part of the world. More specifically, the development of Greek philosophy with its sustained abstraction of thought could take place only in the wake of the achievements of the previous century. Now we find the elevation of *logos* over *mythos*,[84] the valorization of truth and beauty, the fundamental place of precarious freedom, the nature of democracy, the first elaboration of a system of ethics—in short, the development of full systems of what we now call philosophy—which now, in terms of the classicist narrative, forms the basis of "Western" thought.[85] None of this would have been possible without slavery, although the usual argument is that slavery provided aristocratic thinkers like Plato and Aristotle with the means and leisure to engage in philosophy, or more sharply that the class formations signaled by "slave" and "free" needed the theorists and ideologues to justify such a system.

We add to these arguments the crucial point that the abstraction entailed in slavery went hand-in-hand with the abstraction required for such developments in thought. In short, philosophy as we know it could not have arisen without slavery, since both entail a significant process of abstract thought. However, it fell to the Roman jurists to

---

84. Lincoln, *Theorizing Myth*.
85. Roland Boer, "On the Myth of Classicism," *Journal for the Study of Christian Culture* 31 (2014): 131–51.

pinpoint what had actually been taking place for some time. Earlier laws might have identified a slave as *res* and that such a thing had a master with almost limitless power over the thing. But what did this really mean? For the Roman jurists and their definition of absolute private property, it meant that a distinct, objective, and abstract value could also attach to a human being and not just to a piece of metal or indeed any other object. The condition for such attachment was crucial, for the human being had to become a thing like everything else. This was clearly a step beyond coinage, or even the application of the logic of coinage to a loaf of bread, leek, sheep, mug of beer, or indeed an ancient sex toy. Now human beings could have an abstract value. And the markets in question were retooled to ensure that these objects were sourced, transported, sold, bought, and put to work. Throughout, this *res* was the absolute private property of the *dominus* in question.

Hand of the Master

If every tool could perform its own work when ordered, or by seeing what to do in advance. . . .[86]

At the same time, a slave was a thinking and acting being—a reality that has led some to focus on the slave as a human being with feelings and agency, even to the point of a supposed uneasiness and signs of humanitarianism by masters and the law.[87] From this perspective, signs of affection between slaves and masters, if not the recognition of family relations (despite the laws making it clear that for slaves such relations did not exist), are meant to indicate the human side to slaves as also their roles in responsible positions such as doctors, teachers, and overseers of estates. Here too the fact that slaves undertook most of the exchange activities in markets is supposed to indicate that they were not mere objects. More often than not, slaves were one part— albeit significant—of the goods they sought to exchange. There may have been certain restrictions: a slave could engage in a simple act of transfer (*traditio*), but not the elaborate and choreographed ritual of *in iure cessio*. Debate continues as to whether a slave could undertake a solemn verbal contract (*mancipatio*) for the *res mancipi,* which concerned the

---

86. Aristotle, *Politics*, 1253b34–35.
87. Watson, *Roman Slave Law*, 67–89; Johnston, *Roman Law in Context*, 42–44; Dale Martin, "Slave Families and Slaves in Families," in *Early Christian Families in Context: An Interdisciplinary Dialogue*, eds. David Balch and Carolyn Osiek, 207–30 (Grand Rapids: Eerdmans, 2003); Gardner, "Slavery and Roman Law," 424–26.

transfer of the central production of items of land, horses, cattle, and slaves themselves.[88] It may have been banned in strictly legal terms, but the reality was that such exchange took place all the time at the hands of slaves. They also made and received loans, acknowledged receipts of money, and managed operations (*institores*) for their masters.

The question remains: does this indicate a human dimension to slavery, which was recognized by the Romans? Although it may seem so at first sight, this is not the case, for the Romans lacked a sense and category of direct legal agency.[89] This meant that legal contracts could be made only by the actual persons, or principals, involved in the contract: "If Julius made a contract with Seius, who was acting under instructions from Marcus, and they were all free men, the contract firmly remained between Julius and Seius."[90] A third party was out of the question, or, if employed, the process was extremely circuitous and cumbersome. The crucial issue concerns what counts as a third party: this was another free person or a master's freed person. It did not count slaves or indeed a master's children. And the reason is that slaves and children did not possess *potestas* but were subject to the *potestas* of the master. By contrast, another free person or even a freedperson of a master's household did possess *potestas* independent of the master. To go back to the contract: it could be made between two principals with *potestas*, but not through a third (or fourth party) who also held *potestas*.

This reality relates directly to the question of private property and the nature of markets. The slave who engaged in market transactions and contracts was an extension of the master. It was as though the master himself had acted in this or that transaction, for the slave was subject to his *potestas*, was his absolute private property, and therefore had no ability to act outside that frame. The slave in question may therefore be seen as the hand of the master, or perhaps a puppet, or, most appropriately, as the self-motivated tool or automaton that Aristotle imagined.[91] This image is usually presented as an alternative to slavery or as the only other possibility to slavery, at least in the Greek imagination. But the Romans took it a step further—as they had done with private property—and made it a legal and economic real-

---

88. See Hans Anhum, "Mancipatio by Slaves in Ancient Roman Law?," *Acta Juridica (Essays in Honour of Ben Beinart)* (1976): 1–18.
89. Gardner, "Slavery and Roman Law," 419–20.
90. Watson, *Roman Slave Law*, 90.
91. Aristotle, *Politics*, 1253b34–1254a1.

ity. In many respects, the slave was a thinking automaton acting as an extension of the master. From this reality a whole series of practices flowed, such as appointing the slave as manager (*institor*) of all manner of activities, including cattle or slave merchant, innkeeper, miller, funeral undertaker, brothel manager, and so on; giving the slave a *peculium* (a specific amount of property or money) so that the slave could engage in market transactions directly; the ability to sue a master directly even if the transaction had been undertaken by his slave;[92] and even the limit to the amount sued up to the level of the slave's *peculium* (only when the action was undertaken without the knowledge of the master).[93] Throughout our point here is not simply that these various developments made it easier for masters to use slaves, but that the very nature of markets arose from and responded to the realities of slavery.

Conclusion: From Social Relations to Metaphorical Slaves

To sum up, we have argued that slavery determined the nature of Roman markets.[94] Slaves were indispensable for the production of surplus for the ruling class; they were ubiquitous in terms of tasks expected and in the mechanisms of Greek and Roman markets; they were the impetus for the definition of absolute private property, which was defined as a relationship between a human being (*dominus*) and a human being that had been reduced to a thing (*res*); they signal another dimension of abstraction related to coinage and provide the inescapable context of philosophy; and they were seen as the hands of the master, as self-acting automatons who could undertake the bulk of market activities as though they were the master.

We have restricted the analysis of this chapter to the economic role of the slave-relation, although much more can be said—as we will do in the chapter on the mode of *régulation*. At a social level, the ubiquity and sheer normality of slavery meant that social relations became thoroughly mediated. Even more, this mediation also appears at a metaphorical level, if not in human consciousness, literature, lin-

---

92. The *peculium* also meant that the slave could not alienate the master's property, but only the *peculium*. Clearly, the *peculium* served to protect the master's property.
93. For detail, see Watson, *Roman Slave Law*, 90–101.
94. We have consciously avoided comparisons with slavery in the United States, which is common in much of the secondary literature. Although insights may be gained, the risk is that such comparison can skew analysis of the ancient world. However, our argument that the slave-relation is an institutional form that can be recalibrated in distinct regimes and modes of production would provide a way for understanding the economic role of slavery in different contexts.

guistic forms, and even religions produced at the time. Such was the saturation that slaves need no longer be actually present, for mediation itself became central to the way people thought and behaved. Hence our decision to name this institutional form: the slave-relation.

5

Regimes, or, Dealing with Resistance

Thus far, our analysis has been mostly synchronic. This is as it should be for economic reconstructions since they concern longer term patterns, which endure through day-to-day events. But now we turn to more synchronic matters where regimes come into their own. To recap: a regime is a constellation of institutional forms in which one form becomes dominant over the others. A regime is usually an effort at and signal of *relative* stability, entailing compromises and control (both ideological and physical). In the previous chapters, we have identified four institutional forms: subsistence survival, *polis-chōra*, tenure, and the slave-relation. Out of these forms, we identify three combinations as regimes: the slave regime, dominated by the slave-relation; the colonial regime, dominated by *polis-chōra*; and the land regime, dominated by tenure in which peasants were tied to a specific location (*origo*). The difference between the slave and colonial regimes is regional more than temporal, for they operated at the same time in different parts of the Greek and especially Roman era. In particular, the colonial regime held sway in Syria-Palestine during the complex formation of Christianity. Only later did what we call the land regime come to the fore, marked by the colonate. In this case, tenure was the dominant institutional form, subordinating both *polis–chōra* and the slave-relation.

Why not the market, patronage, and the household, the focus of so many studies of the Greco-Roman era? The market we have located as part of the slave-relation, for slavery—economically, socially, and politically—determined the nature of markets. In other words, the market was a byproduct of the need to acquire a steady stream of slaves, providing one of the logistical mechanisms for doing so. The subordination of patronage to other institutional forms may surprise some, for patronage, with its attendant honor-shame dynamic (if not the infamous "status" championed by Weber and Finley among others), seemed to play a significant role among the Romans, if not in the Mediterranean as a whole.[1] However, we have argued that honor-shame and its attendant patronage was mostly the preserve of the obscenely wealthy and politically powerful, as well as criminal gangs (and in our day, some academics). This means it finds a proper place in discussions of the household, particularly that of the *polis*. For this reason, patronage forms part of the *polis-chōra* institutional form. And we have not identified the household as an institutional form in its own right. Initially, we had planned to do so[2] but it soon became clear that the households in question bifurcated along the lines of the distinction between *polis* and *chōra*. It was then a small step to see the different types of households as part of the institutional forms of subsistence survival and *polis-chōra*. We also seek to resist the common notion that the household was the basic economic unit of the ancient world, an assertion that dates back not merely to origins of "household archaeology," but back much further to the *oikos* debate itself.[3] The implicit moral and indeed theological undertones of such an assertion should not be missed.

1. Saller, *Personal Patronage Under the Early Empire*; Malina and Neyrey, "Honor and Shame in Luke-Acts"; Crook, "Honor, Shame, and Social Status Revisited."
2. Especially since it was identified as such in the economics of ancient Southwest Asia in Boer, *Sacred Economy*, 82–104.
3. Wilk and Rathje, "Household Archaeology"; Neyrey, "Managing the Household"; Osiek and Balch, *Families in the New Testament World*; Saller, "Pater Familias, Mater Familias"; Saller, "Household and Gender"; Sivertsev, "The Household Economy"; Assaf Yasur-Landau, Jennie R. Ebeling, and Laura B. Mazow, eds., *Household Archaeology in Ancient Israel and Beyond* (Leiden: Brill, 2011); Berlin, "Household Judaism." For the oikos debate, see the chapter on theory.

The Ghost of Subsistence Survival

I am afraid the peasantry will strike me down.[4]

A little more should be said on why we do not find that subsistence survival at any time was able to establish itself as the main institutional form in a distinct regime, which would then be a subsistence regime. In such a regime the primarily allocative nature of subsistence survival dominated with a focus on agricultural production and reallocation determined socially by the dynamics of the rural household and the village community. Apart from the risk mitigation entailed with practices of crop-growing and animal husbandry, it also contained internal patterns of exploitation (by big peasants) that were in tension with the allocative drive. However, left to its own devices, a subsistence regime was able to contain these extractive tendencies, as also the hovering presence of other institutional forms.[5] The last time a subsistence regime held sway for a considerable period was during the long economic "crisis" in the few centuries at the turn of the first millennium (on this period and its relevance for the Greek articulation of the slave regime, see below).

By the time of the classical era (fifth century BCE), a subsistence regime was no longer able to assert itself. This may seem like a grim situation in which rural laborers were unable to make the most of a period of sustained crisis and break away from external exploitation by one or more of the other largely extractive institutional forms. At the same time, we argue that subsistence survival was the persistent form of resistance inside the other three regimes, a ghost that refused to disappear. Indeed, we propose that since it was the institutional form that was primarily allocative, the slave, colonial, and land regimes may be understood as efforts to deal with and negate the constitutive resistance of subsistence survival.[6]

We draw the category of constitutive resistance from Antonio Negri and his collaborators. The main point of this theory is that resistance does not take place in response to oppressive power but is constitutive of that power: "Even though common use of the term might suggest

---

4. *EA* 77; in William Moran, *The Amarna Letters* (Baltimore: Johns Hopkins University Press, 1992), 148.
5. For a full explication of the subsistence regime in the context of ancient Southwest Asia, see Boer, *Sacred Economy*, 195–202. It was able to sideline the institutional forms of patronage, estates, and tribute-exchange.
6. Many are the proposals for the origins of slavery (or what we call the slave regime) but none have seen it in this light.

the opposite—that resistance is a response or reaction—*resistance is primary with respect to power.*"[7] The real driving force of history is precisely this constitutive resistance to which extractive economic forces and oppressive political powers must constantly adapt and attempt new modes of containment. In other words the dominant and driving reality is precisely this resistance, which can never be contained and harnessed by the powers that be—hence the efforts by the latter at ever-new ways of attempting to do so. The slave regime, colonial regime, and the land regime may thereby be seen as efforts to overcome and control the resistance of subsistence survival.

Negri develops the theory of constitutive resistance from his earlier discovery of *operaismo* (workerism) in relation to capitalism. In this case working class resistance is both outside and against capitalism. While it can never be absorbed by capitalism, and while it holds out the perpetual threat of subversion and revolution, its sheer creativity is also constitutive of capitalism for the forces of the latter constantly need to adapt and find ways to deal with resistance. The idea and practice of *operaismo* was first developed in Italy in two journals by Negri and his comrades, *Red Notebooks* (*Quaderni Rossi*, 1961–65) and *Working Class* (*Classe Operaia*, 1963–66). Negri explains later:

> *Operaismo* builds on Marx's claim that capital reacts to the struggles of the working class; the working class is active and capital reactive. Technological development: Where there are strikes, machines will follow. 'It would be possible to write a whole history of the inventions made since 1830 for the sole purpose of providing capital with weapons against working-class revolt' (*Capital*, Vol. 1, Chapter 15, Section 5). Political development: The factory legislation in England was a response to the working class struggle over the length of the working day. 'Their formulation, official recognition and proclamation by the State were the result of a long class struggle' (*Capital*, Vol. 1, Chapter 10, Section 6). *Operaismo* takes this as its fundamental axiom: the struggles of the working class *precede* and *prefigure* the successive re-structurations of capital.[8]

---

7. Michael Hardt and Antonio Negri, *Multitude: War and Democracy in the Age of Empire* (New York: Penguin, 2004), 64. See further pp. 64–91 for a brief account of the way such a perspective changes the way one understands history since the sixteenth century.

8. Antonio Negri and Michael Hardt, "Marx's Mole is Dead! Globalisation and Communication," *Eurozine*, February 13 (2002), http://www.eurozine.com/articles/2002-02-13-hardtnegri-en.html. For an excellent account of the development of the theory and practice of *operaismo*, see Yann Moulier, "Introduction," in *The Politics of Subversion: A Manifesto for the Twenty-First Century*, 1–44 (Cambridge: Polity, 2005). Later, Negri would develop the idea in relation to feminist and other movements in late capitalism, the biblical book of Job, and in terms of the common and the multitude. Antonio Negri, *The Porcelain Workshop: For a New Grammar of Politics* (Los Angeles: Semiotext(e), 2008), 91–125; Antonio Negri, *The Labor of Job: The Biblical Text as a Parable of Human Labor*,

Immediately a potential problem arises: how can a theory specifically developed with workers in the context of capitalism be applied to the ancient world? *Carefully* is the obvious answer, for the principle of constitutive resistance is applicable to many different contexts in time and place, albeit sensitive to specific issues and data. At the same time, this adaptation requires the constant awareness called a narrative of difference in which the theory itself always maintains the awareness of the differences and similarities between distinct times and places (and modes of production), and even more importantly does so through an account of how these differences manifest themselves through historical narrative.

The Slave Regime

A slave is a living tool, just as a tool is an inadequate slave.[9]

The slave regime is the first that sought to respond to the constitutive resistance of subsistence survival. Within this regime the three institutional forms of subsistence survival, *polis-chōra*, and tenure were subordinated to the slave-relation. It would be tempting to suggest that the slave regime was dominant only during the periods of high slavery, in the fifth and fourth centuries BCE in many parts of Greece, and over the second century BCE to the second century CE of Roman hegemony (at times restricted to the first century BCE). The criterion in these periods then becomes quantitative, determined by the sheer numbers of slaves in the economic system. By contrast, we argue that the slave regime can be found from the fifth century BCE to the third century CE, when Diocletian's decree formally established the colonate. This is clearly an issue of the *longue durée,* covering some eight centuries.

The reason for the persistence of the slave regime is that it involved much more than quantitative factors. Ste. Croix provides the initial insight: slaves provided the main source of surplus for the ruling class, which we now translate into the realities of the slave regime. In other words, when slavery provided the primary means of surplus, the slave

trans. Matteo Mandarini (Durham: Duke University Press, 2009); Hardt and Negri, *Multitude: War and Democracy in the Age of Empire*, 41–45; Antonio Negri, *Time for Revolution*, trans. Matteo Mandarini (London: Continuum, 2003); Michael Hardt and Antonio Negri, *Commonwealth* (Cambridge, Massachusetts: Belknap, 2009); Antonio Negri and Anne Dufourmantelle, *Negri on Negri*, trans. M. B. DeBevoise (New York: Routledge, 2004), 11–13, 149–50; Antonio Negri, *Empire and Beyond*, trans. Ed Emery (Cambridge: Polity Press, 2008), 225–61.

9. Aristotle, *Nicomachean Ethics*, trans. Harris Rackham, Loeb Classical Library (Cambridge: Harvard University Press, 1934), VIII.xi.6.

regime was in place. Further, this dominance entailed the determination of markets in the Greco-Roman world, the telltale signal of which being the invention of the legal definition of private property by the Roman jurors of the second century BCE. This moment was also the crystallization of a longer process in which a new level of abstraction arose, for now abstract value could be attached to a human being, but only insofar as this human being was assumed to be an object (*res*). We add here the mediation of social relations entailed with slavery, as well as the metaphorization of slavery in all levels of thought, philosophy, literature, art, and religion. When this complex was in full flight, it dominated and infiltrated the other institutional forms and produced the slave regime.

Greek Slavery: Valorizing the Big Peasant

The initial shape of the slave regime appeared in Greece in the fifth century after it emerged from the "dark age" of the late second millennium BCE to the early centuries of the first millennium.[10] Mycenaean forms of power and civilization "collapsed" in the twelfth century BCE and the ensuing "crisis" lasted well into the tenth century, although it was not until the eighth or even seventh century BCE that anything like the classical Greece as we know it began to appear. This development was by no means isolated, for the "crisis" also characterized ancient Southwest Asia. Larger powers crumbled and the signs of their power went with them, with nothing to take their place until the Neo-Assyrians emerged late in the tenth century BCE. That story is not our concern here, but the period of "crisis" is.

The dark age of Greece happened at the same time but its effects lasted longer, well into the eighth century BCE. This period is usually characterized as one of economic decline, population decrease, regionalism, and local production and consumption. But this is to take the perspective of the ruling classes, whose traces dominate the archaeological record. Widespread destruction of ruling class centers, eager participation in such destruction by disgruntled peasants with very long memories, as well as the helpful marauders, indicate a rather different situation. This was no collapse or crisis for the majority of rural laborers for whom the process of putting the ruling class out

---

10. Anthony Snodgrass, *The Dark Age of Greece: An Archaeological Survey of the 11th to 8th Centuries BC* (Edinburgh: Edinburgh University Press, 2000); James Whitley, *Style and Society in Dark Age Greece: The Changing Face of a Pre-literate Society 1100–700 BC* (Cambridge: Cambridge University Press, 2003).

of its misery was a pleasant task indeed. All the indications are that subsistence survival dominated during this period, so much so that a subsistence regime was the norm. Crucially during this period, two important inventions appeared (as is characteristic with subsistence regimes): the process of producing iron and, later, the first alphabet. The second claim needs a little further justification, for the Greeks are known to have drawn their inspiration from the Phoenicians. However, the Phoenicians used what is called an *abjad* (the word is drawn from the first letters of the Arabic script and their assumed order) in which the characters represent consonants. By contrast in an alphabet, the characters represent consonants and vowels.[11] This the Greeks invented during their "dark age."

Paradoxically, inventions like these are often used by new ruling classes keen to establish another form of exploitation. This is precisely what happened when the classical age of Greece began to emerge. However, our main point is that the development of the slave regime functioned as a response to the preceding subsistence regime. It was simply inconceivable for an aspiring ruling class to leave peasants to their own devices, focusing on their regions, on livable levels of self-subsistence, and on the production of small surpluses for the inevitable lean season. Some testosterone-charged Greeks took a direct path and enslaved whole peoples, such as the Spartan subjection of their Messenian neighbors or the Thessalian *penestai*, the *klarotai* of Crete, and the *mariandynoi* of Heraclea Pontica.[12] Others took a more indirect path to enslavement, albeit with a double twist. Rather than direct state-sponsored subjection of a conquered people to a position of slavery, they developed a very limited form of democracy—restricted to adult males who were resident in the confines of the *polis* and its *chōra*. This is of course a political form but we are interested in its economic dimensions. Rather than forcing slaves to work in estates with the landlords residing in the *polis*, the landholders tended to stay with the land and use a smaller number of slaves. To be sure, a few of the older ruling class had larger holdings and thereby more slaves[13] but the majority were relatively small farmers.

11. Peter Daniels, "The Study of Writing Systems," in *The World's Writing Systems*, eds. Peter Daniels and William Bright, 3–17 (New York: Oxford University Press, 1996), 4.
12. We do not enter the debate here as to whether this was "full slavery." Ste. Croix calls them "serfs" rather than slaves, but they were forced to work in mainly in agriculture and subject to the control and direction of the minority Spartans.
13. For example, Xenophon's *Oikonomikos* (which was translated by Cicero and cited by Columella) is a treatise on the "good"—that is, morally "sound" and economically prudent—management of the large estate of a fictionalized rich Athenian of the turn of the fifth and fourth centuries.

Now we come to the double twist. To begin with, Greek democracy demanded a level of involvement by the males in question that meant they could not remain with their farms all year. Participation was expected in the assembly, as was service in the army, in liturgies and festivals, and in many other civic activities. This was possible only with slave labor in the fields. The much-vaunted Greek "freedom" and "democracy" and the glories of its political life—let alone the economic requirements of such a life—could happen only with the economic deployment of slaves. Earlier, we argued earlier that the *polis* could not exist without its *chōra*, and that this symbiotic relationship was the basis of Greek expansion. Now we add that the *chōra* in question had to be worked by slaves in order to enable the *polis* to function at all. This entailed the development of slave markets, which provided the logistical means to acquire slaves.

The second twist is that the type of farmer valorized also shifted. The farmer in question may have seemed like a relatively small one, but only in relation to the old wealth of a ruling class that was disgruntled with the development of Greek democracy. In fact, the type of farmer held up as a model was the big peasant who exploited others within subsistence survival. We find the beginning of such a valorization in Hesiod's *Works and Days*,[14] and by the fifth century BCE this model big peasant came to be seen as the norm. Only such a farmer could afford the requirements of service in the *polis*. Let us give the example of hoplite service, in which they had to supply their own armor and weapons, be attended by a slave or two, and be away from the farm during the seasonal warfare. Indeed, the much-vaunted phalanx symbolized the solidarity of the big peasant, who was the true citizen of the Greek *polis*. And these big peasant citizens were also not so keen on other practices within subsistence survival, such as field shares and reallocation of shares, tasks, and produce. In sum, the formation of the Greek classical age, especially in places like Athens and Corinth, may be seen as a novel response to the constitutive resistance of subsistence survival—a response perpetrated by the big peasants.

Roman Slavery

Roman slavery came late on the scene, as indeed did the Romans as

Xenophon, "Oeconomicus," in *Memorabilia, Oeconomicus, Symposium, Apology, Loeb Classical Library,* 381–558 (Cambridge: Harvard University Press, 2013).

14. Hesiod, "Works and Days."

such. Yet, they produced the most long-lasting and—relative to the context—one of the largest projects in the ancient Mediterranean world. Never enthusiasts for the limited exercise of Greek democracy, they developed the slave regime more extensively and efficiently than the Greeks were ever able to do. Politically, the Roman state may have bent and creaked as it adjusted to the demands of the common people, handing out consolation prizes that were wrapped up to look much better than they actually were. Through it all, the ruling class held onto power and ensured they were not replaced. This reality enabled a thorough transformation of the Italian economic landscape, and then in a more gradual process much of the rest of the empire when it was attained. The effect on the Italian peninsula was to roll back as far as possible the persistent small farmers and their local version of subsistence survival.

The angles of attack were multiple, but four stood out. The first was the constant demand of military service—initially on the Italian peninsula with its Carthaginian and Celtic invasions—along with the local wars and conflicts as Rome established its dominance. The side effect of the local conflicts provides a second and unwitting attack, which was the devastation wrought by war. The third was far more substantial: the conversion of significant portions of the Italian landscape into estates (the "villa system"), which entailed taking over *ager publicus* and driving rural farmers off the land they farmed.[15] The peasants went to more marginal areas, drifted into Rome, made the most of increasing military demands, or, especially under Julius Caesar and Augustus, were resettled as colonists in other parts of the empire. Yet, the effect was the same: their preferred mode of subsistence survival was undermined. As the second century BCE opened out and as ever more slaves were dragged from the latest battlefield, estates covered more and more of Italy—especially in the lower, fertile areas close to waterways for transport. The reasons for such a shift are many, but one factor at least played a significant role: this was the transformation of Rome from a provincial town to an imperial city with an exponential leap in the produce to which it felt entitled. In this context, slave-worked estates provided higher yields (up to fifty percent) compared to taxes from rural villages and their farmers. Rather than estates run by the state itself, they tended to be the preserve of the ruling elite, who also felt it a civic duty to display their wealth ostentatiously in the

15. Hopkins, *Conquerors and Slaves*, 1–74.

city itself. And this brings us to the fourth angle of attack on subsistence survival. While the preferred form of labor on the estates was by slaves, tenure was also deployed. It was not uncommon to find estates with slaves and indentured laborers, if not occasional hired labor when demands were high during sowing and reaping. But the point is that tenure too was a mechanism—through eviction, displacement, debt, coercion, or violence—by which rural laborers were tied into situations of dependence.

The nature of the labor expected of slaves, especially in terms of its sheer range, has already been covered. But here we address the perpetual debate over slave labor and tenure on the estates. Was it predominantly slave labor, tenure, or (a rarer position) hired labor? The reality was a complex mix.[16] Indeed, the model of regimes that we have developed is able to deal with this debate in a way that takes into the account the variety of practices. The slave-relation may have been the predominant institutional form in the slave regime, particularly during the massive influx of slaves and the thorough transformation of the Italian peninsula and then the occupied territories of the empire. But within this regime the institutional form of tenure may also be found alongside subsistence survival and *polis-chōra*, albeit in subordinate positions. Thus, we find tenure alongside slavery, but also rural farmers continuing to find space for subsistence survival and the development of the relations between *polis* and *chōra* (Rome being the preeminent example).

The Colonial Regime

Classical civilization . . . was inherently *colonial* in character.[17]

The second major constellation was the colonial regime. The reason for naming it as such is that it tended to appear in the areas conquered and occupied by Rome. Here the spatial re-production entailed with *polis* and *chōra* was the determining factor, with the other institutional forms sinking to subordinate positions. They were now geared to deal with the expectation that the *chōra*—in its colonial rather than classical Greek shape—supplied the local and more distant *poleis* (in the cases of Rome, Alexandria, and other comparable centers). The *chōra*, of course, was the zone for subsistence survival agriculture. In marginal zones

16. Banaji, *Theory as History*, 104–7.
17. Anderson, *Passages from Antiquity to Feudalism*, 28.

such as the southern Levant subsistence survival had often found space to breathe, even with the periodic tramp of armies on the move to more desirable areas. Home-grown great powers did not arise in this part of the world with the "little kingdoms"[18] of Israel and Judah (and the later Hasmoneans) barely causing a ripple on the world stage. But this did not mean that the "big kingdoms" left the area and its rural laborers alone. These laborers may have flourished, in subsistence survival terms, during the three centuries or so of "crisis" (see above) at the turn of the first millennium BCE. But the Neo-Assyrians, Persians, and above all the Greeks had their own ideas as to what should be done to undermine the resilience of subsistence survival.

We pick up the story with the foundations of the colonial regime in the wake of Alexander of Macedon's conquests. New *poleis* were established and peopled with decommissioned soldiers and locals, especially the various members of the ruling class who were keen to make the most of the new imperial order for the sake of their life's calling of self-aggrandizement and the exercise of power.[19] Other places were transformed into *poleis*, with the requisite "civilized" appurtenances such as temples, theaters, gymnasia, slaves, and the Greek language. Not only did the "city become an instrument of empire"[20] but it also meant a new economic reality. To be sure, the local people had been required to provide the large Persian administration with internal plunder, euphemistically known as taxes. From this perspective, it may seem as though the overlords had changed but that the demands remained the same. However, the spatial reconfiguration in terms of *poleis* and the colonized *chōra* meant that the ever-multiplying new centers demanded provision. The lesser lights—the Diadochi—who inherited and squabbled over Alexander's conquests continued to establish even more *poleis*. The Seleucids in particular did so across their vast western Asian realm, although the Ptolemies encouraged the growth of Alexandria in Egypt to become one of the preeminent cities in the ancient

18. "Little kingdom" is the term used by those in ancient Southwest Asia, and defines a single territorial community or collection of close-knit communities, with security depending on mountains, the sea, or the desert. Mario Liverani, "Ville et campagne dans le royaume d'Ugarit: Essai d'analyse economique," in *Societies and Languages of the Ancient Near East: Studies in Honour of I. M. D'iakonoff*, eds. Muhammad Dandamaev, et al., 250–58 (Warminster: Aris and Phillips, 1982), 250; Mario Liverani, *Israel's History and the History of Israel*, trans. Chiara Peri and Philip Davies (London: Equinox, 2005), 7.

19. Plutarch famously mentions that Alexander founded more than 70 cities, although the number has more to do with ideal numbers than reality. Approximately twenty "Alexandrias" can be identified today. Plutarch, *Moralia IV*, trans. Frank Cole Babbitt, Loeb Classical Library (Cambridge: Harvard University Press, 1936), 328E.

20. Freyne, "Cities of the Hellenistic and Roman Periods," 30.

world. And during Ptolemaic control of the southern Levant, Tyre and Sidon were transformed into Greek cities, along with Ptolemais (Acco), Philoteria (Beth Yerach), and Scythopolis in Galilee.

The Romans came, saw, conquered, and realized that the colonial system in place was already working quite well. Under their various puppets, more *poleis* were established or refounded. Wider afield, Corinth, Carthage, and Philippi were rebuilt as Roman cities with the necessary bathhouses, aqueducts, and amphitheaters, while in Galilee under the Herods, we find Sepphoris, Tiberias, Caesaria Philippi, Caesaria Maritima, and the Dekapolis.[21] One correlate of this rapid increase in the number of *poleis* was the increase in settlements in areas that were widely regarded as pestilential—precisely those that were well watered and fertile. Here disease was more endemic, which explains the relative absence of earlier settlements. However, by the first century of the common era when the colonial regime came into its own, such areas began to see significant growth in small settlements. Less a sign of relative prosperity, this pattern was due to increased pressure to supply the *poleis*. For example, various estimates for Galilee alone indicate that settlements in low-lying areas increased between 60 and 142 percent. Clearly, subsistence survival agriculture was being bent and reshaped to the new spatial and economic configuration. There was yet another shift, the model of which may well have been provided by Ptolemaic Egypt. As the Zenon archive reveals, all of the lands under Ptolemaic control were required to supply the major centers in Egypt itself. Although grain was sequestered only in emergencies, other produce—such as salted fish—was required for Egyptian consumption.[22] But the demands of Rome itself were of another order, manifesting at this empire-wide level the connection between *polis* and *chōra*. As we indicated earlier, a population of above one million, with the *frumentationes* and grain for those not so supplied, demanded supplies from across the empire. Once the eastern Mediterranean was conquered, Egypt itself became a major source, but anywhere would do if grain could be found.

The Roman transformation of cities turned them also into means of managing and pacifying the local populations. Violence and terror were tried methods, as we find in Syria-Palestine after the two revolts of 70 CE and 132–35 CE, if not in the everyday workings of the local *poleis*. But alongside coercion is persuasion, as Machiavelli knew so

21. Freyne, "Cities of the Hellenistic and Roman Periods."
22. Freyne, *Galilee from Alexander the Great to Hadrian*, 173.

well.[23] For the Romans, this entailed enticing the local ruling class to become part of the administrative structures of occupied territories for which the cities played a key role. The ultimate interest of the Romans was for the ever elusive *pax Romana,* since it enabled a much smoother operation of the economic patterns of exploitation and expropriation. As we stressed earlier, a symbiotic and integrated relationship of *polis* and *chōra* was the most desirable, precisely because it enabled more efficient mechanisms of economic exploitation. In other words the debate is not over symbiosis or conflict, for this is a false opposition.[24] Instead, it was simultaneously symbiosis and economic conflict, or indeed economic exploitation (and its attendant inequality and conflict) through integration.

Two questions remain: how did the institutional forms of slavery and tenure work within the colonial regime? And what was the regional and temporal spread of this regime? In this case, whatever would work to ensure the patterns of exploitation for the sake of the *polis* were deployed. If rural laborers could be coerced into producing goods for the local *polis,* well and good. This would work if the villages in question were within enforceable distance. For example, within a ten kilometer radius around Sepphoris in Galilee lie villages such as Nazareth, Kefar Shikhin, Karm-er-Ras, Kafr Kanna, Khirbet Ruma, Yodefat-Jotapata, and Khirbet Qana. Even with the basic pathways between them, the sheer proximity meant that these villages could be pressed to produce goods for Sepphoris itself. At the same time, the ubiquity of slaves in everyday life meant that slave labor would appear not only in the *poleis* themselves, but also in the fields of the estates that can be found even in the occupied territories. Although we discuss the land regime in more detail below, it should be noted here that Egypt was the prime instance of an estate system that included not only slaves, but also tenants who worked in a village context. As for Syria-Palestine, the rearrangement of the production of villages in the vicinity of local *poleis* indicates a similar process, albeit determined initially by the needs of the *polis* in question.

The second question concerns the regional and temporal spread of the colonial regime. Since our interest is in the eastern Mediterranean, bending towards the area in which Christianity first arose, we pro-

---

23. Machiavelli, *The Prince* (Cambridge: Cambridge University Press, 1988).
24. For example, Jensen's approach is rather simplistic, postulating that rapid change is bad for the "lower orders" and stability is good. His conclusion—that the situation in Galilee was quite stable, perhaps growing, and therefore good for the rural laborers—simply misses the point that stability and symbiosis enable greater exploitation. Jensen, "Rural Galilee and Rapid Changes."

pose that the colonial regime dominated in such an area if not in most other parts of the eastern Mediterranean. A major reason is the immediate history of Greek colonization, which the Romans were more than happy to adopt, albeit with modifications. Another reason is that it worked quite well alongside the slave regime in other parts of the empire. So we find that on the Italian peninsula, if not in Greece, the slave regime was dominant. It also featured in the western expansion of the empire. Perfected in Italy, it was transplanted across the western Mediterranean and into Europe. Here too the bulk of the provincial ruling class that rose to power with the Principate tended to live. And here Latin was spoken, eventually to become the basis of many of the European romance language. By contrast, in the eastern colonized areas the colonial regime was preferred, during the very same period. In short, they complimented one another for the sake of the economic structures of an empire that had to rely on its agricultural base to function at all.

The Land Regime

We have argued that both the slave and colonial regimes may be seen as ever-changing responses to the determined constitutive resistance of subsistence survival. In this light, the third regime we identify signals the eventual failure of both the slave and colonial regimes to contain such constitutive resistance.[25] This is what we call the land regime, which comes into its own only with the colonate in the third century CE. Why the land regime? This regime marks a fundamental shift from a focus on labor to land. The shift from the slave regime was more substantial for it was clearly focused on labor (albeit labor reduced to a thing and then given an abstract value). The colonial regime was in some respects closer, for it was driven by the reproduction and reconfiguration of space. It was a smaller step to a regime in which labor was fixed to a particular place (*origo*) with the consequent restriction of movement.

The core of the land regime was the colonate to which we now turn in more detail. The determining institutional form was tenure, concerning which we identified three conditions during the sway of the slave and colonial regimes: 1. Village communities and their laborers under no tenure; 2. Lifetime tenure on condition of military service

---

25. For an excellent account of the rolling crises that effected the slave regime in particular, see Anderson, *Passages from Antiquity to Feudalism*, 76–93.

and subject to the will of the ruler; 3. Tenure for either (a) for a given number of years with the option of renewal, or (b) for an unspecified period, with ejection and change of terms possible at any time. The desire of the ruling classes was clearly to reduce as many peasants as possible to the third category. Estates and debt may have played a role, but the consummate effort appears with the colonate and thereby the land regime.

Colonate

The paths to the colonate differed depending on the many regions of the empire, and our systematic exposition risks simplifying the sheer complexity of regional arrangements. However, we are committed to discerning deeper patterns beneath the chatter of detail—and the colonate is one such pattern.[26] This shift to the colonate took some centuries to bring into being, and its "progress" went at various rates depending on the region, but it was the source of yet another form of consistent disruption to the institutional form of subsistence survival.

The key moment was the recognition and consolidation of this new situation by the dramatic reform of Diocletian late in the third century CE. The ostensible purpose was reform of the Roman taxation system through a thorough census (to enable effective poll taxes), but the deeper effect was to lock in—theoretically—the whole of the working agricultural population throughout the empire, to which end a whole series of subsequent laws were aimed.[27] An individual tenant, or, rather a tenant and his extended family was henceforth tied to the farm or plot under rent, was entered into the census in such a category, and would remain so on a hereditary basis. They began to be designated in the tax rolls as *colonus originalis, originarius,* or *adscripticius,* and the new abstract noun, *colonatus,* began to be used.[28] More significantly, individuals who lived in villages (the vast majority) were tied to those villages, even if they also farmed some land under tenure. In some cases, such as Egypt and Palestine, peasants who farmed only under tenure were enrolled in villages. In sum, the result was:

26. Inspired by Igor M. Diakonoff, "Slaves, Helots and Serfs in Early Antiquity," in *Wirtschaft und Gesellschaft im alten Vorderasien,* eds. János Harmatta and Geörgy Komoróczy, 45–78 (Budapest: Akadémiai Kiadó, 1976), 56; Wallerstein, *The Modern World-System I,* 10.
27. In Judea and Galilee, such an arrangement is assumed in the Mishnah by the third century CE. Kloppenborg, "The Growth and Impact of Agricultural Tenancy," 32–36.
28. Pieter Willem De Neeve, *Colonus: Private Farm-Tenancy in Roman Italy During the Republic and the Early Principate* (Amsterdam: J.C. Gieben, 1984), 121.

1. Peasants not exclusively under tenure were enrolled in the census under the name of their village and so tied to the village.

2. Peasants only under tenure fell into two categories: a) in some areas, such as Palestine, Egypt, and Gaul, they were tied to their villages; b) in other areas, such as Asia Minor, the Greek islands, Thrace, and Illyricum, they were listed under the landlord's census return and tied to the actual plot rented. Both of these types were known as *adscriptii*.[29]

Debate continues as to why these transformations took place. Although it is not our task to enter this debate,[30] we stress the complex overlays of practices in relation to the dominant colonial regime in this part of the world. The *polis-chōra* interaction, which was the key to the colonial regime, sought to lock the villages of the *chōra* into the realms of the *poleis*. In this light should we understand the relative concentrations of production in some places close by *poleis*. For example, Galilee saw the development of so-called "industrial" processes relating to wool, wine, olive oil, pottery, stoneware, lamps, and even glass production.[31] Thus, the villages closest to the *poleis*—such as Shikhin, Yode-

29. Ste. Croix, *Class Struggle*, 250. Landlords and "head lessees" were of course not so tied.
30. As a sample of the wide range of opinions: a response to the combined problems of a growing resistance from slaves and the pressures of ever larger estates; the relatively higher cost of breeding slaves in comparison with the earlier cheapness of prisoners-of-war; rolling economic crises in the later empire; the large numbers of "barbarians" settled within the empire; disjointed estates that made tenants more viable; inefficiency of peasant agriculture; land allotments to army veterans; fiscal constraints for an imperial government seeking to secure its tax, with the by-product of tying farmers to their land; a favoring of landowners who wished to secure hired labor; a changed tax system that was determined primarily by the concept of *origo* (specific land or estate). Elena Mikhaĭlovna Shtaerman, *Krizis rabovladel'cheskogo stroia v zapadnykh provintsiiakh Rimskoĭ imperii (Italiâ)* (Moscow: "Nauka", 1957); Anderson, *Passages from Antiquity to Feudalism*, 93–95; Jones, *Roman Economy*, 293–307; Bruce Frier, "Law, Technology, and Social Change: The Equipping of Italian Farm Tenancies," *Zeitschrift der Savigny-Stiftung für Rechtsgeschichte, Romanistische Abteilung* 96 (1979): 204–28; Guiseppe Giliberti, *Servus quasi colonus: forme non tradizionali di organizzazione del lavoro nella societ'a romana* (Naples: E. Jovene, 1981); Guiseppe Giliberti, *Servi della terra: ricerche per una storia del colonato* (Turin: Giappichelli, 1999); Ste. Croix, *Class Struggle*, 226–59; De Neeve, *Colonus*, 122–74; C. R. Whittaker, "Circe's Pigs: From Slavery to Serfdom in the Later Roman Empire," *Slavery and Abolition* 8, no. 1 (1987): 88–122; P.A. Brunt, *The Fall of the Roman Republic and Related Essays* (Oxford: Clarendon, 1988), 240–80; Pascale Rosafio, "Slaves and *Coloni* in the Villa System," in *Landuse in the Roman Empire*, eds. Jesper Carlsen, Peter Ørsted, and Jens Erik Skydsgaard, 145–59 (Rome: "L'Erma" die Bretschneider, 1994); Jairus Banaji, *Agrarian Change in Late Antiquity: Gold, Labour and Aristocratic Dominance* (Oxford: Oxford University Press, 2001), 190–212; Banaji, *Theory as History*, 155–81; Cam Grey, "Contextualizing *Colonatus*: The *Origo* of the Late Roman Empire," *Journal of Roman Studies* 97 (2007): 155–75; Kehoe, *Law and the Rural Economy in the Roman Empire*, 163–72; Grey, "Slavery in the Late Roman World," 503–6; Kloppenborg, "Growth and Impact of Agricultural Tenancy," 51–52. Kloppenborg (61) somewhat strangely suggests—to bolster his argument for estates—that the colonate is not attested until the time of Constantine.
31. Freyne, *Galilee from Alexander the Great to Hadrian*; Fiensy, "Galilean Village," 173–76; Safrai, "Urbanization and Industry in Mishnaic Galilee"; Aviam, "Transformation from *Galil Ha-Goyim* to Jewish Galilee," 15–16; Strange, "Kefar Shikhin"; Mordechai Aviam, "Yodefat-Jotapata: A Jewish Galilean Town at the End of the Second Temple Period," in *Galilee in the Late Second Temple and Mishnaic Periods. Volume 2: The Archaeological Record from Cities, Towns, and Villages*, eds. David Fiensy and James

fat, Khirbet Qana, Kefar Ḥananya—had production facilities geared for the local *poleis* like Sepphoris and Tiberias. Further, the subordinate practices relating to tenure and estates in this part of the world were influenced by complex overlays from different directions (as we discussed in chapter 3). One practice followed in the wake of the Persians (and Seleucids), who deployed a system of tribute, taxation, and exchange—along with brutal enforcement—that sought to ensure as large a number of villages kept providing what they were supposed to provide. From the Egyptian direction, the elaborate system of estates developed by the Ptolemies included villages within them—a practice they also enacted when they held sway over Syria-Palestine. On top of all this came Roman preferences, although they initially liked what they saw and kept the former systems largely in place. The *polis* and its linked *chōra* was re-geared for yet more local *poleis*, as well as the demands from Rome. The Roman love for censuses tended towards an identification of people with place, so as to enable the significant increases in extraction of the middle and later Roman Empire. All of these forces served to intensify the tying of peasants to their villages so that by the time of Diocletian's decree, the identification of the *origo* as the village itself seemed quite logical and practical.

Overcoming Resistance

Three questions remain. First, what was the rate of extraction under tenure? On this matter, we must rely on calculations, for the only information available relates to flat or customary rates.[32] Oakman provides the most detailed calculations although these are necessarily speculative given the variables.[33] He begins with the proposal that the minimum amount of land needed to feed an adult (excluding land in fallow and land needed for tenure rent and taxes) was 0.6 hectares (1.5 acres). He arrives at an estimate that each adult would on average need 352 liters (10 bushels) of grain per year or 2,400 calories per day. Assuming that the average seed-to-yield ratio was 1:5, this means that one-fifth,

Strange, 109–26 (Minneapolis: Fortess, 2015); C. Thomas McCollough, "Khirbet Qana," in *Galilee in the Late Second Temple and Mishnaic Periods. Volume 2: The Archaeological Record from Cities, Towns, and Villages*, eds. David Fiensy and James Strange, 127–45 (Minneapolis: Fortess, 2015); David Adan-Bayewitz, "Kefar Ḥananya," in *Galilee in the Late Second Temple and Mishnaic Periods. Volume 2: The Archaeological Record from Cities, Towns, and Villages*, eds. David Fiensy and James Strange, 181–85 (Minneapolis: Fortess, 2015).

32. Thus, in ancient Southwest Asia the assumed level (from Uruk onwards) was usually one-third to one-half from palatine estates.

33. Oakman, *Jesus and the Economic Questions of His Day*, 59–72.

or 20 percent, was required for seed for the next sowing season. If one estimates other needs—such as fodder for livestock, reserves for the sake of exchanging for various goods and services, a Temple tithe (as in Palestine), which might fluctuate if it had to be converted into coinage, and the need for a surplus for a bad year, taxes and rents (imperial, local, and landlord)—the amount left over for feeding one's own immediate circle, clan, or village was rather small. Or, as Oakman concludes, what was left was between one-fifth and one-thirteenth for the actual use of the peasant.

Second, why not seek to reshape the colonial and slave regimes, given that they had already been in place for centuries, operating side by side throughout the empire? We identify two main reasons. First, as Anderson already pointed out many years ago,[34] classical European antiquity is notable for its technical stagnation. To be sure, scattered technological improvements can be found, such as rotary mills for grain, screw presses, developments in glass-blowing, refinements of heating systems, improvements of field drainage, and slightly more efficient weaving methods. However, there was no major collection of inventions that would enable a qualitative economic shift. When one has a mass of manual labor through slavery, there is no need for such developments. Further, the disproportion between *polis* and *chōra* meant that the much admired developments of the ancient *polis* relied on agricultural techniques that changed relatively little over the centuries in question. A key factor in all of this was the inescapable association of manual labor with a servile condition, a denigration that had profound effects on the function and nature of that labor, and removed interest in improving that labor. We would add that crucial inventions usually happen during times of "crisis," when subsistence survival dominates. The last such breakthroughs had happened before classical antiquity appeared on the scene with the invention of iron implements and the alphabet. The subsequent effort to suppress subsistence survival, at ideological, social, and economic levels, meant that any technological breakthrough was stifled. Second and at the same time, both the colonial and slave regimes were ultimately unable to squash the resistance of subsistence survival. Try as they might to reduce peasants to the most servile condition, these extractive regimes failed to achieve their aims. Unwilling laborers, either on slave estates or in villages required to supply a local or even imperial *polis,* are

---

34. Anderson, *Passages from Antiquity to Feudalism*, 26–27.

not only reluctant, finding all manner of quotidian resistance along-side ever new ways to revert to their preferred mode of existence.[35] In response, the land regime sought to find a new way to cut through this apparent "problem." The colonate was both the culmination of a centuries-long development and the beginning of a whole new series of steps to lock in peasants. Diocletian's decree may have tied peasants and estate laborers to their *origo*, but this required subsequent polic-ing and further measures to ensure that it was carried out. For exam-ple, in the early fourth century, Constantine instituted a law that any *coloni* who sought to escape their *origo* should be chained as slaves and fulfill their allotted tasks as slaves. This practice became widespread afterwards.[36] This law indicates that slavery continued both as an ide-ological framework and as an economic practice, for the slave-relation itself was part of the land regime, albeit now in a subordinate position. Thus, by 370 CE, agricultural slaves could not be sold without the land on which they were registered in the census.[37] Further, as Valentin-ian I (364–75 CE) put it, *coloni* were seen not as slaves of a master, but as "slaves of their land."[38] Agricultural village laborers became *colonus quasi servus*. The crucial shift was to the land as *origo* with the attendant restriction on freedom of movement and thereby effort to control the agricultural laborers in question.

Third, why tie peasants to the land? The major reason again was the constitutive resistance of peasants to the impositions from without. This resistance took many forms, but the most threatening was move-ment away from land. This resulted in removing labor from land—an indication that the shortage of able-bodied labor remained a crucial issue, as it had done for millennia.[39] Land without labor was useless for those who did not work but needed the produce of the land for the life to which they had become accustomed.[40] Thus, the workers of land in village communities knew well the effects of removing their labor: they

---

35. Another later example of this resistance may be found in the sheer disaffection for the Roman Empire and disinterest in its collapse. As we noted in the first chapter, stiff penalties were insti-tuted for aiding the "enemy," as well as revolts and even "defections."
36. Kehoe, *Law and the Rural Economy in the Roman Empire*, 174.
37. Ste. Croix, *Class Struggle*, 255; Miroslava Mirkovic, *The Later Roman Colonate and Freedom* (Philadel-phia: American Philosophical Society, 1997), 29–30.
38. Kehoe, *Law and the Rural Economy in the Roman Empire*, 185.
39. Horsley calls this a form of "peasant strike." Horsley, "Social Movements in Galilee." For the con-stitutive role of the shortage of able-bodied labor, which was restricted to perhaps a decade and half of an adult who lived to the age of 30, see Jones, *Roman Economy*, 307; Ste. Croix, *Class Struggle*, 217; Davies, "Classical Greece: Production," 352; Boer, *Sacred Economy*, 228. Hopkins, with a focus on Italy, tries to have it both ways, stressing land and labor. Hopkins, *Conquerors and Slaves*, 6–8. Of course, one must take into account regional variations and the effects of disease, military con-scription, and incursions by hostile forces.

were willing to move and resettle if the burdens imposed became too much—disease, famine, onerous pressures of taxation, military service, requisitioned labor, or pressure for labor-intensive work.[41] For example, viticulture demanded four times the workers required for cereal and vegetable crops, and three times that demanded by olive cultivation.[42] Along with the increase in numbers of *poleis* and their consequent demands, the expansion of such labor-intensive activities saw governing authorities pressure peasants to move into fertile but disease-ridden lands—as we find with Palestine during the early Roman period when Herod and his offspring oversaw the construction of many *poleis* and lower-lying areas began to fill up with new settlements and village sizes increased. In these contexts, peasant removal of labor was a potent form of resistance.[43] The most telling signal of this tendency is "brigandage," although many forms of resistance appeared. For millennia, peasants had joined brigand groups, often by night while they worked the land by day. The ruling classes saw them as threatening "mountain men" and "nomads," gave them fictitiously archaicized names such as the Gutians, or became known as *'abiru*—in our day they would be called "terrorists."[44] By the Greco-Roman era, specific names of leaders appear, although we need to distinguish between brigand chiefs (such as John of Gischala) and royal pretenders (such as Simon bar Giora).[45] That they were sometimes village big men, draw-

---

40. The focus on land rather than labor is the basic mistake made by Pastor, *Land and Economy in Ancient Palestine*.

41. Ste. Croix, *Class Struggle*, 215–17. Even in Egypt, with the reclaimed Fayum under the Ptolemies, able labor remained in chronic short supply and peasants left the land frequently and revolted. Manning, "Hellenistic Egypt," 449.

42. Kloppenborg, "Growth and Impact of Agricultural Tenancy," 54–56.

43. In-between strategies included attacking agents of the landlord (Mark 12:2–8), resisting pressures to move into pestilential fertile lands (such as the new polis of Tiberias), and shifting from one form of tenure to another—as in the fourth and fifth centuries CE, when whole villages and *coloni* at times opted to place themselves under the patronage of a *dux* (local military commander), whose help would then be enlisted to resist the landlord's rent collectors or the local government's tax agents. See Ste. Croix, *Class Struggle*, 224–25.

44. "Throughout antiquity mountains preserved their reputation among the cultured urban elite as the haunt of the brigand, the barbarian and the savage, man and beast." Garnsey, Saller, and Goodman, *Roman Empire*, 26.

45. See further Josephus, *Bellum Judaicum*, 1.201–5; 2.56, 118, 427–48, 585–94, 652–53; 4.503–13, 529–34. Not only was Jesus crucified between two *lestai* (Mark 15:27, 32; Matt 27:38, 44; Luke 23:33, 39–43), but he accused the temple traffickers of turning it into a "robbers' cave" (Mark 11:17). Paul too mentions that he would at times fall victim to "bandits" (2 Cor 11:26). The most comprehensive studies remain Horsley and Hanson, *Bandits, Prophets, and Messiahs: Popular Movements in the Time of Jesus*; Richard Horsley, *Jesus and the Spiral of Violence: Popular Jewish Resistance in Roman Palestine* (Philadelphia, PA: Augsburg Fortress, 1992). See also Horsley, "Social Movements in Galilee"; Freyne, *Galilee from Alexander the Great to Hadrian*, 208–55; James Anderson, "The Impact of Rome on the Periphery: The Case of Palestina-Roman Period (63 BCE–324 CE)," in *The Archaeology of Society in the Holy Land*, ed. Thomas Levy, 446–68 (London: Leicester University Press, 1998); Peter Richardson and Douglas Edwards, "Jesus and Palestinian Social Protest: Archeological and Literary

ing on rural networks of support and using systems of hiding places found in many villages[46] only enhances the enmeshment of brigandage with this institutional form. This creativity required ever new efforts by the ruling class to curb peasant ingenuity and secure agricultural production, whether through military campaigns, censuses, estates, or the colonate in which a peasant was tied to the land and movement was severely restricted.

The colonate thereby formed the basis of the land regime. Its genealogy can be traced back to the third century BCE, with the institutional form of tenure finding a place in either the slave or colonial regimes. But it was only later that tenure came to dominate as the earlier regimes ran out of ways to respond to the constitutive resistance of subsistence survival. With the land regime, the institutional form of tenure determined the other forms. This reality makes sense of the continued presence of slaves, which more than one commentator has sought to emphasize,[47] if not the mindset in which the *coloni* themselves were often seen in terms of slaves. The solution to this argument is simple, for the slave-relation continued as a subordinate institutional form within the land regime. Further, the land regime did not suddenly do away with the relations between *polis* and *chōra*, for now this particular connection was recalibrated to fit into the new regime in which and its peasants became the determining feature.

Conclusion

We have proposed that the slave and colonial regimes existed side-by-side in different parts of the Roman empire, with the colonial regime being the norm in the eastern parts of the empire (including Syria-Palestine), or what we prefer to call the occupied territories. Only later, by the third century CE, did a substantial shift take place. As the former two regimes ran out of ways to contain the resistance of peasants

Perspectives," in *Handbook of Early Christianity: Social Science Approaches*, eds. Anthony Blasi, Jean Duhaime, and Paul-André Turcotte, 247–66 (Walnut Creek: Altamira, 2002); John Kloppenborg, "Unsocial Bandits," in *A Wandering Galilean: Essays in Honour of Seán Freyne*, eds. Zuleika Rodgers, Margaret Daly-Denton, and Anne Fitzpatrick McKinley, 451–84 (Leiden: Brill, 2009); Thomas Scott Caulley, "Notable Galilean Persons," in *Galilee in the Late Second Temple and Mishnaic Period, Volume 1: Life, Culture, and Society*, eds. David Fiensy and James Strange, 151–66 (Minneapolis: Fortress, 2014).

46. These hideouts, underground or in caves dug into the mountainside and accessed through sealed entries, were expanded at the time of the Jewish revolts. Mordechai Aviam, *Jews, Pagans, and Christians in the Galilee: 25 Years of Archaeological Excavations and Surveys, Hellenistic to Byzantine Periods* (Rochester: University of Rochester Press, 2004), 123–32; Killebrew, "Village and Countryside," 197.

47. Whittaker, "Circe's Pigs," 108–9; Grey, "Slavery in the Late Roman World," 485; Garnsey, Saller, and Goodman, *Roman Empire*, 97–99.

and their subsistence survival, a new regime gradually came into place, with its focus on tying such peasants to land. At this point, we enter the transition not between regimes but between modes of production themselves.

We understand a mode of production as the most inclusive of all economic models, incorporating economic matters (the traditional Marxist "base" or "infrastructure"), relations of productions (the questions of class and class conflict), and the crucial role of ideologies, cultures, beliefs, and ways of being (the traditional "superstructure," or what we prefer to call the mode of régulation). We add here the definition of Jessop and Sum: "In general terms a mode of production can be defined as a specific combination of forces and relations of production so organized that it can sustain a distinctive mode of appropriating surplus labour."[48] It is therefore a matter of the *longue durée*, which is the least perceptible to its actors and the slowest of all historical time. We have sought to provide some detail to how the staggering of such modes of production may work, using the terminology of institutional forms and regimes. Even so, a mode of production is measurable only across centuries.[49]

We have not yet named the mode of production we have been examining over the previous pages. Here we follow conventional Marxist terminology and call it the ancient mode of production, although we have analyzed it in terms of the slave, colonial, and land regimes. It may appear to have been rather long-lived, running from the fifth century BCE (in Greece) to the fifth century CE. But this was nothing to what had preceded it, at least in ancient Southwest Asia. Here the sacred economy (at times known as the Asiatic mode of production) stretched over almost four millennia, from the time of Ur to the end of the Persian Empire in the fourth century BCE (although the Sasanian Empire may be seen in some respects as its afterlife until the seventh century CE). But what was to follow the ancient mode of production, at least in the anomalous part of the world known as Europe?[50] Nothing less than feudalism. The precursor, however, was the land regime, for the first steps in the long gestation of feudalism entailed taking over

48. Bob Jessop, "Mode of Production," in *Marxian Economics*, eds. John Eatwell, Murray Milgate, and Peter Newman, 289–96 (London: Macmillan, 1987), 290.
49. Banaji, *Theory as History*, 87.
50. Here we follow Diakonoff, who notes that the path of European modes of production is actually an anomaly in terms of world history. The catch is that, due to European colonialism from the sixteenth to nineteenth centuries CE, this anomalous path has been assumed to be a global norm. Igor M. Diakonoff, *The Paths of History* (Cambridge: Cambridge University Press, 1999), 3.

and transforming the key feature of this regime—the fixing of rural laborers to the land—and making it a central feature of a whole mode of production. But that is another story.

6

Christianity as a Mode of Régulation

For though I am free with respect to all, I have made myself a slave to all, so that I might win more of them. To the Jews I became as a Jew, in order to win Jews. To those under the law I became as one under the law (though I myself am not under the law) so that I might win those under the law. To those outside the law I became as one outside the law (though I am not free from God's law but am under Christ's law) so that I might win those outside the law. To the weak I became weak, so that I might win the weak. I have become all things to all people [men] that I might by all means save some. I do it all for the sake of the gospel, so that I may share in its blessings. (1 Cor 9:19-23)

The present chapter on Christianity as mode of *régulation* addresses the flexibility and malleability of early Christianity, a flexibility which meant that it was a product of the slave and colonial regimes, and as such could undergird and develop these regimes, as well as facilitate the transition to the land regime.

By mode of *régulation*, we understand a set of behavioral patterns and institutions that enable and challenge the ideological reproduction of a given regime. All of this takes place in three domains: those of (1) constraint (laws and rules) and compromises; (2) patterns of behavior and assumptions; and (3) the methods by which these are socially reinforced and undermined. A mode of *régulation* need not be religious, but in the context of the first centuries of the Common Era, the primary nature of such a mode was deeply and inescapably religious. Further, during periods of relative stability, a mode of *régulation* provides the necessary social and ideological glue to enhance such stability. Yet, during times of turbulent change, modes of *régulation* become plural, exploring ways to challenge the problematic status quo, and attempting to find ways through times of troubles. This is how we understand the rise of early Christianity, as both challenge and promise. That it would also fulfil the role of constraint and stability is to be seen when the Emperor Constantine adopted Christianity as the ideology of empire. While the earlier chapters have included references to examples from the New Testament in the discussions of the institutional forms, what we propose here is to use the regimes to examine the ideologies of early Christian material.

A significant contention in light of the previous chapter is then that such a viewpoint necessarily regards early Christianity as an important ideological tool in the fight *against* subsistence survival, rather than the more ingrained assumption which sees the Jesus movement as an organic peasant movement. For this reason, we begin with the colonial regime. Taking our cue from Milton Moreland's article on earliest Christianity in Early Roman Galilee, we recall his pertinent question: why did Christianity so quickly become part of the Early Roman urban setting? And we explore his equally pertinent suggestion that the "eventual failure of Christianity to establish a viable community in Galilee in the first century . . . can be found in the intense opposition among peasant populations to disruptions in their protective social fabric."[1] Although Ste. Croix does not pose this question, it is nevertheless contained within his observation that within a generation, the transfer of Christian ideas from the *chōra* to the *polis* had taken place.[2] While the argument unfolds spatially, its kernel, however, is the question of property: since the Greco-Roman world was obsessed with wealth and status, Jesus's views on property had to be modified or explained away in order for Christianity to avoid "a fatal conflict with the all-powerful propertied classes."[3]

We propose to examine this argument in greater detail, and question

1. Moreland, "Galilean Response to Earliest Christianity," 37.
2. A similar idea is found in Edwin Judge, *The Social Pattern of the Christian Groups in the First Century: Some Prolegomena to the Study of New Testament Ideas of Social Obligation* (London: Tyndale, 1960), 49–61. Heinz Kreissig also notes that if we leave the "palästinensischen Urgemeinde" to one side, then the peasant population does not seem to exist for the Christian communities. Heinz Kreissig, "Zur sozialen Zusammensetzung der frühchristliche Gemeinden im ersten Jahrhundert u.Z.," *Eirene* 6 (1967): 91–100, 96.
3. Ste. Croix, *Class Struggle*, 427.

some of Ste. Croix's assumptions, especially regarding the relationship between the Gospels and Jesus. To do so, we will initially bracket out the question of property, and focus on the representation of *polis–chōra* in the Gospels, moving from the ostensibly most *polis*-oriented (John) through Mark to end up in the rural refuge of the parables. We return to the question of property in the following section on the slave regime and finish with deliberations over productions of space, spatial redistribution, and transitions within the mode of production.

The Colonial Regime

With the *polis-chōra* institutional form in mind, we now turn to the New Testament. We do so with the warning that we must always remember that the very distinction between *polis* and *chōra* reflects a *polis* perspective—that is, of the Greco-Roman colonial presence—for the literature available provides the perspective of those who were the colonizers. This reality also applies to the New Testament, which may be seen at a number of levels. To begin with, the fact that Gospels such as Luke have a tendency to call even the smallest hamlet a *polis* indicates a perspective that seeks to elevate the narrative from a somewhat embarrassing provincial context—a strategy to which a snob like Pausanius might respond: "if indeed one can give the name of city to those who possess no public buildings (*archeia*), no gymnasium, no theatre, no market-place, no water descending to a fountain, but live in bare shelters just like mountain huts on the edges of ravines."[4] Nonetheless, Luke tries his best. Further, this situation is compounded by the fact that the language of the Gospels is the language of the *polis*, namely Greek. This is reinforced by the fact that grapho-literacy—the ability to read and write—was very limited in the *chōra*. It was the preserve of scribes upon whom peasants relied for the occasional written document.[5] A text like the New Testament implies a greater literacy, which was largely restricted to the *polis*. All of this requires a dual reading

4. Quoted in Ste. Croix, *Class Struggle*, 9–10. Ste. Croix curiously uses this tendency to argue for a *chōra* perspective. See also Richard Rohrbaugh, "The Pre-Industrial City in Luke-Acts: Urban Social Relations," in *The Social World of Luke-Acts: Models for Interpretation*, ed. Jerome Neyrey, 125–50 (Peabody: Hendrickson, 1991).
5. John Poirier, "Education/Literacy in Jewish Galilee: Was There Any and at What Level?," in *Galilee in the Late Second Temple and Mishnaic Period, Volume 1: Life, Culture, and Society*, ed. David Fiensy and James Riley Strange, 253–60 (Minneapolis: Fortress, 2014). For a moderate contrary, which suggests a modicum of literacy among artisans, see Esther Eshel and Douglas Edwards, "Language and Writing in Early Roman Galilee: Social Location of a Potter's Abecedary from Khirbet Qana," in *Religion and Society in Roman Palestine: Old Questions, New Approaches*, ed. Douglas Edwards, 49–55 (New York: Routledge, 2004).

strategy: the first is to keep in mind the overarching *polis* perspective of these texts, while the second is to read dialectically, which entails examining such a perspective's contradictions that are manifested in unexpected ways.

Let us pick up again our touchstone, Ste. Croix. He does not distinguish between the Gospels, but takes them as trustworthy conveyors of "a true picture of the general sources of the activity of Jesus."[6] He does acknowledge the disagreements as to the historical reliability of the Gospels ("even the Synoptics"), but insists that he neither draws conclusions from the use of the word *polis*, nor the accuracy of the topographical information, but rather uses the narratives to demonstrate that the synoptic Gospels unanimously and consistently place Jesus's mission in the countryside and thus outside the limits of colonial economics and Hellenistic "civilization." Ste. Croix offers a careful analysis of the terms used in the Gospels,[7] in order to make the point that close by Nazareth were Sepphoris (seven kilometers away), and Tiberias, on shore of Lake Galilee at almost the point closest to Nazareth. Both were "the only two real cities of Galilee." "Yet, it need not surprise us to find no record of Jesus's presence in either of these cities,"[8] for they were viewed with suspicion, belonging to an alien and colonizing world. The *polis-chōra* opposition explains—argues Ste. Croix—the challenge of Jesus's words, especially his approach to property and wealth and thereby the ruling class. For Jesus, property was an evil and a huge hurdle to entering the Kingdom of God. By contrast, Jesus values simplicity (or, in our terms, subsistence survival) over luxury and rejects the power that comes with wealth. Everything about Jesus stands against the deeply-held values of the Greco-Roman ruling class, almost uniquely in the literature of the ancient world. Many biblical scholars, theologians, and even some Marxists would agree.[9] So problematic are the records of Jesus's words that the early Christians "had to play down those ideas of Jesus which were hostile to the ownership of any large quantity of property."[10]

6. Ste. Croix, *Class Struggle*, 430; Ste. Croix, *Christian Persecution, Martyrdom, and Orthodoxy*, 337.

7. Ste. Croix, *The Class Struggle in the Ancient Greek World: From the Archaic Age to the Arab Conquests*, 427–30; Ste. Croix, *Christian Persecution, Martyrdom, and Orthodoxy*, 330–36.

8. Ste. Croix, *Class Struggle*, 429.

9. As a sample: John Dominic Crossan, *The Historical Jesus: The Life of a Mediterranean Peasant* (San Francisco: HarperSanFrancisco, 1993); John Dominic Crossan, *Jesus: A Revolutionary Biography* (San Francisco: HarperSanFrancisco, 1995); Gustavo Gutiérrez, *The Power of the Poor in History* (Maryknoll: Orbis, 1983); Gustavo Gutiérrez, *A Theology of Liberation*, trans. Caridad Inda and John Eagleson (London: SCM, 2001); Juan Luis Segundo, *The Historical Jesus of the Synoptics* (Maryknoll, New York: Orbis, 1985); Terry Eagleton, *Jesus Christ: The Gospels (Revolutions)* (London: Verso, 2007).

10. Ste. Croix, *Class Struggle*, 426–27. Note also: "I am tempted to say that in this respect the opinions

The question remains, why did Christianity so quickly become part of the early Roman urban setting?[11] While Ste. Croix does not pose this question, it is, as mentioned earlier, contained within his observation that within a generation the transfer of Christian ideas from the *chōra* to the *polis* had taken place. This thorough shift pertains not merely to issues of private property, but also to slaves and women.[12] If we assume that the Gospels are snapshots of Jesus's life in Galilee, then we might end up with a conclusion like that of Ste. Croix. However, if we assume that the Gospels are second-generation texts, generated from within a *polis* perspective, then our conclusion would look somewhat different. One point can illustrate why this is a potentially fruitful pursuit. Ste Croix insists that the *poleis* through which Jesus passes are not genuine *poleis*, for the use of the term is to be understood in a "loose and untechnical sense," which bolsters his assumption that the parables express a *chōra* viewpoint. However, if we transfer his point about the *poleis* being used in a loose and untechnical sense, to the *chōra*, also here we find a strange impression. As Moxnes points out, "'the parables of the Kingdom do not give names of villages or towns, and they speak in general terms."[13] Moxnes interprets this as being a matter of course, because they are general depictions of village life; we should not expect to find "direct references to specific towns or persons." However, one could say that it is because it is a representation several times removed from what it intends to depict. This will be our argument in the following.

Turning to the gospel texts themselves, we begin with what appears to be the most extreme example of a *polis* outlook, namely John.

John

Meanwhile his disciples urged him, "Rabbi, eat something." But he said to them, "I have food to eat that you know nothing about." Then his disciples

of Jesus were nearer to those of Bertolt Brecht than to those held by some of the Fathers of the Church and by some Christians today" (433).

11. Moreland, "Galilean Response to Earliest Christianity," 37. See also Deines, "Religious Practices and Religious Movements in Galilee."

12. On the matter of private property, see Ste. Croix's analysis of Paul and then a host of church leaders (Irenaeus, Tertullian, Cyprian, Lactantius, Hilary of Poitiers, Jerome, Augustine, John Cassian, Clement of Alexandria, Paulinus of Nola, Gregory of Nyssa, Gregory of Nazianzus, John Chrysostom, and Theodoret) who twist uncomfortable biblical texts in order to suit a *polis* ideology. Ste. Croix, *Class Struggle*, 433–38; Ste. Croix, *Christian Persecution, Martyrdom, and Orthodoxy*, 355–68. For slavery and women, see Ste. Croix, *Class Struggle*, 103–11, 418–25; Ste. Croix, *Christian Persecution, Martyrdom, and Orthodoxy*, 345–55.

13. Moxnes, *Putting Jesus in His Place*, 155–56.

said to each other, "Could someone have brought him food?" "My food," said Jesus, "is to do the will of him who sent me and to finish his work. Do you not say, 'It's still four months until harvest'? I say to you, open your eyes and look at the fields (*tas chōras*)! They are white for harvest. Even now the one who reaps draws a wage and harvests a crop for eternal life, so that the sower and the reaper may be glad together. In this the saying, "One sows and another reaps," is true. I sent you to reap what you have not worked for. Others have done the hard work, and you have reaped the benefits of their labor."

This particular text (John 4:31–38) is one of three instances of the word *chōra* in John—the others are in 11:54 concerning the area around Ephraim, and 11:55, the area around Jerusalem. This conversation between Jesus and the disciples takes place immediately after the encounter between Jesus and the Samaritan woman. The woman has gone back to fetch the villagers, and they are on their way out to Jesus, as this conversation takes place. This pericope is one of the few places in John that uses the agricultural imagery otherwise so significant in the synoptic Gospels. And while great attention has been given to the process and significance of the spiritualization of, for example, space, temple, and Judaism in John,[14] the spiritualization or re-signification of *chōra* here has generally gone unquestioned.

Most analyses of this pericope (4:31–38) note that it continues the misunderstanding at work in the dialogue between the Samaritan woman and Jesus. Whereas in the case of the Samaritan woman it was water which led to revelation, here it is food and agricultural imagery that becomes the point of departure for an instruction on mission, which is expressed in terms of reaping the harvest. However well this pericope fits within the larger epistemological framework of John, the imagery is somewhat out of character. As noted, Ste. Croix argues that the whole imagery of Jesus's speech in the synoptic Gospels is based on life in the *chōra*, representing the unique viewpoint of the peasant over against that of the ruling classes.[15] But this is clearly not the case in John: this reference to the fields and harvest is a decided anomaly.

However, an important feature of this pericope is its post-resurrection perspective, which is present in verse 38 and the aorist *apesteila*. This perspective means that the Gospel narrative is constructed on the

14. Musa Dube and Jeffrey Staley, *John and Postcolonialism: Travel, Space and Power*, The Bible and Post-colonialism (London: Continuum, 2002).
15. Ste. Croix also sees Jesus in the synoptic Gospels as a spokesperson for the perspective of the colonized, who are not given voice in any literature. John is thereby an exception in this respect as well.

presupposition that the spiritual has full precedence over the material, despite the constant contradictions breaking through this presentation.[16] This means that for John there is no *chōra*, which then becomes spiritualized. Rather, the *chōra* and the "harvest" are both materializations produced by the text. *Chōra* then is a product of the spiritual order of the gospel, and is thereby already shaped so as to meet its needs. Hence the move is not from the material to the spiritual but from the spiritual to the material.

In other words, it may be argued that John displays an "aristocratic," or rather a "ruling class ideology," since the text obfuscates the relations of production.[17] For example, in the denigration of the hired hand in John 10:11–13, Jesus expresses a "born to rule" attitude that already appears in 2:1–11.[18] Indeed, John's epistemological framework serves to deploy conditions and relations of production as symbols of false understanding and unbelief. More examples of this ideology would include the building of a temple (2:19–21), drawing water (4:7–15), food (4:31–32), and the reinterpretation of *ergon* and *ergazomai* in 6:22–40.[19] Thus, in the bread of life discourse in chapter 6, there are several ideas of bread presented: the bread which was eaten in the feeding, manna, and the bread of life. And while the crowds ask for bread, they are chastised for not seeking the bread of life. A fundamental concern, which most of us in this business have never encountered, is the need to feed ourselves and our families. Yet, this is dismissed as a base and truly mistaken obsession about something, which, under the aegis of the heavens, simply does not matter. Class struggle is thus present not only in the narrative, but the text itself is the result of class struggle, and as such, a participant in current class struggles. This obliteration of the conditions of production may be seen as part of ruling class ideology, or, in the terms of this chapter, the viewpoint of the *polis* over against that of the *chōra*.

---

16. As Stephen Moore has aptly demonstrated: Stephen Moore, "Are there Impurities in the Living Water that the Johannine Jesus Dispenses?" in *A Feminist Companion to John I*, ed. Amy Jill Levine and Marianne Blickenstaff, 78-97 (Sheffield: Sheffield Academic Press, 2003).

17. What John does here is not far removed from what Plato is doing in Timeaus, where Plato introduces the concept of *chōra* into his philosophical paradigm as that which is necessary for transmitting the true forms, accessible only to "the gods and a small group of people," into objects perceptible by sense.

18. Robert Myles, "Opiate of Christ; or, John's Gospel and the Spectre of Class," *Postscripts: The Journal of Sacred Texts and Contemporary Worlds* 7, no. 3 (2016): 255–77, 263–66.

19. See full analysis of this in Christina Petterson, *From Tomb to Text: The Death of Jesus in the Book of John* (London: T&T Clark, 2016).

Mark

The Gospel of Mark is often assumed to be the text closest to the rural "roots" of Jesus and early Christianity, if not "folk literature" that presents the itinerary of an "organic intellectual" and that may have been composed in Galilee.[20] While we are sympathetic to this approach, our hypothesis is that Christianity was primarily a *polis*-based movement. So the question arises as to how the rural, subsistence survival dimension of life is represented in such a text. We propose that it should be seen as form of responsive metaphorization in which the text responds in complex and mediated ways to a multilayered situation: it emerges from the period after the Roman legions of Vespasian and Titus carved a bloody path, with the customary Roman practice of widespread terror, through the troublesome region; it constructs its narrative when the process of indenture was well under way, leading to the colonate; the founder of the movement came from a context, the *chōra*, where it did not take root.[21]

This response has two pertinent features: the depictions of the countryside features laborers who were negotiating the process of indenture; the primary contradiction (to gloss Mao Zedong) is between *polis* and *chōra*, which is presented in a cosmological framework. To begin with, Mark's gospel is replete with signals of rural laborers, so much so that land, labor, and economic contentions form the background of many key episodes. Obviously, tenants appear, as do the various tasks peasants would undertake, such as sowing, harvesting, cultivating longer yield trees, and fishing (Mark 1:16–20; 4:3–9, 26–29; 12:1–11; 13:28–31). More importantly, the many "possessed," "unclean," "diseased," and "deformed" of the miracle stories (1:23–34, 40–45; 2:1–12; 3:1–6, 11; 4:1–20; 5:21–43; 6:56; 7:24–36; 8:22–26; 9:14–29, 38–40; 10:46–52) function not so much as echoes of the tough realities of life where disease and hard, repetitive labor reshaped bodies, but as *polis*-based perceptions of the working rural population. Throughout Greek and Roman literature, peasants appear as misshapen, ugly, and unlucky, in contrast to the properly formed (*kairos*), beautiful, and

---

20. Adela Yarbro Collins, *Mark: A Commentary*, Hermeneia (Minneapolis: Augsburg Fortress, 2007), 41; Cadwallader, "Peasant Plucking in Mark"; Joel Marcus, "The Jewish War and the *Sitz im Leben* of Mark," *Journal of Biblical Literature* 111, no. 3 (1992): 441–62. We leave aside the question of the hypothetical Q document, concerning which similar arguments are made. See Horsley, "Language(s) of the Kingdom," 416–24. We do not wish to enter the endless debate over the geographical provenance of the Gospel.

21. Moreland, "Galilean Response to Earliest Christianity."

lucky dwellers of the *poleis*.[22] This is not to say that Mark offers a ruling class perspective per se, but that the ideological framework of representation is one informed by the *polis*. This perspective appears in the way the "disabled" become "abled" and functional through the healing stories. They are transformed to conform to what a *polis*-dweller may assume to be a conventional and proportional body.[23] In the background are continuous allusions to Roman presence and control (Mark 12:13–17; 6:14–29; 15:1–25),[24] especially in light of the fact that the Gospel was written at a time when the colonate was well underway to becoming the overarching determinant of rural life (see also Mark 15:39–45).

Second, Mark opposes from its first moment the rural reaches of the backwater of Galilee to the *polis* of Jerusalem. Yet, by the time of the Gospel, Jerusalem no longer existed as such but was on its way to becoming a truly Roman *polis*—Aelia Capitolina. So the *polis* exists only as an image, a recreation by the text that destroys it (Mark 13). This situation enables the mythologizing of the opposition, which appears as a cosmological opposition between wildness and the *polis* (and all that it embodies). Here the ideological dimension of the literary response to a conflicted economic situation takes full flight. The countryside may be a place of resistance, but the *chōra* is also a wild place. From the first moments of the narrative, the arrow of authority and significance points away from the *polis*: evoking the Exodus traditions, Jesus's ministry grows from the "wild places" of desert (1:3–4), of camel's hair and locusts (1:6), Jordan river (1:5, 9), Holy Spirit (1:10–11), and "the

---

22. Here the Platonic search for the true, good, and beautiful must be located, for these philosophical and moral categories were redolent with class assumptions. See further, Ste. Croix, *Christian Persecution, Martyrdom, and Orthodoxy*, 338–39; Ste. Croix, *Origins of the Peloponnesian War*, 371–76. See also a study that highlights the use of commonality of disability, the use of the disabled as spectacles, and the reality of many artisans being disabled in some way: Nicole Kelley, "Deformity and Disability in Greece and Rome," in *This Abled Body: Rethinking Disabilities in Biblical Studies*, ed. Hector Avalos, Sarah Melcher, and Jeremy Schipper, 31–45 (Atlanta: Society of Biblical Literature, 2007). Thank you to Anna Rebecca Solevaag for clarifying discussion on this matter.

23. Indeed, in the very effort to reveal the transformative power of Jesus, Mark unwittingly gives voice to such a perspective. We draw here on some disability studies that highlight the normative role of the abled body. Holly Joan Toensing, "'Living among the Tombs': Society, Mental Illness, and Self-Destruction in Mark 5:1–20 " in *This Abled Body: Rethinking Disabilities in Biblical Studies*, ed. Hector Avalos, Sarah Melcher, and Jeremy Schipper, 131–43 (Atlanta: Society of Biblical Literature, 2007), 140–41; David Mitchell and Sharon Snyder, "'Jesus Thrown Everything Off Balance': Disability and Redemption in Biblical Literature," in *This Abled Body: Rethinking Disabilities in Biblical Studies*, ed. Hector Avalos, Sarah Melcher, and Jeremy Schipper, 173–83 (Atlanta: Society of Biblical Literature, 2007), 178–83.

24. See further Ched Myers, *Binding the Strong Man: A Political Reading of Mark's Story of Jesus* (Maryknoll: Orbis, 1988); Alan Cadwallader, "In Go(l)d we Trust: Literary and Economic Exchange in the Debate over Caesar's Coin (Mark 12:13–17)," *Biblical Interpretation* 14, no. 5 (2007): 486–507; Cadwallader, "Peasant Plucking in Mark."

sea" (1:16; 2:13; 3:7; 4:35–41; 5:1, 13, 21; 6:45–56; 9:42; 11:23). People flow from the *polis* to the wild *chōra* (1:5; 3:8). Jesus immediately turns not to the *polis*—from where scribes, chief priests, elders, and Roman authorities come, who seek to test, torment, and ultimately execute Jesus (3:22; 7:1; 11:27; 12:38–40; 14:1–2, 43, 53; 15:1, 31)—but to the wilderness and deserted places (1:12, 35) where one encounters demons, Satan, wild beasts, and angels (1:13). Indeed, Jesus himself is suspected by some of being possessed (3:21–22). Here mythology can run riot, where fabulous occurrences, crazy prophets, miracles,[25] heavens torn apart (1:10), transfigurations (9:2–8), and the whole spirit world are on full display. Here too mustard seeds grow (4:30–32) in untamed and wild growth, loaves and fish multiply uncontrollably (6:30–44; 8:1–10), and the Sabbath can be disregarded (2:23–28; 3:1–6). The *chōra* is nature out of control, which no amount of culture can tame. The value of this rampant, wild nature is ambivalent, for it may be a sign that even the most intense effort at domination cannot succeed (resistance), or it may be a negative depiction of all that is fearful about the *chōra*. But this ambivalence is part of a *polis*-based depiction of the countryside: it is a place of both freedom and danger, of promise and risk. This tension appears above all in the story of the Gerasene Demoniac, who is called "Legion"—tellingly, the longest story in Mark (5:1–20). Who is the *legiōn*, which the man himself claims as a title (5:9)? Alongside the multitude of interpretations,[26] we suggest it functions as a signal of the wild *chōra* in which myriad possessions flourish—"for we are many" (*hoti polloi esmen*, 5:9). The untamed nature of the wilds is simultaneously a place of the multiplicity of resistance and a frightening space for those accustomed to the relative and constraining (5:3–4) order of the *polis*.[27] The story is after all set in the Decapolis to which the "healed" man returns. Leaving Mark, we now turn to the last bulwark of rural bliss, the parables and their setting.

---

25. The only miracle in Jerusalem is the anti-miracle of the cursed fig tree (Mark 11: 12–14, 20–24).

26. Interpretations are many: demon possession as a sanctioned way of dealing with Roman scorched-earth policies; a reference to the force of the Roman military; a specific condemnation of the Roman "boar" legion that was present in Galilee. Richard Horsley, *Hearing the Whole Story: Politics of Plot in Mark's Gospel* (Louisville: Westminster John Knox, 2001), 140; Collins, *Mark: A Commentary*, 237; Warren Carter, "Cross-Gendered Romans and Mark's Jesus: Legion Enters the Pigs (Mark 5:1–20)," *Journal of Biblical Literature* 134, no. 1 (2015): 139–55.

27. This constraint may also be seen as a literary trace of Roman practices of enslavement, characteristic of *polis* life. This suggestion was made a research assistant on the project, Niall McKay.

Sheep, Goats, and the Question of Parables

An important feature of subsistence survival was herding, especially of sheep and goats (see chapter 2). A superficial comparison of the appearance of sheep and goats in the Hebrew Bible and the New Testament shows that both tend to favor shepherd and sheep as an image to depict the relation between God and people. For example, 1 Kings 22:17 speaks of Israel scattered on the mountains as sheep that have no shepherd, and Psalm 44, which twice likens the "us" of the psalm to sheep for slaughter (vss 11 and 22).[28] In the New Testament, Matthew's Gospel speaks of the crowds as harassed and helpless "like sheep without a shepherd" (Matt 9:36; Mark 6:34), the "lost sheep of the house of Israel" (Matt 10:6), not to mention the parable of the lost sheep in Luke 15:1–7.[29] An interesting point of difference between the two collections of texts is that in the Hebrew Bible there is ample mention of goats and sheep alongside this metaphorization, while the New Testament mentions goats twice: once in the parable of the Prodigal Son, where the elder son complains about the slaughtering of the fatted calf for the return of his brother, while his father has never given him "even a young goat" to celebrate (Luke 15:29), and once in the so-called "Judgement of the Nations" in Matthew 25:31–46, where Son of Man separates the nations as a shepherd would separate goats from the sheep. Here, the goats signify those who are to go "into eternal punishment." This emphasis on sheep may very well be due to the likening of Jesus to a shepherd or a lamb, but it does not change the fact that with few exceptions, such as Luke 17:7, the use of sheep is a metaphorization of a metaphorization, and as such twice removed from the everyday life of actual husbandry and herding—a similar relation to the one between the patty in a McDonalds burger and the mooing cows in the nursery rhyme, "Old MacDonald Had a Farm." This brings us to the issue of the parables.

In a galaxy far, far away, C. H. Dodd discusses the allegorical understanding of the parables over against a non-allegorical interpretation.[30] For Dodd, the crucial passage is that of Mark 4:11–12: "And he said to them, 'To you has been given the secret of the kingdom of God, but

---

28. See also Lev 17:7; Num 27:17; 1 Sam 16:11, 19; 17:34; 2 Sam 5:2; 7:8; 2 Chr 11:15; 18:16; Pss 23; 74:1; 78:52, 70–72; 95:7; 100:3; Isa 1:11; 13:14, 21; 34:6, 14; 40:11; 53:6–7; Jer 12:3; 23:1; 50:6; Ezek 34:2–16; Mic 2:12.
29. See also Matt 7:15; 9:36; 10:6, 16; 12:11–12; 15:24; 18:12–14; 25:31–46; 26:31; Mark 14:27; John 10:1–18, 26–27; 21:15–19; Acts 8:32; Rom 8:36; Heb 9:11–14, 19; 10:4; 11:37; 13:20; 1 Pet 2:25.
30. C. H. Dodd, *The Parables of the Kingdom*, revised ed. (London: Collins, 1961), 13.

for those outside, everything comes in parables; in order that "they may indeed look, but not perceive, and may indeed listen, but not understand; so that they may not turn again and be forgiven.""" Dodd interprets this saying as very unlike the other sayings of Jesus, for it uses a terminology which is much closer to that of Paul.[31] The facts he lists—the seven central terms—create the presumption that we are dealing with a piece of apostolic teaching rather than the words of Jesus. Furthermore, according to Dodd, among Jewish teachers the parable was a common and well understood teaching method. Thus, the probability that the parables should be seen as allegories in need of unlocking could have happened only in a non-Jewish environment, for example, in Hellenism, where allegory was widespread.[32]

Finally, Dodd suggests that he has earlier shown "what a singularly complete and convincing picture the parables give of life in a small provincial town—probably a more complete picture of *petit-bourgeois* and peasant life than we possess for any other province of the Roman Empire except Egypt, where papyri come to our aid."[33] While Dodd's text is of an older date, we have picked it out, because it expresses in clear form the underlying assumptions of the view of the parables—namely that they express the teachings of Jesus, and as such express genuine Jewish, provincial, peasant-life.

If this is so, then why do so few of the parables actually concern peasant life? As Guijarro points out, "one would expect to find in [the parables] a portrait of the families of peasants, fishermen, or day workers." Instead, "we find a significant number of individuals who belong to the elite families: rulers or aristocrats, who lived in big mansions, had servants to perform different tasks and owned large amounts of land."[34] The explanation given to this disjunction is that the type of story related to peasant families would not have appealed to Jesus's listeners. A similar view is taken by Moxnes, who argues that while the location for the parables are the households of the elite, the various parables may be told "from the perspective of 'below' with neither the implied author nor the audience sharing the social location of the characters in the story, but the large farms nevertheless provide plausible settings for the stories."[35]

31. Ibid., 14.
32. Ibid., 15.
33. Ibid., 21.
34. Santiago Guijarro, "The Family in First-Century Galilee," in *Early Christian Families: Family as Social Reality and Metaphor* ed. Halvor Moxnes, 42–65 (London: Routledge, 1997), 48.
35. Moxnes, *Putting Jesus in His Place*, 43–44.

We are not quite convinced by this explanation and propose to analyze some of the parables in order to bring out their perspective as well as that of the audience: is it one of rural ambience, or, to paraphrase Ernst Käsemann from a different but not unrelated context, do these features of peasant life represent the *absolute minimum* of the costume designed for those of whom one only has the vaguest sense—thus appearing to be of peasant stock, yet without having being subjected to these earthy conditions?[36] In other words, do the parables represent actual rural life, or the representation of rural life as it is imagined by someone not of peasant provenance? While most interpretations assume the former, we argue for the latter, showing how the perspective of the parables has more affinities with the *polis* than with the *chōra*. Consequently, we seek to show how the representation of the *chōra* household is accordingly based on assumptions of the *polis*. We do not contest the idea of the parables as arising from a shared location and perspective between the teller and the audience; we merely question the rural provenance of this location and perspective.

To illustrate, let us begin with the parable of the wicked tenants in Mark 12:1–12 (also Matt 21:33–46 and Luke 20:9–19). This parable has thrown up a host of problems for interpreters committed to a social justice agenda, such as William Herzog III and Luise Schottroff.[37] The difficulty is ultimately a theological one:

> The matter-of-fact interpretation of the vineyard owner as God, which rules in the interpretative tradition with only a few exceptions, must be fundamentally called into question if we take the social-historical analysis of the text seriously. The owner of the vineyard acts like an opponent of God; he does the opposite of what the God of the Torah and the Lord's Prayer desires and does.[38]

It is the delicate issue of an allegorical interpretation that equates God with the owner of the vineyard, the violence perpetrated and also the ensuing dismissal of the Jewish people as the heirs of the vineyard, which Schottroff attempts to combat as part of her larger non-dualist parable theory. This theory intends to emphasize the lives of peo-

---

36. Ernst Käsemann, *Jesu letzter Wille nach Johannes 17* (Tübingen: JBC Mohr, 1980), 10. Käsemann is of course talking about the earthly Jesus and how the features of humanity in John's gospel should be seen as this minimalist costume.

37. William R. Herzog III, *Parables as Subversive Speech: Jesus as Pedagogue of the Oppressed* (Louisville: Westminster/John Knox, 1994); Luise Schottroff, *The Parables of Jesus*, trans. Linda M. Maloney (Minneapolis: Fortress Press, 2006), 15–28.

38. Schottroff, *Parables of Jesus*, 17.

ple in the Roman Empire, instead of treating them as mere signifiers for a theologically relevant meaning.[39] In line with her non-dualist theory, Schottroff reads the behavior of the tenants as reflecting "the economic hopelessness of the increasingly poor agrarian population and their hatred for their new master," so much so that "in this parable we hear how indebtedness turns those burdened with it into violent people filled with hatred."[40] However accurate this may be, we still need to consider the question of *perspective within the parable*, in that the so-called grain of the narrative follows the slave-owning landlord rather than the tenants. The landlord is presented as the one who performed all the labor in establishing the vineyard,[41] and was as such only claiming that to which he was entitled. The tenants attempt to appropriate this through violence and murder.[42]

It is instructive to look at Schottroff's analysis of the individual parables to see which ones she finds outrageously unacceptable. This is possible because she has an excellent eye for the socio-economic conditions and inequalities of the first centuries, and therefore refuses to see God as being represented as complicit in these structures. Thus, a rule of thumb is that any parable which depicts God as a slave-owner, landowner, or cranky king is seen by Schottroff not as an analogy, but as an antithetical parable, which intends to present the listeners with the difference between God's kingdom and the current situation. Examples include the parable of the unforgiving servant (Matt 18:23–36), the laborers in the vineyard (Matt 20:1–16), the wedding banquet (Matt 22:1–13), and the slave parables in Luke (12:35–38; 17:3–10; and 19:11–27) to which we return in the following section.[43]

Schottroff follows Herzog in seeing the parables as expressions of class conflict. In order to do so, both have to read against the grain of the parable to detach God from the rich slave-owner. While Herzog detaches the parables from their later interpretations—as Dodd had

---

39. Ibid., 2. See the methodological sections in part 2, 81–113.
40. Ibid., 17.
41. Schottroff brings out the labor of the slaves nicely: Ibid., 16. We return to this in the discussion of parables in the slave regime.
42. Interestingly, it is especially Mark's version which is the harshest, and attempts to ameliorate the parable may be seen in both Matthew and Luke—versions which are also favored by scholars attempting an interpretation which presents God in a more flattering way. Kenneth Bailey, *Jesus Through Middle Eastern Eyes: Cultural Studies in the Gospels* (Downers Grove: IVP Academic, 2008), 410–26. In fact, Bailey names the parable "The Parable of the Noble Vineyard Owner and his Son," and the tenants are labelled vinedressers, the slaves servants. At one and the same time, Bailey manages to hide and reveal the class issues in the parable. Schottroff, *Parables of Jesus*, 17–25.
43. It is worth noting that the parable of the weeds among the wheat, which also depicts God as a slave-owner, is passed by with only a brief mention of its eschatological significance. Schottroff, *Parables of Jesus*, 207.

done—Schottroff keeps them in their respective contexts, which means that she needs other arguments to support her antithetical readings. The main interpretive tactic she uses is her translation of *homoioun* and *homoios* as "compare" rather than "equate," because "compare" includes the possibility of seeing difference in the comparison rather than similitude. Schottroff and Herzog thus want to separate God from class conflict. Our argument is rather that class conflict is already represented from the viewpoint of a certain class, namely, that of the ruling class or the landlords—a perspective from which the peasants and workers are presented and from which resistance in the parables is depicted as wicked rebellion.[44] This brings us back to the vineyard. In his interpretation of Luke's version, Bailey notes that the title "The Parable of the Wicked Tenants" incorrectly places the emphasis on the tenants. By contrast, for Bailey it is the noble owner who is the hero of the story, because he chooses not to enact his legitimate vengeance on his enemies.[45] The vineyard owner's grievances are depicted as legitimate, while those of the tenants are not. We can reconstruct, flesh out, and read from below all we like, but the fact of the matter is that the text simply does not recognize this viewpoint as valid.

Finally, we return to the question of allegory. As noted above, Dodd and Herzog regard allegory as secondary to the parables themselves. Schottroff does not follow this line, opting instead to combat an allegorical interpretation of the parables. While we are sympathetic to the motivation behind rejecting an allegorical interpretation of the parables because of the propensity of such an interpretation to dismiss the relevance of the signifying material, it must still be discussed whether the parables themselves, with or without the allegorical superstructure, really are as reflective of village life and rural ideology as Schottroff, Herzog, Moxnes, and Dodd assume. Does not the mere existence of the allegorical key to the parables display the contradictions of class struggle? It is telling that Schottroff attempts to get out of trouble with the parable of the wicked tenants by introducing yet another allegorical interpretation, one which connects the parable much more firmly to the Jewish history of the land: "the vineyard itself is not a metaphor that can be understood apart from the history of the fields and vine-

---

44. As an instructive parallel see the example of Ernst Bloch's reading of the sons of Korah (Num 16) in Boer, *Political* Myth, 20–21.
45. Bailey, *Jesus Through Middle Eastern Eyes*, 410.

yards of the land. In this one vineyard, within the narrative, is concentrated the history of the people."[46]

To wrap up, the information on the conditions of production and the socio-economic history of the land, which provide a reading from below, comes not from the New Testament material but rather from historical studies of Roman Palestine and Egypt, all of which suggests that the New Testament texts are not the wonderful sources of the history of the common man as might be wished. As in archaeological excavations, the lower classes are present in the texts only as traces.

The Slave Regime

We now turn to the role of Christianity as mode of *régulation* of the slave regime. The vexed question of the relation between Christianity and slavery has occasioned a monumental amount of research into detailed features of various texts and authors. While reliant on this research, we propose to focus on the "slave-relation," which operated at a social, intellectual, and psychic level. As slavery became integral to economic activity, it influenced the modes of human social interaction. Such interaction became mediated through slaves, but the key is that mediation itself became a wider norm within human consciousness and thereby the literature, linguistic forms, and even religions produced at the time. Such was the saturation that slaves need no longer be actually present, for mediation itself became central to the way people thought and behaved.

In his chapter on exploitation, Ste. Croix juxtaposes two petitions, one from a minor village official to King Ptolomy III Euergetes from 243 BCE, the other from a tenant named Anoup in sixth-century CE Egypt to his landlord, Apion. The earlier example reads: "To King Ptolomy, greeting, from Antigonus. I am being unjustly treated by Patron, the superintendent of police in the lower toparchy." The sixth-century CE example is as follows: "To my good master, lover of Christ, lover of the poor, all esteemed and most magnificent Patrician and Duke of the Thebaid, Apion, from Anoup, your miserable slave [*doulos*] upon your estate called Phacra."[47] It is this groveling self-deprecation that we designate the slave-relation, and, with a nod to Nietzsche, we regard it as inextricable from the ideology of Christianity and its socio-economic context.

46. Schottroff, *Parables of Jesus*, 25.
47. Ste. Croix, *Class Struggle*, 223.

In what follows, we look at slaves in various settings in the New Testament texts. In order to show how Christianity played a major role in the mode of *régulation* relating to the slave regime, we focus on the first and arguably most important Christian ideologue, Paul. From there, we move on to examine the slave-relation in the Gospels, and return to the vexed issue of property, which Ste. Croix identifies as a feature of *polis*-based Christianity and not the *chōra*-based Jesus movement.

Of Slaves and Brothers

It would be self-deception if one failed to see that Jesus of Nazareth, the apostles, and the Church—both in its formative period and its later development—accepted the dominant system of labor of the time, including the slave structure, without hesitation or any expressed reluctance.[48] Further, the overwhelming tendency of biblical studies is to focus on household slavery (see chapter 4), which is unsurprising given that this is also the major focus of the New Testament. This reinforces our argument that the perspective of the New Testament texts is that of the *polis,* especially since the slaves in the parables either belong to a wealthy household or work for an absentee landlord.

Before we examine this perspective in more detail, let us begin by focusing on Paul, whose letters are full of slave metaphors. Above all, there is the letter which concerns a slave directly, namely, the letter to Philemon concerning the slave Onesimus. In order to understand this letter, we draw on the work of Ulrike Roth, which eminently shows how this letter may function as a productive starting point for early Christian attitudes toward slavery.[49] Roth's argument is that Onesimus was a contribution as human chattel to the *koinōnia*, and that Paul was a co-owner of Onesimus. This point is carefully argued through attention to the communication strategies of the letter, analysis of the term *koinōnia* and its practices of pooled ownership of various resources, Paul's display of mastery, and an analysis of the parallel universe of Pauline Christianity which brings the contradiction between Christian brotherhood and the economic system of slavery to the fore. Roth concludes:

---

48. William Westermann, *The Slave Systems of Greek and Roman Antiquity* (Philadelphia: American Philosophical Society, 1955), 150.
49. Ulrike Roth, "Paul, Philemon, and Onesimus," in *Zeitschrift für die Neutestamentliche Wissenschaft und die Kunde der älteren Kirche* 105, no. 1 (2014): 105–30.

Whilst slavery, like citizenship, was irrelevant in the new world order, it was the order of the "old" world, which acknowledged slavery, that allowed Paul a double coup: in his dealings with Philemon and Onesimus, Paul embraces the order of both this world and the next, creating parallel universes that, with regard to slavery, could only have been understood by non-Christians (and probably by some fellow Christians) as an expression of a complete and unreserved acceptance of the slave system.[50]

We would like to address a number of significant points resulting from Roth's article, moving from there to some other New Testament texts. The first and probably least controversial concerns Paul as a slave-holder. Based on a dual reading of *koinōnia* as both a practical association of pooling resources for a specific goal, as well as Paul's spin on this as a community of believers (the *koinōnia tēs pisteōs*), Roth argues that Paul is consciously mingling the two layers in order to assert his authority and undergird his demand for Onesimus. Based on the contractual arrangements inherent in *koinōnia* to which Paul refers several times in the letter, the challenge to Philemon is to honor the agreements in this arrangement. The precise issue is Onesimus, who, if he was a contribution by Philemon to the *koinōnia*, would make Paul the *de iure* part-owner of Onesimus. This situation accords with the agreement entailed in the nature of the *koinōnia*, where material contributions become common property. Slaves, as chattel, would have been part of this contractual arrangement. Roth notes that a similar arrangement could be argued for the relation between Paul and Epaphroditus in Philippi.[51] She argues that there are two particular points in the letter which reinforce the master-slave relation between Paul and Onesimus. The first is Paul's readiness to take on possible debts, which shows him thinking as a slave master and acknowledging his legal responsibilities to Philemon.[52] The second is the presentation of Onesimus as Paul's agent—the physical extension of Paul who is to be received by Philemon both in the flesh and in the Lord, thereby reinforcing Onesimus's status as a "thing," a sentient tool or the hands of Paul's mind, but also "of the old world."[53] This brings us to the second item of interest to take from Roth's article, namely the idea of slave as a thing, used as a slave, *within the church*.

Scholarship on slavery and Christianity has come a long way since

---

50. Ibid., 128.
51. Ibid., 120–21, and note 70.
52. Ibid., 123–24.
53. Ibid., 122.

William Westermann's naïve assertion that the early Christians regarded slaves as human personalities instead of *things* as in Roman law.[54] In particular, the work of Glancy and Harrill has broken much new ground.[55] Another provocative example is Marchal's analysis of Onesimus as a sexual vessel. And yet, it seems to us that there still is another step, which scholars are reluctant to take—namely the use of slave labor within the churches and congregations. These scholars attempt to insert a buffer against such a possibility in various ways: seeing Paul's perspective as *aligning* comfortably with that of the slave owners;[56] Paul's possible interaction with slaves when accepting hospitality of slaveholders;[57] using qualifiers when mentioning ownership ("as though");[58] perhaps even regarding Onesimus as a runaway slave—since this avoids the interpretation put forward by Knox, Winter, and Roth, that Onesimus was sent by Philemon as assistant to Paul, which would make Paul someone who directly benefited from slave labor. It seems that most follow, whether explicitly or implicitly, Byron's point of view in his assessment of the status quo: "As appalling as the notion of slavery is in any society, the fact remains that, in the context of the New Testament, slavery did take on some positive aspects. This is not to suggest, of course, that Paul was a supporter of slavery. But he and other New Testament authors were able to find something that was of 'redeeming' value for their theology."[59]

Following Roth, we prefer to see what the text actually says: slaves were used in the service of Christianity. We mean not only that Paul would have benefited from someone's slave in someone's house, but that the various congregations made use of slave labor within them, as

---

54. Westermann, *Slave Systems of Greek and Roman Antiquity*. See the helpful but already dated survey by John Byron, "Paul and the Background of Slavery: The Status Quaestionis in New Testament Scholarship," *Currents in Biblical Research* 3, no. 1 (2004): 62–72. But see Osiek and Balch, *Families in the New Testament World*. Here they state that "the human dignity of slaves was recognized by their acceptance into the community, without calling into question the mention of slavery itself" (188).

55. Glancy, *Slavery in Early Christianity*; Jennifer Glancy, *Slavery as Moral Problem: In the Early Church and Today* (Minneapolis: Fortress, 2011); Harrill, *Manumission of Slaves in Early Christianity*; Harrill, *Slaves in the New Testament*.

56. Marchal, "Usefulness of an Onesimus."

57. Glancy, *Slavery in Early Christianity*, 45. See also John Barclay, "Paul, Philemon and the Dilemma of Christian Slave-Ownership," *New Testament Studies* 37, no. 2 (2009): 161–86. Barclay states that the slave context that would be most familiar to Paul would have been "that of slaves living in the urban homes of their masters" 165, followed by a number of examples from Paul's letters and their references, for instance, to Chloe's people in 1 Cor 1:11.

58. For "as though he himself was the owner of Onesimus" see Peter Arzt-Grabner, *Philemon*, Papyrologische Kommentare zum Neuen Testament (Göttingen: Vandenhoeck & Ruprecht, 2003), 246. For scare quotes ("elsewhere, the epistle maintains the claim that Onesimus 'belongs' to the apostle"), see Chris Frilingos, "'For My Child, Onesimus': Paul and Domestic Power in Philemon," *Journal of Biblical Literature* 119, no. 1 (2000): 91–104.

59. Byron, "Paul and the Background of Slavery."

was the case with Onesimus and Epaphroditus. For example, the reference to Chloe's house in 1 Corinthians 1:11, suggests for Barclay "probably . . . the presence of slaves in the homes of some of his converts,"[60] and to Osiek and Balch, following Gerd Theissen, "perhaps 'her slaves or dependent workers'."[61] Both Glancy and Nasrallah go a little further and suggest that the message to Paul was conveyed by Chloe's slaves[62] but without pushing through to the obvious, but uncomfortable, conclusion that early Christianity exploited slaves as a matter of course—as did the rest of society.

In her conclusion, Roth follows and expands upon Barclay's point that the hospitality offered in the first house churches is unimaginable without the help of slaves.[63] Roth regards it as impossible that the missionary activity could be carried out without the work of slaves. One of us has suggested as much in a reading of Acts 8:1–5, where Paul works with Aquila and Priscilla, until Silas and Timothy turn up in Corinth.[64] While most commentators assume that Timothy and Silas bring funds or money, which enables Paul to concentrate on preaching,[65] the text actually says nothing about bringing anything. This opens up for the possibility of understanding that Timothy and Silas work to support Paul, enabling him to preach full time. This is emphasized by the order, or command (ἐντολή)[66], issued by Paul to Silas and Timothy in 17:15 to join him as soon as possible. Another place where Paul's use of slaves shows up is in his letters, where he himself (and his disputed alter ego) steps in, indicating that he himself is now writing:[67]

I, Paul, write this greeting with my own hand. (1 Cor 16:21)

60. Barclay, "Paul, Philemon and the Dilemma of Christian Slave-Ownership," 165.
61. Osiek and Balch, *Families in the New Testament World*, 99. The reference is to Gerd Theissen and John Howard Schütz, *The Social Setting of Pauline Christianity: Essays on Corinth* (Edinburgh: T&T Clark, 1982), 93.
62. Glancy, *Slavery in Early Christianity*, 49; Laura Salah Nasrallah, "'You were bought with a price:' Freedpersons and Things in 1 Corinthians," in *Corinth in Contrast: Studies in Inequality*, ed. Stephen J. Friesen, Sarah A. James, and Daniel N. Schowalter, 54–73 (Leiden: Brill, 2014), 64n45.
63. Barclay, "Paul, Philemon and the Dilemma of Christian Slave-Ownership."
64. See Petterson, *Acts of Empire*, 89–91.
65. Bruce speaks of Timothy and Silas bring "supplies." F. F. Bruce, *The Acts of the Apostles: The Greek Text with Introduction and Commentary* (London: Tyndale, 1952), 344. See also I. Howard Marshall, *Acts of the Apostles* (Sheffield: JSOT Press, 1982), 293–94; Richard Pervo, *Acts: A Commentary*, Hermeneia (Minneapolis: Fortress, 2009), 452; Ben Witherington, *The Acts of the Apostles: A Socio-Rhetorical Commentary* (Grand Rapids: Eerdmans, 1998), 448–49.
66. Translations and commentaries usually translate ἐντολή as "instructions," which softens the force of the word and take for granted that they are *co-workers*, and not subservient to Paul.
67. Petterson, *Acts of Empire*, 12.

> I, Paul, write this greeting with my own hand. This is the mark in every letter of mine; it is the way I write. (2 Thess 3:17)

> See what large letters I make when I am writing in my own hand! (Gal 6:11)

> So if you consider me your partner, welcome him as you would welcome me. If he has wronged you in any way, or owes you anything, charge that to my account. I, Paul, am writing this with my own hand: I will repay it. I say nothing about your owing me even your own self. (Phil 1:17-19)

> I, Paul, write this greeting with my own hand. Remember my chains. Grace be with you. (Col 4:18)

And then of course we have the example in Romans 16:22, where Tertius (a typical slave name, suggesting the possibility of a Primus and Secundus also under Paul's *potestas*), inscribes himself: "I, Tertius, the writer of this letter, greet you in the Lord."[68]

Roth pursues the topic of what she calls "Christian Slavery,"[69] situating "Paul's use of slave labor in the wider context of the economic exploitation of slaves in the Roman Empire."[70] The final section of her article deals with slavery and the economics of missionary success, which argues that "slave exploitation was a *systematic* [and, we would add, systemic] feature behind Christianity's (early) success."[71] Beginning with Meggitt's contention that full labor and ministry were incompatible within Paul's modus operandi,[72] and taking into account the efforts at staying connected with various communities, Roth rightly concludes that the "demand for slaves to undertake some of the leg-work—in a literal sense—emerges as very real," of which Onesimus and Epaphroditus are suitable examples.[73] The travels and epistles (from *epistellō*, of course) which made the Pauline mission such a success were unthinkable without slave labor. Here we find offers of accommodation, financial and in-kind travel subventions, and courier

---

68. For indications of Tertius as a slave name see H. Solin, *Die stadtrömischen Sklavennamen: ein Namenbuch. Barbarische Namen, Indices* (Franz Steiner Verlag, 1996), 152–53.

69. Ulrike Roth, "Paul and Slavery: Economic Perspectives," in *Paul of Tarsus and Economics*, ed. Thomas R. Blanton and Raymond Pickett (Minneapolis: Fortress Press, 2016). We would like to thank Roth for generous access to the unpublished version of this paper.

70. Ibid., 1.

71. Ibid., 7. Emphasis in original.

72. Justin Meggitt, *Paul, Poverty and Survival* (Edinburgh: T&T Clark, 1998), 76. However, it must be said that Meggitt's overall thesis, on the poverty of Paul and his communities, falls under what Roth astutely calls the "pauperising approach" to early Christians' social standing, which functions to minimize the possibility of implication in slavery and exploitation (which she also notes is not a given). Roth, "Paul and Slavery: Economic Perspectives," 5.

73. Roth, "Paul and Slavery: Economic Perspectives," 7.

services, as examples of slave-based services which slave-owners may offer Paul.[74] We add the possibility of Paul's own co-owned slaves assisting him on travels, as the above example from Acts shows.[75]

And finally, contradiction. That there is a contradiction between the acceptance of slave-ownership in the early congregations and the ideology of equality espoused by Paul in his epistles is noted by many.[76] However, if it is clear that the early Christian communities exploited slave labor in their missionary activity, then the issue becomes slightly more acute, needing an effort at least at a solution. Here we draw on the theory of an imaginary resolution of a real contradiction, first proposed by Lévi-Strauss and then elaborated by Fredric Jameson in an Althusserian framework.[77] In short, an irresolvable social and indeed economic contradiction so often generates an attempt at resolution at an ideological level. Obviously, such a resolution cannot deal with the real social contradiction, so it reveals, through its very tensions and problems, the irresolvable nature of the problem. In this light, we propose that Paul's use of metaphorical slavery is a desperate and brilliant attempt at attempting to resolve the actual contradiction at an ideological level. It consists quite simply in making everyone slaves, figuratively speaking, while maintaining, supporting, and benefiting from the fundamental inequality of this economic structure in daily life: as Roth says, Paul has his cake and eats it too.[78] The contradiction is not expressed in these terms, but relies rather on a difference between this world and the next, flesh and spirit, death and resurrection, and so on, which revolve around the fundamental problem of the early Christians caught between this world and the next.[79] This means that the metaphor does not simply arise from everyday life,[80] but emerges as an ideological effort to deal with an actual and pressing problem. It also indicates the inability to resolve this problem in actual practice.[81]

---

74. Ibid., 8.

75. Much more research needs to be done. A possible line of questioning, which we cannot pursue here, would be the passive verbs in the texts, since they may conceal the metaphorization of slave labor (eg. 1 Cor 1:11; Mark 12:1; Acts 8:28).

76. Barclay mentions "the central tension in the present status of Onesimus as both slave and brother to Philemon." Barclay, "Paul, Philemon and the Dilemma of Christian Slave-Ownership," 183.

77. Claude Lévi-Strauss, *Tristes Tropiques*, trans. John Weightman and Doreen Weightman (London: Pan, 1989); Fredric Jameson, *The Political Unconscious: Narrative as a Socially Symbolic Act* (Ithaca: Cornell University Press, 1981); Louis Althusser, *Lenin and Philosophy and Other Essays*, trans. Ben Brewster (New York: Monthly Review Press, 1971).

78. Roth, "Paul, Philemon, and Onesimus," 124.

79. Roland Boer, *In the Vale of Tears: On Marxism and Theology V*, Historical Materialism Book Series (Leiden: Brill, 2013), 179–98.

80. As Glancy seems to suggest in her characterization of slavery as "fertile ground for generating metaphorical language." Glancy, "Slavery and the Rise of Christianity," 457.

Parables and Property

This metaphor of slavery took on a life of its own, wresting itself free from the problems which gave rise to it. One place in which the metaphor comes out quite clearly is in the parables of Jesus that deal with slaves and God as the slaveholder. As we mentioned earlier, Schottroff takes particular exception to the parables that present God as a slaveholder and argues that these must be seen as antithetical parables, pointing to the difference between the slaveholder and God. Crucial to her argument is the dubious move of translating of *homoioun* and *homoios* as "compare" rather than "equate," since this loosens the obvious connection in the parables. Shottroff also insists heavily on non-allegorical interpretations of the various parables, because she wants to use the exploitative and violent content of the parables to signify the actual socio-economic context and separate a given parable from the Kingdom of God.

However, many of the parables do contain the "keys" to their own interpretation, either through an extensive one-by-one exposition of the various elements, such as in the parable of the sower (Mark 4:2–20; Matt 13:1–23; and Luke 8:4–15), or weeds in the field (Matt 13:36–43), or in the formula *homoiuon/homoios estin* (Matt 7:24–27 and Luke 6:46–49). As we pointed out earlier, we wonder whether the existence of the allegorical key to the parables displays the contradictions of class struggle, in that the agricultural imagery is used to explain something else. However, the allegorical reading (broadly defined) was in Dodd's analysis set out in terminology much closer to that of Paul than of Jesus.[82] This he understood to mean that the saying in Mark 4:11–12 (And he said to them, "To you has been given the secret of the kingdom of God, but for those outside, everything comes in parables; in order that 'they may indeed look, but not perceive, and may indeed listen, but not understand; so that they may not turn again and be forgiven'") indicates that this is a piece of apostolic teaching. Both Dodd and Schottroff's rejections of the allegorical method are founded in their refusal to acknowledge anti-Judaism in Jesus's teaching, with both seeing this facilitated and encouraged by the allegorical method and its inside-outside structure.[83] However understandable such an ideological posi-

---

81. Contra Geoffrey Turner, "The Christian Life as Slavery: Paul's Subversive Metaphor," *Heythrop Journal* 54, no. 1 (2013): 1–12.
82. Dodd, *Parables of the Kingdom*, 14.
83. Their motivations have different foundations. Over against Schottroff's liberative reading, Dodd's

tion might be, it also seems to close down some valuable interpretative options, which we are keen to pursue— not so much in relation to the question of insiders and outsiders but rather what the abstraction itself indicates.

This allegorical key, which is also present in Matthew and Luke, undergirds the dual nature of the material in question and along with *homoiuon/homoios estin* encourages the allegorical readings.[84] Following on from this point, we suggest that the use of parables in the Gospels is an expression of the abstraction identified in Paul's writings, specifically in his attempt to overcome the contradiction between the use of slaves within the church and the equality of its members.

Let us go further, for Christian metaphors of slavery include both negative and positive connotations: "The Christian can be termed both a slave of Christ and a freed person of Christ."[85] What is crucial in this designation is not the positive or the negative valence, but the characterization of the Christian as a slave, one way or another.[86] This is not only the case in Paul and later uses thereof, but also in Jesus's parables, as we find in Luke 16:13, which concerns a slave not being able to serve two masters. Here God and wealth are personified as masters, which means that the listener is interpellated as a slave. Furthermore, in the various parables where God is characterized as slaveholder, the slaves are either obedient or disobedient, and are rewarded or punished accordingly—all of which provides the listener with a choice between being an obedient or a disobedient *slave*. Finally, Paul's instruction to become slaves to one another through love (Gal 5:13) echoes Jesus's pronouncement in Mark that whoever wants to be first shall become everyone's slave, following Jesus's own example.[87] Following our line of argument, we would see this the other way around.

Let us now return to Ste. Croix's point about slavery and Jesus. On the one hand, Ste. Croix claims that Jesus was against property; on the other hand, he acknowledges that "Jesus accepted slavery as a fact of his environment."[88] In other words, Ste. Croix singles out slavery as a

---

concern is more historically motivated, in his keenness to keep the original Jesus apart from the primitive church. Dodd, *Parables of the Kingdom*, 14–15.

84. This is hardly a controversial point, but the anti-allegorical reading does have its supporters, especially in the liberation theological tradition, of which Schottroff and Herzog are examples, but also outside it, as Dodd testifies.

85. Glancy, "Slavery and the Rise of Christianity," 457–58.

86. See also Wayne Meeks, *The Moral World of the First Christians* (Philadelphia: Westminster John Knox, 1986), 157, 169.

87. Glancy, "Slavery and the Rise of Christianity," 459.

88. Ste. Croix, *Christian Persecution, Martyrdom, and Orthodoxy*, 349.

specific problem, while at the same time recognizing slavery as "one aspect of the larger question of property in general."[89] What do we make of this? Ste. Croix, we suggest, is repeating a contradiction which is present in the Gospels themselves: Jesus at times argues against property, while in no way criticizing the institution of slavery, which he uses as a way of getting theological points across. Here we disagree with Ste. Croix, for if there is a very close connection between property and slavery, as we argued earlier (see chapter 4), it would be possible to see the criticism of property in the Gospel as a criticism also of slavery. At the same time, we want to take our argument in a different direction and point out that the question of property in the Gospels is not without its problems. On the one hand, we do have the various sayings about camels and eyes of needles (Matt 19:23–24; Mark 10:23–25; Luke 18:24–25), as well as the parable of the rich fool (Luke 12:13–21). Yet, we also have the parables about God in which God is cast as a king or slaveholder, to the point of being in charge of substantial property, as we find in the parable of the faithful or the unfaithful slave (Matt 24:45–51; Luke 12:41–48), or the parable of the talents (Matt 25:14–30). A particularly interesting example is the chapter in Luke containing three parables which illustrate repentance. Two of them concern property as metaphors for sinners, namely, the parable of the lost sheep (Luke 15:1–7) and the parable of the lost coin (Luke 15:8–10). Both parables equate the repentance of a sinner with the finding a lost sheep and a lost coin. The third is the parable of the prodigal son (Luke 15:11–32), whose father owns a large slave-run property. In all three cases, God is the property owner who rejoices in the return of something or someone lost.

What we propose, on the basis of these examples, is that the Gospels propagate the slave-ethos, or in our terminology the slave-relation, to the listener—continuing the metaphorical tradition springing from Paul's attempt to overcome the profound tension between slave exploitation and equality. In doing so, the Gospels are not really advocating an alternative society, but remain within the parameters of the status quo. The odd rich person—who sells off property, gives it to the poor, and joins Jesus—does not change the dynamics of slaves and slave-owners. Instead, he contributes towards the endurance of the slave-relation.

---

89. Ibid., 345.

Luke 17:7-10 sums up what we call the slave-relation, namely the extension of the slave ethos to everyone, in submission to God:

> Who among you would say to your slave who has just come in from plowing or tending sheep in the field, "Come here at once and take your place at the table?" Would you not rather say to him, "Prepare supper for me, put on your apron and serve me while I eat and drink; later you may eat and drink?" Do you thank the slave for doing what was commanded? So you also, when you have done all that you were ordered to do, say, "We are worthless slaves; we have done only what we ought to have done!"

We have traced this ideological form back to the contradiction between ideology and practice in Paul's thinking, out of which the metaphorization of slavery arose as an imaginary effort as resolution. As many studies point out, slavery continued well after Constantine, and Christianity's contribution to slavery seems to be more one of undergirding the system with an ideology that did not challenge it but rather strengthened it, in the sense that the servile attitude was imbued as something desirable. This is what we designate the slave-relation.

The Land Regime

Thus far we have argued that Christianity as a mode of *régulation* largely followed in the wake of and provided new and telling ideological justifications for the colonial and slave regimes. The fact that it was a *polis*-based movement indicates that it was enmeshed with the *polis* and saw the *chōra* through such eyes. In terms of slaves, we identified a tension within the early movement between a drive towards equality (Gal 3:28 is the signal text) and the reality of slaves as enabling the spread of the early movement. Indeed Paul—the man who breathed the *polis* and who owned slaves as a matter of course in the context of the Christian *koinōnia*—was precisely the one who saw this contradiction and provided an attempted resolution at an ideological level: the slave metaphor for the Christian life, a metaphor that took on a life of its own in the subsequent Gospels and then in the very structure of Christian teaching and practice afterwards.

However when we turn to the land regime, which came into its own only in the late third century and was cemented by none other than Constantine, Christianity took on a somewhat different role. Here its role was more anticipatory, providing the means in practice and belief for the fundamental shift from labor to land as the focus. The intriguing aspect of this development is that the period in question was deeply formative for the nature of Christianity as an institution and as a set of doctrines. At the same time, since this period draws nigh to the end of our purview in this book we offer in this closing section suggestions of significant connections that really require much further research. So let us lay our proposal on the table. Three significant and overlapping developments indicate the anticipatory role of Christianity: the growth of pilgrimages to the "Holy Land," allegorical interpretation of the Bible (especially as a way of including the Hebrew Scriptures as the Old Testament), and canonization. In a nutshell, our proposal is that the possibility of focusing on the land where Jesus trod was enabled by the process of allegorizing. More sharply, the universal and transcendent features of Christianity enabled the distinct fixation of place, land, and earthly reality that characterized the period of the establishment of the land regime. While the three components of this process are intimately related, so much so that one can begin at any point in this "trinity," we begin with the land as a focus of pilgrimage, moving then to the questions of allegory and canonization. We also stress that these three features were not suddenly invented some time in the third or fourth century CE, but that their threads may already be espied from earlier centuries. By the time Constantine gained power in the 312 CE, these threads had coalesced in way that made his project of turning Palestine into a veritable biblical theme park seem perfectly normal.

And Did Those Feet in Ancient Times

An overwhelmingly pervasive narrative of early Christianity, with many facets and variations, is the passage from the "Jesus movement" to the church, from Galilee to Rome, from an anti-imperial movement to one that was quite at home with the emperor himself. This narrative also applies to the question of "holy places" and pilgrimage, following in the very footsteps of Jesus. So Markus can ask, "How on earth could places become holy?"[90] A majority answer is that the fourth century's fascination with holy places constituted a massive *volte-face* between the time of Jesus and that of Constantine.[91] In other words, earliest

---

90. Robert Markus, "How on Earth Could Places Become Holy? Origins of the Christian Idea of Holy Places," *Journal of Early Christian Studies* 2, no. 3 (1994): 257–71.
91. See also Joan Taylor, *Christians and the Holy Places: The Myth of Jewish-Christian Origins* (Oxford: Clarendon, 1993), 313–14; Brouria Bitton-Ashkelony, *Encountering the Sacred: The Debate on Christian Pilgrimage in Late Antiquity* (Berkeley: University of California Press, 2005), 21–22.

Christianity was not interested in holy places, fostering a universal creed that appealed across space and time (Paul), while fourth-century Christianity could not get enough of the countryside of Palestine festooned with holy places that were filled with hordes of pilgrims.[92] In between these two moments we find only dusty desert space, traversed by odd figures such as Melito of Sardis, Origen, and a couple of Cappadocians.

Yet, this period is hardly blank, hardly a desert which one at most traverses to get from one point to the other. Instead, it is full of developments that play off two sides in what at times begins to look like a dialectic. On the one hand we have Paul, the great universalizer and indeed transcendental thinker, pushing for a form of Christianity that could appeal across peoples, places, and times, all of which was based on his narrative of death and resurrection. On the other hand we have the Gospels which follow in his wake.[93] These texts notably seek to locate Jesus in a particular place and time. Whether or not the compilers of Mark, Matthew, Luke, and John had ever been to Galilee or Judea is of little consequence. What is important is that they all four situated Jesus within the dual kingdom, namely the biblical land of Israel and the *chōra* of the Roman province of Palestine. But they did so via what may appear initially to be a curious mechanism: they viewed the *chōra* in question from the perspective of the *polis*—exactly the same perspective as that of Paul but with a very different result. In other words, the very mechanism of situating Jesus in Palestine is a mediated one. We cannot stress enough this mediation, for it would become a staple of subsequent efforts to focus on the land.

In order to examine this mediation further, let us follow two of the earlier "pilgrims" on their path. The first is Melito of Sardis (died in 180 CE), who visited Palestine "to the place where these things were preached and done" and returned with a list of the books of the Old Testament.[94] The catch is that this very same Melito had argued in his

---

92. In her study of the evolution of Christian holy places in Palestine, Joan Taylor argues that pilgrimage, which regards places as being intrinsically holy, did not exist before Constantine. This is the crucial piece in her overall argument against the Bagatta-Testa hypothesis which argues for an original Jewish-Christian veneration of holy sites in Palestine, which were subsequently appropriated by the Byzantine Church. Taylor, *Christians and the Holy Places.* Most studies of pilgrimage to Palestine in the first four centuries distinguish between earlier "scholarly" visits and later "emotional" pilgrimage. However, this distinction does not have a bearing on our argument. Taylor, *Christians and the Holy Places,* 310–11; E. D. Hunt, *Holy Land Pilgrimage in the Later Roman Empire, AD 312–460* (Oxford: Clarendon, 1982), 92–93; Robert Wilken, *The Land Called Holy: Palestine in Christian History and Thought* (New Haven: Yale University Press, 1992), 108.
93. In other words, we do see a difference between Paul and the Gospels, but in an unlikely place: the concern over the land.

first homily, *Peri Pascha*, that the Jerusalem here below once had value, but now it is without value because of the Jerusalem from above. How can Melito hold both positions, valorizing the heavenly and universal (pace Paul) and yet setting off for Palestine to see where Jesus had been and preached? Before we answer this question, let us now follow none other than Origen, the prince of allegory, who in *Contra Celsum* refuted the idea that the good land was the earthly land of Judea. He nevertheless set out from Caesarea where he lived, "to trace the footsteps of Jesus" in Palestine.[95] He also uses his visit to Bethlehem to refute those who would deny that Jesus was the savior:

> With respect to the birth of Jesus in Bethlehem, if any one desires, after the prophecy of Micah and after the history recorded in the Gospels by the disciples of Jesus, to have additional evidence from other sources, let him know that, in conformity with the narrative in the Gospel regarding His birth, there is shown at Bethlehem the cave where He was born, and the manger in the cave where He was wrapped in swaddling-clothes. And this sight is greatly talked of in surrounding places, even among the enemies of the faith, it being said that in this cave was born that Jesus who is worshipped and reverenced by the Christians.[96]

Thus, if the prophecy in Micah is not enough, and even if the Gospel history is not enough, then —in correspondence with the gospel (which must be the proto-gospel of James)—a cave in Bethlehem is shown as proof with its manger where the Christ was wrapped in swaddling-clothes. Has Origen finally given up on his elaborate flights of interpretation, which would become the basis for a millennium or so of allegorical exegesis, or is something else going on here? To the contrary, we suggest that it was through the universal and transcendent (Melito) and through the allegorical move (Origen) that the fixation on place and land could happen.[97]

94. Eusebius, *Hist Eccl* 4.26.14. See the full list of pre-Constantinian visitors in D. Hans Windisch, "Die Ältesten Christlichen Palästinapilger," *Zeitschrift des Deutschen Palästina-Verein* 48, no. 1–2 (1925): 145–58.
95. Wilken, *The Land Called Holy: Palestine in Christian History and Thought*, 108. There seems to be great discomfort with Origen's trip, and it is hardly mentioned without a speedy qualifier that he was not a pilgrim, but rather a scholar or tourist. See also Taylor, *Christians and the Holy Places*, 311.
96. Origen, *Contra Celsum*, ed. Henry Chadwick (Cambridge: Cambridge University Press, 1980), 1.51.
97. Another interesting feature is that Origen also compiled a biblical onomasticon, which served to explain the Hebrew place names to Greek readers, using the etymological allegorical method. See R. P. C. Hanson, "Interpretations of Hebrew Names in Origen," *Vigiliae Christianae* 10, no. 1 (1956): 103–23. For a good analysis of this form of interpretation, see David Dawson, *Allegorical Readers and Cultural Revision in Ancient Alexandria* (Berkeley: University of California Press, 1991), 24–38. Once again Origen's obsession with the land resurfaces.

Through Allegory to the Canon

So we have two developments that began to happen in the lead-up to the land regime: pilgrimage to the places of where Jesus trod and allegorical exegesis. More to the point, the earliest pilgrims were precisely those interested in transcendent and allegorical approaches. And we have pointed out that the Gospels themselves, mediated through the eyes of the *polis*, played a significant role in this situation. Indeed, since we have the focus on the land—crucial to the land regime—in mind, then the difference between the canonical and extra-canonical gospels becomes apparent, in this register at least. Several reservations notwithstanding—such as the fragmented nature of the texts (due to their non-canonical status), and all of the texts we do not possess—a look through the non-canonical gospels shows a distinct lack of interest in Palestine.[98] This is not to say that there is no mention of, for instance, Bethlehem, Galilee, or the river Jordan,[99] but these are brief occurrences in the texts and do not seem to have quite that same insistence or distention in space as in the canonical Gospels. The non-canonical gospels, in other words, display a more focused transcendent perspective, in contrast to the canonical texts that emphasize in their mediated fashion the historical and geographical perspective.

In the end, it is allegory—deriving from practices in Greek texts and philosophy—that provides the key form of mediation not only for fixing on the land, but also for the process of canonization, the third development intimately connected with the land regime.[100] We noted earlier that Melito of Sardis returned from his trek with a list of the

---

98. In his book on canonization and marginalization, Bart Ehrman paints a vivid picture of the diversity of early Christianity. Was it one God or many? Who created the world? Were the Jewish scriptures inspired? If so, where they inspired by a true God, a Jewish God or an evil deity? Was Jesus either divine or human or both? Did he have flesh or not? Did he die? And if so, did his death bring about the salvation of the world or not? From this bewildering array of possibilities emerged, as we know, the canon of the 27 writings referred to in Athanasius's Easter epistle in 367 CE. Ehrmann describes the process as one where a particular form of Christianity, which he names "proto-orthodox," emerged as "victorious from the conflicts of the second and third centuries" and then proceeded to produce a story describing a process in which, to quote Schröter, "the church ensured continuity with its beginnings and the mutual correspondence of its confession and its writings." Jens Schröter, *From Jesus to the New Testament: Early Christian Theology and the Origin of the New Testament Canon* (Waco: Baylor University Press, 2013), 250; Bart Erhman, *Lost Christianities: The Battle for Scripture and the Faiths We Never Knew* (New York: Oxford University Press, 2003).
99. Thus the Proto-gospel of James has an account of the census-trip to Bethlehem and the birth of Jesus in a cave there; the gospel according to the Hebrews mentions Galilee, Jordan, and Bethany; the Gospel of the Ebionites mentions Capernaum and Jordan; the Gospel of Peter refers to the darkness falling over Judea as well as Golgatha; etc.
100. For a useful study of early Christian allegory, see Dawson, *Allegorical Readers and Cultural Revision in Ancient Alexandria*.

books of the Old Testament and Origen himself compiled a biblical ono-masticon for the benefit of Greek readers. Allegory was the process by which the canon could be formed (turning the Hebrew Bible into the Old Testament), and concomitantly the land could be identified. Crucially, allegory emerged *both* as a weapon to combat heresy *and* as the tool with which to canonize—a tool without which canonization of the Old and the New Testament would have been impossible. Allegory embodies the persistent tension in early Christianity between the ide-alized heavenly homeland and the actual land, which was very much present in the great allegorizer himself—Origen. As Davies points out, the land was one of the "most persistent and passionate doctrines with which the early church had to come to terms."[101] At the very same time that the shift from labor to land, from the slave and colonial regimes to the land regime, was happening, proto-orthodoxy was busy appro-priating the Hebrew Scriptures in their fight against heresy. And it was through the allegorization of the texts that the land came back with a vengeance and had to be reshaped as the land of Jesus. As was the case with the land, the appropriation of the Hebrew Scriptures took place at a practical, earthly level with the copying of Old Testament passages into the notebooks that eventually would become the codices and scriptures of the proto-orthodox church.

Other efforts to deal with this tension, or rather mediate the earthly through the heavenly, may be seen in debates that raged in the fourth century CE and afterwards over the nature of Christ, or indeed the four Gospels and the singular story, but we close by focusing on what is really the end-point of this process that both foreshadowed and then cemented the fixation on the land: the *Onomasticon* by Eusebius from about 330 CE.[102] The title proper is *The Place Names of the Holy Scripture* and it includes a list of about 1,000 entries, most of which refer to Old Testament place names in Palestine. According to Stenger, Eusebius's main concern seems to have been the identification of the ancient places, thus interweaving the spatial and chronological dimen-sions—that is, late-ancient Palestine with a conjunction of Old and New

---

101. W. D. Davies, *The Gospel and the Land: Early Christianity and Jewish Territorial Doctrine* (Berkeley: Uni-versity of California Press, 1974), 5. See also Christina Petterson, "The Land is Mine: Place and Dis-location in the Letter to the Hebrews," *Sino-Christian Studies* 4 (2007): 69–93.
102. It is not his most well-known work, but is nevertheless experiencing renewed interest since the initial surge in the last century. For more recent research see Jan Stenger, "Eusebius and the Representation of the Holy Land," in *Brill's Companion to Ancient Geography: The Inhabited World in Greek and Roman Tradition*, ed. Serena Bianchetti, Michele R. Cataudella, and Hans Joachim Gehrke, 381–98 (Leiden: Brill, 2016).

Testament with Roman times.[103] Correspondingly, Stenger also regards Eusebius's purpose as apologetic and concludes:

> The gazetteer's usefulness lies then not so much in each individual entry but rather in the whole picture it evokes. Only when readers have the geographical inventory of the Bible in accessible presentation before them will they form an image of the territory of Palestine in their mind and recognise it as a coherent and well-defined space that is inscribed with Christian memories.[104]

With Eusebius's *Onomasticon* undergirding Constantine's efforts, the grip on the land and the forced conversion of its peasant inhabitants was well underway.[105]

103. Stenger, "Representation," 388–89. Wolf shows that the items which occur are biblical places with summaries of events, references to Josephus, locations in reference to fourth century towns and roads, modern name of a place and if relevant present inhabitants, Roman garrisons and forts. Carl Umhau Wolf, "Eusebius of Caesarea and the Onomasticon," *Biblical Archaeologist* 27, no. 3 (1964): 65–96, 76.
104. Stenger, "Representation," 396.
105. For an intriguing argument linking peasant with pagan and the violent destruction of peasant shrines in the wake of Constantine, see Taylor, *Christians and the Holy Places,* 301–2.

Conclusion

In this conclusion, we do not offer yet another summary of our main arguments, for such a summary may be found in the introduction. Instead, we broach a couple of matters that are pertinent to ourselves and to potential readers. The first can be dealt with relatively quickly, for it deals with the old charge that Marxism is for some perverse reason "reductionist." Put in terms of the problem of base and superstructure, this charge asserts that a Marxist approach will ultimately lead to a position in which the superstructure is determined by the infrastructure or the base. In our case, this would mean that the economic tensions and shifts between the colonial, slave, and land regimes generated new features in the ideological formulations of an ideology like Christianity. Religion—if not ideology more generally—is supposed to reflect the economic realities of daily life. This approach is at times called "vulgar" Marxism. While space must always be made for a good dose of hardline vulgar Marxism at appropriate moments, this is not one of those moments.

Our argument is different. To begin with, due to its in-between nature, manifested above all in the theological tension between death and resurrection, between life in this world and in the world to come, Christianity was brilliantly placed to become a dominant religious force in not merely the Roman Empire, but eventually the world. Christianity offered a new life, but was also fully aware that the realities of the old life continued to influence the new life. So, one could be comforted by the old familiarities while simultaneously seeking to live in a new way. We see no betrayal here of Christianity's "pure" origins, a fall narrative perhaps that is beloved of historians and many a biblical critic, for this tension appears already in the earliest texts. Further, we have argued that Christianity more often anticipated the economic shifts under way, thereby providing people with the existential, religious, and ideological resources to manage the shift. This was particularly the case with the shift to the land regime in the third century CE. A number of threads indicate this anticipatory feature: the gospel tendency to locate Jesus in specific locations in Galilee, the impetus towards canonization that began in the second century, the development of full-blooded allegory as a way to incorporate the Hebrew texts and their focus on land and land-use, and the growth of pilgrimage to significant gospel locales. Indeed, this anticipatory feature of Christianity applies also to the growth of feudalism for which the land regime provided the bridge between the ancient mode of production and feudalism.

The second matter requires more sustained attention, for it has been the topic of many discussions between us. In short, we differ on the question of resistance to the dominant economic regimes. We do not mean the constitutive resistance of subsistence survival, which the three regimes sought to overcome, albeit unsuccessfully. We differ on the nature of resistance from and within Christianity. Roland is prepared to leave room for resistance, although he sees it as mediated through the dominant ideological and economic framework. By contrast, Christina prefers what some have called a more totalizing approach—or perhaps an "iron cage" approach—in which resistance is generated by the system in question and is thereby contained within the system. Rather than immediately consider a sample text or two to show how our readings differ, let us use an example from an unexpected but pertinent situation: the development of Christian "orthodoxy" through a series of ecumenical councils. In doing so, we return for one last time to Ste. Croix, who has been our touchstone in so many ways (not least because his monumental work has been systematically neglected in classical studies, ancient history, economic reconstructions, and biblical scholarship). We would like to entitle these observations "the spirit works in strange ways."

The material in question appears in the posthumously published collection by Ste. Croix, *Christian Persecution, Martyrdom, and Orthodoxy*.[1] The last topic of this title is our interest, for it takes place at a time both when the land regime came to the fore and when Christianity became a state ideology (the two moments are intimately connected in complex ways). Constantine's decision to make Christianity the religion of

---

1. Ste. Croix, *Christian Persecution, Martyrdom, and Orthodoxy*.

his realm had a number of consequences. More obviously, it meant state funding for the construction of churches and cathedrals, as also for a whole new bureaucracy of religious professionals and their costly vestments. But one outcome was unexpected: the sheer difference of opinion between Christian groups across the empire. We can imagine Constantine's horror at finding religious leaders viciously attacking one another over what must to him have appeared as inconsequential doctrinal differences. What was to be done? Constantine would ensure uniformity! To this end, he called the first ecumenical council to hammer out the differences, in Nicaea in 325 CE. Whatever his failings, Constantine was no fool, so he was hardly one to allow the various bishops and theologians to settle matters in what they claimed would be the spirit of calm debate and brotherly love. No, the emperor himself presided over much of the proceedings, intervening in debates, and, where necessary, enforcing what became "orthodox" positions.

Subsequent emperors followed suit, such the emperor Marcian (392–457 CE) and the council of Chalcedon in 451 CE, which set the agenda for most of the later Christian churches. Indeed, the council itself was called amid controversy, for Marcian (with the reluctant agreement of pope Leo I) wished to overturn the monophysite positions—two natures absorbed into one divine nature—of the second council of Ephesus (459 CE) called by his predecessor, Theodosius II. Given such a background, one could hardly expect Chalcedon to be a peaceful council. Ste. Croix takes great delight in showing, on the basis of council records,[2] how debate often took the form of abusing one's opponent and trying to outshout him. At times of clear division between groups, a quiet show of hands was the last approach on their minds. Instead, the council resembled more of a Roman circus or perhaps a modern-day football match. One group would begin a chant, "*exo bales, exo bales, exo bales*. . ."—"chuck 'em out, chuck 'em out, chuck 'em out." The group in question sought to indicate by sheer volume and venom what an "orthodox" position should be. Presiding officials attempted vainly to regain order: "These vulgar outbursts are not becoming to bishops, nor useful to either party."[3] By this time an insightful device first instituted by Constantine ensured that no-one could leave until agreement was attained; imperial troops were stationed around the council's meeting venue.

The troops also ensured that no-one was actually lynched during the

2. Ibid., 259–319.
3. Ibid., 268.

council. But this did not prevent some from being so dealt with afterwards. If one happened to one of the unfortunate bishops who found himself in a minority that lost out in the final decision, the person in question would literally fear for his life upon returning home. Conversely, the same fear attended those who were appointed to replace a supposedly "heretical" bishop or even patriarch. For example, at Chalcedon, the "heretical" patriarch Dioscurus I was deposed for his key role in the second council of Ephesus a couple of years earlier, and thereby for his monophysite (or miaphysite) Christology. His replacement was Proterius, who, after Chalcedon had come to a close, proudly took his way to Alexandria to claim his new position. Large sections of the Egyptian church refused to accept him. The struggle continued for a few years, until an alternative patriarch (Timothy II) was elected and Proterius was mobbed in his church, dragged out, killed, burnt, and his ashes scattered. By contrast, Juvenal of Jerusalem was a little more careful. Juvenal had been campaigning for some time (since 422 CE) to have Jerusalem elevated to a patriarchate. Sensing the direction of the political wind, Juvenal spoke out of both sides of his mouth. In Jerusalem, he vowed to hold to local positions on the nature of Christ. At the councils, however, he supported what became known as Chalcedonian Christology. Thus, he opposed Nestorian dyophysitism at the first council of Ephesus (431 CE) and monophysitism at Chalcedon.[4] For his trenchant support at Chalcedon, he was rewarded with a patriarchate. But he was also aware of what this might mean upon his return home, for he knew that word of his apparent about-face would not go down well with the large number of monophysites in his see. He requested and received a strong cohort of troops as security. Even with the troops, it took him almost two years to reclaim his see as the new patriarch.

What are we to make of these realities? Does the spirit work in strange ways indeed, as the councils show? Or is Ste. Croix's favorite text from the pagan writer, Ammianus, more pertinent: "Wild beasts are not more hostile to mankind than are *most* Christians (*plerique Christianorum*) in their deadly hatred of one another"?[5]

Roland tends to favor the first position, while Christina bends more towards the latter. Let us give a second example, now from the biblical

---

4. At one level, these debates over the nature of Christ were also debates concerning human nature. A human being may be seen as separated from but close to God (dyophysitism), or a divine figure on earth, distinct from all other creation (monophysitism), or separate from God through sin but closely connected with God through salvation (Chalcedonian "orthodoxy").

5. Ste. Croix, *Class Struggle*, 451; Ste. Croix, *Christian Persecution, Martyrdom, and Orthodoxy*, 222, 260.

parable of the "wicked" tenants (Mark 12:1–12; Matt 21:33–46; Luke 20:9–19). Christina is keen to emphasize the grain of the parable itself. From this perspective, the focus is clearly on the landlord: "A man planted a vineyard, put a fence around it, dug a pit for the wine press, and built a watchtower" (Mark 12:1). He then lets tenants work the vineyard and expects that they provide him with what he is rightly owed. That they do not is due to their wicked, evil intent. They beat and kill the various slaves sent by the landlord to collect his due percentage of the produce, resorting at last to the dastardly act of killing even the landlord's beloved son. Jesus points out: "What then will the owner of the vineyard do? He will come and destroy the tenants and give the vineyard to others" (Mark 12:9). And to make sure the point is clear, Jesus cites Psalm 118 concerning the stone that the builders rejected.

We have used Mark's version of the parable, since it is the toughest (Matthew and Luke tend to soften its edges). For Christina, the parable presents God as the slaveholding landlord and the tenants as believers who must do the right thing. The added touch of the beloved son (and cornerstone) ensures that one can only with difficulty and some deft footwork attempt to drive a wedge between God and the landlord. In other words, in the mouth of Jesus—as presented in the Gospels—God comes through clearly from a ruling class and *polis*-based perspective. Believers are thereby tenants who must pay the appropriate due in produce or in money, or they are—as we find in other parables and sayings—slaves who should be obedient rather than disobedient. Roland agrees and disagrees. He agrees that the tone of the parable is one of a ruling-class perspective, indeed that the class dynamics of the parable determine the relationship between Christians and God, if not Jesus himself. No amount of dexterous interpretation can overcome this tone of the parable. But Roland also wants to challenge this ruling-class perspective in the following way (inspired by Ernst Bloch's enticing work[6]). From such a perspective, one would expect that tenants would be dishonest thieves and murderers, keen to avoid an honest day's work and keen to make off with any of the landlord's rightful property. Even today, unfree labor (workers) are routinely suspected and accused of avoiding work, pilfering, being paid too much, and being part of those "criminal" organizations known as trade unions. But this is a ruling-class approach, a perspective of the bosses. Once this ideological framework of the parable is recognized for what it is,

---

6. Bloch, *Atheism in Christianity*.

we can begin to read the parable in a different way. The actions of the tenants are perfectly in accord with age-old tactics of the exploited. They do the labor upon which the idle rich rely, as 2 Thessalonians 3:10 would have it: "Anyone unwilling to work should not eat."[7] The ones unwilling to work are the rulers, the slave-owners, the landlords, and the bosses. In light of this approach, what is characterized as disobedience, wickedness, if not outright insurrection in the parable can be reread as perfectly justified. In other words, this is a dual reading of the parable, undertaken in light of a class approach. One does not seek to excuse the landlord-God of this parable, since this is a God who has been enlisted without too much trouble to support ruling ideology; but one also sees that the tenants' resistance to this God of white-guard terror is what one may expect. Because it represents the ruling class perspective, the parable must include the insurrection to justify the violent reaction; however, it does not succeed in containing the insurrection, so to speak. By its very presence, the insurrection testifies to its own perspective.

Even Roland's approach may not be palatable for those keen to read the Gospels, let alone the texts of the Apocalypse or even of Paul, as in some sense resistance literature. Christina would say that this is a difficult if not forlorn exercise; Roland would say that he understands and even affirms the underlying impetus to do so, but that the approach needs to be a little more aware of the economic and class dimensions of how such a reading might proceed. We close by observing that we do not want to resolve this difference of approach to early Christianity, for the debate continues. But we do agree that the economic and material realities of the new religious movement are crucial to understanding the nature of the movement itself.

---

7. This interpretation was first clearly articulated by Lenin, only to make its way in the Soviet Union's Constitution of 1936. V. I. Lenin, "The State and Revolution," in *Collected Works*, vol. 25, 385–497 (Moscow: Progress Publishers, 1964 [1917]), 472. V. I. Lenin, "On the Famine: A Letter to the Workers of Petrograd, 22 May, 1918," in *Collected Works*, vol. 27, 391–98 (Moscow: Progress Publishers, 1965 [1918]), 391–92; I. V. Stalin, "Constitution (Fundamental Law) of the Union of Soviet Socialist Republics, With amendments adopted by the First, Second, Third, Sixth, Seventh, and Eighth Sessions of the Supreme Soviet of the U.S.S.R., Kremlin, Moscow, December 5, 1936," in *Works*, vol. 14, 199–239 (London: Red Star Press, 1978 [1936]), article 12.

Bibliography

Adan-Bayewitz, David. "Kefar Ḥananya." In *Galilee in the Late Second Temple and Mishnaic Periods. Volume 2: The Archaeological Record from Cities, Towns, and Villages*, edited by David Fiensy and James Strange, 181–85. Minneapolis: Fortress, 2015.

Alcock, Susan. "A Simple Case of Exploitation? The Helots of Messenia." In *Money, Labour and Land: Approaches to the Economies of Ancient Greece*, edited by Paul Cartledge, Edward Cohen and Lin Foxhall, 185–99. London: Routledge, 2002.

Algaze, Guillermo. *Ancient Mesopotamia at the Dawn of Civilization: The Evolution of an Urban Landscape*. Chicago: University of Chicago Press, 2008.

Althusser, Louis. *Lenin and Philosophy and Other Essays*, translated by Ben Brewster. New York: Monthly Review Press, 1971.

Ambler, Wayne. "Aristotle on Nature and Politics: The Case of Slavery." *Political Theory* 15, no. 3 (1987): 390–410.

Amouretti, Marie-Claire. "L'agriculture de la Grèce antique: bilan des recherches de la dernière décennie." *Topoi* 4, no. 1 (1994): 69–93.

Anderson, James. "The Impact of Rome on the Periphery: The Case of Palestina-Roman Period (63 BCE–324 CE)." In *The Archaeology of Society in the Holy Land*, edited by Thomas Levy, 446–68. London: Leicester University Press, 1998.

Anderson, Perry. *In the Tracks of Historical Materialism*. London: Verso, 2016 [1983].

_____. *Passages from Antiquity to Feudalism*. London: Verso, 1974.

_____. *A Zone of Engagement*. London: Verso, 1992.

André, Christine. "The Welfare State and Institutional Compromises: From Origins to Contemporary Crisis." In *Régulation Theory: The State of the Art*, edited by Robert Boyer and Yves Saillard, 94–100. London: Routledge, 2002 [1995].

Andreau, J., Pierre Briant, and R. Descat, eds. *Économie antique. La guerre dans les économies antiques*. Saint-Bertrand-de-Comminges: Musée Archéologique Départemental, 2000.

_____, eds. *Économie antique. Les échanges dans l'Antiquité: le rôle de l'État*. Saint-Bertrand-de-Comminges: Musée Archéologique Départemental, 1994.

_____, eds. *Économie antique. Prix et formation des prix dans les économies antiques*. Saint-Bertrand-de-Comminges: Musée Archéologique Départemental, 1997.

Andreau, Jean. "Markets, Fairs and Monetary Loans: Cultural History and Economic History in Roman Italy and Hellenistic Greece." In *Money, Labour and Land: Approaches to the Economies of Ancient Greece*, edited by Paul Cartledge, Edward Cohen and Lin Foxhall, 113–29. London: Routledge, 2002.

Anhum, Hans. "Mancipatio by Slaves in Ancient Roman Law?" *Acta Juridica (Essays in Honour of Ben Beinart)* (1976): 1–18.

Applebaum, Shimon. "Economic Life in Palestine." In *The Jewish People in the First Century: Historical Geography, Political History, Social, Cultural and Religious Life and Institutions*, vol. 2, edited by Shemuel Safrai and Menahem Stern, 631–700. Assen: Van Gorcum, 1976.

Arav, Rami, and Carl Savage. "Bethsaida." In *Galilee in the Late Second Temple and Mishnaic Periods. Volume 2: The Archaeological Record from Cities, Towns, and Villages*, edited by David Fiensy and James Strange, 258–79. Minneapolis: Fortress, 2015.

Aristotle. *Nicomachean Ethics*. Translated by Harris Rackham. Loeb Classical Library. Cambridge: Harvard University Press, 1934.

_____. *Politics*. Translated by Harris Rackham. Loeb Classical Library. Cambridge: Harvard University Press, 2005 [1934].

Arzt-Grabner, Peter. *Philemon*. Papyrologische Kommentare zum Neuen Testament. Göttingen: Vandenhoeck & Ruprecht, 2003.

Aubert, Jean-Jacques. *Business Managers in Ancient Rome: A Social and Economic Study of Institores, 200 BC–AD 250*. Leiden: Brill, 1994.

Aviam, Mordechai. "First Century Jewish Galilee: An Archaeological Perspective." In *Religion and Society in Roman Palestine: Old Questions, New Approaches*, edited by Douglas Edwards, 7–27. New York: Routledge, 2004.

_____. *Jews, Pagans, and Christians in the Galilee: 25 Years of Archaeological Excavations and Surveys, Hellenistic to Byzantine Periods*. Rochester: University of Rochester Press, 2004.

_____. "People, Land, Economy, and Belief in First-Century Galilee and Its Origins: A Comprehensive Archaeological Synthesis." In *The Galilean Economy in the Time of Jesus*, edited by David Fiensy and Ralph Hawkins, 5–48. Atlanta: Society of Biblical Literature, 2013.

_____. "The Transformation from *Galil Ha-Goyim* to Jewish Galilee: The Archaeological Testimony of an Ethnic Change." In *Galilee in the Late Second Temple and Mishnaic Periods. Volume 2: The Archaeological Record from Cities, Towns, and Villages*, edited by David Fiensy and James Strange, 9–21. Minneapolis: Fortress, 2015.

_____. "Yodefat-Jotapata: A Jewish Galilean Town at the End of the Second Temple Period." In *Galilee in the Late Second Temple and Mishnaic Periods. Volume 2: The Archaeological Record from Cities, Towns, and Villages*, edited by David Fiensy and James Strange, 109–26. Minneapolis: Fortress, 2015.

Bagnall, Roger, ed. *The Oxford Handbook of Papyrology.* Oxford: Oxford University Press, 2009.

_____. *Reading Papyri, Writing Ancient History.* London: Routledge, 1995.

Bailey, Kenneth. *Jesus Through Middle Eastern Eyes: Cultural Studies in the Gospels.* Downers Grove: IVP Academic, 2008.

Bakhos, Carol. "Orality and Writing." In *The Oxford Handbook of Jewish Daily Life in Roman Palestine*, edited by Catherine Hezser, 482–501. Oxford: Oxford University Press, 2010.

Bal, Mieke. *Death and Dissymetry: The Politics of Coherence in the Book of Judges.* Chicago: University of Chicago Press, 1988.

Banaji, Jairus. *Agrarian Change in Late Antiquity: Gold, Labour and Aristocratic Dominance.* Oxford: Oxford University Press, 2001.

_____. *Theory as History: Essays on Modes of Production and Exploitation.* Historical Materialism Book Series. Leiden: Brill, 2010.

Barclay, John. "Paul, Philemon and the Dilemma of Christian Slave-Ownership." *New Testament Studies* 37, no. 2 (2009): 161–86.

Baslé, Maurice. "Acknowledged and Unacknowledged Institutionalist Antecedents of Régulation Theory." In *Régulation Theory: The State of the Art*, edited by Robert Boyer and Yves Saillard, 21–27. London: Routledge, 2002 [1995].

Becker, Gary S. *The Economic Approach to Human Behavior.* Chicago: University of Chicago Press, 1976.

Bell, Gertrude. *The Desert and the Sown.* London: William Heinemann, 1907.

Beloch, Julius. "Zur griechischen Wirtschaftsgeschichte." *Zeitschrift für Sozialwissenschaft* 5 (1902): 1–97.

Bergheim, Samuel. "Land Tenure in Palestine." *Palestine Exploration Fund Quarterly* 26, no. 3 (1894): 191–99.

Berlin, Andrea. "Household Judaism." In *Galilee in the Late Second Temple and Mishnaic Period, Volume 1: Life, Culture, and Society*, edited by David Fiensy and James Strange, 208–15. Minneapolis: Fortress, 2014.

Berlin, Andrea, and Sharon Herbert. "Kadesh of the Upper Galilee." In *Galilee in the Late Second Temple and Mishnaic Periods. Volume 2: The Archaeological Record* from *Cities, Towns, and Villages*, edited by David Fiensy and James Strange, 424–42. Minneapolis: Fortress, 2015.

Berquist, Jon, and Claudia Camp, eds. *Constructions of Space I: Theory, Geography, and Narrative*. London: T&T Clark, 2008.

_____, eds. *Constructions of Space II: The Biblical City and Other Imagined Spaces*. London: T&T Clark, 2009.

Binford, Lewis. *Constructing Frames of Reference: An Analytical Method for Archaeological Theory Building Using Hunter-Gatherer and Environmental Data Sets*. Berkeley: University of California Press, 2001.

Bitton-Ashkelony, Brouria. *Encountering the Sacred: The Debate on Christian Pilgrimage in Late Antiquity*. Berkeley: University of California Press, 2005.

Blackledge, Paul. *Reflections on the Marxist Theory of History*. Manchester: Manchester University Press, 2006.

Blaug, Mark. "The Formalist Revolution of the 1950s." *Journal of the History of Economic Thought* 25, no. 2 (2003): 145–56.

Bloch, Ernst. *Atheism in Christianity: The Religion of the Exodus and the Kingdom*. Translated by J. T. Swann. London: Verso, 2009.

Block, Fred. "Introduction." In *The Great Transformation: The Political and Economic Origins of Our Time*, xviii–xxxviii. Boston: Beacon, 2001 [1944].

Blum, Jerome. *The End of the Old Order in Rural Europe*. Princeton: Princeton University Press, 1978.

Bodel, John. "Slave Labour and Roman Society." In *The Cambridge World History of Slavery*, vol. 1, edited by Keith Bradley and Paul Cartledge, 311–36. Cambridge: Cambridge University Press, 2011.

Boer, Roland. *Criticism of Theology: On Marxism and Theology III*. Leiden: Brill, 2010.

_____. *In the Vale of Tears: On Marxism and Theology V*. Historical Materialism Book Series. Leiden: Brill, 2013.

_____. "On the Myth of Classicism." *Journal for the Study of Christian Culture* 31 (2014): 131–51.

_____. *Political Myth: On the Use and Abuse of Biblical Themes*. Durham: Duke University Press, 2007.

_____. *The Sacred Economy of Ancient Israel*. Library of Ancient Israel. Lousville: Westminster John Knox, 2015.

Boer, Roland, and Christina Petterson. *Idols of Nations: Biblical Myth at the Origins of Capitalism*. Philadelphia: Fortress, 2014.

Bouquet, A. C. *Everyday Life in New Testament Times*. London: Batsford, 1953.

Bowman, Alan, and Andrew Wilson, eds. *Quantifying the Roman Economy: Methods and Problems*. Oxford: Oxford University Press, 2009.

_____, eds. *The Roman Agricultural Economy: Organization, Investment, and Production*. Oxford: Oxford University Press, 2013.

_____, eds. *Settlement, Urbanization, and Population*. Oxford: Oxford University Press, 2011.

Boyer, Robert. "Introduction." In *Régulation Theory: The State of the Art*, edited by Robert Boyer and Yves Saillard, 1–10. London: Routledge, 2002 [1995].

_____. "The Regulation Approach as a Theory of Capitalism: A New Derivation." In *Institutional Economics in France and Germany: German Ordoliberalism Versus the French Regulation School*, edited by A. Labrousse and J. D. Weisz, 49–92. Berlin: Springer, 2001.

_____. *The Regulation School: A Critical Introduction*. Translated by Craig Charney. New York: Columbia University Press, 1990.

Boyer, Robert, and Yves Saillard, eds. *Régulation Theory: The State of the Art*. London: Routledge, 2002 [1995].

_____. "A Summary of *Régulation* Theory." In *Régulation Theory: The State of the Art*, edited by Robert Boyer and Yves Saillard, 36–44. London: Routledge, 2002 [1995].

Bradley, Keith. "Engaging with Slavery." *Biblical Interpretation* 21, no. 4–5 (2013): 533–46.

_____. "Resisting Slavery at Rome." In *The Cambridge World History of Slavery*, vol. 1, edited by Keith Bradley and Paul Cartledge, 362–84. Cambridge: Cambridge University Press, 2011.

_____. "Roman Slavery: Retrospect and Prospect." *Canadian Journal of History/Annales canadiennes d'histoire* 43, no. 3 (2008): 477–500.

_____. *Slavery and Rebellion in the Roman World, 140 BC–70 BC*. Bloomington: Indiana University Press, 1998 [1989].

_____. "Slavery in the Roman Republic." In *The Cambridge World History of Slavery. Volume 1: The Ancient Mediterranean World*, edited by Keith Bradley and Paul Cartledge, 241–64. Cambridge: Cambridge University Press, 2011.

_____. *Slaves and Masters in the Roman Empire: A Study in Social Control*. New York: Oxford University Press, 1987.

Branting, Scott. "Agents in Motion." In *Agency and Identity in the Ancient Near East: New Paths Forward*, edited by Sharon R. Steadman and Jennifer C. Ross, 47–59. London: Equinox, 2010.

Braudel, Fernand. *The Structures of Everyday Life*. Translated by M. Kochan. revised ed. New York: Collins, 1981.

Braund, David. "The Slave Supply in Classical Greece." In *The Cambridge World History of Slavery*, vol. 1, edited by Keith Bradley and Paul Cartledge, 112–33. Cambridge: Cambridge University Press, 2011.

Brewer, Douglas. "Hunting, Animal Husbandry and Diet in Ancient Egypt." In *A History of the Animal World in the Ancient Near East*, edited by Billie Jean Collins, 427–56. Leiden: Brill, 2002.

Bridges, Edwin Michael. *World Soils*. 3 ed. Cambridge: Cambridge University Press, 1997.

Broshi, Magen. "The Role of the Temple in the Herodian Economy." *Journal of Jewish Studies* 38, no. 1 (1987): 31–37.

Bruce, F. F. *The Acts of the Apostles: The Greek Text with Introduction and Commentary*. London: Tyndale, 1952.

Brunt, P. A. *The Fall of the Roman Republic and Related Essays*. Oxford: Clarendon, 1988.

Bücher, Karl. *Industrial Evolution*. Translated by Samuel Morley Wickett. New York: H. Holt and Company, 1901 [1893].

Buckland, William Warwick. *The Roman Law of Slavery: The Condition of the Slave in Private Law from Augustus to Justinian*. Cambridge: Cambridge University Press, 1908.

Butler, Ann. "Traditional Seed Cropping Systems in the Temperate Old World: Models for Antiquity." In *The Prehistory of Food: Appetites for Change*, edited by Chris Gosden and Jon Hather, 452–67. London: Routledge, 1999.

Byron, John. "Paul and the Background of Slavery: The Status Quaestionis in New Testament Scholarship." *Currents in Biblical Research* 3, no. 1 (2004): 62–72.

Cadwallader, Alan. "In Go(l)d we Trust: Literary and Economic Exchange in the Debate over Caesar's Coin (Mk 12:13–17)." *Biblical Interpretation* 14, no. 5 (2007): 486–507.

_____. "Peasant Plucking in Mark: Conceptual and Material Issues." In *Scriptural Radicalism*, edited by Sean Durbin and Robert Myles. New York: Palgrave Macmillan, In Press.

Caesar, Iulius. *De Bello Galico*. Translated by H.J. Edwards. Loeb Classical Library. London: William Heinemann, 1958.

Capogrossi Colognesi, Luigi. "Grandi proprietari, contadini e coloni nell'Italia Romana (I–II dC)." In *Società romana e impero tardoantico. Vol. I, Istituzioni, ceti, economie*, edited by Andrea Giardina, 326–65, 702–23. Bari: Editori Laterza, 1986.

Carter, Warren. "Cross-Gendered Romans and Mark's Jesus: Legion Enters the Pigs (Mark 5:1–20)." *Journal of Biblical Literature* 134, no. 1 (2015): 139–55.

Cartledge, Paul. "The Political Economy of Greek Slavery." In *Money, Labour and Land: Approaches to the Economies of Ancient Greece*, edited by Paul Cartledge, Edward Cohen and Lin Foxhall, 156–66. London: Routledge, 2002.

Cartledge, Paul, Edward Cohen, and Lin Foxhall, eds. *Money, Labour and Land: Approaches to the Economies of Ancient Greece.* London: Routledge, 2002.

Casana, Jesse. "Structural Transformations in Settlement Systems of the Northern Levant." *American Journal of Archaeology* 112 (2007): 195–222.

Caulley, Thomas Scott. "Notable Galilean Persons." In *Galilee in the Late Second Temple and Mishnaic Period, Volume 1: Life, Culture, and Society,* edited by David Fiensy and James Strange, 151–66. Minneapolis: Fortress, 2014.

Centano, Rui M. S. "De República ao Império: reflexões sobre a monetização no Ocidente da Hispânia." In *Barter, Money and Coinage in the Ancient Mediterranean (10th-1st Centuries BC),* edited by María Paz García-Bellido, Laurent Callegarin and Alicia Jiménez Díaz, 355–67. Madrid: Instituto de Historia, 2011.

Chancey, Mark. "Archaeology, Ethnicity, and First-Century C.E. Galilee: The Limits of Evidence." In *A Wandering Galilean: Essays in Honour of Seán Freyne,* edited by Zuleika Rodgers, Margaret Daly-Denton and Anne Fitzpatrick McKinley, 205–14. Leiden: Brill, 2009.

_____. "City Coins and Roman Power in Palestine: From Pompey to the Great Revolt." In *Religion and Society in Roman Palestine: Old Questions, New Approaches,* edited by Douglas Edwards, 103–12. New York: Routledge, 2004.

_____. "The Ethnicities of Galileans." In *Galilee in the Late Second Temple and Mishnaic Period, Volume 1: Life, Culture, and Society,* edited by David Fiensy and James Strange, 112–28. Minneapolis: Fortress, 2014.

_____. *Greco-Roman Culture and the Galilee of Jesus.* SNTS Monograph Series 134. Cambridge: Cambridge University Press, 2005.

_____. *The Myth of a Gentile Galilee: The Population of Galilee and New Testament Studies.* SNTS Monograph Series 118. Cambridge: Cambridge University Press, 2002.

Chayanov, Aleksandr Vasilievich. *The Theory of Peasant Co-operatives.* Translated by David Wedgwood Benn. Columbus: Ohio State University Press, 1991 [1927].

_____. *The Theory of Peasant Economy.* edited by Daniel Thorner, Basile Kerblay and R. E. F. Smith Homewood: Richard D. Irwin, 1966.

Cherry, David. "The Frontier Zones." In *The Cambridge Economic History of the Greco-Roman World,* edited by Walter Scheidel, Ian Morris and Richard Saller, 720–40. Cambridge: Cambridge University Press, 2007.

Childe, V. Gordon. *Man Makes Himself.* New York: Mentor, 1936 [1951].

Chirichigno, Gregory C. *Debt-Slavery in Israel and the Ancient Near East.* Sheffield: JSOT, 1993.

Choi, Agnes. "Never the Two Shall Meet? Urban-Rural Interaction in Lower Galilee." In *Galilee in the Late Second Temple and Mishnaic Period, Volume 1: Life,*

Culture, and Society, edited by David Fiensy and James Strange, 297–311. Minneapolis: Fortress, 2014.

Christian, David. *Maps of Time: An Introduction to Big History*. Berkeley: University of California Press, 2004 [2011].

Cicero, M. Tullius. *De Officiis*. Translated by Walter Miller. Loeb Classical Library. London: William Heinemann, 1928.

Clark, Elizabeth A. *History, Theory, Text: Historians and the Linguistic Turn*. Cambridge, MA: Harvard University Press, 2004.

Cohen, Edward. "Free and Unfree Sexual Work: An Economic Analysis of Athenian Prostitution." In *Prostitutes and Courtesans in the Ancient World*, edited by Christopher Faraone and Laura McClure, 95–124. Madison: University of Wisconsin Press, 2006.

_____. "Introduction." In *Money, Labour and Land: Approaches to the Economies of Ancient Greece*, edited by Paul Cartledge, Edward Cohen and Lin Foxhall, 1–7. London: Routledge, 2002.

Collins, Adela Yarbro. *Mark: A Commentary*. Hermeneia–A Critical and Historical Commentary on the Bible. Minneapolis: Augsburg Fortress, 2007.

Crook, Zeba. "Honor, Shame, and Social Status Revisited." *Journal of Biblical Literature* 128, no. 3 (2009): 591–611.

Crossan, John Dominic. *The Historical Jesus: The Life of a Mediterranean Peasant*. San Francisco: HarperSanFrancisco, 1993.

_____. *Jesus: A Revolutionary Biography*. San Francisco: HarperSanFrancisco, 1995.

Crossan, John Dominic, and Jonathan Reed. *Excavating Jesus: Beneath the Stones, Behind the Texts*. San Francisco: HarperSanFrancisco, 2001.

Cytryn-Silverman, Katia. "Tiberias, from Its Foundation to the End of the Early Islamic Period." In *Galilee in the Late Second Temple and Mishnaic Periods. Volume 2: The Archaeological Record from Cities, Towns, and Villages*, edited by David Fiensy and James Strange, 186–210. Minneapolis: Fortress, 2015.

D'Arms, John. *Commerce and Social Standing in Ancient Rome*. Cambridge: Harvard University Press, 1981.

Dale, Gareth. *Karl Polanyi: The Limits of the Market*. Cambridge: Polity, 2010.

Dalman, Gustaf. *Arbeit und Sitte in Palästina*. 8 vols Gütersloh and Berlin: Bertelsmann and De Gruyter, 1928–2012.

Dalton, George. "Introduction." In Karl Polanyi, *Primitive, Archaic and Modern Economies*, ix–liv. Boston: Beacon, 1971 [1968].

Dandamaev, Muhammad. *Slavery in Babylonia: From Nabopolassar to Alexander the Great (626–331 BC)*. Translated by Victoria A. Powell. DeKalb: Northern Illinois University Press, 2009 [1974].

Daniels, Peter. "The Study of Writing Systems." In *The World's Writing Systems*, edited by Peter Daniels and William Bright, 3–17. New York: Oxford University Press, 1996.

Dar, Shimon. *Landscape and Pattern: An Archaeological Survey of Samaria, 800 B.C.E.–636 C.E.* BAR International Series. Oxford: BAR, 1986.

Davies, John. "Classical Greece: Production." In *The Cambridge Economic History of the Greco-Roman World*, edited by Walter Scheidel, Ian Morris and Richard Saller, 333–61. Cambridge: Cambridge University Press, 2007.

Davies, W. D. *The Gospel and the Land: Early Christianity and Jewish Territorial Doctrine.* Berkeley: University of California Press, 1974.

Dawson, David. *Allegorical Readers and Cultural Revision in Ancient Alexandria.* Berkeley: University of California Press, 1991.

De Ste. Croix, G. E. M. *The Class Struggle in the Ancient Greek World: From the Archaic Age to the Arab Conquests.* Cornell University Press, 1989.

De Wet, Chris. *Preaching Bondage: John Chrysostom and the Discourse of Slavery in Early Christianity.* Oakland: University of California Press, 2015.

_____. "Slavery in John Chrysostom's Homilies on the Pauline Epistles and Hebrews: A Cultural-Historical Analysis." University of Pretoria, 2012.

Deines, Roland. "Galilee and the Historical Jesus in Recent Research." In *Galilee in the Late Second Temple and Mishnaic Period, Volume 1: Life, Culture, and Society*, edited by David Fiensy and James Strange, 11–48. Minneapolis: Fortress, 2014.

_____. "Religious Practices and Religious Movements in Galilee: 100 BCE–200 CE." In *Galilee in the Late Second Temple and Mishnaic Period, Volume 1: Life, Culture, and Society*, edited by David Fiensy and James Strange, 78–111. Minneapolis: Fortress, 2014.

Denzey, Nicola. "The Limits of Ethnic Categories." In *Handbook of Early Christianity: Social Science Approaches*, edited by Anthony Blasi, Jean Duhaime, and Paul-André Turcotte, 489–507. Walnut Creek: Altamira, 2002.

Diakonoff, Igor M. *The Paths of History.* Cambridge: Cambridge University Press, 1999.

_____. "Slaves, Helots and Serfs in Early Antiquity." Translated by G. M. Sergheyev. In *Wirtschaft und Gesellschaft im alten Vorderasien*, edited by János Harmatta and Geörgy Komoróczy, 45–78. Budapest: Akadémiai Kiadó, 1976.

_____. "The Structure of Near Eastern Society before the Middle of the Second Millennium B.C." *Oikumene* 3 (1982): 7–100.

Diósdi, György. *Ownership in Ancient and Preclassical Roman Law.* Budapest: Akadémiai Kiadó, 1970.

Dodd, C. H. *The Parables of the Kingdom.* revised ed. London: Collins, 1961.

Draper, Jonathan. "Recovering Oral Performance from Written Text in Q." In *Whoever Hears You, Hears Me: Prophets, Performance and Tradition in Q*, edited by Richard Horsley and Jonathan Draper, 175–94. Harrisburg: Trinity Press International, 1999.

Eagleton, Terry. *Jesus Christ: The Gospels (Revolutions)*. London: Verso, 2007.

Edmondson, Jonathan. "Slavery and the Roman Family." In *The Cambridge World History of Slavery*, vol. 1, edited by Keith Bradley and Paul Cartledge, 337–61. Cambridge: Cambridge University Press, 2011.

Edwards, Douglas. "Identity and Social Location in Roman Galilean Villages." In *Religion, Ethnicity, and Identity in Ancient Galilee: A Region in Transition*, edited by Jürgen Zangenberg, Harold Attridge and Dale Martin, 357–74. Tübingen: Mohr Siebeck, 2007.

_____. "The Socio-Economic and Cultural Ethos of the Lower Galilee in the First Century: Implications for the Nascent Jesus Movement." In *The Galilee in Late Antiquity*, edited by Lee Levine, 53–73. New York: Jewish Theological Seminary of America, 1992.

Ekholm, Kajsa, and Jonathan Friedman. "'Capital' Imperialism and Exploitation in Ancient World Systems." In *Power and Propaganda: A Symposium on Ancient Empires*, edited by Mogens Trolle Larsen, 41–58. Copenhagen: Akedemisk Forlag, 1979.

Eliav, Yaron. "Bathhouses as Places of Social and Cultural Interaction." In *The Oxford Handbook of Jewish Daily Life in Roman Palestine*, edited by Catherine Hezser, 605–22. Oxford: Oxford University Press, 2010.

Ellis, Simon. "The End of the Roman House." *American Journal of Archaeology* 92, no. 4 (1988): 565–76.

_____. "Late Antique Housing and the Uses of Residential Buildings: an Overview." In *Housing in Late Antiquity: From Palaces to Shops*, edited by Luke Lavan, Lale Özgenel and Alexander Sarantis, 1–23. Leiden: Brill, 2007.

_____. *Roman Housing*. London: Duckworth, 2000.

Engels, Friedrich. "The Peasant Question in France and Germany." In *Marx Engels Collected Works*, vol. 27, 481–502. Moscow: Progress Publishers, 1990 [1894].

Englund, Robert. "Proto-Cuneiform Account-Books and Journals." In *Creating Economic Order: Record-Keeping, Standardization, and the Development of Accounting in the Ancient Near East*, edited by Michael Hudson and Cornelia Wunsch, 23–46. Bethesda: CDL Press, 2004.

Erdkamp, Paul. "Agriculture, Underemployment, and the Cost of Rural Labour in the Roman World." *Classical Quarterly* 49, no. 2 (1999): 556–72.

_____. "Beyond the Limits of the 'Consumer City'. A Model of the Urban and Rural Economy in the Roman World." *Historia: Zeitschrift für Alte Geschichte* 50, no. 3 (2001): 332–56.

_____. *The Grain Market in the Roman Empire: A Social, Political and Economic Study.* Cambridge: Cambridge University Press, 2005.

Erdkamp, Paul, Koenraad Verboven, and Arjan Zuiderhoek, eds. *Ownership and Exploitation of Land and Natural Resources in the Roman World.* Oxford: Oxford University Press, 2015.

Erhman, Bart. *Lost Christianities: The Battle for Scripture and the Faiths We Never Knew.* New York: Oxford University Press, 2003.

Eschebach, Hans. "Erlauterungen zum Plan von Pompeji." In *Neue Forschungen in Pompeji und den anderen vom Vesuvausbruch 79 n. Chr. vershutteten Stadten,* edited by Bernard Andreae and Helmit Kyrieleis, 331–38. Recklinghausen: Verlag Aurel Bongers Recklinghausen, 1975.

Eshel, Esther, and Douglas Edwards. "Language and Writing in Early Roman Galilee: Social Location of a Potter's Abecedary from Khirbet Qana." In *Religion and Society in Roman Palestine: Old Questions, New Approaches,* edited by Douglas Edwards, 49–55. New York: Routledge, 2004.

Fatum, Lone. "Brotherhood in Christ: A Gender Hermeneutical Reading of 1 Thessalonians." In *Constructing Early Christian Families: Family as Social Reality and Metaphor,* edited by Halvor Moxnes, 183–97. London: Routledge, 1997.

Fiensy, David. *Christian Origins and the Ancient Economy.* Eugene: Cascade, 2014.

_____. "Did Large Estates Exist in Lower Galilee in the First Half of the First Century CE?" *Journal for the Study of the Historical Jesus* 10 (2012): 133–53.

_____. "The Galilean House in the Late Second Temple and Mishnaic Periods." In *Galilee in the Late Second Temple and Mishnaic Period, Volume 1: Life, Culture, and Society,* edited by David Fiensy and James Strange, 216–41. Minneapolis: Fortress, 2014.

_____. "The Galilean Village in the Late Second Temple and Mishnaic Periods." In *Galilee in the Late Second Temple and Mishnaic Period, Volume 1: Life, Culture, and Society,* edited by David Fiensy and James Strange, 177–207. Minneapolis: Fortress, 2014.

_____. *The Social History of Palestine in the Herodian Period: The Land is Mine.* Lewiston: Edwin Mellen, 1991.

Fine, Ben, and Dimitris Milonakis. *From Economics Imperialism to Freakonomics: The Shifting Boundaries between Economics and Other Social Sciences.* London: Routledge, 2009.

_____. "From Freakonomics to Political Economy." *Historical Materialism* 20, no. 3 (2012): 81–96.

Finley, Moses. *The Ancient Economy.* Berkeley: University of California Press, 1999 [1973].

_____. *Ancient Slavery and Modern Ideology.* Princeton: Markus Weiner, 1998 [1980].

_____. *Economy and Society in Ancient Greece*, edited by Brent Shaw and Richard Saller London: Chatto & Windus, 1981.

_____. "Was Greek Civilization Based on Slave Labour?" *Historia: Zeitschrift für Alte Geschichte* 8, no. 2 (1959): 145–164.

_____. *The World of Odysseus*. New York: New York Review Books, 2002 [1954].

Firestone, Ya'akov. "The Land-equalizing Mushâ' Village." In *Ottoman Palestine*, edited by Gad Gilbar, 91–130. Leiden: Brill, 1990.

Fischbach, Michael R. *State, Society and Land in Jordan*. Leiden: Brill, 2000.

Foldvari, Peter, Bas Van Leeuwen, and Reinhard Pirngruber. "Markets in Pre-Industrial Societies: Storage in Hellenistic Babylonia in the English Mirror." *CGEH Working Paper Series* (2011). http://www.cgeh.nl/working-paper-ser ies/.

Fox, Bonnie J., ed. *Family Patterns, Gender Relations*. New York: Oxford University Press, 2008.

Foxhall, Lin. "Access to Resources in Classical Greece: The Egalitarianism of the Polis in Practice." In *Money, Labour and Land: Approaches to the Economies of Ancient Greece*, edited by Paul Cartledge, Edward Cohen and Lin Foxhall, 209–20. London: Routledge, 2002.

_____. "The Dependent Tenant: Land Leasing and Labour in Italy and Greece." *Journal of Roman Studies* 80 (1991): 97–114.

Franco, M.a Isabel Vila. "El proceso de monetización del noroeste de la Península Ibérica: las calzadas romanas." In *Barter, Money and Coinage in the Ancient Mediterranean (10th-1st Centuries BC)*, edited by María Paz García-Bellido, Laurent Callegarin and Alicia Jiménez Díaz, 369–76. Madrid: Instituto de Historia, 2011.

Freyne, Séan. "Cities of the Hellenistic and Roman Periods." In *The Oxford Encyclopaedia of Archaeology in the Near East*, vol. 2, edited by Eric Meyers, 29–35. Oxford: Oxford University Press, 1997.

_____. *Galilee and Gospel: Collected Essays*. Leiden: Brill, 2002.

_____. *Galilee from Alexander the Great to Hadrian, 323 B.C.E. to 135 C.E.: A Study of Second Temple Judaism*. Wilmington and Notre Dame: Michael Glazier and University of Notre Dame Press, 1980.

_____. *Galilee, Jesus, and the Gospels: Literary Approaches and Historical Investigations*. Philadelphia: Fortress, 1988.

_____. "Galilee, Jesus, and the Gospels: Literary Approaches and Historical Investigations." In *Studying the Historical Jesus: Evaluations of the State of Current Research*, edited by Bruce Chilton and Craig Evans, 75–121. Leiden: Brill, 1988.

_____. "Herodian Economics in Galilee: Searching for a Suitable Model." In

Modelling Early Christianity: Social-Scientific Studies of the New Testament in Its Context, edited by Philip Esler, 22–44. London: Routledge, 1995.

_____. "Jesus and the Urban Culture of Galilee." In *Texts and Contexts: Biblical Texts in Their Textual and Situational Contexts. Essays in Honor of Lars Hartman*, edited by Tord Fornberg and David Hellholm, 597–622. Oslo: Scandinavian University Press, 1995.

_____. *Jesus, a Jewish Galilean: A New Reading of the Jesus Story*. London: T&T Clark, 2004.

_____. "Urban-Rural Relations in First-Century Galilee: Some Suggestions from the Literary Sources." In *The Galilee in Late Antiquity*, edited by Lee Levine, 75–91. New York: Jewish Theological Seminary of America, 1992.

Frier, Bruce. "Law, Technology, and Social Change: The Equipping of Italian Farm Tenancies." *Zeitschrift der Savigny-Stiftung für Rechtsgeschichte, Romanistische Abteilung* 96 (1979): 204–28.

Frier, Bruce, and Dennis Kehoe. "Law and Economic Institutions." In *The Cambridge Economic History of the Greco-Roman World*, edited by Walter Scheidel, Ian Morris and Richard Saller, 113–43. Cambridge: Cambridge University Press, 2007.

Frilingos, Chris. "'For My Child, Onesimus': Paul and Domestic Power in Philemon." *Journal of Biblical Literature* 119, no. 1 (2000): 91–104.

Gabba, Emilio. "The Social, Economic and Political History of Palestine, 63 BCE–CE 70." In *The Cambridge History of Judaism*, vol. 3, edited by William Horbury, W.D. Davies and John Sturdy, 94–167. Cambridge: Cambridge University Press, 1999.

Gallant, Thomas. *Risk and Survival in Ancient Greece. Reconstructing the Rural Domestic Economy*. Cambridge: Polity, 1991.

Galor, Katharina. "Domestic Architecture." In *The Oxford Handbook of Jewish Daily Life in Roman Palestine*, edited by Catherine Hezser, 393–402. Oxford: Oxford University Press, 2010.

Gardner, Jane. "Slavery and Roman Law." In *The Cambridge World History of Slavery*, vol. 1, edited by Keith Bradley and Paul Cartledge, 414–37. Cambridge: Cambridge University Press, 2011.

Garlan, Yvon. *Slavery in Ancient Greece*. Rev. and expanded ed. Ithaca: Cornell University Press, 1988 [1982].

Garnsey, Peter. *Cities, Peasants and Food in Classical Antiquity*. Cambridge: Cambridge University Press, 1998.

_____. *Famine and Food Supply in the Graeco-Roman World: Responses to Risk and Crisis*. Cambridge: Cambridge University Press, 1988.

_____. "Grain for Rome." In *Trade in the Ancient Economy*, edited by Peter Garnsey, Keith Hopkins, and C. R. Whittaker, 118–30. Berkeley: University of California Press, 1983.

_____, ed. *Non-Slave Labour in the Greco-Roman World*. Cambridge: Cambridge Philological Society, 1980.

Garnsey, Peter, Richard Saller, and Martin Goodman. *The Roman Empire: Economy, Society and Culture*. Oakland: University of California Press, 2015.

Gianaris, Nicholas. *Modern Capitalism: Privatization, Employee Ownership, and Industrial Democracy*. Westport: Greenwood Publishing, 1996.

Giliberti, Guiseppe. *Servi della terra: ricerche per una storia del colonato*. Turin: Giappichelli, 1999.

_____. *Servus quasi colonus: forme non tradizionali di organizzazione del lavoro nella societ`a romana*. Naples: E. Jovene, 1981.

Glancy, Jennifer. *Corporal Knowledge: Early Christian Bodies*. Oxford: Oxford University Press, 2010.

_____. "Obstacles to Slaves' Participation in the Corinthian Church." *Journal of Biblical Literature* 117, no. 3 (1998): 481–501.

_____. "The Sexual Use of Slaves: A Response to Kyle Harper on Jewish and Christian *Porneia*." *Journal of Biblical Literature* 134, no. 1 (2015): 215–29.

_____. "Slavery and the Rise of Christianity." In *The Cambridge World History of Slavery*, vol. 1, edited by Keith Bradley and Paul Cartledge, 456–81. Cambridge: Cambridge University Press, 2011.

_____. *Slavery as Moral Problem: In the Early Church and Today*. Minneapolis: Fortress, 2011.

_____. *Slavery in Early Christianity*. Minneapolis: Fortress, 2003.

Gleason, Maud. "Greek Cities Under Roman Rule." In *A Companion to the Roman Empire*, edited by David Potter, 228–49. London: Blackwell, 2006.

Godelier, Maurice. *The Mental and the Material: Thought, Economy and Society*. Translated by Martin Thom. London: Verso, 1986 [1984].

Golden, Mark. "Slavery and the Greek Family." In *The Cambridge World History of Slavery*, vol. 1, edited by Keith Bradley and Paul Cartledge, 134–52. Cambridge: Cambridge University Press, 2011.

Goodblatt, David. "Population Structure and Jewish Identity." In *The Oxford Handbook of Jewish Daily Life in Roman Palestine*, edited by Catherine Hezser, 102–21. Oxford: Oxford University Press, 2010.

Goodrich, John. "Voluntary Debt Remission and the Parable of the Unjust Steward (Luke 16:1–13)." *Journal of Biblical Literature* 131, no. 3 (2012): 547–66.

Gordon, W. M., and O. F. Robinson. *The Institutes of Gaius*. London: Duckworth, 1988.

Gotsis, George, and Sarah Drakoupolou Dodd. "Economic Ideas in the Pauline Epistles of the New Testament." *History of Economics Review* 35 (2002): 13–34.

Gotsis, George, and Gerasimos Merianos. "Early Christian Representations of the Economy: Evidence from New Testament Texts." *History and Anthropology* 24, no. 3 (2012): 467–505.

Graeber, David. *Debt: The First 5,000 Years*. New York: Melville House, 2011.

Granott, Abraham. *The Land System of Palestine in History and Structure*. London: Eyre and Spottiswood, 1952.

Gray, Kevin, and Susan Francis Gray. "The Idea of Property in Land." In *Land Law*, edited by S. Bright and J. Dewar, 15–51. Oxford: Oxford University Press, 1998.

Greene, Kevin. *The Archaeology of the Roman Economy*. Berkeley: University of California Press, 1990.

Grey, Cam. "Contextualizing *Colonatus*: The *Origo* of the Late Roman Empire." *The Journal of Roman Studies* 97 (2007): 155–75.

_____. "Slavery in the Late Roman World." In *The Cambridge World History of Slavery*, vol. 1, edited by Keith Bradley and Paul Cartledge, 482–509. Cambridge: Cambridge University Press, 2011.

Grmek, Mirko. *Diseases in the Ancient Greek World*. Baltimore: Johns Hopkins University Press, 1989.

Grotius, Hugo. *Commentary on the Law of Prize and Booty*. Translated by John Clarke. edited by Martine Julia Van Ittersum Indianapolis: Liberty Fund, 2006 [1868].

Guijarro, Santiago. "The Family in First-Century Galilee." In *Early Christian Families: Family as Social Reality and Metaphor*, edited by Halvor Moxnes, 42–65. London: Routledge, 1997.

Guillaume, Philippe. *Land, Credit and Crisis: Agrarian Finance in the Hebrew Bible*. Sheffield: Equinox, 2012.

Gutiérrez, Gustavo. *The Power of the Poor in History*. Maryknoll: Orbis, 1983.

_____. *A Theology of Liberation*. Translated by Caridad Inda and John Eagleson. London: SCM, 2001 [1969].

Halperin, David. *One Hundred Years of Homosexuality: And Other Essays on Greek Love*. New York: Routledge, 1989.

Halstead, Paul. "The Economy has a Normal Surplus: Economic Stability and Social Change Among Early Farming Communities of Thessaly, Greece." In *Bad Year Economics: Cultural Responses to Risk and Uncertainty*, edited by Paul Halstead and Paul O'Shea, 68-80. Cambridge: Cambridge University Press, 1989.

_____. "Traditional and Ancient Rural Economy in Mediterranean Europe: Plus ça Change?" *Journal of Hellenic Studies* 107 (1987): 77–87.

_____. *Two Oxen Ahead: Pre-Mechanized Farming in the Mediterranean*. Oxford: Wiley Blackwell, 2014.

Halstead, Paul, and Glynis Jones. "Agrarian Ecology in the Greek Islands: Time Stress, Scale and Risk." *Journal of Hellenic Studies* 109 (1989): 41–55.

Hanson, R. P. C. "Interpretations of Hebrew Names in Origen." *Vigiliae Christianae* 10, no. 1 (1956): 103–23.

Hanson, Victor Davis. *The Other Greeks: The Family Farm and the Agrarian Roots of Western Civilization.* revised ed. Berkley: University of California Press, 1999 [1995].

Hardin, James. "Understanding Houses, Households, and the Levantine Archaeological Record." In *Household Archaeology in Ancient Israel and Beyond*, edited by Assaf Yasur-Landau, Jennie R. Ebeling, and Laura B. Mazow, 9–25. Leiden: Brill, 2011.

Hardt, Michael, and Antonio Negri. *Commonwealth.* Cambridge, Massachusetts: Belknap, 2009.

_____. *Multitude: War and Democracy in the Age of Empire.* New York: Penguin, 2004.

Harland, Philip. "The Economy of First-Century Palestine: State of the Scholarly Discussion." In *Handbook of Early Christianity: Social Science Approaches*, edited by Anthony Blasi, Jean Duhaime, and Paul-André Turcotte, 511–27. Walnut Creek: Altamira, 2002.

Harrill, J. Albert. *The Manumission of Slaves in Early Christianity.* Tübingen: J.C.B. Mohr, 1995.

_____. *Slaves in the New Testament: Literary, Social and Moral Dimensions.* Minneapolis: Fortress, 2006.

Harris, Edward. "Workshop, Marketplace and Household: The Nature of Technical Specialization in Classical Athens and Its Influence on Economy and Society." In *Money, Labour and Land: Approaches to the Economies of Ancient Greece*, edited by Paul Cartledge, Edward Cohen, and Lin Foxhall, 67–99. London: Routledge, 2002.

Harris, William. "The Late Republic." In *The Cambridge Economic History of the Greco-Roman World*, edited by Walter Scheidel, Ian Morris and Richard Saller, 511–39. Cambridge: Cambridge University Press, 2007.

_____. *Rome's Imperial Economy: Twelve Essays.* Oxford: Oxford University Press, 2011.

Harvey, David. *The Limits to Capital.* 2nd ed. London: Verso, 1999.

Hasebroek, Johannes. *Trade and Politics in Ancient Greece.* Translated by L.M. Fraser and D. C. MacGregor. London: G. Bell, 1933 [1928].

Hayden, Brian. "On Territoriality and Sedentism." *Current Anthropology* 41, no. 1 (2000): 109–12.

Heath, Malcolm. "Aristotle on Natural Slavery." *Phronesis* 53, no. 3 (2008): 243–70.

Heltzer, Michael. *The Rural Community in Ancient Ugarit.* Wiesbaden: Dr. Ludwig Reichert, 1976.

Hesiod. "Works and Days." In *Theogony, Works and Days, Testimonia.* Loeb Classical Library, 86–153. Cambridge: Harvard University Press, 2006.

Hesse, Brian. "Pig Lovers and Pig Haters: Patterns of Palestinian Pork Production." *Journal of Ethnobiology* 10 (1990): 195–225.

Hesse, Brian, and Paula Wapnish. *Animal Bone Archaeology from Objectives to Analysis.* Washington, DC: Taraxacum, 1985.

_____. "An Archaeozoological Perspective on the Cultural Use of Mammals in the Levant." In *A History of the Animal World in the Ancient Near East*, edited by Billie Jean Collins, 457–91. Leiden: Brill, 2002.

Hezser, Catherine. "The Graeco-Roman Context of Jewish Daily Life in Roman Palestine." In *The Oxford Handbook of Jewish Daily Life in Roman Palestine*, edited by Catherine Hezser, 28–48. Oxford: Oxford University Press, 2010.

_____. "Travel and Mobility." In *The Oxford Handbook of Jewish Daily Life in Roman Palestine*, edited by Catherine Hezser, 210–28. Oxford: Oxford University Press, 2010.

Hindess, Barry, and Paul Hirst. *Precapitalist Modes of Production.* London: Routledge and Kegan Paul, 1975.

Hirschfeld, Yizhar. "Farms and Villages in Byzantine Palestine." *Dumbarton Oaks Papers* 51 (1997): 33–71.

_____. *The Palestinian Dwelling in the Roman-Byzantine Period.* Jerusalem: Franciscan Printing Press, 1995.

Hopkins, David. "Agriculture." In *The Oxford Encyclopaedia of Archaeology in the Near East*, vol. 1, edited by Eric Meyers, 22–30. Oxford: Oxford University Press, 1997.

_____. "Cereals." In *The Oxford Encyclopaedia of Archaeology in the Near East*, vol. 1, edited by Eric Meyers, 479–81. Oxford: Oxford University Press, 1997.

_____. *The Highlands of Canaan: Agricultural Life in the Early Highlands.* Sheffield: Almond, 1985.

Hopkins, Keith. *Conquerors and Slaves.* Cambridge: Cambridge University Press, 1978.

_____. "Taxes and Trade in the Roman Empire (200 CE–400 AD)." *The Journal of Roman Studies* 70 (1980): 101–25.

Horace. "Epodes." Translated by Niall Rudd. In *Odes and Epodes.* Loeb Classical Library, 270–320. Cambridge: Harvard University Press, 2004.

Hordern, Peregrine, and Nicholas Purcell. *The Corrupting Sea: A Study of Mediterranean History.* Oxford: Palgrave, 2000.

Horsley, Richard. *Archaeology, History and Society in Galilee.* Philadelphia: Trinity Press International, 1996.

_____. *Covenant Economics: A Vision of Biblical Justice for All*. Louisville: Westminster John Knox, 2009.

_____. *Galilee: History, Politics, People*. Philadelphia, Pennsylvania: Trinity Press International, 1995.

_____. *Hearing the Whole Story: Politics of Plot in Mark's Gospel*. Louisville: Westminster John Knox, 2001.

_____. *Jesus and the Politics of Roman Palestine*. Columbia: University of South Carolina Press, 2014.

_____. *Jesus and the Spiral of Violence: Popular Jewish Resistance in Roman Palestine*. Philadelphia, Pennsylvania: Augsburg Fortress, 1992.

_____. "The Language(s) of the Kingdom: From Aramaic to Greek, Galilee to Syria, Oral to Oral-Written." In *A Wandering Galilean: Essays in Honour of Seán Freyne*, edited by Zuleika Rodgers, Margaret Daly-Denton, and Anne Fitzpatrick McKinley, 401–26. Leiden: Brill, 2009.

_____. "Social Movements in Galilee." In *Galilee in the Late Second Temple and Mishnaic Period, Volume 1: Life, Culture, and Society*, edited by David Fiensy and James Strange, 167–74. Minneapolis: Fortress, 2014.

Horsley, Richard, and John Hanson. *Bandits, Prophets, and Messiahs: Popular Movements in the Time of Jesus*. Philadelphia: Trinity Press International, 1985.

Hunt, E. D. *Holy Land Pilgrimage in the Later Roman Empire, AD 312-460*. Oxford: Clarendon, 1982.

Jameson, Fredric. *The Political Unconscious: Narrative as a Socially Symbolic Act*. Ithaca: Cornell University Press, 1981.

Jameson, Michael. "Agriculture and Slavery in Classical Athens." *The Classical Journal* 73, no. 2 (1976–1977): 122–45.

_____. "On Paul Cartledge, 'The Political Economy of Greek Slavery'." In *Money, Labour and Land: Approaches to the Economies of Ancient Greece*, edited by Paul Cartledge, Edward Cohen and Lin Foxhall, 167–74. London: Routledge, 2002.

Jankowska, Ninel. "Communal Self-Government and the King of the State of Arrapha." *Journal of the Economic and Social History of the Orient* 12 (1969): 233–82.

Jensen, Morten Hørning. "Climate, Drought, Wars, and Famines in Galilee as a Background for Understanding the Historical Jesus." *Journal of Biblical Literature* 131, no. 2 (2012): 307–24.

_____. *Herod Antipas in Galilee: The Literary and Archaeological Sources on the Reign of Herod Antipas and Its Socio-Economic Impact on Galilee*. WUNT 2.215. Tübingen: Mohr Siebeck, 2006.

_____. "Rural Galilee and Rapid Changes: An Investigation of the Socio-Economic Dynamics and Developments in Roman Galilee." *Biblica* 93, no. 1 (2012): 43–67.

Jessop, Bob. "Mode of Production." In *Marxian Economics*, edited by John Eatwell, Murray Milgate and Peter Newman, 289–96. London: Macmillan, 1987.

Jessop, Bob, and Ngai-Ling Sum. *Beyond the Regulation Approach: Putting Capitalist Economies in their Place.* Cheltenham: Edward Elgar, 2006.

Johnston, David. *Roman Law in Context.* Cambridge: Cambridge University Press, 1999.

Jolowicz, H. F., and Barry Nicholas. *Historical Introduction to the Study of Roman Law.* 3rd ed. Cambridge: Cambridge University Press, 1972.

Jones, Arnold Hugh Martin. *The Greek City.* Oxford: Clarendon, 1966.

_____. *The Roman Economy: Studies in Ancient Economic and Administrative History.* Oxford: Blackwell, 1974.

Jongman, Willem. *The Economy and Society of Pompeii.* Amsterdam: J. C. Gieben, 1988.

Josephus, Flavius. *Bellum Judaicum.* Translated by H. St. J. Thackeray. Loeb Classical Library. 2 vols. London: William Heinemann, 1927.

_____. *Vita. Contra Apion.* Translated by H. St. J. Thackeray. Loeb Classical Library. London: William Heinemann, 1926.

Judge, Edwin. *The Social Pattern of the Christian Groups in the First Century: Some Prolegomena to the Study of New Testament Ideas of Social Obligation.* London: Tyndale, 1960.

Käsemann, Ernst. *Jesu letzter Wille nach Johannes 17.* Tübingen: JBC Mohr, 1980.

Kautsky, Karl. *Foundations of Christianity.* Translated by H. F. Mins. London: Socialist Resistance, 2007 [1908].

Kehoe, Dennis. "Landlords and Tenants." In *A Companion to the Roman Empire*, edited by David Potter, 298–311. London: Blackwell, 2006.

_____. *Law and the Rural Economy in the Roman Empire.* Ann Arbor: University of Michigan Press, 2007.

Kelley, Nicole. "Deformity and Disability in Greece and Rome." In *This Abled Body: Rethinking Disabilities in Biblical Studies*, edited by Hector Avalos, Sarah Melcher and Jeremy Schipper, 31–45. Atlanta: Society of Biblical Literature, 2007.

Khalidi, Tarif, ed. *Land Tenure and Social Transformation in the Middle East.* Beirut: American University of Beirut Press, 1984.

Killebrew, Ann. "Village and Countryside." In *The Oxford Handbook of Jewish Daily Life in Roman Palestine*, edited by Catherine Hezser, 189–209. Oxford: Oxford University Press, 2010.

Kim, H. S. "Small Change and the Moneyed Economy." In *Money, Labour and*

Land: Approaches to the Economies of Ancient Greece, edited by Paul Cartledge, Edward Cohen and Lin Foxhall, 44–51. London: Routledge, 2002.

Kloppenborg, John. "The Dishonoured Master (Luke 16:1–8a)." Biblica 70 (1989): 474–95.

_____. "The Growth and Impact of Agricultural Tenancy in Jewish Palestine (III BCE–I CE)." Journal of the Economic and Social History of the Orient 51, no. 1 (2012): 31–66.

_____. The Tenants in the Vineyard: Ideology, Economics, and Agrarian Conflict in Jewish Palestine. WUNT 195. Tübingen: J.C.B. Mohr [Paul Siebeck], 2006.

_____. "Unsocial Bandits." In A Wandering Galilean: Essays in Honour of Seán Freyne, edited by Zuleika Rodgers, Margaret Daly-Denton and Anne Fitzpatrick McKinley, 451–84. Leiden: Brill, 2009.

Knight, Douglas. Law, Power, and Justice in Ancient Israel. Library of Ancient Israel. Louisville: Westminster John Knox, 2011.

Knott, Kim. The Location of Religion: A Spatial Analysis. London: Equinox, 2005.

Kosmin, Paul. The Land of the Elephant Kings: Space, Territory, and Ideology in the Seleucid Empire. Cambridge: Harvard University Press, 2014.

Kotter, Wade. "Settlement Patterns." In The Oxford Encyclopaedia of Archaeology in the Near East, vol. 5, edited by Eric Meyers, 6–10. Oxford: Oxford University Press, 1997.

Kraay, Colin. "Hoards, Small Change and the Origin of Coinage." The Journal of Hellenic Studies 84 (1964): 76–91.

Kreissig, Heinz. "Zur sozialen Zusammensetzung der frühchristliche Gemeinden im ersten Jahrhundert u.Z." Eirene 6 (1967): 91–100.

Kurke, Leslie. Coins, Bodies, Games, and Gold: the Politics of Meaning in Archaic Greece. Princeton: Princeton University Press, 1999.

Kyrtatas, Dimitris. "Domination and Exploitation." In Money, Labour and Land: Approaches to the Economies of Ancient Greece, edited by Paul Cartledge, Edward Cohen and Lin Foxhall, 140–55. London: Routledge, 2002.

_____. "Modes and Relations of Production." In Handbook of Early Christianity: Social Science Approaches, edited by Anthony Blasi, Jean Duhaime, and Paul-André Turcotte, 529–54. Walnut Creek: Altamira, 2002.

_____. "Slavery and Economy in the Greek World." In The Cambridge World History of Slavery, vol. 1, edited by Keith Bradley and Paul Cartledge, 91–111. Cambridge: Cambridge University Press, 2011.

Landry, David, and Ben May. "Honor Restored: New Light on the Parable of the Prudent Steward (Luke 16:1–8a)." Journal of Biblical Literature 119, no. 2 (2000): 287–309.

Laslett, Peter. "Introduction: The History of the Family." In Household and Fam-

ily in Past Time, edited by Peter Laslett and Richard Wall, 1–89. Cambridge: Cambridge University Press, 1972.

Lassen, Eva Marie. "The Roman Family: Ideal and Metaphor." In *Constructing Early Christian Families: Family as Social Reality and Metaphor*, edited by Halvor Moxnes, 103–20. London: Routledge, 1997.

Lefebvre, Henri. *Éléments de rythmanalyse*. Paris: Éditions Syllepse, 1992.

_____. *The Production of Space*. Translated by David Nicholson-Smith. Oxford: Oxford University Press, 1991.

_____. *Rhythmanalysis: Space, Time and Everyday Life*. Translated by Stuart Elden and Gerald Moore. London: Continuum, 2004.

Legros, Jean-Paul. *Major Soil Groups of the World: Ecology, Genesis, Properties and Classification*. Translated by V.A.K. Sarma. Boca Raton: CRC, 2012.

Lekas, Padelis. *Marx on Classical Antiquity: Problems of Historical Methodology*. Brighton: Wheatsheaf, 1988.

Lenin, V.I. "On the Famine: A Letter to the Workers of Petrograd, 22 May, 1918." In *Collected Works*, vol. 27, 391–98. Moscow: Progress Publishers, 1965 [1918].

_____. "The State and Revolution." In *Collected Works*, vol. 25, 385–497. Moscow: Progress Publishers, 1964 [1917].

Lévi-Strauss, Claude. *Totemism*. Translated by Rodney Needham. Harmondsworth: Penguin, 1962.

_____. *Tristes Tropiques*. Translated by John Weightman and Doreen Weightman. London: Pan, 1989.

Lincoln, Bruce. *Theorizing Myth: Narrative, Ideology, and Scholarship*. Chicago: University of Chicago Press, 2000.

Lipietz, Alain. "Accumulation, Crises, and Ways Out: Some Methodological Reflections on the Concept of 'Regulation.'" *International Journal of Political Economy* 18, no. 2 (1988): 10–43.

_____. "Rebel Sons: The Regulation School." *French Politics and Society* 4 (1987): 17–26. http://lipietz.net/spip.php?article750.

Liverani, Mario. *Israel's History and the History of Israel*. Translated by Chiara Peri and Philip Davies. London: Equinox, 2005.

_____. *Prestige and Interest: International Relations in the Near East ca. 1600–1100 BC* Padua: Sargon, 1990.

_____. "Ville et campagne dans le royaume d'Ugarit: Essai d'analyse economique." In *Societies and Languages of the Ancient Near East: Studies in Honour of I. M. D'iakonoff*, edited by Muhammad Dandamaev, I. Gershevitch, Horst Klengel, G. Komoroczy, Mogens Trolle Larsen, and J. Nicholas Postgate, 250–58. Warminster: Aris and Phillips, 1982.

Llewellyn-Jones, Lloyd. *Aphrodite's Tortoise: The Veiled Woman of Ancient Greece*. Swansea: Classical Press of Wales, 2003.

Lloyd, Geoffrey. "Preface." In *Money, Labour and Land: Approaches to the Economies of Ancient Greece*, edited by Paul Cartledge, Edward Cohen, and Lin Foxhall, xv–xviii. London: Routledge, 2002.

Lo Cascio, Elio. "Considerazioni sulla struttura e sulla dinamica dell'affitto agraria in età imperiale." In *De Agricultura: In Memoriam Pieter Willem de Neeve*, edited by Heleen Sancisi-Weerdenburg, Robartus J. Van der Spek, H. C. Teitler, and H. T. Wallinga, 296–316. Amsterdam: J.C. Gieben, 1993.

_____, ed. *Credito e moneta nel mondo romano: Atti degli Incontri capresi di storia dell'economia antica (Capri 12-14 ottobre 2000)*. Bari: Edipuglia, 2003.

_____, ed. *Innovazione tecnica e progresso economico nel mondo romano: Atti degli Incontri capresi di storia dell'economia antica (Capri 13-16 aprile 2003)*. Bari: Edipuglia, 2006.

_____. "The Size of the Roman Population: Beloch and the Meaning of the Augustan Census Figures." *The Journal of Roman Studies* 84 (1994): 23–40.

Locke, John. *Two Treatises of Government and A Letter Concerning Toleration*. Edited by Ian Shapiro New Haven: Yale University Press, 2003 [1691].

Love, John. *Antiquity and Capitalism: Max Weber and Sociological Foundations of Roman Civilization*. London: Routledge, 1991.

_____. "Max Weber and the Theory of Ancient Capitalism." In *Max Weber: Critical Assessments*, edited by Peter Hamilton, 270–90. London: Routledge, 1991.

Love, Serena. "Architecture as Material Culture: Building Form and Materiality in the Pre-Pottery Neolithic of Anatolia and Levant." *Journal of Anthropological Archaeology* 32 (2013): 746–58.

Machiavelli. *The Prince*. Cambridge: Cambridge University Press, 1988. Italian, 1532.

Magness, Jodi. *Stone and Dung, Oil and Spit: Jewish Daily Life in the Time of Jesus*. Grand Rapids: Eerdmans, 2011.

Malina, Bruce, and Jerome Neyrey. "Honor and Shame in Luke-Acts: Pivotal Values of the Mediterranean World." In *The Social World of Luke-Acts: Models for Interpretation*, edited by Jerome Neyrey, 25–66. Peabody: Hendrickson, 1991.

Malinowski, Bronislaw. *Argonauts of the Western Pacific; an Account of Native Enterprise and Adventure in the Archipelagoes of Melanesian New Guinea*. London: Routledge, 1932.

Manning, Joseph Gilbert. "Hellenistic Egypt." In *The Cambridge Economic History of the Greco-Roman World*, edited by Walter Scheidel, Ian Morris, and Richard Saller, 434–59. Cambridge: Cambridge University Press, 2007.

Marchal, Joseph. "The Usefulness of an Onesimus: The Sexual Use of Slaves in Paul's Letter to Philemon." *Journal of Biblical Literature* 130, no. 4 (2011): 749–70.

Marcus, Joel. "The Jewish War and the *Sitz im Leben* of Mark." *Journal of Biblical Literature* 111, no. 3 (1992): 441–62.

Markus, Robert. "How on Earth Could Places Become Holy? Origins of the Christian Idea of Holy Places." *Journal of Early Christian Studies* 2, no. 3 (1994): 257–71.

Marshall, I. Howard. *Acts of the Apostles*. Sheffield: JSOT Press, 1982.

Martin, Dale. "Slave Families and Slaves in Families." In *Early Christian Families in Context: An Interdisciplinary Dialogue*, edited by David Balch and Carolyn Osiek, 207–30. Grand Rapids: Eerdmans, 2003.

_____. *Slavery as Salvation: The Metaphor of Slavery in Pauline Christianity*. New Haven: Yale University Press, 1990.

Marx, Karl. "Economic and Philosophic Manuscripts of 1844." In *Marx and Engels Collected Works*, vol. 3, 229–346. Moscow: Progress Publishers, 1975 [1844].

_____. "The Eighteenth Brumaire of Louis Bonaparte." In *Marx and Engels Collected Works*, vol. 11, 99–197. Moscow: Progress Publishers, 1852 [1979].

Marx, Karl, and Friedrich Engels. *The German Ideology: Critique of Modern German Philosophy According to Its Representatives Feuerbach, B. Bauer and Stirner, and of German Socialism According to Its Various Prophets*. In *Marx and Engels Collected Works*, vol. 5, 19–539. Moscow: Progress Publishers, 1976 [1845–46].

Matthews, John. "Roman Law and Roman History." In *A Companion to the Roman Empire*, edited by David Potter, 477–91. London: Blackwell, 2006.

Mattila, Sharon Lee. "Capernaum, Village of Naḥum, from Hellenistic to Byzantine Times." In *Galilee in the Late Second Temple and Mishnaic Periods. Volume 2: The Archaeological Record from Cities, Towns, and Villages*, edited by David Fiensy and James Strange, 217–57. Minneapolis: Fortress, 2015.

_____. "Inner Village Life in Galilee: A Diverse and Complex Phenomenon ". In *Galilee in the Late Second Temple and Mishnaic Periods: Life, Culture, and Society*, vol. 1, edited by David Fiensy and James Strange, 312–45. Minneapolis: Fortress, 2014.

_____. "Jesus and the 'Middle Peasants': Problematizing a Social-Scientific Concept." *Catholic Biblical Quarterly* 72 (2010): 291–313.

_____. "Revisiting Jesus' Capernaum: A Village of Only Subsistence-Level Fishers and Farmers?" In *The Galilean Economy in the Time of Jesus*, edited by David Fiensy and Ralph Hawkins, 75–134. Atlanta: Society of Biblical Literature, 2013.

Mattingly, David. "The Imperial Economy." In *A Companion to the Roman Empire*, edited by David Potter, 283–97. London: Blackwell, 2006.

McCleary, Rachel, ed. *The Oxford Handbook of the Economics of Religion*. Oxford: Oxford University Press, 2010.

McCollough, C. Thomas. "City and Village in Lower Galilee: The Import of the

Archeological Excavations at Sepphoris and Khirbet Qana (Cana) for Framing the Economic Context of Jesus." In *The Galilean Economy in the Time of Jesus*, edited by David Fiensy and Ralph Hawkins, 49–74. Atlanta: Society of Biblical Literature, 2013.

_____. "Khirbet Qana." In *Galilee in the Late Second Temple and Mishnaic Periods. Volume 2: The Archaeological Record from Cities, Towns, and Villages*, edited by David Fiensy and James Strange, 127–45. Minneapolis: Fortress, 2015.

McGuire, Randall. *A Marxist Archaeology*. New York: Percheron, 2002 [1992].

McKeown, Niall. "Resistance Among Chattel Slaves in the Classical Greek World." In *The Cambridge World History of Slavery*, vol. 1, edited by Keith Bradley and Paul Cartledge, 153–75. Cambridge: Cambridge University Press, 2011.

McKinnon, Susan. *Neo-Liberal Genetics: The Limits and Moral Tales of Evolutionary Psychology*. Chicago: Prickly Paradigm, 2005.

McKown, Niall. *The Invention of Ancient Slavery?* London: Duckworth, 2007.

Meeks, Wayne. *The First Urban Christians: The Social World of the Apostle Paul*. New Haven: Yale University Press, 2003.

_____. *The Moral World of the First Christians*. Philadelphia: Westminster John Knox, 1986.

Meggitt, Justin. *Paul, Poverty and Survival*. Edinburgh: T&T Clark, 1998.

Meikle, Scott. *Aristotle's Economic Thought*. Oxford: Clarendon, 1995.

Meyer, Eduard. "Die wirtschaftliche Entwicklung des Altertums." In *Kleine Schriften zur Geschichtstheorie und zur wirtschaftlichen und politischen Geschichte des Altertums*, 79–168. Halle: Niemeyer, 1910 [1895].

_____. *Geschichte des Altertums*. Stuttgart: J.G. Gotta'sche Buchhandlung Nachfolger, 1907.

Meyers, Carol, and Eric Meyers. "Sepphoris." In *The Oxford Encyclopaedia of Archaeology in the Near East*, vol. 4, edited by Eric Meyers, 527–36. Oxford: Oxford University Press, 1997.

Meyers, Eric. "Jesus and His Galilean Context." In *Archaeology and the Galilee: Texts and Contexts in the Graeco-Roman and Byzantine Periods*, edited by Douglas Edwards and C. Thomas McCollough, 57–66. Atlanta: Scholars Press, 1997.

_____. "The Problems of Gendered Space in Syro-Palestinian Domestic Architecture: The Case of Roman-Period Galilee." In *Early Christian Families in Context: An Interdisciplinary Dialogue*, edited by David Balch and Carolyn Osiek, 44–70. Grand Rapids: Eerdmans, 2003.

_____. "Roman Sepphoris in Light of New Archaeological Evidence and Research." In *The Galilee in Late Antiquity*, edited by Lee Levine, 321–38. New York: Jewish Theological Seminary of America, 1992.

Meyers, Eric, and Mark Chancey. *Alexander to Constantine*. Archaeology of the Land of the Bible. Vol. 3, New Haven: Yale University Press, 2012.

_____. "How Jewish was Sepphoris in Jesus' Time?" *Biblical Archaeology Review* 26, no. 4 (2000): 18–33.

Meyers, Eric, and Carol Meyers. "Meiron in Upper Galilee." In *Galilee in the Late Second Temple and Mishnaic Periods. Volume 2: The Archaeological Record from Cities, Towns, and Villages*, edited by David Fiensy and James Strange, 379–88. Minneapolis: Fortress, 2015.

Meyers, Eric, Carol Meyers, and Benjamin Gordon. "Residential Area of the Western Summit." In *Galilee in the Late Second Temple and Mishnaic Periods. Volume 2: The Archaeological Record from Cities, Towns, and Villages*, edited by David Fiensy and James Strange, 39–52. Minneapolis: Fortress, 2015.

Meyers, Eric, E. Netzer, and Carol Meyers. "Artistry in Stone: The Mosaics of Ancient Sepphoris." *Biblical Archaeologist* 50 (1987): 223–31.

Mieroop, Marc van de. *The Ancient Mesopotamian City*. Oxford: Clarendon, 1997.

_____. "A History of Near Eastern Debt?" In *Debt and Economic Renewal in the Ancient Near East*, edited by Michael Hudson and Marc van de Mieroop, 59–94. Bethesda: CDL, 2002.

Miéville, China. *Between Equal Rights: A Marxist Theory of International Law*. Leiden and London: Brill and Pluto, 2004. Leiden: Brill, 2005.

Milevski, Ianir. *Early Bronze Age Goods Exchange in the Southern Levant: A Marxist Perspective*. London: Equinox, 2011.

Millar, Fergus. *The Roman Near East: 31 BC–AD 337*. Cambridge: Harvard University Press 1993.

_____. "The World of The Golden Ass." *The Journal of Roman Studies* 71 (1981): 63–75.

Milonakis, Dimitris, and Ben Fine. *From Political Economy to Economics: Method, the Social and the Historical in the Evolution of Economic Theory*. London: Routledge, 2009.

Mirkovic, Miroslava. *The Later Roman Colonate and Freedom*. Philadelphia: American Philosophical Society, 1997.

Mitchell, David, and Sharon Snyder. "'Jesus Thrown Everything Off Balance': Disability and Redemption in Biblical Literature." In *This Abled Body: Rethinking Disabilities in Biblical Studies*, edited by Hector Avalos, Sarah Melcher and Jeremy Schipper, 173–83. Atlanta: Society of Biblical Literature, 2007.

Möller, Astrid. "Classical Greece: Distribution." In *The Cambridge Economic History of the Greco-Roman World*, edited by Walter Scheidel, Ian Morris and Richard Saller, 362–84. Cambridge: Cambridge University Press, 2007.

Monier, Raymond. *Manuel élémentaire de droit romain*. Paris: Dalmat-Montchrestien, 1947.

Monson, Andrew. *From the Ptolemies to the Romans: Political and Economic Change in Egypt.* Cambridge: Cambridge University Press, 2012.

Moore, A. M. T. "Villages." In *The Oxford Encyclopaedia of Archaeology in the Near East*, vol. 5, edited by Eric Meyers, 301–3. Oxford: Oxford University Press, 1997.

Moore, Stephen. "Are there Impurities in the Living Water that the Johannine Jesus Dispenses?" In *A Feminist Companion to John I*, edited by Amy Jill Levine and Marianne Blickenstaff, 78–97. Sheffield: Sheffield Academic Press, 2003.

Moran, William. *The Amarna Letters.* Baltimore: Johns Hopkins University Press, 1992.

Moreland, Milton. "The Galilean Response to Earliest Christianity: A Cross-cultural Study of the Subsistence Ethic." In *Religion and Society in Roman Palestine: Old Questions, New Approaches*, edited by Douglas Edwards, 37–48. New York: Routledge, 2004.

Morley, Neville. "Marx and the Failure of Classical Antiquity." *Helios* 26, no. 3 (1999): 151–64.

_____. "Slavery Under the Principate." In *The Cambridge World History of Slavery*, vol. 1, edited by Keith Bradley and Paul Cartledge, 265–86. Cambridge: Cambridge University Press, 2011.

_____. *Theories, Models and Concepts in Ancient History.* London: Routledge, 2004.

Morris, Ian. "Archaeology, Standards of Living, and Greek Economic History." In *The Ancient Economy: Evidence and Models*, edited by Joseph Gilbert Manning and Ian Morris, 91–126. Stanford: Stanford University Press, 2005.

_____. "Hard Surfaces." In *Money, Labour and Land: Approaches to the Economies of Ancient Greece*, edited by Paul Cartledge, Edward Cohen and Lin Foxhall, 8–43. London: Routledge, 2002.

Moulier, Yann. "Introduction." Translated by Philippa Hurd. In *The Politics of Subversion: A Manifesto for the Twenty-first Century*, 1–44. Cambridge: Polity, 2005.

Moxnes, Halvor. *Putting Jesus in His Place: A Radical Vision of Household and Kingdom.* Louisville: Westminster John Knox, 2003.

_____. "What Is Family? Problems in Constructing Early Christian Families." In *Constructing Early Christian Families: Family as Social Reality and Metaphor*, edited by Halvor Moxnes, 13–41. London: Routledge, 1997.

Myers, Ched. *Binding the Strong Man: A Political Reading of Mark's Story of Jesus.* Maryknoll: Orbis, 1988.

Myles, Robert. "Opiate of Christ; or, John's Gospel and the Spectre of Class." *Postscripts: The Journal of Sacred Texts and Contemporary Worlds* 7, no. 3 (2016): 257–77.

Nadan, Amos. "Colonial Misunderstanding of an Efficient Peasant Institution." *Journal of the Economic and Social History of the Orient* 46 (2003): 320–54.

_____. *The Palestinian Peasant Economy under the Mandate: A Story of Colonial Bungling.* Cambridge: Harvard University Press, 2006.

Nafissi, Mohammad. "On the Foundations of Athenian Democracy: Marx's Paradox and Weber's Solution." *Max Weber Studies* 1, no. 56–83 (2000).

Nasrallah, Laura Salah. "'You were bought with a price': Freedpersons and Things in 1 Corinthians." In *Corinth in Contrast: Studies in Inequality*, edited by Stephen J. Friesen, Sarah A. James and Daniel N. Schowalter, 54–73. Leiden: Brill, 2014.

Negri, Antonio. *Empire and Beyond.* Translated by Ed Emery. Cambridge: Polity Press, 2008.

_____. *The Labor of Job: The Biblical Text as a Parable of Human Labor.* Translated by Matteo Mandarini. Durham: Duke University Press, 2009 [2002].

_____. *The Porcelain Workshop: For a New Grammar of Politics.* Los Angeles: Semiotext(e), 2008 [2003].

_____. *Time for Revolution.* Translated by Matteo Mandarini. London: Continuum, 2003.

Negri, Antonio, and Anne Dufourmantelle. *Negri on Negri.* Translated by M. B. DeBevoise. New York: Routledge, 2004.

Negri, Antonio, and Michael Hardt. "Marx's Mole is Dead! Globalisation and Communication." *Eurozine* no. February 13 (2002). http://www.euro zine.com/articles/2002-02-13-hardtnegri-en.html.

Neusner, Jacob. *Judaism: The Evidence of the Mishnah.* Chicago: University of Chicago Press, 1981.

Neyrey, Jerome. "Managing the Household: Paul as Paterfamilias of the Christian Household Group in Corinth." In *Modelling Early Christianity: Social-Scientific Studies of the New Testament in its Context*, edited by Philip Esler, 208–18. London: Routledge, 1995.

O'Connor, Terry. *The Archaeology of Animal Bones.* Stroud: Sutton, 2000.

Oakman, Douglas. "The Countryside in Luke-Acts." In *The Social World of Luke-Acts: Models for Interpretation*, edited by Jerome Neyrey, 151–80. Peabody: Hendrickson, 1991.

_____. "Execrating? or Execrable Peasants!". In *The Galilean Economy in the Time of Jesus*, edited by David Fiensy and Ralph Hawkins, 135–64. Atlanta: Society of Biblical Literature, 2013.

_____. *Jesus and the Economic Questions of His Day.* Lewiston: Edwin Mellen, 1986.

_____. *Jesus and the Peasants.* Eugene: Cascade, 2008.

_____. "Late Second Temple Galilee: Socioarchaeology and Dimensions of

Exploitation in First-Century Palestine." In *Galilee in the Late Second Temple and Mishnaic Period, Volume 1: Life, Culture, and Society*, edited by David Fiensy and James Strange, 346–56. Minneapolis: Fortress, 2014.

Origen. *Contra Celsum*. edited by Henry Chadwick Cambridge: Cambridge University Press, 1980 [1953].

Osborne, James. "Sovereignty and Territoriality in the City-State: A Case Study from the Amuq Valley, Turkey." *Journal of Anthropological Archaeology* 32 (2013): 774–90.

Osiek, Carolyn. "Female Slaves, *Porneia*, and the Limits of Obedience." In *Early Christian Families in Context: An Interdisciplinary Dialogue*, edited by David Balch and Carolyn Osiek, 255–75. Grand Rapids: Eerdmans, 2003.

Osiek, Carolyn, and David Balch. *Families in the New Testament World: Households and House Churches*. Louisville: Westminster John Knox, 1997.

Overman, J. Andrew. "Late Second Temple Galilee: A Picture of Relative Economic Health." In *Galilee in the Late Second Temple and Mishnaic Period, Volume 1: Life, Culture, and Society*, edited by David Fiensy and James Strange, 357–65. Minneapolis: Fortress, 2014.

Palmer, Carol. "Whose Land Is it Anyway? An Historical Examination of Land Tenure and Agriculture in Northern Jordan." In *The Prehistory of Food: Appetites for Change*, edited by Chris Gosden and Jon Hather, 282–99. London: Routledge, 1999.

Pastor, Jack. *Land and Economy in Ancient Palestine*. London: Routledge, 1997.

_____. "Trade, Commerce, and Consumption." In *The Oxford Handbook of Jewish Daily Life in Roman Palestine*, edited by Catherine Hezser, 297–307. Oxford: Oxford University Press, 2010.

Patterson, Orlando. *Slavery and Social Death: A Comparative Study*. Cambridge: Harvard University Press, 1982.

Patterson, Thomas. *Marx's Ghost: Conversations with Archaeologists*. Oxford: Berg, 2003.

_____. "The Turn to Agency: Neoliberalism, Individuality, and Subjectivity in Late-Twentieth-Century Anglophone Archaeology." *Rethinking Marxism: A Journal of Economics, Culture & Society* 17, no. 3 (2005): 373–82.

Pearson, Harry. "The Secular Debate on Economic Primitivism." In *Trade and Market in the Early Empires: Economies in History and Theory*, edited by Karl Polanyi, Conrad Arensberg and Harry Pearson, 3–11. New York: Free Press, 1957.

Pervo, Richard. *Acts: A Commentary*. Hermeneia. Minneapolis: Fortress, 2009.

Peskowitz, Miriam. "Gender, Difference, and Everyday Life: The Case of Weaving and Its Tools." In *Religion and Society in Roman Palestine: Old Questions, New Approaches*, edited by Douglas Edwards, 129–45. New York: Routledge, 2004.

_____. *Spinning Fantasies: Rabbis, Gender and History*. Berkeley: University of California Press, 1997.

Petterson, Christina. *Acts of Empire: The Acts of the Apostles and Imperial Ideology*. Sino-Christian Studies: Supplement Series. Taiwan: Chung Yuan Christian University Press, 2012.

_____. *From Tomb to Text: The Death of Jesus in the Book of John*. London: Bloomsbury T&T Clark, 2016.

_____. "The Land is Mine: Place and Dislocation in the Letter to the Hebrews." *Sino-Christian Studies* 4 (2007): 69–93.

Phaedrus. *The Fables of Phaedrus*. Translated by Henry Thomas Riley and Christopher Smart. Urbana-Champaign: Gutenberg, 2002.

Pliny. *Naturalis Historia*. Translated by Harris Rackham, W. Jones and D. Eichholz. Loeb Classical Library. 10 vols. London: William Heinemann, 1949–54.

Plutarch. *Moralia IV*. Translated by Frank Cole Babbitt. Loeb Classical Library. Cambridge: Harvard University Press, 1936.

Poirier, John. "Education/Literacy in Jewish Galilee: Was There Any and at What Level?" In *Galilee in the Late Second Temple and Mishnaic Period, Volume 1: Life, Culture, and Society*, edited by David Fiensy and James Riley Strange, 253–60. Minneapolis: Fortress, 2014.

Polanyi, Karl. "The Economy as Instituted Process." In *Trade and Market in the Early Empires: Economies in History and Theory*, edited by Karl Polanyi, Conrad Arensberg and Harry Pearson, 242–70. New York: Free Press, 1957.

_____. *The Great Transformation: The Political and Economic Origins of Our Time*. Boston: Beacon, 2001 [1944].

_____. *The Livelihood of Man*. Edited by Harry Pearson New York: Academic Press, 1977.

_____. *Primitive, Archaic and Modern Economies*. Boston: Beacon, 1971 [1968].

Polanyi, Karl, Conrad Arensberg, and Harry Pearson, eds. *Trade and Market in the Early Empires: Economies in History and Theory*. New York: Free Press, 1957.

Polanyi, Karl, and Abraham Rotstein. *Dahomey and the Slave Trade: An Analysis of an Archaic Economy*. Seattle: University of Washington Press, 1966.

Pollard, Nigel. "The Roman Army." In *A Companion to the Roman Empire*, edited by David Potter, 206–27. London: Blackwell, 2006.

Polybius. *The Histories*. Translated by W. R. Paton. Loeb Classical Library. 6 vols. London: William Heinemann, 1922–29.

Proudhon, Pierre-Joseph. *Qu'est-ce que le propriété? Recherche sur le principe du droit et du gouvernement. Premier mémoire*. Paris: J.-F. Brocard, 1840.

Qin, Yicheng. "Archaeological Research and Guidance of Marxism." *Marxist Studies in China* 2014 (2014): 287–307.

Rawson, Beryl. "Death, Burial, and Commemoration of Children in Roman

Italy." In *Early Christian Families in Context: An Interdisciplinary Dialogue*, edited by David Balch and Carolyn Osiek, 277–97, 2003.

Redding, Richard. "A General Explanation of Subsistence Change: From Hunting and Gathering to Food Production." *Journal of Anthropological Archaeology* 7 (1988): 56–97.

_____. "Subsistence Security as a Selective Pressure Favoring Increasing Cultural Complexity." *Bulletin on Sumerian Agriculture* 7 (1993): 77–98.

_____. "Theoretical Determinations of a Herder's Decisions: Modeling Variation in the Sheep/Goat Ratio." In *Animals in Archaeology 3: Early Herders and Their Flocks*, edited by J. Clutton-Brock and C. Grigson, 223–41. Oxford: British Archaeology Reports, 1984.

Reed, Jonathan. *Archaeology and the Galilean Jesus: A Re-Examination of the Evidence.* Harrisburg: Trinity Press International, 2000.

_____. "Mortality, Morbidity, and Economics in Jesus's Galilee." In *Galilee in the Late Second Temple and Mishnaic Period, Volume 1: Life, Culture, and Society*, edited by David Fiensy and James Strange, 242–52. Minneapolis: Fortress, 2014.

Reibig, André. "The Bücher-Meyer Controversy: The Nature of the Ancient Economy in Modern Ideology." PhD, University of Glasgow, 2001.

Retief, François, and Louise Cilliers. "Malaria in Graeco-Roman Times." *Acta Classica* 47 (2004): 127–37.

Richardson, Peter. "Khirbet Qana (and Other Villages) as a Context for Jesus." In *Jesus and Archaeology*, edited by James Charlesworth, 120–44. Grand Rapids: Eerdmans, 2006.

_____. "Towards a Typology of Levantine/Palestinian Houses." *Journal for the Study of the New Testament* 27 (2004): 47–68.

Richardson, Peter, and Douglas Edwards. "Jesus and Palestinian Social Protest: Archeological and Literary Perspectives." In *Handbook of Early Christianity: Social Science Approaches*, edited by Anthony Blasi, Jean Duhaime and Paul-André Turcotte, 247–66. Walnut Creek: Altamira, 2002.

Rihll, T. E. "Classical Athens." In *The Cambridge World History of Slavery*, vol. 1, edited by Keith Bradley and Paul Cartledge, 48–73. Cambridge: Cambridge University Press, 2011.

Roaf, Michael. *Cultural Atlas of Mesopotamia and the Ancient Near East.* London: Equinox, 1990.

Robbins, Lionel Charles. *An Essay on the Nature and Significance of Economic Science.* London: Macmillan, 1935 [1932].

Roberts, Brian. *Landscapes of Settlement: Prehistory to the Present.* London: Routledge, 1996.

Rodbertus, Johann Karl. "Untersuchungen auf dem Gebiete der Nationalökonomie des klassischen Alterthums. II. Zur Geschichte der römischen Tributsteuern seit Augustus." *Jahrbücher für Nationalökonomie und Statistik* 4 (1865): 341–427.

Rohrbaugh, Richard. "The Pre-Industrial City in Luke-Acts: Urban Social Relations." In *The Social World of Luke-Acts: Models for Interpretation*, edited by Jerome Neyrey, 125–50. Peabody: Hendrickson, 1991.

Root, Bradley. *First Century Galilee*. Tübingen: Mohr Siebeck, 2014.

Rosafio, Pascale. "Slaves and *Coloni* in the Villa System." In *Landuse in the Roman Empire*, edited by Jesper Carlsen, Peter Ørsted, and Jens Erik Skydsgaard, 145–59. Rome: "L'Erma" die Bretschneider, 1994.

Rosenfeld, Ben-Zion, and Joseph Menirav. *Markets and Marketing in Roman Palestine*. Translated by Chava Cassel. Leiden: Brill, 2005.

Roskams, Steve. "The Urban Poor: Finding the Marginalised ". In *Social and Political Life in Late Antiquity*, edited by William Bowden, Adam Gutteridge, and Carlos Machado, 487–532. Leiden: Brill, 2006.

Rostovtzeff, Mikhail. *The Social and Economic History of the Hellenistic World*. 3 vols Oxford: Clarendon, 1941.

_____. *The Social and Economic History of the Roman Empire*. 2 vols Oxford: Clarendon, 1957 [1926].

Roth, Martha. *Law Collections from Mesopotamia and Asia Minor*. SBL Writings from the Ancient World Series. 2nd ed. Atlanta, Georgia: Scholars Press, 1997.

Roth, Ulrike. "Paul and Slavery: Economic Perspectives." In *Paul of Tarsus and Economics*, edited by Thomas R. Blanton and Raymond Pickett. Minneapolis: Fortress Press, 2016.

_____. "Paul, Philemon, and Onesimus." In *Zeitschrift für die Neutestamentliche Wissenschaft und die Kunde der älteren Kirche*, 105, no. 1 (2014): 102–30.

Rothbard, Murray. *An Austrian Perspective on the History of Economic Thought I: Economic Thought Before Adam Smith*. Auburn: Ludwig von Mises Institute, 2010 [1995].

Safrai, Shemuel. "Home and Family." In *The Jewish People in the First Century: Historical Geography, Political History, Social, Cultural and Religious Life and Institutions*, vol. 2, edited by Shemuel Safrai and Menaḥem Stern, 728–92. Leiden: Brill, 1988.

Safrai, Ze'ev. "Agriculture and Farming." In *The Oxford Handbook of Jewish Daily Life in Roman Palestine*, edited by Catherine Hezser, 246–63. Oxford: Oxford University Press, 2010.

_____. *The Economy of Roman Palestine*. London: Routledge, 1994.

_____. "The Roman Army in the Galilee." In *The Galilee in Late Antiquity*, edited by Lee Levine, 103–14. New York: Jewish Theological Seminary of America, 1992.

_____. "Urbanization and Industry in Mishnaic Galilee." In *Galilee in the Late Second Temple and Mishnaic Period, Volume 1: Life, Culture, and Society*, edited by David Fiensy and James Strange, 272–96. Minneapolis: Fortress, 2014.

Sahlins, Marshall. "Tribal Economics." In *Economic Development and Social Change: The Modernization of Village Communities*, edited by George Dalton, 43–61. New York: Natural History Press, 1971.

Sallares, Robert. *Malaria and Rome: A History of Malaria in Ancient Italy.* Oxford: Oxford University Press, 2002.

Saller, Richard. "Household and Gender." In *The Cambridge Economic History of the Greco-Roman World*, edited by Walter Scheidel, Ian Morris, and Richard Saller, 87–112. Cambridge: Cambridge University Press, 2007.

_____. "Pater Familias, Mater Familias, and the Gendered Semantics of the Roman Household." *Classical Philology* 94, no. 2 (1999): 182–97.

_____. *Patriarchy, Property, and Death in the Roman Family.* Cambridge: Cambridge University Press, 1994.

_____. *Personal Patronage Under the Early Empire.* Cambridge: Cambridge University Press, 1982.

_____. "Women, Slaves, and the Economy of the Roman Household." In *Early Christian Families in Context: An Interdisciplinary Dialogue*, edited by David Balch and Carolyn Osiek, 185–204. Grand Rapids: Eerdmans, 2003.

Sasson, Aharon. *Animal Husbandry in Ancient Israel: A Zooarchaeological Perspective on Livestock Exploitation, Herd Management and Economic Strategies.* London: Equinox, 2010.

Schäbler, Birgit. "Practicing Musha': Common Lands and the Common Good in Southern Syria under the Ottomans and the French (1812–1942)." In *Rights to Access, Rights to Surplus: New Approaches to Land in the Middle East*, edited by Roger Owen, 241–309. Cambridge: Harvard University Press, 2000.

Schäfer, Peter. *The History of The Jews in the Greco-Roman World.* revised ed. London: Routledge, 2003.

Scheidel, Walter, ed. *Debating Roman Demography.* Leiden: Brill, 2001.

_____. "Demography." In *The Cambridge Economic History of the Greco-Roman World*, edited by Walter Scheidel, Ian Morris, and Richard Saller, 38–86. Cambridge: Cambridge University Press, 2007.

_____. "Disease and Death in the Ancient Roman City." *Princeton/Stanford Working Papers in Classics* (2009): 1–14. http://www.princeton.edu/~pswpc/pdfs/scheidel/040901.pdf.

_____. "Epigraphy and Demography: Birth, Marriage, Family, and Death." *Princeton/Stanford Working Papers in Classics* (2007): 1–25. http://www.princeton.edu/~pswpc/pdfs/scheidel/060701.pdf.

_____. "Explaining the Maritime Freight Charges in Diocletian's Prices Edict." *Journal of Roman Archaeology* 26 (2013): 464–68.

_____. "The Greek Demographic Expansion: Models and Comparisons." *Journal of Hellenic Studies* 123 (2003): 120–40.

_____. "Population and Demography." *Princeton/Stanford Working Papers in Classics* (2006): 1–16. http://www.princeton.edu/~pswpc/pdfs/scheidel/0406 04.pdf.

_____. "Quantifying the Sources of Slaves in the Early Roman Empire." *The Journal of Roman Studies* 87 (1997): 156–69.

_____. "The Roman Slave Supply." In *The Cambridge World History of Slavery*, vol. 1, edited by Keith Bradley and Paul Cartledge, 287–310. Cambridge: Cambridge University Press, 2011.

_____. "Slavery in the Roman Economy." *Princeton/Stanford Working Papers in Classics* (2010): 1–22. https://www.princeton.edu/~pswpc/pdfs/scheidel/091003.pdf.

Scheidel, Walter, Ian Morris, and Richard Saller, eds. *The Cambridge Economic History of the Greco-Roman World*. Cambridge: Cambridge University Press, 2007.

Schottroff, Luise. *The Parables of Jesus*. Translated by Linda M. Maloney. Minneapolis: Fortress, 2006.

Schröter, Jens. *From Jesus to the New Testament: Early Christian Theology and the Origin of the New Testament Canon*. Waco: Baylor University Press, 2013.

Schwartz, Seth. "Political, Social, and Economic Life in the Land of Israel, 66–c. 235." In *The Cambridge History of Judaism*, vol. 4, edited by Steven Katz, 23–52. Cambridge: Cambridge University Press, 2006.

Scobie, Alex. "Slums, Sanitation and Mortality in the Roman World." *Klio* 68, no. 2 (1986): 399–433.

Scott, James. *The Moral Economy of the Peasant: Rebellion and Subsistence in Southeast Asia*. New Haven: Yale University Press, 1976.

Segundo, Juan Luis. *The Historical Jesus of the Synoptics*. Maryknoll, New York: Orbis, 1985.

Sen, Amartya. *Poverty and Famines: An Essay on Entitlement and Deprivation*. Oxford: Clarendon, 1981.

Shaked, Idan, and Dina Avshalom-Gorni. "Jewish Settlement in the Southeastern Hula Valley in the First Century CE." In *Religion and Society in Roman Palestine: Old Questions, New Approaches*, edited by Douglas Edwards, 28–36. New York: Routledge, 2004.

Shanin, Teodor, ed. *Peasants and Peasant Societies: Selected Readings*. Harmondsworth: Penguin, 1971.

Shaw, Brent. *Bringing in the Sheaves: Economy and Metaphor in the Roman World.* Toronto: University of Toronto Press, 2013.

Sherratt, Andrew. "Cash-Crops Before Cash: Organic Consumables and Trade." In *The Prehistory of Food: Appetites for Change*, edited by Chris Gosden and Jon Hather, 12–32. London: Routledge, 1999.

_____. "Plough and Pastoralism: Aspects of the Secondary Products Revolution." In *Pattern of the Past*, edited by I. Hodder, G. Isaac, and N. Hammond, 261–306. Oxford: Oxford University Press, 1981.

Sherwin-White, Susan, and Amélie Kuhrt. *From Samarkhand to Sardis: A New Approach to the Seleucid Empire.* Berkeley: University of California Press, 1993.

Shtaerman, Elena Mikhaĭlovna, *Krizis rabovladel'cheskogo stroia v zapadnykh provintsiiakh Rimskoĭ imperii (Italiâ).* Moscow: "Nauka", 1957.

Sivertsev, Alexei. "The Household Economy." In *The Oxford Handbook of Jewish Daily Life in Roman Palestine*, edited by Catherine Hezser, 229–45. Oxford: Oxford University Press, 2010.

Smith, Adam. *An Inquiry into the Nature and Causes of the Wealth of Nations.* Oxford: Oxford University Press, 1979 [1776].

Smith, Bruce. *The Emergence of Agriculture.* New York: W.H. Freeman, 1994.

Snodgrass, Anthony. *The Dark Age of Greece: An Archaeological Survey of the 11th to 8th Centuries BC.* Edinburgh: Edinburgh University Press, 2000 [1971].

Soja, Edward. *Thirdspace: Journeys to Los Angeles and Other Real-and-Imagined Places.* Oxford: Basil Blackwell, 1996.

Solin, H. *Die stadtrömischen Sklavennamen: ein Namenbuch. Barbarische Namen, Indices.* Franz Steiner Verlag, 1996.

Sorel, Georges. *Reflections on Violence.* Translated by T. Hulme and J. Roth. New York: Collier, 1961.

Stalin, I. V. "Constitution (Fundamental Law) of the Union of Soviet Socialist Republics, With amendments adopted by the First, Second, Third, Sixth, Seventh and Eighth Sessions of the Supreme Soviet of the U.S.S.R., Kremlin, Moscow, December 5, 1936." In *Works*, vol. 14, 199–239. London: Red Star Press, 1978 [1936].

Ste. Croix, G. E. M. de. *Christian Persecution, Martyrdom, and Orthodoxy.* edited by Michael Whitby and Joseph Streeter. Oxford: Oxford University Press, 2006.

_____. *Athenian Democratic Origins and Other Essays.* Edited by David Harvey, Robert Parker, and Peter Thonemann. Oxford: Oxford University Press, 2004.

_____. *The Class Struggle in the Ancient Greek World: From the Archaic Age to the Arab Conquests.* London: Duckworth, 1981.

_____. *The Origins of the Peloponnesian War.* London: Duckworth, 1972.

Stegemann, Ekkehard, and Wolfgang Stegemann. *The Jesus Movement: A Social*

History of Its First Century. Translated by O.C. Dean, Jr. Minneapolis: Fortress, 1999.

Steinkeller, Piotr. "The Money-Lending Practices in Ur III Babylonia: The Issue of Economic Motivation." In *Debt and Economic Renewal in the Ancient Near East*, edited by Michael Hudson and Marc van de Mieroop, 109–38. Bethesda: CDL, 2002.

———. "The Ur III Period." In *Security for Debt in Ancient Near Eastern Law*, edited by Raymond Westbrook and Richard Jasnow, 47–61. Leiden: Brill, 2001.

Stenger, Jan. "Eusebius and the Representation of the Holy Land." In *Brill's Companion to Ancient Geography: The Inhabited World in Greek and Roman Tradition*, edited by Serena Bianchetti, Michele R. Cataudella, and Hans Joachim Gehrke, 381–98. Leiden: Brill, 2016.

Strange, James. "First Century Galilee from Archaeology and from the Texts." In *Archaeology and the Galilee: Texts and Contexts in the Graeco-Roman and Byzantine Periods*, edited by Douglas Edwards and C. Thomas McCollough, 39–48. Atlanta: Scholars Press, 1997.

———. "The Galilean Road System." In *Galilee in the Late Second Temple and Mishnaic Period, Volume 1: Life, Culture, and Society*, edited by David Fiensy and James Strange, 263–71. Minneapolis: Fortress, 2014.

———. "The Jewel of the Galilee." In *Galilee in the Late Second Temple and Mishnaic Periods. Volume 2: The Archaeological Record from Cities, Towns, and Villages*, edited by David Fiensy and James Strange, 22–38. Minneapolis: Fortress, 2015.

———. "Kefar Shikhin." In *Galilee in the Late Second Temple and Mishnaic Periods. Volume 2: The Archaeological Record from Cities, Towns, and Villages*, edited by David Fiensy and James Strange, 88–108. Minneapolis: Fortress, 2015.

———. "The Sepphoris Aqueducts." In *Galilee in the Late Second Temple and Mishnaic Periods. Volume 2: The Archaeological Record from Cities, Towns, and Villages*, edited by David Fiensy and James Strange, 76–87. Minneapolis: Fortress, 2015.

Strange, James, and Eric Meyers. *Excavations at Ancient Meiron, Upper Galilee, Israel 1971-72, 1974-75, 1977*. Cambridge: American Schools of Oriental Research, 1981.

Suetonius, Gaius. *De Vita Caesarum*. Loeb Classical Library. London: William Heinemann, 1914.

Swedborg, Richard. *The Max Weber Dictionary: Key Words and Central Concepts*. Stanford: Stanford University Press.

Tacitus, P. Cornelius. *Dialogus, Agricola, Germania*. Translated by William Peterson and Maurice Hutton. London: William Heinemann, 1914.

Taylor, Joan. *Christians and the Holy Places: The Myth of Jewish-Christian Origins* Oxford: Clarendon, 1993.

Tcherikover, Viktor. *Palestine Under the Ptolemies: A Contribution to the Study of the Zenon Papyri, Mizraim IV-V*. New York: G.E. Stechert, 1937.

Temin, Peter. *The Roman Market Economy*. Princeton: Princeton University Press, 2013.

Theissen, Gerd, and John Howard Schütz. *The Social Setting of Pauline Christianity: Essays on Corinth*. Edinburgh: T&T Clark, 1982.

Toensing, Holly Joan. "'Living among the Tombs': Society, Mental Illness, and Self-Destruction in Mark 5:1–20." In *This Abled Body: Rethinking Disabilities in Biblical Studies*, edited by Hector Avalos, Sarah Melcher, and Jeremy Schipper, 131–43. Atlanta: Society of Biblical Literature, 2007.

Turley, David. *Slavery*. Oxford: Wiley-Blackwell, 2000.

Turner, Geoffrey. "The Christian Life as Slavery: Paul's Subversive Metaphor." *Heythrop Journal* 54, no. 1 (2013): 1–12.

Udoh, Fabian. "Taxation and Other Sources of Government Income in the Galilee of Herod and Antipas." In *Galilee in the Late Second Temple and Mishnaic Period, Volume 1: Life, Culture, and Society*, edited by David Fiensy and James Strange, 366–87. Minneapolis: Fortress, 2014.

Vélissaropoulos-Karakostas, Julie. "Merchants, Prostitutes and the 'New Poor': Forms of Contract and Social Status." In *Money, Labour and Land: Approaches to the Economies of Ancient Greece*, edited by Paul Cartledge, Edward Cohen and Lin Foxhall, 130–39. London: Routledge, 2002.

Villeval, Marie-Claire. "*Régulation* Theory Among Theories of Institutions." In *Régulation Theory: The State of the Art*, edited by Robert Boyer and Yves Saillard, 291–98. London: Routledge, 2002 [1995].

Viner, Jacob. *Essays on the Intellectual History of Economics*. Princeton: Princeton University Press, 1991.

Von Reden, Sitta. "Classical Greece: Consumption." In *The Cambridge Economic History of the Greco-Roman World*, edited by Walter Scheidel, Ian Morris, and Richard Saller, 385–406. Cambridge: Cambridge University Press, 2007.

Wallace-Hadrill, Andrew. "*Domus* and *Insulae* in Rome: Families and Housefuls." In *Early Christian Families in Context: An Interdisciplinary Dialogue*, edited by David Balch and Carolyn Osiek, 3–18. Grand Rapids: Eerdmans, 2003.

Wallerstein, Immanuel. *The Modern World-System I: Capitalist Agriculture and the Origins of the European World-Economy in the Sixteenth Century*. Berkeley: University of California Press, 2011 [1974].

_____. *The Modern World-System IV: Centrist Liberalism Triumphant, 1789-1914*. Berkeley: University of California Press, 2011.

Wapnish, Paula, and Brian Hesse. "Archaeozoology." In *Near Eastern Archaeology: A Reader*, edited by S. Richard, 17–26. Winona Lake: Eisenbrauns, 2003.

Watson, Alan. *The Digest of Justinian*. 4 vols. Philadelphia: University of Pennsylvania, 2009 [1985].

_____. *Roman Slave Law*. Baltimore: Johns Hopkins University Press, 1987.

_____. *Rome of the XII Tables: Persons and Property*. Princeton: Princeton University Press, 1975.

_____. *The Spirit of Roman Law*. Athens: University of Georgia Press, 1995.

Weber, Max. *The Agrarian Sociology of Ancient Civilizations*. London: Verso, 1976 [1896, 1909].

_____. *Economy and Society: An Outline of Interpretive Sociology*. New York: Bedminster, 1968.

_____. *General Economic History*. Translated by Frank Knight. New York: Collier, 1961.

Weintraub, E. Roy. *How Economics Became a Mathematical Science*. Durham, North Carolina: Duke University Press, 2002.

Weiss, Alexander. *Sklave der Stadt: Untersuchungen zur öffentlichen Sklaverei in den Städten des Römischen Reiches*. Stuttgart: Franz Weiner, 2004.

Weiss, Zeev. "From Galilean Town to Roman City, 100 BCE–200 CE." In *Galilee in the Late Second Temple and Mishnaic Periods. Volume 2: The Archaeological Record from Cities, Towns, and Villages*, edited by David Fiensy and James Strange, 53–75. Minneapolis: Fortress, 2015.

Westermann, William. *The Slave Systems of Greek and Roman Antiquity*. Philadelphia: American Philosophical Society, 1955.

Wharton, Clifton. "Risk, Uncertainty, and the Subsistence Farmer: Technological Innovation and the Resistance to Change in the Context of Survival." In *Studies in Economic Anthropology*, vol. 7, edited by George Dalton, 152–80. Washington: American Anthropological Association, 1971.

White, Hayden. *The Content of the Form: Narrative Discourse and Historical Representation*. Baltimore: The Johns Hopkins University Press, 1987.

_____. *Metahistory: The Historical Imagination in Nineteenth-Century Europe*. Baltimore: The Johns Hopkins University Press, 1973.

_____. *Tropics of Discourse: Essays in Cultural Criticism*. Baltimore: The Johns Hopkins University Press, 1978.

White, Lynn. "The Expansion of Technology 500–1500." In *The Fontana History of Europe, I: The Middle Ages*, edited by Carlo Cipolla, 143–74. London: Fontana, 1972.

Whitley, James. *Style and Society in Dark Age Greece: The Changing Face of a Pre-literate Society 1100–700 BC*. Cambridge: Cambridge University Press, 2003 [1991].

Whittaker, C. R. "Circe's Pigs: From Slavery to Serfdom in the Later Roman Empire." *Slavery and Abolition* 8, no. 1 (1987): 88–122.

_____. "The Consumer City Revisited: The *Vicus* and the City." *Journal of Roman Archaeology* 3 (1990): 110–18.

_____. *Land, City and Trade in the Roman Empire*. Aldershot: Variorum, 1993.

Wickham, Chris. *Framing the Early Middle Ages: Europe and the Mediterranean, 400–800*. Oxford: Oxford University Press, 2005.

_____. *Land and Power: Studies in Italian and European Social History, 400–1200*. London: British School at Rome, 1994.

_____, ed. *Marxist History Writing for the Twenty-First Century*. Oxford: Oxford University Press, 2007.

Wilk, Richard, and William Rathje. "Household Archaeology." *American Behavioral Scientist* 25 (1982): 617–39.

Wilken, Robert. *The Land Called Holy: Palestine in Christian History and Thought*. New Haven: Yale University Press, 1992.

Wilkinson, Tony. *Archaeological Landscapes of the Near East*. Tucson: University of Arizona Press, 2003.

_____. "The Tell: Social Archaeology and Territorial Space." In *Development of Pre-State Communities in the Ancient Near East*, edited by Dianne Bolger and Louise C. Maguire, 55–62. Oxford: Oxbow, 2010.

Willcox, George. "Agrarian Change and the Beginnings of Cultivation in the Near East: Evidence from Wild Progenitors, Experimental Cultivation and Archaeobotanical Data." In *The Prehistory of Food: Appetites for Change*, edited by Chris Gosden and Jon Hather, 468–89. London: Routledge, 1999.

Windisch, D. Hans. "Die Ältesten Christlichen Palästinapilger." *Zeitschrift des Deutschen Palästina-Verein* 48, no. 1–2 (1925): 145–58.

Witham, Larry. *Marketplace of the Gods: How Economics Explains Religion*. Oxford: Oxford University Press, 2010.

Witherington, Ben. *The Acts of the Apostles: A Socio-Rhetorical Commentary*. Grand Rapids: Eerdmans, 1998.

Wolf, Carl Umhau. "Eusebius of Caesarea and the Onomasticon." *Biblical Archaeologist* 27, no. 3 (1964): 65–96.

Wolf, Eric. *Peasants*. Englwood Cliffs: Prentice-Hall, 1965.

Wolff, Hans Julius. *Roman Law: An Historical Introduction*. Norman: University of Oklahoma Press, 1951.

Wood, Ellen Meiksins. *Democracy Against Capitalism: Renewing Historical Materialism*. Cambridge: Cambridge University Press, 1995.

_____. *Peasant-Citizen and Slave: The Foundations of Athenian Democracy*. London: Verso, 1997 [1988].

Xenophon. "Oeconomicus." Translated by E. C. Marchant, O. J. Todd, and Jeffrey

Henderson. In *Memorabilia, Oeconomicus, Symposium, Apology*. Loeb Classical Library, 381–558. Cambridge: Harvard University Press, 2013.

Yasur-Landau, Assaf, Jennie R. Ebeling, and Laura B. Mazow, eds. *Household Archaeology in Ancient Israel and Beyond*. Leiden: Brill, 2011.

Yoffee, Norman. *Myths of the Archaic State: Evolution of the Earliest Cities, States, and Civilizations*. Cambridge: Cambridge University Press, 2005.

Zangenberg, Jürgen. "Review of David A. Fiensy and James Riley Strange, eds. Galilee in the Late Second Temple and Mishnaic Periods, Volume 1: Life, Culture, and Society." *Review of Biblical Literature* 2016, no. 02 (2016): 1–7.

Zangenberg, Jürgen, and Dianne Van der Zande. "Urbanization." In *The Oxford Handbook of Jewish Daily Life in Roman Palestine*, edited by Catherine Hezser, 165–88. Oxford: Oxford University Press, 2010.

Zeder, Melinda A. "The Origins of Agriculture in the Ancient Near East." *Current Anthropology* 52 (2011): 221–35.

Zohary, Daniel, Maria Hopf, and Ehud Weiss. *Domestication of Plants in the Old World*. 4th ed. Oxford: Oxford University Press, 2012.